HENRI BERGSON

HENRI
BERGSON

VLADIMIR JANKÉLÉVITCH

ALEXANDRE LEFEBVRE & NILS F. SCHOTT, EDITORS

TRANSLATED BY NILS F. SCHOTT

INTRODUCTION BY ALEXANDRE LEFEBVRE

DUKE UNIVERSITY PRESS

Durham & London 2015

Henri Bergson by Vladimir Jankélévitch
© Presses Universitaires de France, 1959
English translation © 2015 Duke University Press
All rights reserved
Printed in the United States of America
on acid-free paper ∞
Typeset in Adobe Caslon Pro by Westchester Publishing Services

Library of Congress Cataloging-in-Publication Data
Jankélévitch, Vladimir.
[Henri Bergson. English]
Henri Bergson / Vladimir Jankélévitch ; edited by Alexandre
Lefebvre and Nils F. Schott ; translated by Nils F. Schott ;
introduction by Alexandre Lefebvre.
pages cm
Includes bibliographical references and index.
ISBN 978-0-8223-5916-6 (hardcover : alk. paper)
ISBN 978-0-8223-5935-7 (pbk. : alk. paper)
ISBN 978-0-8223-7533-3 (e-book)
1. Bergson, Henri, 1859–1941. I. Lefebvre, Alexandre, 1979–
II. Schott, Nils F. III. Title.
B2430.B43J315 2015
194—dc23
2015003367

Cover art: Henri Bergson (1859–1941), French philosopher, sitting
in his garden. World History Archive/Alamy.

Preface to *Bergson* (1930) by Henri Bergson © Presses Universitaires de France. Letters to Vladimir Jankélévitch by Henri Bergson
were originally published in *Correspondances* (2002) and *Mélanges*
(1972) © Presses Universitaires de France. "Letter to Louis Beauduc
on First Meeting Bergson" was originally published in *Une vie en
toutes lettres* (1995) © Editions Liana Levi. "What Is the Value of
Bergson's Thought? Interview with Françoise Reiss" and "Solemn
Homage to Henri Bergson" were originally published in *Premières
et dernières pages* by Vladimir Jankélévitch, edited by Françoise
Schwab © Éditions du Seuil, 1994.

CONTENTS

EDITORS' PREFACE vii

ACKNOWLEDGMENTS ix

INTRODUCTION. Jankélévitch on Bergson: Living in Time xi
Alexandre Lefebvre

INTRODUCTION I

CHAPTER ONE. Organic Totalities 3
    I. *The Whole and Its Elements* 4
    II. *The Retrospective View and the Illusion of the Future Perfect* 11

CHAPTER TWO. Freedom 23
    I. *Actor and Spectator* 24
    II. *Becoming* 30
    III. *The Free Act* 49

CHAPTER THREE. Soul and Body 66
    I. *Thought and Brain* 66
    II. *Recollection and Perception* 79
    III. *Intellection* 89
    IV. *Memory and Matter* 94

CHAPTER FOUR. Life 109
    I. *Finality* 109
    II. *Instinct and Intellect* 119
    III. *Matter and Life* 137

CHAPTER FIVE. Heroism and Saintliness 151

   I.   *Suddenness* 152

   II. *The Open and the Closed* 156

   III. *Bergson's Maximalism* 159

CHAPTER SIX. The Nothingness of Concepts and
the Plenitude of Spirit 167

   I.   *Fabrication and Organization: The Demiurgic Prejudice* 167

   II. *On the Possible* 179

CHAPTER SEVEN. Simplicity... and Joy 191

   I.   *On Simplicity* 191

   II. *Bergson's Optimism* 203

APPENDICES 211

SUPPLEMENTARY PIECES 247

   Preface to the First Edition of Henri Bergson (1930) 247

   Letters to Vladimir Jankélévitch by Henri Bergson 248

   Letter to Louis Beauduc on First Meeting Bergson (1923) 250

   What Is the Value of Bergson's Thought? Interview with
   Françoise Reiss (1959) 251

   Solemn Homage to Henri Bergson (1959) 253

NOTES 261

BIBLIOGRAPHY 299

INDEX 315

"Jankélévitch's works," Arnold Davidson writes, are characterized "by his inimitable style of writing, his invention of a vocabulary, and a rhythm of prose whose texture is a perpetual challenge for any translator to try to capture."[1] This is true of *Henri Bergson* in more ways than one. Its recomposition for the second edition of 1959—on which this translation is based—combines a very early treatise with a text in which Jankélévitch has found his voice. It brings together a reenactment of Bergson's philosophy in an often breathless current with a melodic interweaving of motifs. Yet it also implies the occasional disparity. This is a stylistic matter, but concerns documentation, for example, as well. Our goal in editing and translating the texts included in this volume, which comprises nearly all of Jankélévitch's writings on Bergson,[2] has thus been twofold: on the one hand, to remain close to the text with its idiosyncrasies and, on the other, to make it as accessible as possible to a wider audience without intimate knowledge of Ancient Greek, Latin, Russian, and German (languages in which Jankélévitch not only quotes but in which he even writes on occasion) and who may not have the wide-ranging philosophical knowledge (to mention but one field) Jankélévitch seems to presuppose in his readers but in fact may have been one of the few to possess.

We have, therefore, retained Jankélévitch's capitalization, punctuation, and so forth, wherever doing so does not contravene American usage outright. That said, we have adapted the use of tenses, for example, and changed what would appear in English as incomplete sentences by supplementing subjects and verbs, by dropping prepositions (where warranted), or by combining sentences. More often, however, we have broken up sentences, as Jankélévitch uses semicolons the way others use periods. Further, suspension points (...) are a central rhetorical device for him, and distinct from ellipses (...). To reveal the structure of Jankélévitch's argument and to make the text more manageable, we have broken down paragraphs, which in the original can run to several pages.

There are relatively few direct quotations in the book. Jankélévitch instead weaves references into his text, frequently without marking them. Very often, these seem less to refer to any specific passage of a text than to possible connections to be established with the discussion he is currently engaged in. Quotations from texts written in Greek, Latin, and German have been replaced by translations, and the number of terms and phrases in other languages has been greatly reduced. Where they are available, we have used existing translations but modified them, when needed, to conform to Jankélévitch's reading of a text. This applies in particular to Greek texts but, of course, to Bergson's books as well. We have also kept parenthetical mentions of French terms to a minimum.

All references have been checked. In the 1959 edition of *Henri Bergson*, Jankélévitch refers to the original Alcan editions for some of Bergson's books and the newer Presses Universitaires de France (PUF) editions for others, but does not do so consistently. Although we have taken on what Jankélévitch calls the "long and tedious labor" of aligning these references,[3] this means that occasionally, it is not entirely clear what passage exactly Jankélévitch meant to point to. In such cases, references are to entire paragraphs (which can span several pages) or longer discussions. Missing references have been supplied, evidently incorrect ones silently corrected. All references are found in the notes.

References to other authors have been specified where possible, although some—like the reference to Lermontov's poetry—are too general to be pinpointed, others simply too obscure. Where possible, Jankélévitch's references have been updated to refer to newer translations or more accessible editions. Given the richness of the text, which would require a critical apparatus of immense proportions, we have opted to provide only a minimum of explanatory notes.

ACKNOWLEDGMENTS

We are grateful for the funding provided by the School of Philosophical and Historical Inquiry and the School of Social and Political Sciences at the University of Sydney. We warmly thank Sophie Jankélévitch, Joanne Lefebvre, Anne Eakin Moss, Melanie White, and Frédéric Worms for their invaluable assistance, the anonymous reviewers for Duke University Press for their helpful comments, and especially our editor, Courtney Berger, for her support, hard work, and good cheer.

In the process of editing and translating the book, we have been greatly helped by the staff of a large number of libraries, including, in Paris, the various branches of the Bibliothèque nationale de France, the Bibliothèque Sainte Geneviève, the libraries of the Sorbonne and the American University of Paris, the American Library in Paris, and the Bibliothèque publique d'information; in the United States, the Library of Congress, the New York Public Library, and the Sheridan Libraries of the Johns Hopkins University; in Berlin, the University and Philological Libraries at the Free University and the Staatsbibliothek; and the University of Sydney Library.

This project has brought us together many years after our graduate studies in the Humanities Center at The Johns Hopkins University. We dedicate this volume to our teachers there, Paola Marrati and Hent de Vries.

JANKÉLÉVITCH ON BERGSON: LIVING IN TIME

Alexandre Lefebvre

Just twenty-one years old and a doctoral student of the École Normale Supérieure, Vladimir Jankélévitch met Henri Bergson at his Paris home. This was a big moment for the young student. France's greatest living philosopher was not only a hero to him but, on top of that, also the subject of his very first article, which only weeks previously had been accepted for publication.[1] Keen to speak with the master himself, the two met for an hour and a half. These are the first impressions he noted down for a friend:

> Speaking of Bergson: last Sunday, I finally saw the great man at his home; we chatted for a good hour and a half. His is a charming simplicity, and I beg you to believe that one feels much more at ease with him—great man that he is—than with that fussy B[réhier]. Picture a little bony fellow (and I imagined him to be tall) whose 65 years show, with very round blue eyes that seem to latch onto something in the distance when he speaks. His speech is slow (an academic's deformation!) but very simple and without affectation, despite some surprising images that, bursting into the conversation with abrupt impertinence, remind the listener that it is Bergson he's listening to.[2]

This meeting took place in 1923 and, over the years, a close intellectual friendship blossomed between them that would last until the end of Bergson's life.[3] The pattern of their exchanges was for Jankélévitch to send an article that he had written on Bergson's philosophy for comment, and, in turn, receive a warm and encouraging reply. So, for example, in 1924 Jankélévitch passed along his "Two Philosophies of Life: Bergson, Guyau" and in 1928 sent "Prolegomena to Bergsonism" and "Bergsonism and Biology."[4] Thanks to the reputation gained from these early writings, not to mention the high esteem Bergson held him in, Jankélévitch was soon asked by a former student of Bergson's if he would write a short book. He accepted enthusiastically. "Delacroix has asked me for a book on Bergson for the 'Great Philosophers' series (to be published by Alcan)," he told his friend. "I accepted. I can say that the book is almost done. All that's left is to write it. It's a one- or two-year job."[5]

Perhaps this statement was a little brash on Jankélévitch's part. But, then again, it didn't prove untrue. The first edition of *Henri Bergson* was published in 1930 and to acclaim. It received very positive reviews.[6] And, most impressively, it included a fulsome preface in the form of a letter by Bergson himself.

> Dear Sir,
>
> You have done me the honor of dedicating a work to the whole of my writings. I have read it closely, and I want you to know the interest I took in reading it and the delight it has given me. Not only is your account exact and precise; not only is it informed by such a complete and extended textual study that the citations seem to answer, all by themselves, the call of ideas; above all, it also demonstrates a remarkable deepening of the theory and an intellectual sympathy that led you to discover the stages I went through, the paths I followed, and sometimes the terms that I would have used if I had expounded what remained implicit. I add that this work of analysis goes hand in hand with a singularly interesting effort of synthesis: often my point of arrival was for you a point of departure for original speculations of your own.
>
> Allow me to send my compliments and thanks for this penetrating study, and please trust, dear Sir, in my highest regard.
>
> H. BERGSON.[7]

These glowing lines are helpful to introduce the flavor of Jankélévitch's reading of Bergson. First of all, it is clear that Bergson did not see this book as merely an exegesis of his work. Neither did he think of his relationship to Jankélévitch as a one-way street where the master would simply lead his disciple. His preface points instead to a mutual enrichment of young and old philosopher. And this wasn't mere politeness or fine words on Bergson's part. The proof is that several of his own key later essays— most notably, "The Possible and the Real" and the "Introductions" of *Creative Mind*—would be devoted to amplifying themes from his own work that Jankélévitch had originally highlighted in his study, such as the critique of retrospection and the categories of the possible and nothingness.[8] Truly, what higher praise is there?

Another notable feature of Bergson's preface is his gratitude to Janké-lévitch for treating his oeuvre as a living doctrine, as something that was unpredictable in its development and that continues to grow in new directions. This is significant in light of the reception of Bergson at the time, which was undergoing a major shift. Prior to the First World War, Bergson had been the philosopher of the avant-garde par excellence. True, he was world famous. And yes, the educated public and high society flocked to his lectures. But he was also the vital point of reference for leading artistic and political movements of the day, no matter how diverse. Cubism, symbolism, literary modernism, anarchism, and many others, all took their cue from him.[9] Yet despite this tremendous success and effect—or likely, because of it—Bergson remained a relative outsider in academic philosophy.[10]

After the Great War, however, all that changes. On the one hand, the onetime patron saint of youth, art, and culture is dismissed as a dated establishment figure. And, on the other hand, the onetime renegade philosopher is elevated to the position of a historical "great," one perfectly at home on a shelf with Descartes, Pascal, and Kant.[11] Raymond Aron, a classmate of Jankélévitch's, sums up Bergson's reversal of status particularly well: "Bergson is someone everyone knows, to whom some people listen, and who nobody regards as contemporary."[12] A great merit of Jankélévitch's book for Bergson, then, is to resist this rather unhappy experience of being embalmed alive, of being canonized and shelved all at once. By plumbing the undiscovered depths of his works, and by glimpsing the paths by which it could be renewed and extended, Jankélévitch reinvigorates the élan of a doctrine that was at great risk of becoming a classic.[13]

Bergson thus praises Jankélévitch for representing a vital doctrine still in the making. This, however, is itself a tricky point; and, after Bergson's death in 1941, things get more complicated. The reason is that Janké-lévitch will write not just one but two versions of *Henri Bergson*. There is the first 1930 edition, and then another in 1959. It is this second edition that we have prepared for the present volume. What is the difference between the two? The 1959 edition has three more chapters.[14] By and large, these extra chapters treat Bergson's final work, *The Two Sources of Morality and Religion*, which had not yet appeared when the first volume was published in 1930. Thus, Jankélévitch adds one chapter on heroism and sainthood, another on simplicity and joy, and an appendix on Bergson's thought and Judaism. He also writes a new introduction and conclusion.

Stated in these terms, however, the difference between the two editions appears to be merely quantitative: the 1930 edition has five chapters, the 1959 edition has eight. But, in truth, there is a more basic and yet less tangible difference. It relates to the lavish praise given by Bergson in his preface to the first edition. What he admires in Jankélévitch is his ability to place the reader within a process of philosophical creation, one in which the doctrine is in the midst of working itself out and with all the risks and unpredictability that this involves. But the situation is different, of course, in 1959. Then, nearly twenty years after Bergson's death, the object of Jankélévitch's commentary effectively changes. No longer working on a philosophy that is flying and running, he is, instead, writing on one that has flown its course and run its race. He is, in other words, addressing a completed doctrine. The result is a fascinating overlay. By necessity, Jankélévitch's second edition (1959) combines the original commentary of the first edition (1930)—which, as Bergson said, does its utmost to honor a living and breathing philosophy—together with a later perspective that now has the whole and complete philosophy before it.

The marvelous texture of Jankélévitch's book can be put in other, more Bergsonian terms. At its most basic level, Bergson's philosophy boils down to an awareness (or perhaps better, a perception) that the past and the present are very different from one another. The past is time that is done and gone, and, because of that, can be analyzed, broken down, and reconstructed in a great many ways. But that's not the case for the present. Because it is in the making, the present is open-ended, unpredictable, and resistant to analysis. Seen from the perspective of this difference, then, Jankélévitch's *Henri Bergson* is something more than a substantively rich commentary on Bergson. Thanks to its creation in two different editions, it is also a work that uniquely presents—or rather, that uniquely *is*—the temporalities that Bergson had labored his whole life to present and distinguish: a living present, thick and unforeseeable; and an accomplished past, available to analysis and retrospection.

Why Read Jankélévitch's Henri Bergson?

Here, then, is one tempting reason to read Jankélévitch's *Henri Bergson*: its composition exhibits the very temporalities that Bergson sought to represent. But there are, of course, other reasons. Some, we might say, concern Jankélévitch's own philosophical development; others concern his interpretation of Bergson and the features that distinguish it from existing commentaries.

Let's begin with the first point: *Henri Bergson* is not only a great book *on* Bergson; it is also a great book *by* Jankélévitch in his own right and a key point of reference for his oeuvre. Here a remark of Bergson's is particularly apt. In "Philosophical Intuition," he claims that any great philosopher has, in all honesty, only one or two "infinitely simple" ideas that are elaborated over the course of his or her life.[15] Taking up the suggestion, what would we say is Jankélévitch's "big idea"? What single idea could possibly span a most prolific and diverse oeuvre, one that includes over forty books in philosophy and musicology?[16] The answer is given in his letters: irreversibility. "Irreversibility," he says, is "the primitive fact of spiritual life . . . [it is] the very center of moral life."[17] What does he mean by irreversibility? Nothing other than the fact that we live in time and that we cannot, in a literal sense, undo what has already been done:

> It strikes me that irreversibility represents *objectivity* par excellence. Objectivity, experientially speaking, is that on which we can't do anything. . . . The will can do anything—except one thing: undo that which it has done. The power of undoing is of another order: of the order of grace, if you will. It is a miracle. Orpheus could have not looked back. But the moment he did, Eurydice is lost forever. God alone could do it, if he wanted. The mind [*l'esprit*] thus carries in itself the supreme objectivity, and yet it is true, as idealism tells us, that this objectivity depends on us. It would take too long to tell you how this can be confirmed in all the domains of spiritual life.[18]

When we scan the titles of Jankélévitch's oeuvre we see that they revolve around the problem of irreversibility. His works on forgiveness, bad conscience, the instant, nostalgia, evil and harm, and above all, on death, are all meditations of how moral, aesthetic, and religious life responds to and accommodates, for better or worse, the basic fact of irreversibility.[19] It is for this reason that Jankélévitch's writings on Bergson have a very special place in his corpus.

Put it this way: if we were to turn the tables on Bergson and ask him to identify his own big idea, an excellent candidate would be irreversibility. Underlying Bergson's conception of lived and effective time (what he calls "duration") is an awareness that it cannot be broken down, reordered, and reconstructed without distortion, without betraying its nature *as* time and turning into something else (that which he calls "space"). As one commentator puts it, "Bergson will affirm a dynamic ontology of irreversible time."[20] In this respect, we might say that Jankélévitch is a Bergsonian moralist (and, in another register, a Bergsonian musicologist). His writings recast a range of moral problems and topics through Bergson's appreciation of the irreversibility of time. His book on Bergson, then, could rightfully be called the ground zero of his own philosophical project. Not just because it is his first work, but more importantly, because it is his original (and with the second edition following later, a renewed) attempt to formulate what will become the defining theme of his philosophy.

Let's turn now to his reading of Bergson. What makes it special? To my mind, its great virtue is to present Bergson as a philosopher of existence. By this, I mean that the defining feature of Jankélévitch's exposition is to consistently couple Bergson's insights on the nature of time, memory, evolution, and morality, together with Bergson's (and also his own) reflections on a concrete way of life that would be in harmony with these realities. Understood in this way, the great end of Bergson's philosophy is to present a mode of living that would be more intensely present, receptive, loving, and ultimately joyful. That is Jankélévitch's accomplishment. He convincingly portrays Bergson as a philosopher who strives to effect a personal or "existential" transformation in his readers just as much as he seeks to furnish a theoretical discourse to explain reality.

My introduction to this volume will flesh out this line of interpretation. Right away, though, I should say that Jankélévitch is not alone in reading Bergson this way. Just recently, for example, I was happy to discover a volume on Bergson in the popular "Life Lessons" book series.[21] Moreover, two of Bergson's greatest readers—William James and Frédéric Worms—place a philosophy of existence at the center of their respective interpretations of Bergson. James, for his part, affirms that Bergson exacts a "certain inner catastrophe"—that is, a reorientation of perception and attitude—in each of his readers.[22] Likewise, Worms argues, "It is as if Bergson's philosophy rediscovered from the outset the most ancient task of philosophy, which is not to distinguish between concepts, but between ways of conducting oneself, not only to think, but also to intervene in life, to reform or transform it."[23] Other readers have also been drawn to Bergson for this reason. Pierre Hadot, the contemporary thinker who more than anyone has revived an appreciation of philosophy "as a way of life," describes his attraction to Bergson and Bergsonism precisely in these terms. "For me," he says in an interview, "the essential of Bergsonism will always be the idea of philosophy as transformation of perception."[24] For Hadot as well, the basic aim of Bergsonism is to transform our everyday orientation or way of life.

Although such interpretations of Bergson abound, Jankélévitch's book is the most determined and comprehensive effort in that direction. This makes it an especially important text for an English-speaking audience. Why? Because the English-language reception of Bergson's philosophy has been dominated by another great work of interpretation that sidelines the philosophy of existence: Gilles Deleuze's *Bergsonism* (1966). This book almost single-handedly revived interest in Bergson in the English-speaking world. But it is interesting in light of Jankélévitch's efforts that it deliberately underplays the psychological, spiritual, and existential aspects of Bergson's thought. I would like here to briefly turn to Deleuze's interpretation and mark out its basic differences from that of Jankélévitch's.

Deleuze's Bergsonism

It is not at all controversial to claim that Deleuze effectively revived interest in Bergson for English speakers. Indeed, the "Henri Bergson" entry for the *Stanford Encyclopedia of Philosophy* begins on just this note: "While such French thinkers as Merleau-Ponty, Sartre, and Lévinas explicitly acknowledged his influence on their thought, it is generally agreed that it was Gilles Deleuze's 1966 *Bergsonism* that marked the reawakening of interest in Bergson's work."[25] Consider too that most of the recent major works on Bergson in English are guided by Deleuze's interpretation, such as John Mullarkey's *Bergson and Philosophy* (1999), Keith Ansell-Pearson's *Philosophy and the Adventure of the Virtual* (2002), and Leonard Lawlor's *The Challenge of Bergsonism* (2003).

Why is Deleuze's interpretation so prominent? Certainly Deleuze's status and the key role that Bergson plays in his own thought is a significant reason, along with the fact that *Bergsonism* is a short book and that it was translated into English relatively early in relation to his other works. But most importantly, *Bergsonism* is an indisputably powerful work of interpretation. It is tremendously systematic, tightly presented, and speaks in a commanding no-nonsense tone. For all its strengths, though, balance is not one of them. Deleuze is highly selective in terms of the concepts he chooses to exposit. And he is determined to demonstrate a clear-cut progression in Bergson's thought.

It's helpful here to draw out these two features in order to contrast Deleuze's and Jankélévitch's respective interpretations. First, Deleuze interprets Bergson's philosophy in terms of a progression, wherein the insights of his early writings are fully realized only in his later work. And it's not as if Deleuze is coy about this feature of his interpretation. To the contrary, he couldn't be more up front about it! Just look at the famous first lines of *Bergsonism*: "Duration, Memory, *Élan Vital* mark the major stages of Bergson's philosophy. This book sets out to determine, first, the relationship between these three notions and, second, the progress they involve."[26] With his talk of stages and progress, this is a bold opening move. Indeed, it is a highly—an incredibly!—anti-Bergsonian gambit. No doubt, it buys Deleuze a sharp and systematic presentation; but it comes at the price of faithfulness to precisely what Jankélévitch labored hard to capture: the real duration and lived development of Bergson's philosophy. Or, to put the point in more technical terms, at the outset of his interpretation of Bergson, Deleuze avowedly (I am tempted to say, brazenly) occupies the very standpoint that Bergson had spent a lifetime problematizing: a retrospective vision that sees movement only in terms of the destination it reaches.

What is that destination according to Deleuze? It is Bergson's eventual realization of the ontological, and not merely psychological, nature of duration. Bergson's trajectory, in other words, is said by Deleuze to trace a progressive realization that the notion of duration he uncovers in his early work cannot be confined to merely psychological or subjective experience. Duration, instead, comes to be recognized as the very substance of life and being. As Suzanne Guerlac states, for Deleuze it is as if Bergson's thought "self-corrects" as it moves away from "the phenomenological cast of the early work, toward the purely ontological character of *Creative Evolution*."[27] At every point in his interpretation Deleuze is keen to push past Bergson's analysis of subjective experience toward an ontological—or, as he puts it, an "inhuman" or "superhuman"[28]—register of duration.

This brings us to the second feature of *Bergsonism*: Deleuze's select concentration on themes and concepts from Bergson's philosophy. Because Deleuze is keen to demonstrate that psychological duration is only a particular case of ontological duration, he systematically underplays the subjectivist, spiritualist, and phenomenological dimensions of Bergson's thought. Here again, Guerlac is helpful to characterize this bent of Deleuze's interpretation: "It is as if, in *Le bergsonisme* (1966), Deleuze had carefully edited out all those features of Bergson's thought that might appear 'metaphysical' (the soul, life, value, memory, choice), all those features that distinguish the human being from the machine, that suggest an appeal to experience and a phenomenological perspective. It is perhaps this gesture that most clearly delineates the contours of the New Bergson."[29] In Deleuze's interpretation, then, there is a studied avoidance of precisely those psychological and existential features of duration that Jankélévitch foregrounds.

This tendency to avoid the psychological and subjective has consequences for which texts Deleuze decides to focus on. In a nutshell, the more ontological works (especially *Matter and Memory* and *Creative Evolution*) are in; the more psychological (or "phenomenological" or "existential") texts are out. Deleuze, for example, largely restricts his discussion of Bergson's first work, *Time and Free Will: An Essay on the Immediate Data of Consciousness* (1889), to its mathematical theory of multiplicities. He also makes no reference to Bergson's essay on laughter and the comic. Yet by far the most significant omission of Deleuze's text concerns Bergson's final great work, *The Two Sources of Morality and Religion* (1932). In *Bergsonism*, Deleuze devotes a scant seven pages to it. And it's not difficult to see why given that *Two Sources* is, in large measure, a book on the emotions and has as its centerpiece an account of the pressure and pull of obligation and the aspiration to love.[30] Clearly, for Deleuze, this feature of *Two Sources* does not sit well within a narrative that recounts Bergson's career as progressively moving away from a theory of subjective experience toward an ontological account of duration.[31]

Did Deleuze read Jankélévitch's book on Bergson? It is hard to believe he didn't. The second edition of *Henri Bergson* was published well before Deleuze would have begun writing *Bergsonism*. Yet there is not a single mention of Jankélévitch's book.[32] In light of their basic differences of approach, this is perhaps not so surprising. In terms of style and composition, and also with respect to their substantive and textual focal points, the two books are at opposite ends of the spectrum. First, Jankélévitch writes out Bergson's philosophy from the perspective of the lived present, whereas Deleuze explicitly adopts a retrospective position. Second, Jankélévitch privileges the psychological dimensions of Bergson's work that Deleuze eschews. And third, Jankélévitch gives special attention to those texts that Deleuze downplays (namely, *Time and Free Will* and *Two Sources*). But while these differences may once have marked a contest over Bergson's philosophy, today they are a genuine boon. For as Nietzsche said with respect to the ancients, "we will not hesitate to adopt a Stoic recipe just because we have profited in the past from Epicurean recipes."[33] So too with us. English readers of Bergson have long enjoyed Deleuze's interpretation. Jankélévitch's book will hopefully provide just as rewarding fare. To continue Nietzsche's metaphor, we could say that by holding the divergent but not incompatible perspectives of *Henri Bergson* and *Bergsonism* in mind, we have the unique chance to have our Bergsonian cake and eat it too.

Jankélévitch on Bergson

Jankélévitch's *Henri Bergson* is a comprehensive commentary on Bergson's philosophy, with chapters devoted to all four of his major books. But, as is the nature of Jankélévitch's writing, it also includes a series of what one might call improvisations on Bergsonian themes, such as life, embodiment, and joy. At times this interweaving of interpretation and improvisation makes it difficult to keep the principal lines of the book in sight. To conclude this introduction I would like to briefly sketch its structure and a few of its animating problematics.

The structure is relatively straightforward. Jankélévitch lays it out early in chapter 1:

> The experience of duration determines [the] true and internal style [of Bergson's philosophy]. Duration is what we find in the "infinitely simple" image at issue in the lecture "Philosophical Intuition," and it is really the lively source of Bergson's meditations. Before we follow its successive incarnations by way of four problem-types—the *effort of intellection, freedom, finality, heroism*—we have to go back to the "primitive fact" that, in matters of the soul, governs all of Bergson's ascetic approach. (4)

Duration and the experience of duration is the core (or "primitive fact") of Bergson's philosophy according to Jankélévitch. As such, chapter 1 is dedicated to an exposition of its three modalities: past (which he calls "succession"), present (which he calls "coexistence"), and future (which he calls "becoming"). From there, as Jankélévitch says, he takes up the theme of duration within the context of four "problem-types" that map, with some degree of overlap, onto each of Bergson's major works. Thus, chapters 2 and 3 treat duration in relation to intellection and freedom in *Time and Free Will* and *Matter and Memory*; chapter 4 addresses duration with respect to finalism and teleology in *Creative Evolution*; and chapter 5 addresses the temporality of heroism and love in *Two Sources*. The final two chapters work a bit differently. Here Jankélévitch's aim is to make explicit certain understated motifs that traverse Bergson's philosophy. In this vein, chapter 6 (which, in the 1930 edition, was the final chapter) extracts Bergson's tacit critique of the categories of "nothingness" and "possibility."[34] Chapter 7 does the same but this time with positive concepts: the presence of joy and the imperative of simplicity that imbue all of Bergson's writing. Finally, as a kind of coda, the book compares conceptions of time in Judaism and Bergson.

As I've suggested, Jankélévitch interprets Bergson in terms of a philosophy of existence: namely, as a doctrine that sets out a way of life attuned to the nature of duration. But why is a life lived in sync with time, so to speak, so important for Bergson? What are the stakes? Jankélévitch identifies them straightaway in chapter 1: human beings, and us moderns in particular, have an inveterate tendency to deny and repress time and movement, such that we both misapprehend the world and also close off pathways of self-understanding and experience. He calls this tendency the "illusion" or "idol" of retrospectivity (16).

Like the devil it is, this idol has many guises. Truth be told, it takes a different form for each facet of human life, whether it is our self-understanding, our conception of freedom, our appreciation of nature, our depiction of morality, or how we envisage the future. As Jankélévitch puts it, "Bergson for his part never relented in denouncing, more or less implicitly, this idol in all problems of life" (16). But underlying all of its manifestations, the core of the illusion of retrospectivity is to reconstruct any event or phenomenon as a modification of already given parts. Its essence, in other words, is to deny novelty in favor of an explanation that represents any process of change either as an increase or decrease of existing elements or else as a rearrangement of them. From the perspective of this illusion, then, a new sensation or feeling is seen as an intensification or diminution of a previous one; freedom is envisaged as a deliberation between alternatives; an organism is comprehended as the product of its combined parts; all-embracing love is grasped as the expansion of exclusive attachments; and the future is seized as the predicted outcome of a reshuffled present. Jankélévitch will track down all of these permutations. But again, if we can set aside the details of his reading, the overarching point is that for Bergson the illusion of retrospection isn't just an error of understanding. Its failing is not simply that it gets the world, or ourselves, or the nature of change "wrong." Its effects, rather, are practical. The distortion we suffer is not merely cognitive but also existential.

Here we can speak concretely. One way to approach Jankélévitch's *Henri Bergson* is as a treatise on the different dispositions or moods that are vitiated by the retrospective illusion. He highlights three in particular: naivety, wonder, and simplicity. Indeed, the threatened loss of one of these dispositions is at the heart of each of his readings of Bergson's major works: naivety in *Time and Free Will* and *Matter and Memory*, wonder in *Creative Evolution*, and simplicity in *Two Sources* and *Creative Mind*. In each case, Jankélévitch demonstrates that for Bergson the retrospective illusion confounds our knowledge of the world and of ourselves, that it undermines particular experiences, and most disastrously, that it blocks joyful and intense modes of life. I will briefly summarize each in turn.

NAIVETY

"Naivety" is a keyword in *Henri Bergson*, especially in the early chapters on *Time and Free Will* (chapter 2, "Freedom") and *Matter and Memory* (chapter 3, "Soul and Body"). With it, Jankélévitch marks Bergson's goal to "place us, once again, in the presence of *immediately perceived qualities*" (29). But for Jankélévitch this term is also an exegetical device. He uses it, on the one hand, to mark the fundamental continuity between Bergson's first two books in that both seek to recover a capacity for unprejudiced and immediate perception. But he also uses it, on the other hand, as a foil to contrast these same works and show genuine evolution—in the sense of an unplanned and innovative development—in Bergson's oeuvre.

Let us consider the contrast. Jankélévitch says that Bergson seeks "immediately perceived qualities." But perceived qualities of what? What is the "object," for lack of a better word, that Bergson seeks a naive perception of? Jankélévitch observes that it changes over the course of the two books. In *Time and Free Will*, Bergson seeks an unmediated perception of spiritual life and consciousness. The problem in this text, according to Jankélévitch, is how to regain a naive (or pure, or exact) perception of ourselves in light of the abstract and distancing nature of intellection. *Matter and Memory*, by contrast, has a slightly but significantly different goal. Certainly, the desire for naive perception remains; but, at the same time, Jankélévitch notices that its object changes. Whereas before in *Time and Free Will* it was a question of perceiving ourselves, now, in *Matter and Memory*, it becomes a question of how to perceive things in the world ("images," as Bergson would say) outside the associations, opinions, and prejudices we foist on them. As Jankélévitch puts it, Bergson's thrust in *Matter and Memory* is "to dissociate the immediate given from the 'suggestions' of habit and association" (88). The conclusion Jankélévitch draws from this comparison is brilliant. He demonstrates that the very reality Bergson uncovers in his first book (i.e., the rich thickness of spiritual life and the deep self) becomes a key obstacle to confront in his second book: namely, how the wholeness of the person obtrudes his or her past (i.e., his or her memory) on the world, such that, in the end, true knowledge and experience of things fall into mere recognition and familiarity.

In one sense, then, Jankélévitch's analysis of naivety shows variation in Bergson's work. Yet to fixate on this variation is to miss the forest for the trees. We must not forget that Jankélévitch is equally keen to prove just how steadfast Bergson is in his search for lost naivety and unprejudiced perception. This is, indeed, the ambition that links *Time and Free Will* and *Matter and Memory*. Driving the critique of intellection and retrospection in *Time and Free Will*, Jankélévitch returns time and again to Bergson's concrete ambition: to show the possibility of a pure perception of the self so that we may become fully present to our own experience. His aim, in Jankélévitch's words, is to release us from the state of living as a "posthumous consciousness [that] lets the miraculous occasions of contemporaneity pass by forever" (17). The same holds, mutatis mutandis, for *Matter and Memory*. While Bergson's critical apparatus may take aim at a different target, Jankélévitch is clear that his goal remains constant: to regain an immediate perception of the world—a "learned naivety"—that is nothing short of a mode of life, a way of being that is more receptive, sensitive, and present. "No other theory has ever shown more forcefully and more lucidly to what extent learned simplicity, which separates us from our dear and old superstitions, in reality brings us closer to the center of the mind. Those who recollect too much will always remain ignorant of the innocence of life. But those who know how to renounce memory will find themselves, and in themselves, reality" (105). "That," he concludes, "is what Bergson's philosophy asks of us."

WONDER

Jankélévitch's commentary on Bergson's most famous book, *Creative Evolution*, begins with an examination of a particularly entrenched idol of retrospection: finalism or teleology. Finalism is the doctrine that natural processes and evolution are directed toward a goal. Or, in Jankélévitch's more pointed definition, its essence is to "subject life to the execution of a transcendent program." Its principal sin, he elaborates, is "to exhaust the unforeseeable movement of life in advance, in a fictitious future that is not 'to come' (except on paper) and that, mentally is already past" (110). In chapter 4 ("Life") Jankélévitch enumerates the manifold errors of understanding that finalism commits. These include misrepresenting immanent or vital causality, not acknowledging discontinuity in evolution, and failing to grasp the pluri-dimensional character of evolution.

But along with these errors of understanding, Jankélévitch also diagnoses a moral (or rather, an existential) failing that stems from finalism and retrospection. He calls it, borrowing from Schopenhauer, "teleological astonishment" (114). Such astonishment happens, according to Jankélévitch, when finalism is combined—as it almost always is—with a conception of nature as created by a demiurge or creator. The result is the discourse of creationism: a view that evolution is purposive and that biological life is made the same way that an artisan produces his work, namely by crafting parts into a whole. Creationism is thus, for Jankélévitch, a striking case of the retrospective idol. Or more exactly, it is a species of that idol: it is the form retrospection takes when confronted with the plurality and movement of life. Creationism both eliminates the creativity of time by turning evolution into design and also portrays vital creation in terms of an unfathomably complicated combination of parts. For these reasons, Jankélévitch charges it with the errors of retrospection. Fair enough. But why, then, does he see in it a moral failing as well? Because it is narcissistic. "In thus reducing the operation of nature to a procedure of the mechanical type," writes Jankélévitch, "our intellect in a way admires itself. It is in fact one of the intellect's most absurd manias to thus create within things a certain complicated order in order to enjoy the spectacle. It is perpetually lunatic and loses itself in the ridiculous contemplation of its own image" (114).

The casualty of this kind of astonishment is wonder. For when we gape at the so-called complexity of this kind of artisanal creation, or when we reel at the so-called greatness of the craftsman behind it, what we really opt for is admiration of feats drawn from our own likeness. This is why, according to Jankélévitch, Bergson's efforts in *Creative Evolution* seek to regain a disposition of wonder: "For the one who adopts an entirely different scale from the beginning, who from the outset conceives an entirely different metempirical and supernatural order, stupid *amazement* would no doubt make way for *wonder* and veneration of the sublime thing" (116). No doubt, inculcating a disposition of wonder is difficult. It requires us to swim against a very strong current. For to do so we must resign ourselves to remain contemporary with the history of vitality and not subject it to a transcendent plan. Or positively speaking—and in a line that might as well have come from the pen of Deleuze—we must reorient ourselves according to a "nominalism of the virtual," in which open-ended tendencies are acknowledged as the genuine realities of life (181). But the upshot of an attunement to duration is to attain an adequate comprehension of life as process and movement and, in so doing, rescue wonder—that existential attitude at the heart of philosophical inquiry—from its degradation into a merely astonished contemplation of ourselves.

SIMPLICITY

In French as in English, the word "simplicity" has several meanings. It can designate something that is undivided and unalloyed. And it can also refer to a way of being that is plain, unpretentious, and uncomplicated. For Jankélévitch, the virtue of Bergson's work—the "beautiful aridity" of his philosophy (203)—is that it combines these different meanings. And in the three concluding chapters of *Henri Bergson*, he sets out to show how Bergsonian simplicity can infuse all the different dimensions of our life: moral (chapter 5, "Heroism and Saintliness"), intellectual (chapter 6, "The Nothingness of Concepts and the Plenitude of Spirit"), and affective and aesthetic (chapter 7, "Simplicity... and Joy").

Consider intellectual simplicity. Like so many other major philosophers of the twentieth century—such as the later Wittgenstein, J. L. Austin, Stanley Cavell, John Dewey, Jacques Derrida, and Richard Rorty—Bergson advances a method (he calls it "intuition") to release us from long-standing but ultimately fruitless problems of philosophy. These problems include, for example, Zeno's paradoxes on movement, the Kantian relativity of knowledge, as well as vexing concepts of possibility and nothingness. But while there are innumerable pseudo-problems and idle concepts according to Bergson, for him they all stem from one and the same fault: our inveterate tendency to confuse time with space and quality with quantity. What is the solution? A critical method able to distinguish these categories and analyze each on its own terms, pure and unalloyed. That, as Jankélévitch explains at length, is precisely what Bergson's philosophy provides: a means to think "quantity quantitatively" and "quality qualitatively" (152). Or, to revert to the language of simplicity, Bergson's achievement is to furnish a way of thinking of time, space, quality and quantity "simply" (i.e., as unalloyed with one another) in order to attain a tranquil or "simple" mind.

Readers steeped in interpretations of Bergson will know that this aspect of Jankélévitch's analysis is not unique. Other commentators stress the link between Bergson's method of intuition and simplicity of mind. It is, for example, a staple of Deleuze's first chapter in *Bergsonism* ("Intuition as Method"). However, Jankélévitch goes a step further in positing that for Bergson intellectual simplicity cannot be isolated from simplicity in other walks of life. He recognizes, in other words, the internal connection between intellectual simplicity on the one hand, and moral, affective, and aesthetic simplicity on the other.

These latter kinds of simplicity go by different names in Jankélévitch's interpretation: love, grace, and charm. And his passages on these distinct virtues are among the most moving in the book. But if we view them together, it becomes clear why Jankélévitch represents Bergson's philosophy as renewing *l'esprit de finesse* and culminating in a great "thawing of the soul" (201). For the simplicity sought by his philosophical method aims, in the final analysis, at the simplicity of what ancient philosophers would have called a "philosophical" way of life: a mode of being that upends not just our mental habits but also our moral and affective constitution. "Perhaps," Jankélévitch proposes, "there is even only one Simplicity, or rather one single spirit of simplicity... There is thus no difference whatsoever between the pure movement that swallows up all Zeno's aporias and the ascetic who leaps over [merely material] well-being in a single jump. For intuition is the asceticism of the mind; and asceticism, in turn, is nothing but intuition become the diet, catastasis, and permanent exercise of our soul" (165). Put this way, the simplicity that Bergson urges is comprehensive. Indeed, it is more than that. In touching the different areas of our life, and in urging a change in all of them, it might be called maximalist.

If we were to boil down Jankélévitch's reading of Bergson to its essence, we could say that for him Bergson's philosophy rests on the affirmation—and not just the recognition—that we live in time. As he states in the appendix, "There is no other way of being for man than becoming. Becoming, namely being while not being, or not being while being, both being and not being (is this not the way it is conceived in Aristotle's *Physics?*)—this is the only way man has of being a being! Man, turning his gaze away from the mirage of the timeless, put down roots in the joyful plenitude" (223–24). Now, when we hear a line like this today our first reaction may be to think we already know the lesson. Yes, yes: movement and flux is our own reality. We've heard it before and since Bergson! But to read Jankélévitch's interpretation of Bergson may raise a nagging sense that our assent to this proposition is only notional or theoretical. Because what Jankélévitch is talking about is something different. It is real assent. It is an awareness that assenting to this proposition—that is, that our mode of being is becoming—involves our entire being and that to adhere to it will change our entire life, right down to our habits and ethos. It involves, to use a term Jankélévitch raises time and again, a conversion.

Speaking at a gathering to commemorate the hundred-year anniversary of Bergson's birth, Jankélévitch begins his address by adapting Kierkegaard's observation that the least Christian person in the world is, in fact, not the atheist or pagan but instead the satisfied soul who goes to church once a week on Sunday and forgets about Christ the rest of the time. The same goes, Jankélévitch says, for Bergson and Bergsonism.

We know that at the end of his life, Bergson preached the return to simplicity. One may wonder whether what we're doing here tonight is very Bergsonian. One may wonder whether it is very Bergsonian, generally, to commemorate Bergson. There are two ways not to be Bergsonian. The first is to be Bergsonian only on anniversaries, as if that exempted us from being Bergsonian all the other days, as if we had to square accounts once and for all. On that account, we may say, we might be better off being anti-Bergsonian. This anniversary must not resemble the all soul's days that the living invented in order to think of their dead only once a year and then to think of them no more. I hope, therefore, that it is about a renewal of Bergson's thought and that we won't wait for the second centenary to talk about it again.

The second way not to be Bergsonian is to treat Bergson like a historical sample, to repeat what he said instead of acting the way he did, or to "situate" Bergson's philosophy instead of rethinking Bergson the way Bergson wanted to be rethought. These two pseudo-Bergsonisms, that of the anniversary Bergsonians and that of the historians, bring me to the two main points of this speech.[35]

Henri Bergson takes aim at these kinds of "holiday" Bergsonians. In this category are those who think of Bergson only now and again, but it also includes professional philosophers and philosopher tourists for whom Bergson's work would be just another doctrine or method among others— as if his insights could be hived off to a specialist set of questions on time, memory, or life. It is to this casual reader—whether lay or professional— that Jankélévitch opposes his maximalist interpretation. For what drives his book is the attempt to interpret each line Bergson wrote as if it could invite or initiate, as he puts it, "a conversion that implies a reversal of all our habits, of all our associations, of all our reflexes" (239). Or, in the more laconic phrase of his 1930 preface, Jankélévitch seeks "less to give an exposition of Bergson's philosophy than to make it understandable."[36] Those are, for him, related but distinct tasks.

INTRODUCTION

There is only one way to read a philosopher who evolves and changes over time: to *follow the chronological order of his works and to begin with the beginning.* This order, to be sure, does not always correspond to the order of increasing difficulty; for example, reading *Matter and Memory*, which dates from 1896, is much more arduous a task than reading the 1900 text *Laughter.* But Bergson's philosophy [*le bergsonisme*] is neither a mechanic fabrication nor an architecture built step by step, as some of the great "systems" are. *All* of Bergson's philosophy figures, each time in a new light, in each of his successive books—just as, in Plotinus's doctrine of emanation, all hypostases figure in each hypostasis. In the same way, Leibniz presents his entire philosophy in each of his works: does not each monad express the entire universe from its individual point of view? Is not the entire universe mirrored in the *Monadology*'s drop of water? The microcosm is a miniature of the Cosmos. Schelling, another philosopher of becoming, writes, "what I consider is always consider the totality," and this totality he calls potential (*Potenz*).[1] Bergson writes each of his books oblivious of all the others, without even worrying about the inconsistencies that might at times result from their succession. Bergson delves into each problem as if this problem were the only one in the world. He follows each "line of facts" independently of all the other lines, just as the *élan vital* follows divergent lines of evolution. He leaves it to the commentators to resolve possible contradictions and to harmonize these divergences. The conciliation will no doubt work itself out infinitely. It will work itself out, not within the coherence of logic but in the musical affinity of themes and in the continuity of an *élan*. For in Bergson *order* resembles a kind of obsessive digression[2] more than it resembles the patient work of the system builders' marquetry. Bergsonian intuition, always total and undivided, simple and whole, grows continually in a single organic thrust. In this sense Bergson's philosophy is as complete in the eighteen pages of the essay on "The Possible and the Real" as it is in the four hundred pages of *Creative Evolution*.

Bergson, this great genius in perpetual becoming, was very impressionable. The essay on "The Possible and the Real," which is of capital importance for understanding Bergson's philosophy, appeared (in Swedish) in November 1930, after Bergson had read my *Bergson*. In this book, which had come to his attention at the beginning of 1930,[3] I had shown the importance of the *illusion of retrospectivity*, talked about the possible in the *future perfect*, and signaled the central character of the critique of the Nothing, already anticipated by Bergson himself in his 1920 address to the Oxford meeting. Bergson thus became aware of the brilliant originality, the creative fecundity of his own intuitions only bit by bit. The intuition is born in 1906, in an article in the *Revue philosophique* about the idea of Nothing; then in 1907, in the pages of *Creative Evolution* dedicated to the ideas of Nothing and Disorder; in 1920, it first becomes aware of itself; at the end of 1930 and in 1934, in *The Creative Mind*, Bergson finally, influenced by his interpreters, reconstitutes the movement that has carried him from the originary dawning to the metaphysics of change and creative plenitude. In Bergson's evolution, as in all volition or causation, there is a retroaction of the present on the past and, after the fact, an ideal reconstruction of becoming. The end, as Schelling says, testifies to the beginning.[4]

A melody played backward, going upstream beginning with the last note, will only be an unspeakable cacophony. This is what *Time and Free Will* lets us understand. How could we ever understand a living philosophy that develops irreversibly in the dimension of becoming if we began at the end or in the middle? The temporal order of a sonata is not an accident but its very essence. In Bergson's philosophy, the temporal order and the succession of moments are not details of protocol: they are Bergson's philosophy itself and the Bergsonian ipseity of a philosophy unlike the others. The first requirement for understanding Henri Bergson's Bergsonism is not to think it against the flow of time. Bergson's philosophy wants to be thought in the very sense of futurition, that is to say, *in its place*.

CHAPTER 1

ORGANIC TOTALITIES

Take comfort; you would not seek me
if you had not found me.—Pascal

Bergson's philosophy is one of the rare philosophies in which the investigation's theory blends with the investigation itself. It excludes the kind of reflexive doubling that gives rise to gnoseologies, propaedeutics, and methods. In a sense, we may repeat à propos of Bergson's thought what has been said about Spinoza's philosophy, in which there is no method substantially and consciously distinct from the meditation of its objects.[1] Instead, the method is immanent to this meditation whose general figure, as it were, it traces out. Bergson has carefully insisted on the vanity of the ideological phantoms that perpetually insinuate themselves in-between thought and facts and mediatize knowledge.[2] The philosophy of life embraces the sinuous curve of the real, and no transcendent method of any kind weakens this strict adherence. Better still, its "method" is the very line of the movement that leads thought into the thick of things. In Friedrich Schlegel's profound words, the thinking of life does without any propaedeutic because life presupposes nothing but life, and a living thought that adopts the rhythm of life goes straight to the real without troubling itself with methodological scruples.[3] The difference between timid scholastic abstractions and the generosity of concrete philosophy is that the former are *eternally preliminary* or—which amounts to the same thing—relative to something *absolutely ulterior* that would constitute their application or would derive from them, while the latter is at every moment present to itself. The former refer to some kind of future from which a gaping void separates them; the latter on the contrary is enveloped in what is presently evident and visibly certain: it accepts no transcendent jurisdiction because it carries its law and its sanction within itself. The method, thus, is already true knowing. Far from preparing a doctrinal deduction of concepts, it comes into being by degrees as spiritual progress unfolds, a progress of which the method, in sum, is nothing but the physiognomy and internal rhythm.

Let us, therefore, not seek the starting point of Bergson's philosophy in a critique of knowledge or (the way Høffding seems to do) in a gnoseology centered on the idea of intuition. Such an exposition retains of Bergson's thought only a certain system of formulas, a certain *ism* (in this case, "intuitionism"). It condemns the interpreter to confront *Bergson's philosophy all said and done* instead of witnessing its generation and penetrating its meaning [*sens*]. Incidentally, in the response he sent to Høffding, Bergson protests quite clearly (and perhaps without giving all of his reasons) against so *retrospective* an exposition, alleging that Duration, much more so than Intuition, is the living center of his doctrine.[4] As a metaphysics of intuition, Bergson's philosophy is only one system among others. But the experience of duration determines its true and internal style. Duration is what we find in the "infinitely simple" image at issue in the lecture "Philosophical Intuition,"[5] and it is really the lively source of Bergson's meditations. Before we follow its successive incarnations by way of four problem-types—the *effort of intellection, freedom, finality, heroism*—we have to go back to the "primitive fact" that, in matters of the soul, governs all of Bergson's ascetic approach.

I. *The Whole and Its Elements*

This ascetic approach is necessary because a method that works only on the level of material realities (what, to abbreviate, I will call *mechanisms*) has been extended erroneously to spiritual—mental and vital—realities (what I will call *organisms*). The truly fundamental fact, both in the order of the mind and in the order of life, is the fact of "enduring" [*durer*] or, which amounts to the same, the mnemic property. This property, when properly considered (as it is by Richard Semon)[6] is the only guarantee of perpetuating our experiences at each moment of life. Memory is not, as has been claimed, a derivative and belated function.[7] Before it becomes an independent organ, a methodical faculty for classifying and distributing, memory is nothing but the spiritual face of a duration internal to itself. Some persist in treating it as something like the agenda or the calendar of the soul when it simply expresses the following: our person is a world in which nothing is lost, an infinitely susceptible environment in which the slightest vibration calls up deep and prolonged resonances. Memory is but my experiences' entirely primitive perseverance in surviving themselves. It is that which *continues* innumerable contents, continues the ones through the others; these contents, together, form at any moment the current state of our interior person. But to say "continuity" is to say "infinity," and the *immanence of everything in everything* thereby becomes the law of the mind...

Not that memory is literally the thesaurization or capitalization of recollections. Philippe Fauré-Fremiet has lucidly shown that memory is the exercise of an ability rather than the augmentation of a possession, that it is the "re-creation" or active actualization of the past rather than a recording of this past. Bergson himself, hostile as he is to spatial metaphors, refuses to consider the brain as a receptacle of images and refuses to consider these images as contents in a container, and he is certainly not going to turn time itself into a receptacle for recollections! Yet (as a reservoir!) conservation is a spatial image...

It remains no less true that the past imperceptibly qualifies our current being and that it can be evoked at any moment, even if such conservation is simply inferred from the immediate givenness of the recall, even if the past neither literally survives *in* us nor lies dormant *in* the unconsciousness of becoming. Is Bergsonian time not this paradoxical latency without either *inesse* or *being-in*, without either virtual conservation or virtual reservation? Is Bergsonian time not this non-representable survival in which there isn't anything that survives or anything in which the surviving past could survive? Is it not creative conservation, conservation without conservatory? This provision granted, we retain the right to compare (as Bergson does in *Creative Evolution*)[8] duration to a snowball that grows in an avalanche. May the discontinuity of recall not keep us from having the continuity of becoming subtend it!

What we have here, then, is a first opposition between the life of organisms and the existence of mechanisms. A material system *is entirely what it is at any moment one observes it, and it is nothing but that.* Since it does not endure, it is in a way eternally pure because it has no past whatsoever to color and temper its present. And this is why Bergson, on this subject, reminds us of Leibniz's expression, *mens momentanea.*[9] Is this not the instantaneous consciousness that Plato, in the *Philebus*,[10] attributes to oysters? A rock can change and, apparently, "age"; but in this case, its successive states will remain external one to the other without any transition, no matter how imperceptible, succeeding in soliciting the old in the new. For we may very well say, in a paraphrase of a well-known verse, that without duration, "things would indeed only be what they are."[11] And that is the case for material things that are always and totally themselves.

A spiritual reality, which serves as a vehicle for impalpable and subtle traditions, on the contrary, perpetually takes on innuendos [*sous-entendus*]. Thanks to all of its supposed implicit allusions and accumulated experiences, each of its contents is so to speak venerable and profound. The most mediocre human emotion is a treasure whose riches we will never be able to enumerate because it testifies to a continuous past in which a person's innumerable experiences have silently settled like sediment. To be sure, there isn't any sedimentation in the literal sense because all localization is deceptive. Nor do experiences accumulate the way staples pile up in a pantry. But there is nonetheless an enrichment and a continual modification of the way the mind lights up.

This first opposition gives rise to a second that completes it. To make up the duration of the mind [*esprit*], conservatory memory must in fact have an auxiliary. Temporal "immanence" by itself would not suffice irreducibly to differentiate organisms and mechanisms. For it to be possible to talk about, if not a veritable implication of the past in the present, then at least a certain presence of the past, a kind of immanence of coexistence must immediately accompany the immanence of succession. Because the spiritual is in many respects more "elastic" than it is malleable, that is to say, because it records and perpetuates all the modifications of which it is the theater, it also tends to reconstitute at each moment its own totality: at every moment, we may say, it remains organically complete. But since it has conserved "adventitious" experiences and bears no trace of profound breaking or plurality, we must admit that it has assimilated, digested, totalized them and that they have modified it as it has modified them. All spiritual reality thus by nature possesses a certain totalizing power that makes it engulf all imported modifications and reconstitute at each step its total but continually transformed organism. And as this totalization applies at every moment to all elements of the spiritual organism, we have to say that the contents of life not only survive themselves in time, they so to speak revive themselves—partially in each of the contemporaneous contents and totally in the spiritual person they express.

This mutual immanence horrifies our understanding. The arts, on the contrary, seek to imitate it. None, however, succeeds better than music, no doubt because, thanks to polyphony, it has more means at its disposal than any other art to express this intimate copenetration of states of mind. Does not polyphony make it possible to conduct several superposed voices in parallel, voices that express themselves simultaneously and harmonize among themselves and all the while remain distinct and even opposed to one another? Recall, for example, the mysterious prelude to *Pelléas et Mélisande* which, starting in the eighteenth bar, sets Golaud's theme against Mélisande's and thereby expresses the tragic union that will tie the two destinies together. And how can one not admire the marvelous subtlety with which Liszt's *Faust Symphony* meshes the most opposite emotions: Faust's love and his speculative unrest in the first movement, Faust's love and Gretchen's love in the second? The themes confront, blend with, contaminate one another, and each of them bears the signature of all the others. This is what the inner life does at every moment: in paradoxical counterpoints, it associates experiences that appear to us as without connection, such that each of them bears witness to the entire person. Is the "total blending" that the Stoics articulated as a paradox not a reality we continually live?[12]

The distinctive and truly inimitable trait of spiritual things—organisms, works of art, or states of mind—is thus to always be *complete*, to perfectly suffice onto themselves... The distinction between partial and total makes sense only in the world of inert bodies. These, subsisting outside of one another, can always be considered to be parts of a larger set and have an entirely external relation with this set—a topographical relation. The universe of life, on the contrary, is a universe of individuals,[13] of "insular" totalities and, in the proper sense of the word, of masterpieces. Like Plotinus's intelligibles,[14] these masterpieces are total parts, that is to say, each expresses the complete set of the world of which they seem to be the parts. "Thus *all* is Dionysus," Schelling says.[15] And for Plotinus, *panta pasai*, all souls are all things!

This is proven, first, by the study of *instinct*.[16] We cannot imagine instinct to be mutilated or fractional any more than we can conceive of half an emotion or of a piece of sensation. From one species to the next, instinct varies simply in quality, but the theme is entirely present in each of the variations in which it clothes itself. In each, the original theme tends to grow, to set itself up in the center of a private domain. Only raw bodies allow for gradual transitions between the whole and the part. One of the roles of science is to skillfully appropriate insensible transitions and to turn them into pretty genealogies that erase the originality of individuals. The biologist Vialleton, whose acute sense for discontinuity leads him even to negate transformism, affirms Bergson's intuitions on this point. Every species has to emerge such that it is viable from the beginning. Correlations appear sufficient for allowing the organism to live *from the outset.* There are no drafts of organs, no rudiments of function: those are fictitious intermediaries destined to complete our genealogies.[17] In reality, every form is necessarily determinate because it subsists, and the function makes the organ all at once. Elsewhere,[18] Vialleton shows that the least of single-cell organisms is already a complete being and that there is, really, no such thing as an "elementary" individual. The organism is in its entirety or it is not at all.

This is shown even more clearly by the distinction between pure or spiritual recollections and motor recollections.[19] Pure recollection is perfect at once. While habit constitutes itself little by little as an effect of repetition, veritable recollection, like Minerva, is born an adult. Repetition has no hold on pure recollection, which is at any moment determinate and autonomous. Its essence is to be presently experienced and lived by a consciousness: it must therefore momentarily fill all of the mind and from the outset appear as organized and independent. That is why the pure past sometimes surges up in us as abruptly as do biological species in Vialleton's theory, through sudden fits and ruptures of experience. As in Proust, it is an invasion and a surge, a sudden irruption, an abrupt transformation. Spiritual things are thus always whole; that is no doubt why there are no fragments of life to correspond to fragments of matter, just as there are no pieces of ideas to correspond to pieces of a sentence.[20] And we can already foresee that between the two kinds of texts, so unlike each other, between the spiritual text of which every fragment is total and the material text of which every fragment is fragmentary, there is no conceivable literal parallelism, no juxtalinear transposition. The poem always lies beyond its own text.

This particularity of matters of the soul requires us to adopt a method that is entirely paradoxical. We cannot quite say that Bergson's philosophy, a philosophy of plenitude, admits the absolutist and totalitarian law of all-or-nothing, a law that, according to the Stoics, is valid for the alternative between virtue and vice, between wisdom and folly... Nor does Bergson adopt Hamlet's abrupt ultimatum, to be or not to be! What is true is that only sudden mutation results in qualitative newness, which the scalar gradations of geneticism will never obtain. "Love begins with love," La Bruyère writes,[21] and in the same way we may say that the mind begins with the mind. There is no chance we will encounter an emotion on the path of our deduction unless we give ourselves this emotion at the outset in its entirety, in its specificity, and its irreducible originality. In opposition to "reductionism," to the mania of reducing... or deducing, Bergson wants every experience, every problem to be thought apart and for itself as if it were by itself. Nothing is won, therefore, by engendering one living reality from another: instinct from intelligence, recollection from habit, the human from the animal, the complete emotion from the embryonic one.

That is why, as we shall see, the act of understanding does not proceed from words to meaning but from meaning to meaning; not from part to whole, but from whole to whole; and in just this way, there is nothing prior to meaning if not meaning, since meaning is the whole [*le sens est tout*]. Leibniz, whose analytical theory of Expression, on this point, is perhaps not as different from Bergson's immanentism as one might believe, has given profound expression to this particularity of the spiritual. Essentially, albeit in different terms, he writes that what differentiates a machine from a living being is that a part of a machine is truly and purely *a part*, whereas a part of the organism is yet another organism and so is a part of this part, and so on ad infinitum.[22] The infinitely great just like the infinitesimal, in this regard, challenge the principles of identity and conservation: just as the monad is the microcosmic expression of the macrocosm, the organism, down to the least of its microscopic elements is still organic. This seems to be the case for magnets, which are infinitely magnetic...

But life is particularly hard for the organism! An organism remains total in the least of its parts, while a machine is total only as the result of its elements. And this is equally valid for the mind. In material systems, an isolated piece in itself is deprived of all internal and autonomous signification. It is simple and truly *partial* because it is entirely relative to another complementary piece and because this relation precisely exhausts its raison d'être. But emotions, recollections, volitions, cut from the fabric of life, tend instantaneously to regenerate a spiritual environment, to regroup in a complete universe. No fiction, no analysis can cause them to lose their significant plenitude and the kind of spiritual gravity that we sense, instinctively, in all works of life. The totality of an inner world is present here and it acts here, surrounding, as it were, the humblest of our gestures with a halo of spirituality.[23]

The immanence of spiritual matters thus presents a double face, but we can see that it has a single source. All our current experiences have something familiar about them, each is capable of expressing or representing our complete self, because through memory they attach themselves to a common germ whose energies and tendencies they set free. Our duration, blossoming in multiplicity, thickens and so to speak becomes polyphonic. A deep kinship binds separate experiences together. Spiritual realities are doubly internal to themselves because they perpetuate themselves and because they totalize themselves; mechanisms remain external to themselves. A mechanism implies no beyond, and the enumeration of its parts literally exhausts all of its reality. With a perfect machine there never really are any deceptions, but there are also never any surprises. There are none of the failures but also none of the miracles that are, in a way, the signature of life. A perfect machine, like an instinct without intelligence, gives everything it promises but gives only what it promises. Its optical reality is capable of offering everything that our intelligence is right to expect from it. But we also know that it would be in vain to demand more from it. A mechanism leaves nothing to be guessed, to be sensed, nothing to look for. It does not create new solutions. It is not inventive. There are situations for which it is made, others for which it is not: that's all.

The eloquence of life, on the contrary, is above all made up of reticences. When life is somewhere, we feel confusedly that everything becomes possible. Organisms are deep. They are beyond themselves, so to speak, or, better: they are not what they are and are what they are not. They are something other than themselves, much more than themselves: they are becoming. Becoming is nonbeing continually on the point of positing itself as being, it is alteration, it is the same becoming other. Becoming is thus the natural dimension of organisms' depth. Doesn't the mystery of great souls, for example, lie in everything they conceal from us, in what they could nonetheless, we're certain, tell us if we knew how to attentively and seriously ask them? This deep organization, this immanent infinity, which characterizes the continuous duration of life, thus escapes all logic. Noncontradiction by itself represents a demand for intellectual purity and simplicity, and this demand naturally invites the mind to eliminate time, to separate mixed-up entities and to distill existences. And we can already see that the method this density proper to the matters of the soul makes necessary cannot but be entirely "irrational." Philosophy is thus no longer, as it is in Plato, a synoptic panorama of the macrocosm; rather, it is a subterraneous dig and an intense deepening of particular realities.

II. *The Retrospective View and the Illusion of the Future Perfect*

We now have to define the constitutional illusion of the intellectualist view, that is to say the approach that applies methods to interiority that were developed for mechanic existences. When presented with problems, the natural reaction of the intellect is to dismember its objects to understand them or, as Descartes puts it, to divide the questions.[24] But this attitude corresponds to the primitive moment of the discovery, and heuristic thinking tends to veer into didactic thinking wherever possible, that is, everywhere, if we may say so, that thinking tends to become doctrinal. And as the *analysis* of difficulties is relative to the knowledge sought, so the recomposition of entities is relative to the existing science. The mind that is in possession of constituted science adapts from instinct only the most soothing attitudes and relaxes until the acquired movement is exhausted, according to an order of exposition that goes from more to less. Yet it happens that the concern with *explication* leads didactic thinking to progress, in appearance, from less to more or from the part to the whole. Yet this doctrinal thesis is but an illusory denial of the law of economic mechanisms that governs the completed science: the elements with which it starts and which it puts together do not, psychologically, represent a true *minus* in relation to the whole it pretends to restore. For the parts of a whole really to be parts, that is to say, for them to be thought as partial and for their totalization, in consequence, to be able to represent a true psychological enlargement or dilation of thinking, their anteriority in the movement of synthesis would have to be not only ideal but chronological, and it would have to precede absolutely the composite.

Yet the dismembered parts are, precisely, more abstract than the whole and result themselves, within the accomplished science, from a prior analysis; or, rather, they are less concrete "parts" than they are *elements* that are elaborated, derivative, reflexively extracted from a primitive totality in the course of solving a problem.[25] Parts are obtained by a spatial *division* of totalities, and these parts reproduce the complication of the totality. But the elements are the term of an intellectual and purifying *analysis* that follows the logical articulations of things. "To know a living thing and describe it," Mephistopheles tells the student, "First they drive out the vital bit / And hold the parts but not the soul, / Alas, that made the parts a whole."[26] To be able to work undisturbed, our thinking thus tends to choose, as much as possible, these simple, pure, and homogenous elements. Despite their formal purity, they represent a long prior effort— which explains the extensive and inert character of the combinatory technique by means of which thinking assembles them. The movement of synthesis that presides over their grouping completes a reductive analysis and, effacing itself, restores a totality that is already known. We may thus very well say that intelligence is the *thinking of elements* in that it starts *apo stoikheiōn*, from the elements. It is comfortable only where it has succeeded in minting things into elementary parts, into concepts, or into indivisible atoms, where all it has to manipulate are elements.

This is how, for example, Spencer's evolutionism or associationism proceeds,[27] which puts together the whole from belated and artificial elements and replaces concrete things with what Bergson in the "Introduction to Metaphysics" calls the "intellectual equivalent" of reality.[28] This concern is manifest in the "atomistic" psychologies of Condillac or Taine[29] as well, as it is generally in all systems that are designed to put totalities together from simple elements—transformed sensations or nervous shocks. This also holds, therefore, in an area where the thinking of elements is doing rather well, namely for the ideal that opposes a concrete physics that still respects qualities and individuals with a physics according to which the syllables of things are reduced to homogeneous elements. Nature in its entirety would then be nothing but a vast "panspermia," that is to say, a store of entirely similar seeds. All one would have to do to reconstitute bodies would be to draw on this store, and science would become a relaxing game for the mind. As for philosophy, it would be nothing but an *ars combinatoria*, an amusing rearrangement of elements already known.

The likely rejoinder is that the element is *more simple* than the whole and that what is simple, de jure and de facto, exists before what is complex. Bergson, in dealing with a different problem,[30] counters this prejudice by distinguishing between two kinds of simplicity, which to abbreviate I will call logical simplicity and chronological simplicity. In the first sense, the condition is obviously simpler that the conditioned, the principle simpler than the consequence, the reason simpler than the effects, and, I would add, the element simpler than the whole. The relationship of the simple to the complex is thus originarily an ideal relationship. But in the second sense, the only criterion of simplicity is priority in the historical order of lived experience, an internally experienced *autarky*, so to speak, not a logical or transcendent autarky. In the first sense, one would say that the idea of inertia is "simpler" than the idea of spontaneity the way the homogeneous, in Spencerian mechanism, is "older" than the heterogeneous and the way the abstract is "older" than the concrete. But, as in dynamism, one would say in the second sense of simplicity that spontaneity is more simple because from within (and in Bergson there is no higher authority) we know ourselves immediately to be free. There is thus, I would add, a naive simplicity and a clever one, the concrete and so to speak genealogical simplicity of life experienced and the abstract simplicity one gives to oneself in moving away from positive facts. Abstract simplicity is nothing but a reality impoverished, stripped, reduced to uniformity. But in the unity of an all-natural and almost insignificant movement, life hides infinite promises of complication and multiplicity; it is not insipid, color- and odorless like abstract simplicity.[31]

Abstract simplicity is first only *pros hēmas*, in appearance and for the eye, or, put differently, for that optical part of the intellect that has a hold only on surfaces. It is only for the eye that letters are prior to words because, in truth, nobody ever began to speak with letters to then agglomerate them into words. And likewise, it is only for the eye that words precede sentences, for has anyone ever seen someone use words before organizing them into sentences, however incorrect and unsound these might be? Grammars, which doctrinally lay out for us an accomplished science, first teach the alphabet, then morphology, then syntax. Yet this didactic order is an order of fabrication that itself presupposes a long preparatory work. What appears "elementary" in this inventive work of elaboration is not the alphabetic atom—the secondary fruit of an abstraction—it is spoken totalities. The proof for this is that the "direct methods" that aim at accelerating the learning of living languages strain to imitate the living order and to create these spoken totalities as quickly as possible by working simultaneously with all grammatical entities: nouns, verbs, conjunctions… Instead of requiring us to have read a whole grammar book before we begin to speak—for we speak not only with adjectives, nor only with prepositions, nor only with pronouns— these methods seek to give us the totality of the sentence from the outset and then deploy it with increasing precision.[32]

Let us also note that letters and syllables have only *graphic* reality; orally, that is to say, in the life of language, there are no letters, no syllables, but relations, intellectual movements that labor to express themselves. Only barely do words themselves have a little more reality than just a written or visual reality. In spoken language, words that are used in isolation are themselves almost always implicit propositions or verbal "gestures." In other words, they are still totalities, albeit totalities in which the mental distinction between subject, copula, and predicate has not yet articulated itself in speech. Does not Bergson himself point to a natural tendency in words to "anastomose" in sentences?[33] Extracted from the proposition—which, as Delacroix remarks,[34] is the true unit of language—words become indifferent and indeterminate atoms. Yet when they intersect in the play of grammatical relations, all these generalities acquire a precise and particular meaning.

That is why the intellectual effort goes from meaning to signs, and not from signs to meaning: our ideas can only be thought within a spiritual context that orients them. When it is a matter of understanding a foreign word (and "foreign" here means above all isolated), we in a sense forge a possible context for it, an environment in which it could become intentional and significant. In music, this infinite totalization reconstitutes the entire melody around each note. Just as "the whole of every curve lies dormant, as it were, in each" of its segments,[35] just as an infinitesimally small fragment of a hyperbole is already hyperbolic, so each word implies the total meaning and will, if we delve into it, reconstitute the sentence that expresses this meaning. This explains the importance of the copula. The copula is a nascent sentence. It is not the copula that is added to subject and predicate: it is the subject and the predicate that we take from the copula. Le Roy compares this phenomenon of internal polarization to cell division. Is not the prologue, Unamuno writes, posterior to the tale?[36]

Despite the satisfaction our intellectual view derives from the grammatical order of composition, it is thus true to say that the organism is really older than its elements: it is *presbyteron* in the word's real sense, i.e. both more primitive and more venerable. *Time and Free Will* tells us that the pseudo-elements of mechanism generally proceed "by . . . blending together several richer notions that seem to be derived from it, and that have more or less neutralized one another in this very process of blending, just as darkness may be produced by the interference of two lights."[37] Goblot did not say anything different when he laid out the reasons why the study of the concept—a "virtual" judgment—seemed to him to follow the study of judgment and not to precede it (as the logical tradition requires).[38] Most of the time, in fact, the ideally pure elements on which the intellect works are "deposits" of a movement that preexists them. In denouncing their belated origin, logicians and psychologists have done nothing but displace the center of gravity from the purified result onto the purifying effort, from the simplified product onto the simplifying dynamic that completes itself and dies in it. There are, Brunschvicg writes, no simple terms that precede the judgment because the term is itself a relationship.[39] Concepts, these billions of intellectual exchanges, do not exist prior to mental relations except by the authority of fiction and only for the one who, turning his back on their history, manipulates them in a kind of nontemporal passivity. Attribution is thus older than the attributes, and logical simplicity is always an endpoint.

There are two aspects to the confusion of the *primitive* with the *elementary*.

(1) Construction *apo stoikheiōn* or, as Bergson himself writes,[40] *fabrication* is absolutely legitimate where mechanisms are concerned. Machines are indeed made up of simple "pieces" and there is no other way of "assembling" them. Just as there is nothing more, in fact, in the morphological totality of a material system than there is in the finite sum of its assembled parts, so this totality can be reconstructed by an exhaustive enumeration that is, so to speak, "without remainder." And yet we know very well that the value of this synthesis is purely demonstrative and pedagogical but by no means genetic. We only pretend to construct; we reconstruct according to the order indicated by an analysis that is always latently there, like a watermark. The soldier who reassembles his gun would have the illusion he was fabricating it were he not obediently following the mechanic relations that are already preformed in the construction of the machine and in the mutual adjustment of its pieces. This, in fact, is the intimate opposition between the parts of an organism and the elements of a mechanism. The former (e.g., a sensation) are veritable microcosms, autonomous entities, although they "immanently," as Leibniz would say, reflect the entire universe. Inversely, the latter, though simple and pure, are absolutely complementary to each other. Like Goblot's concepts, they are functions, and their very solidarity betrays their real elaboration; otherwise, their coming back together would be a marvelous chance and a continual miracle instead of being a game and the effect of a technique.[41]

Applied to life and to matters of life, this artifice would not be of interest even as a verification because in life, there are no parts external to one another and because organicity is in a way present everywhere.

Every analysis of the mind thus gives in to the attraction of the infinite,[42] just as, inversely, every synthesis of the elements of the mind has to renounce putting spiritual reality together from pieces. A state of mind is not arithmetically equal to the sum of its elements: it is not a plural but an original and concerted unity, an individual.

(2) The essence of "fabrication" is to presuppose something it does not admit to, to play the comedy of synthesis, and to operate on the passive past participle, never on the active present participle. Fabrication, as such, is thus always a *retroactive* operation, just as the order of exposition that simulates a synthesis is a *retrospective* order, entirely posterior to the invention. Mistaking this order for an order of generation, the intellect is fooled by an "ideology," to take up Renouvier's expression,[43] that we may justly consider to be *the* intellectualist sin. Bergson for his part never relented in denouncing, more or less implicitly, this idol in all problems of life.[44]

This idol is what I would like to call the *illusion of retrospectivity.* The intellect, Bergson writes somewhere, eternally looks back; *delay,* I say in turn, constitutes its natural weakness.[45] The delaying intellect is competent only for things already accomplished, and the symbols with which it works are always posterior to the event. This method has nothing but advantages when it is applied to the beings without duration and without memory that constitute the kingdom of matter. There is no profound difference here between *during* and *after,* and we may say that it is never too late to come to know things without duration. But beings that are becoming have future and past. Here, it is not at all the same thing whether one arrives "during" the event or "after," whether one is on this side of the event or on the other, or whether one surprises the present instant in the act, flagrantly and in vivo. Better still, there is a *kairos,* an event irrevocable and unique like all events, and this new circumstance imposes on us an obligation to opportunity that matter knows nothing of. In a moment, it will be too late and the lost occasion will never come back. Depending on whether I am a contemporary of these events or whether I come in after the fact, I will obtain veridical or illusory knowledge of them: during the fact and in the moment, they appear to me with all the vivacity and freshness of a particular, present, effective experience; after the fact and in the perspective of the past, on the contrary, they become indifferent and noncurrent generalities.

Intelligence is perpetually delayed, it lags behind living duration; it will nonetheless try to represent to itself, in the future perfect, the way in which things should have happened to conform to its own immobile scheme. Isn't the future perfect a future that anticipation has made fictitiously past? The retrospective illusion is nothing but this fiction. At the same time *anterior* and to come, the future perfect is the archetype of the *anachronisms* that prohibit us from having a *synchronous* vision of the present: incapable of making up for the lag, posthumous consciousness lets the miraculous occasions of contemporaneity pass by forever. In our perpetual delay vis-à-vis life, in the awkwardness of our reconstitutions, the *Laughter* book discovers the main source of the comical.[46] Practically all pseudo-problems have to do with this *untimely* approach. The teleological idols that make us believe in an intelligent finality of life arise because we cease to be contemporaneous with evolution. Because we place ourselves after the accomplished perception, it seems to us that recollection should follow it like a deadened echo.[47] Freedom, mobility, finality thus are absurd or miraculous only out of season and retrospectively. If for once we renounce looking behind us, we will see that recollection accompanies perception at every moment like an original reality, that life radiates in organized bodies that concentrate life more than they express it.

But this is asking our intellect to make a tough sacrifice. As Berkeley says, we first raise a dust and then complain we cannot see.[48] Even where machines are concerned, the illusion of retrospectivity appears as soon as we pretend to undertake a psychology of invention with the recipes of fabrication. Thanks to this illusion, once the movement of relaxation that *ends with* "simple" terms is completed, we unwittingly reverse the direction of life and decree that the endpoint ought to be the point of departure since, being the most intelligible for reason, it ought also to be the principle of a real filiation. The retrospective illusion consists in leaving what is *in the making*, in placing oneself *after the fact*, and in performing, a posteriori, a little justificatory reconstruction thanks to which belated abstractions become primitive only because they are simple and poor.

In this intellectual conjuring, in this magic trick, there is something analogous to the forms of affective reasoning that Ribot, in the footsteps of Pascal, has studied in his *Logic of Emotions*. Are *justification* and *defense* [*plaidoyer*] not founded on a belief? The essence of justificatory reasoning consists in *pretending to obtain something that is already all posited*, in simulating a spontaneous dialectical conquest where there is no primary and current discovery, only a secondary and retrospective restoration. A veritable demonstration admits and knows itself to be a demonstration because it proves a thesis that is explicitly anterior. Justification, however, is a shameful demonstration that, instead of proffering its proofs, smuggles them in. The lawyer's art, for example, rests on a fiction:[49] the defense will come to a certain conclusion propelled by the internal thrust of its argument—when in fact it comes to that conclusion because the conclusion itself wants it to. It is in this sense that one may speak, like Ribot, of a passionate teleology, and we will see later why Bergson rejected finality thus understood.

Considered in all of its magnitude, the retrospective illusion is a fiction whose social importance and disastrous tenacity cannot be exaggerated. It is truly the "idol" par excellence: it shifts the virtue of organization onto fabrication and, by dint of logicizing us, keeps us from knowing ourselves. Lot's wife, looking back, turns into a pillar of salt, that is to say, she becomes an inanimate and sterile statue. Orpheus, looking back, forever loses the one he loves. If we want to chase out the throng of retrospective prejudices, we need to adopt a perfectly paradoxical movement whose accent and critical virtue would focus on the very conquest of those totalities that, for intelligence, are the secondary product of a fiction. This movement would *find* the totality, far from *pretending* it exists; that is to say, instead of constructing organisms from their elements, it would seize them first and "globally" (*hathroōs*, as Plotinus has it).[50] But in its richness and its profundity, the current, instantaneous, and immediate grasping of an infinite reality implies a sharp contradiction that is only resolved outside of logic. The act of intuition dissolves the paradox that surges up, and it puts an end to the crisis.

If philosophy chooses the totality itself as its starting point, it becomes central again, or rather, centrifugal. As Bergson says, dissociation is older than association and analysis is older than synthesis.[51] All the virtue of the philosophical approach would amass in the center, in a germinative intuition experienced directly. There is infinitely more in this intuition than in the signs in which it expresses itself: more in the dynamic schema than in the completed work, more in the meaning than in the sounds and signs, more in thinking than in the brain, more, finally, in the *élan vital* than in all of the morphology of all living beings. This central totality encloses inexhaustible possibilities that will not actualize themselves: it denies itself in determining itself. To go from the center to the periphery is thus not to add anything but rather to take away; so much so that an interpretation oriented by this radiating movement, far from groping around in arbitrariness, will march with a self-assured and infallible attitude, since who can do the most can do the least. Living under different circumstances, Spinoza and Berkeley would undoubtedly have written different works, formulated different theses than the ones we know: but we would certainly have Spinoza's philosophy or Berkeley's nonetheless. Our tendencies will express themselves in various ways according to the accidental factors that channel them:[52] that is not what is important. What is important is a mind convinced before all conviction, passionate before all passion, resolved before all justification.

A thinking that works the other way around, that is to say, starting on the periphery, on the contrary places itself in a state of permanent inferiority: far from advancing in complete safety, with that frank and direct attitude that distinguishes centrifugal thinking, it is, in the words of *Mind-Energy*, always embarrassed, continually wandering.[53] This is what happens, for example, to anyone who explains meaning by words: since the same miserable alphabet with its twenty-four [*sic*] letters serves to express the most profound philosophical ideas and the most marvelous inflections of emotion, it is a vain enterprise to try to find out how such indigence can attract such richness, according to what law poor sounds, always the same, choose in our memory among so many delicate recollections and subtle thoughts. At every step our fabricating thinking will hit on a new stroke of luck: it will never be able to stop invoking miracles. Is this not, in Leibniz's parlance, "like drinking the ocean"?[54]

The same has to be said of associationism,[55] which pieces the mind together from inert, indifferent, and equivalent recollections. Resemblance or contiguity does not explain the essentially *elective* character of evoking a recollection in a perception. Why this recollection *rather than* that other? Why this affinity of certain determinate recollections with certain determinate perceptions? Bergson here reproaches associationism with what Leibniz, the finalist, objected to Descartes, the mechanist, namely that he did not at all explain why this mechanism exists "rather than any other."[56] It is this *potius quam*, this "rather than" that needs to be explained. Why this aggregate and not that other? Why a selection? Mechanicism can only answer these questions by invoking fortuitous encounters, a lucky chance a thousand times renewed; associationist reconstitution is thus given over to the whims of chance. We will find out later that only a perception's tendency to associate with a recollection with a view to action provides the "sufficient" or "appropriate reason" of these elective attractions. Like associationism, atomistic psychology, which assembles extension from inextensive sensations,[57] stumbles over the explanation of the "rather than." It does not explain the preference of certain sensations for certain points in space, the determination of a particular order of extension. Biological mechanicism, finally, especially in its neo-Darwinian form, deprives itself of an internal principle of direction that could provide it with the notion of a vital and central élan.[58] It exhausts itself in restoring life through contingent variations. Lost in the labyrinth of an organism whose complexity defies all our schemas, it spends itself in cumbersome complications in which the arbitrary and the fortuitous vie with one another for primacy. It cannot see that the élan is precisely this very simple, economical, instantaneous principle that our laborious approximations imitate so badly.

The discussion of relativist Space-Time is ample proof:[59] fabricating thinking places itself outside of real generation, which is always a unique and well-determined becoming, and in so doing admits an infinity of other processes by which these fictions could have been constructed just as well. For in the end, fabrication consists much more in unmaking than in making. Yet "what could be built only in a certain order can be demolished any which way."[60] To follow the centrifugal movement of organization is to find, beyond the thousands of possible operations by which an automaton is built, the only effective labor that results in a living being. That is why, no doubt, our intellect flaunts so zealous a predilection for the "average" [quelconque]. It makes a virtue of necessity. Incapable of reaching effective reality, it vaunts itself with this failure and pretends that its indifference to the real infinitely expands the horizon of its competence—an illusionary pretense. Who would believe that a thousand inexistent possibilities are worth a single solid and effective existence?

To tell the truth, fabricating thinking rarely dares to proceed openly. Nobody would believe it if it openly claimed to get "from the elements" to the soul, to life, to freedom and all the other valuable things that we can only discover if we start with them. To deceive us, those who reverse the genealogical order of experience must willy-nilly *anticipate*, at each step, on what is to follow. This surreptitious anticipation is truly the mechanicist conjuring par excellence. Since every explanation descends—it explains matters by proceeding a fortiori or from stronger reasons and it necessarily goes from more to less—the mechanicists' philosophy-in-reverse functions only by taking from superior realities that with which it feeds the explanations it gives of these very realities! It addresses the mind to capture it and deprives it of its own subsistence.

The vicious circle is thus the fundamental sin of mechanicism[61]—and we may very well say that mechanicism is the permanent presupposition of the totality to be explained. At every turn, Bergson denounces this mechanicist contraband: those who construct meaning from words take words to be already significant.[62] Those who juxtapose sensations to obtain extension already, on the sly, take sensations to be extensive.[63] It is impossible to engender the mind without presupposing the mind and we will see later how skepticism itself gives in to this necessity of employing a thinking it claims to destroy. As Jules Lequier says so forcefully on the subject of freedom, you cannot answer but with the question.[64] And thus materialism "perishes in this fatal clash between what it says and what it is forced to do to say it."[65] Precisely because they reconstitute the movement of the mind after the movement has been completed, the logicians already "know," and if they appear to start with elements to compose the whole, it is only a professorial showing-off. In fact, the act of abstraction with which we posit "elements" in our mind anticipates the notion of the whole that it simultaneously affirms and negates. One can reconstruct a melody from the notes *because* one already knows the melody and because it lies dormant, invisible and latent, in each note. If it did not, we would only find the song by a marvelous chance a thousand times renewed. This is the cheat of a comprehension that follows in the footsteps of creation, but does so reluctantly, the cheat of a fabrication that is a reversal of organization, the cheat of a centripetal reflux that is the inverse of centrifugal influx. The myth to be destroyed is the rhetoric of symmetries.

It is thus by way of a remarkable detour via internal experience that Bergson rehabilitates the critiques materialism has classically confronted. No order is possible in the material universe: there are only coincidences, given direction by incredible randomness, by prodigious chance. The only philosophy that does not add to the mystery is the one that starts with this mystery, that takes it on in its entirety without initially explaining it by anything other than itself. In that case, everything becomes easy, direct, assured. But we then also go from discovery to discovery, from novelty to novelty. No longer obliged to presuppose or anticipate anything, we experience—between the possible and the act, between the germ and the organism, between the intention and the free gesture—all of the anxiety of searching and creation. But the fictions of the technicians, which are laughable syntheses, prefer the quiet pleasure of construction games to these intellectual adventures.

Bergson's method is thus perpetually *contemporaneous* with the progress of life. This progress henceforth appears to us as a movement that, without *anticipating* anything, nonetheless presupposes a certain spiritual preexistence. "Take comfort; you would not seek me if you had not found me": this is the very meaning of the free Act.[66]

CHAPTER 2

FREEDOM

One only knows how to reply but keeps
marching along.—de Maistre

It is a stroke of luck for interpreters of Bergson's philosophy that the chronological order of Bergson's works corresponds quite evidently to the order of the problems he discusses. Bergson himself readily scoffs at the excellent intentions of those of his commentators who seek all too eagerly to introduce a doctrinal coherence into his speculations, a coherence they perhaps lack. At bottom, he has never stopped practicing the method he himself points out in one of his English lectures: setting out to follow *lines of fact* rather than building a system.[1] The unity of Bergson's philosophy thus truly has to be a unity *post rem*, and not at all a unity *ante rem*; not a principle but an outcome. We may say of this theory generally what *Creative Evolution* was to say of life: that it is oriented toward an end without all the same fulfilling a program.

This is what the definition of Definition in the same volume shows us as well: definition cannot radically separate living beings; at the most, it can point to their dynamic tendencies and their dominants, so to speak.[2] Just as a living organism implies characteristics that all other organisms have as well, so the totality of problems is present in each of the tasks separated by reflection. Yet the stress shifts as we move from one problem to the next. It is not entirely clear where one begins, where another ends. What is certain, however, is that going from one to the other, we have changed worlds and climates. In each problem we thus come across all problems, yet we do so according to a particular perspective (the way each treatise of Plotinus's *Enneads* or each short work by Leibniz reiterates, from various points of view, the total system). It is always very tempting to make natural limits out of these conventional boundaries;

here, we must content ourselves with separating "the centers around which the incoherence crystallizes."[3]

I. *Actor and Spectator*

Philosophers' supreme authority and the only jurisdiction they fall under is inner experience. Thought does not need to test its own operations against a truth criterion that transcends knowledge itself before it gets to work. The theory of knowledge does not substantially precede knowledge proper. Philosophers do not assume the place of the spectator but that of the actor: they are, as we say today, immediately committed. As we will see, the false perspective of intellectualism derives largely from the fact that the mind perpetually splits; it projects an image of its own activity away from itself in order to contemplate it objectively. For the mind to come to know itself through reflection, it is certainly necessary that the mind abandon itself.

Yet a singular irony of culture demands that this objective knowledge is bought at the price of innumerable illusions. Zeno's sophisms, just like Einstein's paradoxes, thus arise from a misunderstanding. Does Bergson not dedicate an entire book to showing that the aporias raised by the theory of Relativity arise from this deceptive and yet so necessary distance that intervenes between the observer and the thing observed?[4] The relativist's fictitious times are times "where one is not." Since they have become exterior to ourselves, they break up into multiple durations in which an effect of illusionary refraction draws simultaneity out into succession. They belong to the order of the *idols of distance*, that is to say, to the order of those fictions that circle like shadows around a mind absent from itself. (Such fictions, incidentally, are inevitable and often even very useful.)

But in matters of the soul this absence-from-oneself, which in the contemplation of material nature is a happy guarantee of disinterestedness and veracity, multiplies the number of unsolvable problems (or, as Bergson calls them, phantasms). Zeno's questions arise from a vision of movement and time that is no less phantasmatic, and we dare say that the Eleatics' "Achilles," just like Paul Langevin's "projectile travel,"[5] belongs to the *idola distantiæ*. If movement is impossible, if duration is smashed into instants, if Einstein's times stretch out, if simultaneities draw out, they all do so for a spectator who refuses to coincide with Achilles's movement and the traveler's real movement and whose corrosive dialectic converts the most common and obvious of facts into mysteries.[6] But as soon as the spectator in turn also gets up on stage and mingles with the play's characters, as soon as the mind, no longer entrenched in the impassiveness of speculative knowledge, agrees to participate in its own life, we see Achilles catch up with the tortoise, we see the javelin hit its mark, we see everyone's universal time chase away the physicists' vain phantoms like a bad dream. The natural, obvious facts of life regain the legitimate place that had been usurped by the impostures of dialectics. Liberty, which is impenetrable only to the spectator, once more becomes what it has never ceased to be for consciousness: the clearest and simplest thing in the world.

Bergson's philosophy thus represents the point of view of a consciousness that *necessarily takes sides*. That, no doubt, is what Bergson gets at when he defines his intuition as a kind of *sympathy*. Every time our soul is in play [*en jeu*], this demand for sympathy is there to remind philosophers that we are not dealing with just any problem but with a debate in which we are wholly engaged, in which we are always at the same time judge and party, in which we have to relive, redo, and re-create instead of knowing. Ultimately, as Pascal says, "it is a question of ourselves."[7] Strong minds pretend to look down on intuition as the mind's vegetative numbness, a confusion of subject and object. But intuition is very simply the mind as it is when it has *definitively returned to itself*, the full-blown certainty of a knowledge that is entirely present to itself. Intuition, which is sympathy, thus presents itself to us as a certain kind of philosophical partiality that is nothing but a superior impartiality. The mind, liberated from all heteronomous jurisdiction, is at the same time spectator and spectacle; unconcerned with the contradictions with which self-splitting consciousness obsesses, it thrives as Consciousness. Is intuition not a primary commitment of the whole soul?

Here, too, *Duration and Simultaneity* offers the clearest answers.[8] In that book, Einstein's paradoxes oblige Bergson to draw the line between the real and the fictitious once and for all. *Real is everything that is perceived or perceptible*. To know if a thing is real, all you need to find out is whether it is or could be the object of an actual experience of the mind. There is no other sign of truth than the possibility for a real fact to be experienced or lived by a consciousness. A real simultaneity, for example, is the simultaneity of two events that can be captured in a single instantaneous act of the mind. A real and concrete time is a time that is immediately perceived by our consciousness. More generally, an idea is *effective* to the extent that it is truly present to the mind. The only index of "effectiveness" is this very presence—"presence" taken both in its temporal sense ("the present") and in its physical sense of *parousia*. This idea is expressed particularly well in Russian: while the English and French word "reality" derives from *res*, which means the Thing, i.e. the all-accomplished, *deĭstvytelny*, real, suggests a drastic activity (*deĭstvovat'*, to be effective, to be in effect, etc., *delo*, deed, act, work, etc.) that expresses the living collaboration of the mind in the apportionment of facts and the lived presence of facts in the mind.[9] Taken this way, "effective" means first of all "efficacious"; yet, as Henri Poincaré and Edouard Le Roy have shown, "facts" are less given than they are ideal works of the mind.[10]

We are thus in a position to separate unequivocally the effective from the fictitious. The effective opposes the fictitious like the real opposes the symbol or the "lived" the "attributed." In this manner, we find in *Duration and Simultaneity* an entire table of antitheses it would well be worthwhile to make a list of. On the one hand, there are the lived realities of the philosopher or the metaphysician; on the other, all the symbols of Physics, all the abstractions of notional conceptualism. Real, or metaphysical, is the duration that I personally *try out* within my "system of reference"; symbolic are the durations that I *imagine* to be lived by phantasmatic travelers, movements I *attribute* to the arrow, to the tortoise, and to Achilles. For the same reason, the movement that Kelvin attributes to his vortex atoms is nothing but "a relation between relations,"[11] a conception of the mind and not a real event.

The distinction between the real and the symbol ultimately goes back to the distinction between the immediate and the mediate. The real is the set of presences I "perceive" (in Berkeley's sense) directly and by simple contact, or a tête-à-tête of the mind with its own experiences. But a symbol is rather more conceived than it is perceived, supposing this doubling or, as I put it here, this distance, which is, we have to admit, the condition of intellectual levelheadedness. To conceive is thus at most to perceive a perception; it is a secondhand perception, a perception to the second power, where there is time for error to slip in, just as negation is an affirmation about an affirmation or a judgment advocated by someone.[12] Symbolic thought thus does not draw the real from its source. It is content with a replica whose abstract simplicity makes it manageable but which no longer has the freshness of the original. It condemns itself to the uncertainty that afflicts all unconscious symbolism, all thought absent from itself. While immediate perception is directly the thought of things, the concept is directly only the thought of another, an artificial and fabricated perception. It has forever renounced knowing anything other than substitutes of the real, captured by way of an interposed mediator.

In the presence of an idea, a theory, a notion, the first thing we have to ask ourselves, therefore, is this: does it really correspond to anything *thinkable*?[13] This essentially nominalist concern, a concern Bergson raises in every discussion, will no doubt reveal the secret of his argumentation, which is always so elegant, so subtle, so persuasive. That is why Bergson's criticism spends so much ingenuity on dissipating the pseudo-problems that are tied up with pseudo-ideas.[14] The problem of freedom and the problem of nothingness feed a whole crowd of vain quarrels and opposing theories, defended with gravity by their partisans who believe themselves to be thinking of something when in truth they are not thinking of anything. Such problems are but phantasms and vertigoes,[15] comparable to the "inner cinematograph" thanks to which the intellect, to dizzy itself, gives to itself the illusion of movement. This is one of those intellectual vertigoes that Bergson knows so marvelously to undo in the most varied theories and whose diagnosis reveals an entirely nominalist method:[16] the mind, refusing to come to rest anywhere, jumps from one false idea to another false idea "like a shuttlecock between two battledores"[17] without ever positively and particularly thinking of anything at all.

It is easy to see in this ambivalence the vicious circle that is the bane of fabricating and retrospective geneticism. Such is the "psycho-physiological paralogism" in which Bergson, with admirable penetration, discovers an intellectual sleight of hand. The idealist parallelism becomes realist at just the moment in which its idealism is recognized to be contradictory; but realism in turn is quick to become idealist the moment in which its absurdity is about to break out into the open. The parallelist thinker benefits from this confusion and exploits this coming-and-going. He is never wrong since he cannot be trapped anywhere. He is an illusionist who, the moment he is about to be caught in the act is already somewhere else. In reality, however, he does not think of anything. He bestrides two equally false ideas that call each other forward.

There is an analogous marvel to be found in the interference between two kinds of order, the vital order and the mechanical order. Thought denies both orders simultaneously to create a phantom of disorder or randomness. Yet at least one of the two orders necessarily subsists when the other disappears. Their double exclusion, like the psycho-physiological paralogism, is thus nothing but an empty thought, a refusal to posit itself.[18]

The same is true, once again, for creating the idol of nothingness, for which we at once suppress both external reality and inner world even though one cannot deny the one without positing the other and vice versa. This double negation, too, is phantasmatic and unthinkable.[19] Nihilating thought treats its nothingness now as a Nothing from which, thanks to its marvels, it draws the entire world, now as a Something and even as an All from which it is not surprising to see all things proceed since they were all previously contained in it—what say I?—this rather vague nothingness is at once all and nothing, and the fog of ambiguity that envelops the being of its nonbeing and the nonbeing of its being makes the most enchanting prodigies plausible.

We see the same illusory game of an intellect mounted on two intermediate concepts in the sleight of hand that refers the biologist's mind from the idea of mechanical adaptation to the idea of active adaption or tosses him back and forth between two possible meanings of the word "correlation." But if we were to list all the problems in which Bergson's dialectic finds an oscillation of this kind to be at work, we would never see the end of it. Such is the typical problem of general ideas: generalization does not come without abstraction, which itself presupposes generalization.[20] Nominalism, which defines an idea by its extension, thus ends up in conceptualism, which defines an idea in terms of comprehension. Yet conceptualism in turn is defensible only on the condition that it surreptitiously ends up in nominalism. The mind is thus always up in the air, between the two. Each of the two theories, on the point of being captured, manages a pirouette and takes on the features of the other.

Does this reversal from the pro to the contra not provide a curious illustration of the play of contraries that Jean Wahl has studied with such penetration in Hegel's thought? Wahl tells us about the same ambiguity between two conceptions of causality, one dynamic, the other mechanic; and, in physics, between two conceptions of relativity, one abstract, the other full of imagery, between two kinds of simultaneity, conceptual simultaneity and intuitive simultaneity.[21]

This entire mythology is greatly favored by language.[22] Words, devoid of thought and intuition, have the property, if we so wish it, to have nothing to do with anything at all. They can be everywhere at once, that is to say nowhere, and remain suspended in midair, halfway between two ideas. Since the concept virtually represents an infinity of particular things, we seriously believe that in thinking of the concept we think of something when [in fact] we think of nothing.

Bergson's philosophy thus assumes its nominalism, and its affinity to Berkeley's philosophy has rightly been pointed out. Like Berkeley, Bergson resolutely excludes the phantom of an occult or neutral matter without relation to our consciousness. Matter, even while we believe to conceive of it absolutely, is, as we will see, nothing but pure perception, that is to say, still a spiritual reality and effective presence; there is an intuition of matter, albeit of an entirely different kind than purely spiritual intuition. Let us therefore renounce, once and for all, all "unknowables," all beings of reason, all the generic *universalia* of knowledge by concepts. For the same reasons, the labor of Bergson's criticism consists in finding out what an "unprejudiced" (so *Time and Free Will*'s very Cartesian expression)[23] consciousness would obtain, a consciousness that seeks to purge the recollections that, in us, are accredited by habit, language, traditional prejudices, or, as Descartes might say, nursery tales. The intuition of pure quality is born from this purification, just as the idol of nothingness faints away for those who have recognized that matter is neither an amorphous *hypokeimenon* nor an indeterminate substance or a substance indifferent to all determination. In this sense—but only in this sense—Bergson's philosophy could be said, as has all too often been done, to be an "impressionism." Proust's Elstir, too, wants to dissociate what is sensed from what is known, to dissolve the aggregate of reasonings that substitutes itself for the naive vision of qualities.[24]

What this theory asks of us is a kind of philosophical ingenuity that is profound because it is innocent and superficial and places us, once again, in the presence of *immediately perceived qualities*. Quality draws all its value from itself, from its own irreducible specificity, and in no way from its relation to something it is not; it demands to be known in itself.[25] We need to speak the language of quality with the sui generis and incomparable originality of quality. For their justification, the facts perceived no longer await the investiture of some transcendent authority, the sanction of an absolute entity: they are justified by the irresistible force of their presence alone, by the irreplaceable value with which effective and actual experiences are endowed. The philosopher thus effortlessly surrounds herself with unshakable truths and persuasive evidences; she leaves the burden of proof to those who contest them and prefer to beg from apodictic reasoning the alms of an always meager and fragile certainty.[26] Only lived experiences comprehend themselves.

This is so true that the various symbolisms owe what little reality they possess to intuition and to intuition alone. If the mathematicians' instant does not entirely reduce itself to the geometrical point, it is because it carries with it a recollection of that real time that our intellect's artifices have not managed to disfigure completely. And in the same way that abstract simultaneity, however inhuman it may be, still borrows from intuitive simultaneity the semblance of reality it conserves so, mathematical time, more generally, which is already so little, would be nothing at all if true becoming were not there to perpetually "temporalize" it, to infuse it with a little warmth and life. The crude symbolism that so gravely adulterates our inner truth in turn lets itself be taken by the beneficent contagion of intuition. The "fourth dimension" thus subsists only thanks to a diminished vitality for which it goes begging from veritable intuition. Intuition metes out life to the very fictions that aspire to drive it out. As the concept only breathes in an atmosphere of intuition, as speech only advances driven by intuition, so everything solid about our space, about our caricatures of duration comes from the spirit they do their best to abuse.[27]

II. *Becoming*

If, then, we consult a "non-prejudiced" thought entirely present to itself, if we discard the idols of distance that intercept our gaze and take us away from ourselves, this is what we will discover: the human is a certain almost inexistent and equivocal something [*je ne sais quoi de presque inexistant et d'équivoque*], which is not only in becoming but is itself a becoming incarnate that is entirely duration, an itinerant temporality! It is not, nor isn't it not: thus, it is becoming... "It either does not exist at all or barely, and in the obscure way," Aristotle says about time. "One part of it has been and is not, while the other is going to be and is not yet."[28] It is not what it is, and it is what it is not, because the same always becomes other in continual alteration. Even more precisely: our states of consciousness concatenate according to an uninterrupted becoming without relation to number.

To designate this concatenation, Bergson uses the word "organization," which an analysis of organic totalities will presently allow us to better understand. First of all, "organization" overcomes the alternative of Same and Other; the aporias relative to the One and the Many discussed in Plato's *Philebus* and *Parmenides* are false problems. Bergson is no more astonished by the One being capable of being many than by the many being capable of being but one.[29] Life ignores the contradictions that drive the intellect to despair. Does becoming, this mix of being and nonbeing, not elude the principle of the excluded middle? When life falls into order in lived duration, it is not bound to choose between the one and the many, between identity without nuances and alterity without coherence. Bergson refuses to get caught between these opposites just as he refuses to be caught between unilateral causality and finality. For life, there are no irresolvable dilemmas. Schelling already said it: life is a thousand times more ingenious than dogmatic philosophy, which comes up against the principle of disjunction and lets itself be torn apart between the extremes.

First of all, life does not have to choose precisely because it endures. Material bodies, which do not age at all but subsist in the intemporal juxtaposition of their parts, will remain eternally homogenous or eternally multiple according to whether they adopt the form of unity or the form of plurality—there is no cure for that. But what keeps the same consciousness from being one today, many tomorrow? Time does not tolerate definitive predicates. It loans but never gives, as Lucretius says: "possession to none . . . unto all mere usufruct."[30] But while time readily revokes its own gifts, it is also a great healer. Time heals all wounds, lubricates, fluidifies, and pacifies painful contradictions, dilates unsolvable conflicts, brings pleasant variety into brutal unity. Opposites, incapable of coexisting *uno eodemque tempore* [at one and the same time] can at least succeed one the other. One *first, then* the other: that is the ruse of futurition that prevents the contemporaneity of the Not-yet, the Now, and the Already-no-longer. Had to think of it! An absurd contradiction, which is an evil, makes way for a scandalous denial, which is a lesser evil. The inexhaustible subtlety and ingeniousness of temporal solutions are disconcerting for the intellect because the intellect is not made for understanding the successive; it readily shuts itself away in the dead end of incompossibles, incompatibles, and irreconciliables.

But have we not learned that personality evolves by divergence and radiance, deploying little by little a plurality of tendencies primitively compressed in the unity of our virtual character?[31] The image of the sheaf is everywhere in Bergson. And just as the whole person complicates itself in multiple tendencies, so each tendency taken by itself within the person proliferates itself in variegated emotions that in turn disperse into a multitude of sufferings and joys that become more and more particular. Evolution in general is nothing but this continuing transition from the one to the many, this progressive blossoming of an identity that matures in plurality.

But at the same time at which unity breaks up into particular tendencies, these tendencies are resorbed in an inverse and proportional movement. Plurality is mended, so to speak, to the extent to which unity dislodges itself. At each moment of its becoming, consciousness thus presents us with the spectacle of a rich and varied identity or, as Schopenhauer says,[32] of a *concordia discors* [discordant concord] in which neither the abstract one nor the abstract many can boast of a definite superiority. The criticist idea of Synthesis obtains an admirably clear, new, and spiritual sense. The unity of the mind is a "choral" unity like the *sobornost*'s "conciliary" unity in Sergeĭ Trubetskoĭ, Semyon Frank, and Russian Slavophilism. It rests on the exaltation of singularities and not on their leveling; it does not reign in the desert of concertante multiplicities because it is not a solitary identity but the perpetual victory over alterity.[33] Time is thus not simply the absence of contradiction. It is contradiction vanquished and perpetually resolved; better still, it is this resolution itself, considered in its transitive aspect. Hence the thickness, the concrete plenitude and animation of becoming: unity is never done with putting the recalcitrant originalities in their place, for the protest of the multiple is not easily stifled.

On the other hand, duration overcomes the antinomy of the continuous and the discontinuous just as it overcomes the antinomy of the one and the multiple, and just as Jean Wahl's metaphysics stands beyond such antitheses. Our lived time certainly is continuity itself, like the space of the painter Eugène Carrière. But this continuity does not exclude—what am I saying?—it necessarily presupposes the fundamental heterogeneity of the states it organizes. And reciprocally, thanks to its very homogeneity, homogenous space lends itself to the most trenchant discontinuities. That is the second paradox of becoming. In bare space, there are none of the natural articulations, the great organic divisions that delimit from the outside and the inside the individuals of a group, the parts of a living body, the feelings of a consciousness. Bare space is the realm of uniformity, the desert-like *khōra* [space] that we can arbitrarily slice up one way or another, cut up into the artificial fragments that the demands of action have shown us to be useful. This bare space does not by itself manifest any preference for certain kinds of division over others. Faced with this indifference, all we have to do is cut up this material extension according to our needs; we portion it into pieces we call things, bodies, phenomena. This is what Bergson calls "breaking up" [*morcelage*].[34] Did not Plotinus and Damascius already speak of a *merismos*, of division and distribution?[35]

Duration, on the contrary, is heterogeneous but cannot be broken up. Breaking up is an artificial operation that the intellect operates on its own works and one that space can withstand because space, precisely, is a relaxation, an abstraction of the intellect. But our duration already possesses its objective divisions and does not indifferently withstand no matter what kind of analysis. Duration is thus fundamentally heterogeneous. But, because our crude breaking up has no bearing on it, we say that duration is "continuous," thereby expressing that the utilitarian analysis that eats into space glides along time without finding the slightest fissure in it. In reality, this continuity only signifies that becoming tolerates no discontinuity whatsoever. It does not in any way signify that becoming fades away in a haze or excludes all kinds of variety. Continuity is neither vagueness nor indifferentiation, and time is indivisible rather than undivided. Put differently, we cannot hew it as our fantasy bids us, even if we sense in it natural and profound distinctions. The continuous, in this sense, is the infinitely discontinuous...

It is this aspect of disjunction and determination that is fully brought out by the Bergsonian philosopher Albert Bazaillas or in a pluralism along the lines of William James and Charles Renouvier.[36] Pluralist unilateralism, for that matter, seems much more Bergsonian than Bazaillas's, and if I had to choose, I would prefer to linger on the "varieties of experience." As Schelling, hesitating between "heterousia" and "tautousia" or, perhaps, between polytheism and monotheism, says: *Better too much than too little!* But we do not have to choose because life does not shut itself away in scholastic dilemmas. In fact, pluralism simply signifies that in all respects, the given exceeds what is explained and that the experience of duration is a dramatic experience. Deep down, "explanation" is always monistic, and the breaking up it boasts simply plays the comedy of plurality. We know very well that there is nothing serious underneath because this breaking up is our own work, and if we operate it, we do so because it is convenient for us. Nonetheless, we are quite serene, we are sure to regain our dear unity, since the breaking up, far from excluding this unity, presupposes it. We substitute conventional slicings to the diversity and heterogeneity of qualities, slicings that do not seriously compromise the uniformity of the system. This is how mathematical space can appear to be fundamentally homogenous, precisely because it lends itself to any discontinuity whatsoever. We go all the way in this parceling out so that the multiple destroys itself. Breaking up reverts to unity but that is because it has never really left unity behind. Its "plural" is not a true plural. The qualitative heterogeneity of time, on the contrary, implies unity at the very moment in which time most violently contradicts unity, a bit like the coincidence of opposites in mystical experiences. This is the mystery on which we now need to shed light.

The unity of becoming results from an acute crisis from which it emerges resilient and enriched. Bergson, in his examination of the intellectual effort, brilliantly demonstrates how this dynamic unity is opposed to the unity of a dialectic modeled on space.[37] In the horizontal or visual dialectic, there is only one image but it is representative of different objects; in the vertical or penetrating dialectic, on the contrary, there is an infinity of images for one and the same object. That is to say, I think, that in the first case there is a *discontinuous* progress across a *homogenous* world; and we will see how in Bergson the refusal of Nothingness explains the refusal of this discontinuity. Inversely, in the second case, it is the universes traversed that are by nature heterogeneous: the only thing that connects them is the continuity of the effort by which we pass from one to the other. Unity, in the first case, is so to speak substantial and morphological,[38] and it is functional in the second. In the latter, it no longer has its principle in the rigid identity of a form but in the orientation of a certain power and the perpetuity of a melodic theme, something like that *inner voice* whose immaterial song Robert Schumann, in his piano works, sometimes felt compelled to note down, and which seems to entrust to a "third hand" the invisible harmony hidden underneath the visible harmonies.

In a sense, it is really diversity that governs the horizontal dialectic, and the superficial unity of the milieu it adopts only serves to highlight all the more brutally the fundamental plurality of its matter. Thanks to a singular reversal of things, the flat unity that had not wanted to take the multiple into account rests eternally torn, just as it appeared to us earlier to be eternally solitary. Time is no longer there, and time alone could sew its wounds back up. All our divisions are fatal to it because they are definitive, incurable. But the qualitative diversity that we discover at the root of consciousness immediately resolves itself in the circulation of duration.

Thus musical tonalities: tonal universes address our emotion like so many irreducible worlds. Only the miracle of modulation achieves the copenetration of these incommunicable universes and the continuity of the inner voice heard by Florestan. Discontinuities melt, without losing themselves, into the depth of the modulating dynamic that traverses them. Is not the dense cantilena kept up from beginning to end in the capriccio of Gabriel Fauré's *Pièces brèves* an admirable example of this versicolored continuity? Like the effort of understanding, modulation thus implies the intuition of a certain thickness of originalities to break through. For that matter, it is only this spiritual circulation that can resorb so profound a diversity because only life can disregard the conflict of contradictions. And if the mechanical intellect operates in a world of homogeneity it does so because it would be quite incapable of overcoming so many originalities springing up if it had only a static identity at its disposal. Bergson readily applied to mutation the concept of the qualitative leap with which Kierkegaard explains the instant of sin.[39] The specificity of qualities resists the uniformity of quantity.

For quality will not be ruled. We saw earlier how every state of consciousness left to itself tends to round itself off, to organize as a complete universe. Every feeling is a world apart that is lived for itself and where I am wholly present to some degree.[40] The difference between two emotions is as great as that between silence and sound, between darkness and light, or between two musical tonalities. In Antonín Dvořák, G minor is an original universe that the musician entrusts with his most precious emotions. Liszt, whose nature is magnanimous and prodigious by itself, thinks spontaneously in the sharpest and most triumphant tones: E major, F-sharp major—nothing is too rich for this generous sensibility. E minor is Tchaikovsky's autumnal and melancholic kingdom, and Sergeï Prokofiev's games are usually played in the white and innocent light of C major. Fauré, Albéniz, Janáček display a faithful predilection for flattened tones; in Fauré, these tones have quite different values and powers, and it is impossible to think of them as interchangeable. Each state of sensibility thus expresses itself in a one-of-a-kind tonality that is independent of all the others: such is, no doubt, the function of D-flat major in Fauré. These are, perhaps, so many absolutes between which there is no conceivable equivalence, no conceivable parity.

Fechner's psychophysics already makes this point, since it shows us how sensation varies in leaps when the stimulation grows in a scaled and continuous crescendo.[41] Mechanicism can indefinitely insert transitions between two quantities: such is the method Descartes suggests in the twelfth of his *Rules for the Direction of the Mind*. There, he interprets the differences between colors with the help of geometrical figures, "avoiding the useless assumption and pointless invention of some new entity."[42] But what middle term could ever link a pain and a joy? And yet duration works this miracle. That is the reason why a consciousness that is truly contemporaneous with its own duration is not afflicted, as discourse is, by the fatality of mediation. The intermediaries that lengthen discourse are only delay, detour, and the cause of slowness. They exist only with a view to the end to which they are the means. If it could, the mind would skip over them. Each moment of becoming, on the contrary, has its own value and its own dignity; each is its own means and its own end. There is succession but no discursion: here, one must sometimes "wait." Certain ends are privileged, but this wait is always full of interest, events, and fascinating surprises. Each instant of our inner history is immensely rich in the unforeseen. Better than anyone, Goncharov has managed to enter into this infinitesimal drama in which one sees details bustle, novelties spring up, and opposites link up.

We will see later what importance Bergson's philosophy attaches to discontinuity, both in the relationship of soul and body and in the relationships between biological species. It does so because the exaltation of plurality honors the becoming that triumphs over it and assigns a singular price to it. Mechanicism devalues this plurality and endows itself with a hollow duration by superimposing on changes a numerical scale that makes our feelings gradable and measurable. Always positive, always current, becoming is succeeded by a measurable and fantastic time that one may well call, as Plato does in the *Timaeus*, a "moving image of eternity,"[43] or, as does Joseph de Maistre, "a forced thing that only asks to end."[44] This, perhaps, keeps us from despairing of attenuating Bergson's opposition to Greek philosophy. The time disparaged by Plato, Aristotle, and Plotinus is generally either grammatical discursion or astronomical time; in both cases, overall, a numerical time that "revolves according to a law of number."[45] Yet that time is indeed a delay, something negative that the mind would readily do without if it were more perfect; it simply expresses that which we have not been able to do. We may thus very well say, and undoubtedly, Bergson would not deny this, that such a time does violence to our true nature in the sense that intuition in all its purity seeks to attain the real immediately and not at the end of a laborious stroll across the syllogisms. This is a limitation, a weakness, a deficit, and we firmly hope, like the angel of the Apocalypse, that the day will come when this time will be no more.[46]

But condemning this insipid time in no way prejudges true time or, better, duration, which is the experience of continuation.[47] On the contrary, there are many opportunities for "eternity" (thus defined in opposition to the time of *logismoi*) to turn out to be related to the duration Bergson purified of all arithmetical fictions. This is the epitome of spiritual density. The mind, instead of ceaselessly lagging behind a far-off goal, instead of roaming like an absentee among provisional and subaltern ideas, finds itself continually at the heart of its own effort, in the very midst of problems. To pass from this living eternity to the time of grammar, one does not need to add anything; on the contrary, one has to take something away, to absent oneself from oneself and scatter among the concepts. This is perhaps the true sense of the metaphysicians' "eternal Now": at every moment, we feel ourselves to be present to ourselves, surrounded by certainties and essential things.[48] Bergson's philosophy is time regained.

Our mathematical intellect cannot stand diversity. The essence of measuring is, in fact, less to classify, organize, and compare magnitudes than it is to make things comparable by quantifying them. Measuring standardizes the given and extracts the simple element shared by all things, the numerical element. Measuring thus assimilates more than it separates. And precisely there where it keeps extreme terms at a distance, as in the difference between the maximum and the minimum, this distance still implies an essential parity that makes the comparison possible. What brings the greatest and the smallest together is that they are both quantities. Like Aristotle's *enantia* [opposites],[49] they are the most distant terms within the same genre. Yet the most extreme opposition can only exist between comparable magnitudes. The equal is given virtually where the greatest and the smallest are, or else no gradations are possible. Number is precisely the middle term shared by objects that cannot be compared directly, and the sciences of measuring, like the syllogism itself, consist entirely in the ever more sophisticated mediations that allow us to assimilate these disparities.

Yet qualitative changes exclude virtual equality. The only thing the successive states through which a subject passes have in common is the continuous movement that carries us from one to the other. The unity that is substantial and transcendent in increase and decrease—since it comes from an implied middle term whose magnitudes are more or less involved and which is (rightly) called "unit"—becomes, in alterations, immanent and dynamic. It is no longer to be sought outside of transformed stages but characterizes the appearance of transformation itself. The successive phases of becoming can no longer be numbered along a straight scale. They confront the surveyors of the mind with a sort of profound fantasy that we will see again later in the undisciplined pure recollections of dreams or in the singular whims of phylogenetic evolution. The contradictions become so unforeseen that no extrinsic mediation whatsoever could find the least communality it could increase. Presently, the successive moments must come to an arrangement and consent to a pact that trumps all their mutual loathing. This tour de force is called duration. Duration is not a thing apart: it is but the spontaneous continuation of these dissonances infinitely organizing and resolving themselves.

In a way, the brutal homogeneity of increases and diminutions, owing nothing to the movement according to which quantities organize themselves, leaves bare the fundamental discontinuity of the entities being compared. Quantitative assimilation is clear, flat, and without nuances. It crumbles and levels every whole. It disguises spiritual facts as "transformed sensations" or as "nervous shocks," and it ends up being incapable of explaining the magical affinity that attracts them. Atomism in vain reduces the joyful variety of becoming to "units." Our states of consciousness, submitted to the reductive analysis of associationism, will certainly end up resembling each other on the outside. Yet this resemblance remains as unilateral as it is superficial since to obtain it, one has had to deprive the spiritual facts of all their singularities and retain only one very general and very abstract property. Duration, on the contrary, first accepts the irreconcilable originalities of our feelings and our states of mind, their unsettling reversals, their contradictory claims. Unity, here, thus presupposes not a partial assimilation but a total consent. Just as everything divided us, everything will reunite us. What thus takes place in duration, at every moment, is the fusion of opposites the mystics speak of, which we experience, precisely and totally, in the whimsical concatenation of our emotions.

The discovery and exploration of becoming presuppose a critical labor that gives rise, in *Time and Free Will*, to the first antitheses of Bergson's philosophy. Becoming is what remains when I have separated my intimate personality from the official self that usurps its dignity, when I have become, as Plotinus says, internal to myself—"having entered myself, going out from all things."[50] In Bergson, the spirit of soliloquy and recollection, the spirit of the *Phaedo*, of Saint Augustine, and of Louis Lavelle, often takes a critical form. Bergson's entire effort tends to dissociate "spurious concepts" [*concepts bâtards*]—number, speed, simultaneity—that result from an encroachment: for space encroaches on time, the line traveled along on movement, the point on the instant, quantity on quality, and finally, physical necessity on free effort.[51] The Relativists' space-time, the "fourth dimension" rests on an ambivalence of this kind, as do Fechner's logarithms, which blend sensation and stimulation, mental facts with their causes, and mix up competences. This constitutes—and this is the word used—a veritable phenomenon of moral endosmosis and, so to speak, an exchange of substance between time and space. Bergson's temporalism throws all these monsters out. Time must be thought apart and primarily and not be reduced to something else: symbolisms and myths of symmetry are dismissed. Bergson denounces, above all, the contamination of the mind by exteriority: a Kantianism in reverse.

But he does not for all that neglect the reaction of quality on quantity: for the hybrid concepts of associationism spring from a bilateral and reciprocal encroachment. Bergson's philosophy in *Time and Free Will* is above all a dualist affirmation, a refusal to accept the compromises of science and the half-measures of practice: there are two times and two selves. Henri Bremond, too, distinguishes between *Animus* and *Anima*, opposing "the fine point, the center or the apex of the soul," our mystical essence, to "the self of anecdotes and petty events."[52]

And there are even two memories. In one sense, memory is duration itself as continuation of change; it expresses that there is no duration without a consciousness capable of prolonging its past into its present. But there is another memory—or rather, the same, considered after the fact. This one is but the survival of a bygone past; this one remains external to the things it conserves. Bergson opposes it to "judgment" in terms that recall Montaigne; it is less "continuation" than it is "retention" and limits itself to jealously guarding the traditions whose meaning it has lost, an inert past it truncates and disfigures.[53]

At one point, Bergson even affirms that time and space are two contradictory terms[54]—in *Creative Evolution*, we will read: two inverse movements. Of these two times, of these two selves, only one is true; the other is but a counterfeit of the first, which alone holds the privilege of vitality. Or, even more exactly: mathematical time is an adulterated time only insofar as it claims to play the role of true time. Static science, which is true when it comes to accomplished facts, becomes fraudulent only when it also claims to legislate for facts accomplishing themselves, for the present *in the process of* accomplishing itself. What is false and unreal, in a word, is the "amalgamate," the intrusion of space and of language into a domain in which they are no longer competent—for the truth lies in the dissociation of competences.

Bergson thus distinguishes between the true and the false a little like Berkeley explains the illusions of optics. Everything is true when perceived for itself, and left to themselves our senses never deceive us. Error begins at the precise point where the mind, grown strong with recollections and prejudices, begins to interpret the pure given. Error is born with association and, in consequence, with relation. And, in the same way, the false optic of space-time and the four-dimensional non-Euclidian *continuum* originate in an unfounded association that the mind establishes between two equally real givens. For there is a "real space" that is no less true than real duration.[55] *Time and Free Will* does not tell us any more than that, and we will have to wait until *Matter and Memory* to obtain some clarifications on the pure intuition of which real space can be the object, the intuition that is matter itself.

Can we say, however, that already from this point on Bergson no longer attempts to overcome the dualism? The primary objective of *Time and Free Will*, to be sure, is to dissociate mixed concepts, to separate the confused levels whose collaboration Bergson will later focus on. The immediate givens to which we thus gain access are in no way of the entirely ideal nature of "pure recollection" and "pure perception." Even dreams do not offer us anything that the duration of the profound self does not daily accomplish, as an attentive introspection will show.[56] The objective of *Time and Free Will*, to sum up, is to find the *givens* that an incredible negligence has caused us to lose, and one still wonders how a reality so natural, so close to us, could have escaped us for so long. That is why there is no "intuition" yet in *Time and Free Will*: there, it is enough to eliminate the entirely negative symbolics of space to find oneself face to face with one's true self. From this time on, certain passages[57] invite us to believe that the incriminated amalgamate responds to an organic demand of the mind and that we may have to pay a heavy price for its exclusion. In fact, discourse and intuition collaborate at every moment. The space that disfigures our profound self also allows it to express itself, to declare itself before our philosophical vision. But what is tragic is precisely that duration cannot express itself without perishing; we will learn later that it is nonetheless knowable, albeit by other means than by discourse. But intuition properly speaking does not appear at all before *Creative Evolution*.[58]

On the other hand, although duration still remains a privilege of consciousness, Bergson already seems to have a sense that duration may perhaps not be limited by consciousness. This is proven, even in *Time and Free Will*, by the discovery of pure "mobility." As a phenomenon situated on the border between the mind and the external world, spiritual in its essence, physical in its effects, tangential to both universes, movement in a way is objective spirit. Without further explanation, Bergson already states that there is "some incomprehensible reason,"[59] "some inexpressible reason"[60] that gives material things the appearance of duration. This mystery, this je ne sais quoi also seems to him to pertain more to the presence of the mind than to a property of the things themselves.

It cannot meanwhile be contended that Bergson's philosophy leaves it at an affirmation of a universal duration. It is true that the duality is thus enlarged rather than abolished. There is time and creation in the world as in the human being, and if the opposition is no longer between the memory of subjects and the space of things, it subsists, across the whole of reality, between two inverse movements, the one a movement of materialization, the other of living evolution. Duality, meanwhile, has become very subtle and much less brutal. Bergson's speculation thus little by little discovers an irreducible element of succession in the history of things. It is this historical residue that prevents the physicists' causality from completely resembling an identity. It is this residue, too, that makes mathematical time plausible and usable. After *Creative Evolution*, Bergson will even go so far as to enlarge the share of this universal duration at the expense of the self.[61]

If duration does not express a simple deficiency of our knowledge it is because duration is a characteristic of things no less than it is a property of consciousness—better still: because there is consciousness everywhere. It is really the events that happen to us, not we that happen to them. "To take place" is not by any means, and whatever Eddington may think, a superfluous formality, and those who have tasted the bitterness of action know that duration is the thing in this world that is the most real. Why do we sometimes have to wait for the next day, why is the future not given to us with the present, unless it is because there is a temporality with which we do not do as we please and because the interval is irreducible? This is not a formality; on the contrary, nothing belongs more to experience. The world's greatest philosopher has to wait for the sugar to dissolve in his professor's glass...[62] But, from another perspective, this very resistance of the given is reassuring to us. Dialectical time is really negative because, supposing its object to be given in eternity, it has to accomplish great circuits before finding it; only its constitutional weakness is at issue. But why would the duration of things remain silent about our inner duration? Change is made to know change, and our intuition sets out on the path of the absolute itself.

In fact, only duration can reveal the absolute, or, perhaps better put, only duration provides us with an entirely *determined* reality because it is sanctioned by lived and perceived experience, which is always determined, that is to say, particular.[63] All duration in fact constitutes an oriented, irreversible series. Because it is oriented, this series is not to be taken up indifferently at whatever end; it is, depending on the case, enrichment or impoverishment.[64] Duration thus represents a kind of dramatic order whose episodes cannot be reversed at will, a biography in which the succession of lived experience[65] has itself something intentional and organic about it. A philosophy that would remain true even if everything went backward would discount itself. Only *orientation* and direction count. Science only calculates relations between simultaneities, and that is why it can presuppose intervals of time that are infinitely accelerated or decelerated without having to change its equations.[66] This utopia, abstract and about as serious as the traveling twins, proves the absurdity of relativism!

Only the period in between simultaneities is temporal, only this in-between is an undivided transition and a continuous interval. "I am not portraying being but becoming," Montaigne said.[67] Every lived duration possesses a certain specific quality, a determined value, an affective coefficient it takes from my effort, my expectation, or my impatience: yet this impatience or this effort is a qualitative change, that is to say, an absolute. Discursion draws its only value from the goal it mediates. The interval itself is but a deficit and annoying delay, the principle of pure expectancy. It is a replaceable tool (replaceable because other means could, in theory, serve the same end), and the ideal would even be to do completely without it. But lived duration is in itself its end; what is important here is the interval, which is all plenitude. It is not a lost time of any kind, not a duration of expectation I would pass waiting for this or that event, like those who "kill" time twiddling their thumbs: it is a one-of-a-kind progress in the course of which I age and which will be a loss or a gain for me. True time thus brings into play the history of the entire person. It is to fantastic time what the instinct of *Creative Evolution* is to the intellect: true time is of a "categorical" nature while the mathematicians' time only has "hypothetical" existence, like Hegelian dialectics, which Schelling and Kierkegaard reproach for being notional and deplorably ineffective. What will the *quoddity* of history yield for us? How do we regain this "lived time," which Minkowski has described with such profundity?

All of *Duration and Simultaneity* is thus dedicated to showing that the immediate intuition of time provides us with a natural and absolute system of reference and that the commonsense belief in a universal time has a philosophical foundation. "Common sense," which *Time and Free Will* had held responsible for the ambiguous symbolisms of vulgar science, becomes the vehicle of a great truth that allies it to the philosophers against the physicists. This is an apparent "reversal from for to against": lived duration once again becomes the stronghold of common obvious facts that previously it had seemed to deny. Does Bergson's theory of matter not indirectly prove commonsense realism right?[68] That is because there is a learned naivety that is a thousand times more profound than the erudites' vain subtleties. This naivety commands us to believe in the universality of time, in the absolute reality of movement. Relativist science evaporates, turns into fantasies all these things that are so simple, so solid, so natural because it has taken up the habit of looking at phenomena *perspectively*, that is to say, from variable points of view that it chooses, one after the other, as its systems of reference.[69]

Intuitive duration thus provides us with the principle of a kind of higher anthropocentrism. The distinctive feature of Bergson's philosophy is its affirmation that there is, under each and every circumstance, a *privileged system*, no longer a system of reference but a system higher than any reference, the system I experience from within the instant I speak. No paradox can defeat the certainty of a thought internal to itself that experiences itself as willing, living, and enduring. Each of us possesses a duration (since duration equals consciousness) and therefore we rightly each take ourselves as our "referrer" on this privileged level, so much so that universal reciprocity destroys itself and restores absolute time.

But the essence of the relativist paradoxes consists in placing on one level all the fantastic visions a referring consciousness obtains from the consciousnesses referred to, in thus misunderstanding the metaphysical distance of the real from the virtual. More than that, the real becomes a particular case of the virtual. Just as we pretend to take the various phantasms seriously that we felt like imagining, just as we surreptitiously infuse our "referred" observers with life, so effective duration ceases to exert that incomparable superiority over fictitious durations that distinguishes a living being in flesh and bones from a wax doll. A number of "proper times" have been devised and even hypostasized where perhaps there was simply a plurality of metrics.

Bergson on the contrary has too high an opinion of the real—as is evident in the distinction between recollection and perception—to place it on the same level as these counterfeits. He is not the man to take for true beings all these tortoises, these middle school Achilles, these dialectical or mathematical puppets called traveling twins, space-time, light figures. The things I can experience effectively and personally—my duration, my labor, my effort—are privileged and painfully certain realities to which no other experience compares. These movements are relative for the eye, i.e. for the geometer, who holds on only to the visual aspect of things; but they are not relative for my muscles, for my action, for my exhaustion.[70]

Nobody gets this wrong. Just as duration is irreversible, that is, it implies events that are absolutely anterior and events that are absolutely posterior, an order in which one cannot intervene, so the intuition of duration restores to the universe the hierarchies and prerogatives an egalitarian relativism sets out to abolish. The title "reality" no longer designates a provisional emblem wandering from phenomenon to phenomenon, varying according to the perspective of an observer, decorating at will the system we arbitrarily subject to our point of view: it is a natural privilege that unilaterally belongs to perceived or perceptible things. The primacy of intuition no longer depends on a revocable convention or an arbitrarily chosen point of view. It is a birthright of the mind. For the things of the mind are not things like all the others. They constitute a domain of the chosen, a world completely apart where there are only effective realities, where one is paid in gold and no longer in currency. In terms borrowed from the *Phaedo*, we may say that it is for these things that all other values are to be exchanged. Intuitionism is the true metaphysics of the mind and intuition is the true center of the world.

There are prophetic views on the relation of duration to space to be found in Guyau's psychology,[71] and it seems all the more useful to point these anticipations out as *The Origin of the Idea of Time* may have been retrospectively affected by Bergson's discovery.[72] Like Bergson,[73] Guyau begins by criticizing the English school's geneticist thesis according to which the idea of space is to be construed with the idea of time. Underneath the theories that grant time a semblance of primacy, Bergson, faithful to true duration, sets out above all to frustrate the prestige of an illusory time that is nothing but space; in the same way, he will fight classical indeterminism to better be able to save freedom. Is Guyau's argumentation as subtle?

The time of Herbert Spencer, of Alexander Bain, and of Sully is certainly the "amalgamate" *Time and Free Will* so detests. In this sense, it is indeed space that serves to construe a notion of time. Duration is not measurable until it has been translated into the terms of space. Measuring, Guyau asserts, is always a comparison, by means of superposition, between two extensions. Yet "I cannot *directly* superimpose a standard interval on another time interval because time is in constant flux and never repeats itself. . . . This is why giving a certain permanence to this incessant flow of time requires its being presented in spatial form."[74] And Guyau arrives at formulas that might well be inspired by Bergson: "Time acts, initially, as a fourth dimension of the objects in space."[75] Spencer would thus never manage to extract time from space if this time were not already a phantom of space. For Guyau, this vicious circle, in which Bergson sees an expression of the impossibility of deducing one metaphysically distinct reality from another, proves nothing more than the spatial origin of calendars and temporal emblems.

Guyau furthermore distinguishes between the "bed" and the "stream" of duration.[76] The pseudo-duration of the Spencer school is a "static form" opposed to the "living and moving basis," the extensive alignment according to which concrete elements organize themselves, the empty pathway that is to be animated by the mobile circulation of my experiences. The "stream" of time, Guyau writes, is "change caught in the act [*saisi sur le fait*]."[77] In the act! Or, as Bergson would say, "as it comes [*au fur et à mesure*]," for there is no time to lose if we want to experience the originality of this dynamic. The least delay of memory, the least anticipation of the imagination, substitutes space for the intuition of a change always contemporaneous with itself.

To tell the truth, Guyau limits himself to confronting abstract space and abstract time. But in this case, he may rightly be said to be preaching to the choir. For if there really is no other time than the one geneticism employs for construing space, then there is no problem in reserving the monopoly of originality for space. But that might be taking the easy way out. Bergson himself was well aware of this in a short review of *The Origin of the Idea of Time* he published in the *Revue philosophique* in February 1891. For him, there is no doubt that Guyau admits only one kind of multiplicity, numerical multiplicity, and hence "*there is no use in wanting to picture time without space because one started out by putting space into time.* To say numerical multiplicity is to say multiplicity of juxtaposition, multiplicity in space."[78] Guyau conceives of no other than the following alternative: either it is time that serves to construe space or it is space that serves to construe time—the time of our clocks and our calendars. But is there not an autonomous order of duration that is neither anterior nor posterior to space and represents an absolutely original metaphysical reality? As to this "stream" of time that is opposed to chronometric time as "content" is opposed to "form," we can probe it as much as we like, we won't find anything that would merit the name of real Duration.

Guyau calls the common source of notions of time and space "intention." He defines this intention in terms that are clearly influenced by utilitarianism and pragmatism. Pierre Janet would no doubt have agreed to these terms more readily than Bergson: intention is "the movement following a sensation," the motor reaction provoked by acting and being acted on; it is desire and willing, and it goes back to the "distinction between what one needs and what one has," to the distance between "'the goblet and the lips.'"[79] This intention, which differs from the mathematicians' "constant and necessary succession," differs no less from pure duration: "The future is that which is in front of the animal and what it is looking for; the past is what is behind it and what it can no longer see." To be aware of time means to know "the *prius* and *posterius* of the expanse." For Guyau, "*succession* is an abstraction of *motor effort* produced in *space*; an effort which, when it becomes conscious, is *intention*."[80] Time is an abstraction from movement, from *kinesis*... What creates time in human consciousness is movement. No time without movement. Even Aristotle, despite his refusal to identify time with movement, admits that there is no time without movement ("evidently time is not independent of movement and change"), that time is the "number of motion in respect of 'before' and 'after'" or, more precisely, the numbered ("what is counted"), better, the measure (*metron*).[81]

Bergson, however, endeavored to show (and *Duration and Simultaneity* goes back to this demonstration) that movement, on the contrary, is the intermediary thanks to which duration becomes measurable, that is to say, extensive. Far from engendering the idea of time, movement is, rather, the expedient that allows us to confuse duration and trajectory. Everything positive about movement—the mobility of the act of changing—is of a spiritual and temporal nature.

Guyau thus does not manage to overcome the idea of a time that is, in a sense, muscular and affective, a time he interprets as the distance between need and satisfaction.[82] What his book promises us is a study on the *idea* of time, not on the *feeling* of duration. The "stream" of duration is a representation a little more elementary than the "static form" of time, but a representation nonetheless. Pierre Janet would have called it a comportment. When Bergson denounces the spatial artifice at the basis of the erudites' mendacious duration, we see that his only goal is to isolate the philosophers' pure duration and that he casts out illusionary time in order to regain real time all the more successfully. It is to be feared, in turn, that Guyau's critique attains time in general, not only the mathematicians' deceptive time. He so insists on the priority of space that one loses hope of ever seeing pure time free itself of impure time: "Time is the abstract formula for describing change in the universe."[83] It is the form according to which our sensations organize, our reactions orient themselves, and our desires are ranked.

We are even permitted to think that the reason why Guyau goes so far in his critique of impure duration is that he knows that his entire psychology could only succeed in pure duration. False duration is not as false as all that; it would not even have the appearance of time if the intuition of true duration were not there to maintain and vivify it. It supplies the phantoms of the cinematic with a reminiscence of this intuition and with something like a timid presentiment of its return. We would not for a second have faith in all these equations unless we knew that they can at any moment be converted into direct experience, just as we would stop having faith in banknotes if they were not promises of well-being, comfort, and pleasure. The mathematicians' duration is spatial so long as it pleases Guyau: it is a fact that it is not to be confused with space pure and simple. It would be inexplicable if the appearance did not presuppose its model.

And the model is within us. In us, there is all life, all reality. No "comportment," be it waiting, be it intention, would ever yield duration if it did not imply, in advance, the intuition of duration; for comportments, left to themselves, only yield comportments. Because we know that our meager symbols will become pure duration again the moment we want them to, we never refrain from realizing them and, in our ingratitude, we forget the true time that makes them live. Nonetheless, the return to intuition cannot be perpetually postponed. No one will continue to accept symbols in which none of all the solid and effective good things that nourish intuition are to be found sooner or later. For we cannot live without the absolute.

Time is neither a dimension, nor an attribute among others of the human being, nor a partitive property of this being; time is not a certain mode of being of Being, for Being, in this case, could de jure be conceived as an intemporal substance outside of all chronological modality. Nor does Bergson distinguish between a form that would be furnished, secondarily, i.e. accidentally, with temporal contents... All these abstractions give life again to the Orphic, Platonic, perennial prejudice of a loss of wings and calamitous fall into temporality: for if temporality is a punishment, it is by this very fact epigenesis and contingency. The origin of this prejudice, in turn, is the fixist and substantialist superstition of the system of reference. Just as substantialism pictures a neutral and non-qualified substratum that would come before all ways of being circumstantial, so specious transformism pictures evolution as being sewn onto an immutable background. An unchanging type, changing only its coat, plumage, or fancy dress, i.e. modifying its modalities by "metamorphosis," would operate some small pellicular variations on the theme of the species. For this mutationism, modification, *trans*formation, *trans*figuration are nothing but a stroll from form to form or a transition from figure to figure. As for alteration, it is defined in relation to the Same. Time is thus the secondary characteristic of a being that *is* first and only then becomes or operates, for Being preexists Action. Evolutionism, which reconstitutes evolution from fragments of the evolved, treats change as a superficial arrangement of old elements, that is to say, as a paraphrase of immutability. It is, in other words, the art of making the old new again... Take the same elements and start anew!

Yet, the human being is not only "temporal," in the sense that temporality would be a qualifying adjective of its substance: it is the human being who is time itself (and nothing but time), who is the ipseity of time. To apparent changes, Bergson opposes the metempirical idea of a "transubstantiation," of a central becoming that carries all being into another being, and contradicts the principle of identity. To partitive metabolisms, *Creative Evolution* will oppose the prodigy of radical mutation, to evolutionist pseudo-historicism, revolutionary change. To the static prejudice of a pellicular temporality, the second Oxford lecture on "The Perception of Change" will oppose the paradoxical and almost violent idea of an "ontic becoming": a contradictory idea that constrains us to invert all our habits, to distort our logic, and to undertake a profound inner reform. Does not the inversion of the relation between time and eternity already presuppose a "conversion"? The change without a subject that changes, which this radical relativism tells us about, is the correlate of the qualities without a substrate of perceptionist impressionism. Time is consubstantial with the entire thickness of Being, or, rather, it is the only essence of a being whose entire essence it is to change! It is thus the whole being, down to its root and its ipseity, that is taken up in the movement of becoming. In other terms: being has no other way of being than to become, that is to say, precisely, to be by not being, to be an Already-no-longer or a Not-yet.

Freedom, like time, is the very substance of the human being. For dogmatic indeterminism, liberty designates a partial characteristic of this being. It is, for example, the unassailable stronghold to which a will on the defensive retreats. Freedom is not a negative exception in the tracks of determinism; it is a creative positivity. It does not modify the arrangement of the parts but delivers matter by way of a revolutionary decision. The human being is all freedom, as it is all becoming. It is a freedom on two legs that comes, that goes, that talks, and that breathes. This is what I have to show now.

III. *The Free Act*

Nowhere has the idol of explanation given rise to more irresolvable aporias than where the question of freedom is at issue.[84] Nowhere else does the concern with explanation more readily betray its true nature and retrospective consequences. *Explanation* is, precisely, never contemporaneous with the things to be explained. It replaces the empirical history of events with the intelligible history of phenomena and has to wait for the former to be completely told before it can reconstitute the latter. What opposes narrative [*récit*] to explanation is that in a narrative, biographers or narrators are, by convention, always contemporaneous with the novelistic chronicle that unfolds, while in an "explanation," moralists or historians are fictitiously posterior to the chronicle they unfold. Explanation is thus not only an abolishment of time, as Émile Meyerson has set out to show: the very act of explanation presupposes time to be abolished, the chronicle to be unfolded.[85] What is free will when it is distorted by the optics of retrospectivity? And what is freedom during the free act?

(1) Traditional spiritualism has bequeathed on us a bookish formula for the free voluntary act (which has often been criticized, notably by

Charles Blondel). That, no doubt, is what one is looking for in books. Perhaps the examination of a caricature of volition will shed some light, indirectly, on the authentic freedom of willing. The textbooks, as we all know, distinguish between four successive moments in volition, which they call conception, deliberation, decision, and execution. Do we first need to show how absurd and arbitrary it is to introduce such a division, which distinguishes between operations that are presupposed to be incommunicable and substantially distinct? At the root of this model volition, we recognize above all the tenacious prejudice that all of Bergson's philosophy fights against: the mind waits for the free act to have unfolded all of its mental episodes instead of seizing, live, as it were, their concrete immanence. One thus gives oneself a skeleton of will that perhaps belongs to the ideal homunculus of Wolffian psychology but not to the real, willing, and acting individual. In fact, vulgar substantialism wants at all costs for deliberation to precede and prepare resolution just as resolution precedes, for example, execution.[86] It does so because, "logically," one must hesitate *before* deciding, because the act must be possible before being real, because volition must resemble a fabrication in the course of which the act is constructed piece by piece by passing gradually from virtual or deliberate existence to actual or resolved existence.

But an experience truly contemporaneous with action shows, on the contrary, that we deliberate *after* having resolved much more than before resolving. This seems absurd, but the very uselessness of so "posthumous" a deliberation testifies to the disinterestedness of the speculative intellect, which, to satisfy its predilection for the mechanic, would willingly logicize our entire life. It is as if, by dint of seeking everywhere the order of fabrication, the order of technics, in short, a "useful" order, its constitutional inertia has driven it to reconstitute such an order even when it is too late. In fact, everything is as if the moment of hesitation were in a way nothing but a small unconscious comedy that we perform for ourselves to be in conformity with the intellect and to retrospectively legitimate a decision that, basically, has been made in our minds well in advance.

Far from proceeding from deliberation and following an abstract verdict, decisions thus most of the time are preformed in deliberation, which they govern from the inside. And, in fact, a rigorous examination of our consciousness shows us that the will, originally, has decided without answering *because* to all *whys*. Ideological motives are invented for the needs of the cause, and we confuse our real comportment with an ideal scenario that we sort out after the fact. In a way, we enjoy imagining the way in which things *ought to have* taken place in order to be "reasonable." The vice of retrospective arrangements is that they only make sense in the *future perfect* and never according to the true future.[87] The future in the strict sense is that of which nothing can be prejudged because it is *absolutely "after."* The particularity of the future perfect, in contrast, is to be a future time that has psychologically become past, fictitiously outpaced by the imagination, anticipated and therefore negated as future. Explication thus gets ahead of the action to be explained and, in a way, tells it what to do. It's not about being true but simply about *being in order,*[88] conforming to the grammar of life and concealing the black logic, the shameful logic of our acts with the noble reasons of an official logic controlled by the pilot-intellect.

It is the illusion of retroactivity that governs this inversion of the real chronology. The etiology such as it ought to be, such as it is *supposed* to be, substitutes itself for the etiology such as it is. A causality as glorious as it is conventional—causality of the chief idea, causality of hegemonic reason and of the immaculate mind—reestablishes in us the order of the model child. If an unmotivated decision, made passionately, i.e. without reason, was the mother of posthumous justifications, the justifications pay it back in spades: this late-born progeny, acting backward, now pretends to be the reasonable cause of the decision, the conversion, or the preference. The red-hot order of spontaneity yields to the reheated order of artifice. Our entire life, encumbered by parasitic reconstitutions, disappears underneath such a piling up of logic. The profound and central significance of freedom becomes impenetrable for us. We end up living a second life, a retrospective life, always lagging behind the life really lived—the life we should have lived to serve as models for others or simply to be able to connect our actions with a certain conventional type that figures in books alone. Those who want to leave a faction, Nietzsche remarks, first feel obliged to refute it.[89]

The social and moral illusion to which Scheler devotes an incisive analysis in his *Idols of Self-Knowledge* is but a particular case of this false perspective.[90] For it is not just about assigning honorable motives to our actions after the fact in order to embellish them in the eyes of public opinion; it is an entirely primitive need of logic. We are troubled and scared by everything about our options that is unique, personal, truly irrational, and unmentionable. We prefer asking the reassuring classifications of textbooks and the rubrics of common morality for the scholastic satisfactions that will save us the trouble of placing ourselves in the very center of our will. It's not that we do not suspect what this free will would be if we really accepted being contemporaneous with it; but the central source of our actions scares us a little and, for that matter, it is so comforting to rely on the crutches of formulas! After the act has been accomplished, we have time, we always find something with which to justify ourselves before logic, and we hasten to conceal the truth we glimpsed sincerely underneath the fragile heap of "good reasons." Then we completely forget this true cause, and the retrospective justification definitively acquires the privilege of having engendered the deciding act. We all more or less resemble someone proffering bad excuses for always being late, now because he has overslept, now because he has missed his train, now because he has forgotten his watch—and who, after all, will always be late because the cause of his being late lies in him, in his style of existence and his mental makeup.[91] The very plurality of his pretexts only traces the outlines of the central destiny that engenders, with these delays, the bad reasons invoked to excuse the delays.

Emotionalist and intuitionist philosophers, generally more attentive than others to the central source of actions, have always also more clearly denounced the dressed-up, artificial, anachronistic aspect of justificatory superstructures. In defending the rights of the heart, Pascal, for example, attributes the following to Artus Gouffier de Roannez: "The reasons occur to me afterwards, but first of all the thing pleases or shocks me without my knowing why, and yet it shocks me for reasons I only discover later." And he adds, "I do not think that it shocks us for reasons we discover afterwards, but that we only discover the reasons because it does shock."[92] And Spinoza, too, who is nonetheless not an anti-intellectual by any means but pays homage to the priority of the *Conatus*, reverses the order of causality and professes that "it is clear that we neither strive for, nor will, neither want, nor desire anything because we judge it to be good; on the contrary, we judge something to be good because we strive for it, will it, want it, and desire it."[93] Someone who wants to drink alcohol always discovers, at just the right time, a medical prescription that enjoins him to do so. This is the place to recall, as Léon Brunschvicg has done, La Rochefoucauld's maxim that "[t]he mind is always deceived by the heart"[94] ...or by instinct.

Such, in fact, is the radiating force of the center that Pascal here calls the heart that it radiates not only in actions but also in ideological justifications destined to legalize these actions. The justificatory systems thus represent, on the surface of the mind, a secondary vegetation with no autonomy of its own. It is the essence of "justification" to appear to proceed in a spontaneous movement and to string together proofs that are, at bottom, entirely secondary. Here we have the entire opposition between the impartiality of *reasoning* and the servility of *arguments*. Arguing thought is a prejudiced thought. It is always the *ancilla* of something. It is always *interested* in some thesis. That is why it is above all apologists and master rhetoricians who are preoccupied with it, concerned as they are more with activist logic than with true speculation. The source that inspires our actions, the true genius of our freedom, thus does not lie in a choice of professed theories and deliberate arguments. Almost always, these theories are in themselves indifferent, since the central tendency can always find something else to legalize itself with. Thus Frederick II found authentic titles to the possession of Silesia, which he coveted. Someone who has, for unmentionable reasons, decided to drown his dog, discovers as if by accident that the dog has rabies. Is this not the very definition of bad faith?

In criticizing the traditional schema of the voluntary act this way, we might seem to provide ammunition to determinism. At all times, in fact, humans have believed they could discern the signature of freedom in the moment of choice, i.e. of discursive deliberation. Yet deliberation now seems to us to be a posthumous legalization, a useless formality we superstitiously perform when confronted with the accomplished fact. It no longer has any influence on the true generation of acts—a little like the regrets of those timid monarchs who, making a virtue of necessity, hurry to legitimate a minister's inevitable coup d'état to appear to impose the dictatorship they will in fact be subjected to. All the productivity of action has taken refuge, so to speak, in the beginning, in the conception of a certain result that inspires both our movements and their justification.

Decision is thus no more constructed from motives and motivations than meaning, in intellection, is constructed from elementary signs.[95] Motives and motivations are psychological "nodes" where several directions of thought intersect, directions that are given a convergent orientation by our will. They are thus no more simple than are the concepts of psychological "Atomism." They are even much more complicated. For what do we call "motivation" or "motive" if not a mental content (feeling, idea) considered to have *weight*, i.e. to be a factor that can be balanced out in an oscillating deliberation? Nietzsche denounces the complicity the myth of free will and the atomistic isolation of psychical "facts" have entered into; the substantialism of language naturally favors this complicity.[96] But if, due to their "weight," motives can act on a decision, it is because they are themselves taken up in a network of spiritual relations and reflect the subtle tension that already orients our hesitation along a path traced out in advance. Each motive by itself testifies to my intimate preferences, just as each word of a sentence testifies to the whole meaning of which it, morphologically, only bears a part, and tends to reconstitute its context. An act that contained the entire self would, as Bazaillas rightly observes, be a parody of volition.[97] For common sense, every deliberation takes the form of an alternative whose two branches are said to correspond to two quite distinct series of motives. But the alternative, like the motives themselves, is an effect of retrospection: such is perhaps the abstract *liberum arbitrium* of which Kierkegaard says that it is a "nuisance for thought."[98]

The illusion of having been able to do otherwise—*aliter*, Leibniz would have said—is thus a posthumous fabrication. It is easy to understand why the exemplary freedom of common sense must be situated at just the point where the two possible solutions bifurcate. And yet it is rare that life accepts such clear and brutal dilemmas, that a consciousness lets itself be split this way between opposing possibilities. For the will, there is no thesis that does not imply its antithesis. But above all it is the choice itself that, fixing the decision, creates, along with the decision, the entire procedure—alternatives and motives—that will be supposed to have brought it about. As Lequier says so forcefully in a nice fragment, "my choice suits me; it pleases me that it pleases me."[99] In the *Euthyphro*, Plato has Socrates ask "whether the pious or holy is beloved by the gods because it is holy, or holy because it is beloved of the gods."[100] One might wonder, in that same sense, whether we prefer an act because we choose it or choose it because we have preferred it. The answer, I think, has to be the following, no matter how paradoxical it may seem: if the act is a free act, it is preferable because it is chosen. *Because* the fiat decides in its favor, reason has to come around and legalize it. But we may rest reassured, it always comes around. That is an effect of retrospection. Once the adventure of choice has been undertaken, a reassuring labor of inversion sets in. We will consent to everything, even the most desperate determinism, rather than admit the priority of an arbitrary willing, gratuitous and absolute, or the circularity of a response that answers the question with a question instead of answering with an explanation. The lover pretends he loves the beloved because she is lovable, not because it is she and because it is he: for that would be to avow that he loves without reasons or that he has no account to give... Bergson's philosophy is certainly not a philosophy of indifference (something we will ascertain later).

And yet what we have here is what lends psychological legitimacy to the theological hypothesis of an autocratic God, indifferent and unfathomable, superior even to eternal truths: nothing precedes the pure will, the matrix of existences and values themselves. Just as before the "*élan vital*" there is no transcendental program that would be actualized by this élan,[101] so the considerate will is never outpaced by motives whose impulse it would take up; or rather, if these motives exist, they are the entire will reduced to the scale of a state of the mind. But nothing is more irritating, frightening, terrifying than the irrational priority of a willing. To begin an action, we demand a principle that is, in turn, no longer the action but a something all done. The exceptional intuition that alone would coincide with the very emergence of our acts then becomes useless.[102] Rather than penetrate into the obscure laboratory of freedom, we prefer to find out how the decision is fabricated little by little from the wise words of deliberation.

Were we to hold on at all costs to the classical vocabulary, we would say that freedom is not in deliberation. It must thus be somewhere along the decision that is its real end, its apparent effect. To remain faithful to Bergson's thought, we must somehow distinguish between two views of volition.

(a) Through the prism of deliberation, volition appears as determined because deliberation generally is *actually* posterior to the decision; and this proves that there is a way of bringing out the voluntary finality that proves determinism right. To be sure, an appeal *formally* precedes the thesis it is to demonstrate; but in that case one would have to say that effects can in a sense be anterior to their causes. Untiringly, Bergson's dialectics is devoted to showing that in that case—the case of teleology—it is still, psychologically, a matter of causality, but of a shameful causality that for the eye has taken the form of finality: this is what the entire first chapter of *Creative Evolution* demonstrates.[103] Pascal had already noted this reversal and changed the meaning of the "because." Bergson, for his part, implicitly distinguishes between two types of causality that I will call *thrust-causation* and *attraction-causation*. In the thrust, i.e. in efficiency of the usual type, effects succeed their cause, which "produces" them—in the literal sense of the term—by pushing them along. Such is the impulse of a shock, of an efficient or efferent cause. But all of Bergson's dialectic consists, precisely, in showing that basically, the same is the case for "final" causality—in which it is the effect that precedes. If the cause "attracts" the effects, it is because in lived duration, it exists prior to them; its posteriority is a fiction that only becomes possible because we place ourselves outside of this duration, over against the accomplished fact. If, then, our free acts depended entirely on the finality of justificatory schemes that reconstitute them, we would have to say that our action is foreseeable in its entirety. When a lawyer opens his mouth at a hearing, we know that he will, no matter what, maintain the innocence of the accused; and when the preacher goes up to the rostrum, we know that he will demonstrate the existence of God and the bliss promised to those who do good. This is not where freedom lies.

(b) Looked at *as it ripens*, by way of a meditation that is truly contemporaneous with its growth, the free act appears as an *inspired act*[104]— inspired (for lack of a better word) by the genius of my person, by this center from which free actions spring forth, by this heart of hearts, finally, that one may call, borrowing an expression of Meister Eckhart's, "little spark" [*Fünklein*].[105] Are we thus going back to the idea of production-causality and, once more, to determinism? But what is most important here is to distinguish between *divination* and *anticipation*. The inspiring initiative, which is all invention and improvisation, does not go back to a "thesis" that is despotically anterior to the becoming of the action. "Theses" discourage more than they inspire. They give us so clear-sighted and provident a vision of the future that all possibilities of renewal are thereby exhausted in advance.[106] But premonitions are inspiring; the intuition we owe to them is of the same order as the efferent, centrifugal "dynamic schema" from which the intellect's movement proceeds. This glimpse, so contrary to all foresight, is a very plastic kind of intention or a kind of *intentional* state that, as it emerges, contains in its virtual state what the motivated choice will preferentially actualize. Life thus already appears to us to be an intermediary between the transcendence of "impulsive" causes and the transcendence of final causes.[107] Life is, so to speak, on the path from the former to the latter—not at all in what is all ready-made but in what is *making itself*; and it is this transitivity, it is this "present participle," that represents the very mystery and ipseity of freedom.

(2) We have thus localized free will. The idea of the dynamic schema, applied to the free act—i.e., in our terms, the action's "intentionality"— already indicates the path on which the philosopher will encounter freedom. The intention to come to a decision is entirely "an impulse to act," as Aristotle said about the will.[108] In this intention, as in the an-

ticipations of the intellect's effort, the future act is already entirely pre-formed, not morphologically but dynamically and, so to speak, function-ally. That is why the reconstitution of the act from its elements generates so many irresolvable aporias. These elements are never *constitutive* of the action; they are *expressive* of it. Experience reveals to us moments of a his-tory, not fragments of a system. In this sense, but only in this sense, one can say that the free act is foreseeable. The prediction of a voluntary act is a matter of premonition analogous to the one described by Bergson in his discussion of "false recognition":[109] I foresee that I will act this way or that, and yet I only know it in acting. Abandoned to my hesitations, I am incapable of anticipating their outcome, but I foresee that I will recognize this outcome as the only possible one when I commit myself to it. *I do not know, but I foresee that I will have known.* I find myself, in sum, in the ambiguous "position of a person who feels he knows what he knows he does not know."[110] The feeling of freedom is nothing but *this knowledge, then this ignorance.*[111] A murky and singular feeling if ever there was one, for it carries within itself the threat of a rigorous necessity. This is what Renouvier expresses when he says that "automotive" action always seems to be determined after the fact and to be free before the fact.[112] The ne-cessity of acts, like the finality of evolution, is never just retrospective. Ul-timately, the determinism of someone like John Stuart Mill says nothing more than this: once made, a decision always seems to us to be the only possible and the only natural decision because there is always some way of explaining the decision to oneself by reconstituting the deliberation that prepared it. I am sure, before I act, that my choice will surprise me; and yet I know very well that my choice will be a function of what I am now. When I coincide more and more intimately with my deep desires, I even come to read in them the concluding words. But, alas! Only the conclusion itself can tell me with certainty. I thus acquire certainty only when it is too late, when the secret of the future has become the reality of the present. But in this case, determinism is no longer a prediction: it is an observation. My freedom's life is thus in danger at every moment: it only becomes active by negating itself. "The faculty of choosing cannot be read in the choice we make by virtue of it."[113] The accomplished act turns against the act to be accomplished, and obliging reconstitutions pour in from all directions to show us our servitude.

This explains, in particular, the illusion of the Eleatics.[114] Dialectics forbids Achilles to catch up with the tortoise; and yet it is a fact that he catches up with it and even overtakes it. The geometers, Bergson writes elsewhere,[115] explain the curve to be the union of an infinity of small straight lines because, ultimately, the curve at each point merges with its tangent. And yet it is a fact that curved lines are curved and the most trained of eyes won't manage to break the continuity of their inflection. Achilles doesn't care about dialectics, doesn't move like dialectics does, placing lengths of space end to end: he runs, and he solves this vain problem. Tolstoy, meditating on the historical becoming of humanity put it this way: the continuity of movement has become unintelligible to us because of the intermittent motions we discern in its flux. And Tolstoy asks us to calculate the differential of history, to "integrate" the innumerable and infinitesimal free wills that drive human becoming forward.[116]

Movement—the real movement of things that move, the movement suggested by Rodin's cinematics—is an organic totality, and if one seeks to explain it at all costs "from the elements," its dynamic continuity must be explained with an actual and positive infinity of elements. Yet dialectical construction, which brings a finite number of conceptual atoms into play, is no more capable of justifying true motility than it is able to restitute the smoothness of melodies, the sinuous flexibility of curves, and the living grace of free actions.[117] We therefore cannot really understand movement and action otherwise than by moving and acting. Only the act itself, or the function of knowledge that imitates it—that is, intuition—measures up to the living. This, at bottom, is what Aristotle says in the *Physics* when he writes that "there is no absurdity ... in supposing the traversing of infinite distances in infinite time."[118] On the other hand, he objects to the Eleatics, those instants you obtain from an infinite division of time exist in time only potentially and not actually at all. Does not Bergson see in this, as he says, "virtual stops"?[119] It is an artificial and accidental act of representation that allows us to actualize these possible stops, but in fact, time is no more made up of instants than the spatial continuum is made up of indivisibles or movement of *kinēmata*.[120] While points actually section the line, instants divide time only virtually.[121] Nonetheless, nothing prevents a moving object from running through an infinite number of virtual points as long as this infinite is not actualized. "Have no fear, Sir," Leibniz writes, of

> the tortoise the Pyrrhonians had running as fast as Achilles. You are right to say that all magnitudes can be infinitely divided. There is none so small that one could no longer conceive of an infinity of divi-

sion never to be exhausted. But I do not see what evil there is in this or what need there is to exhaust them. A space divisible without end takes place in a time divisible without end, too.[122]

Pascal, grappling with the geometry of indivisibles, uses this same argument in a dialectical form when he tries to refute Méré's objection against infinite divisibility: how can one, in a finite time, run through this infinity of infinitely small spaces that constitute extension?[123] But it is time in its entirety, Pascal replies, that is coextensive with the entirety of space, and movement runs through an infinity of points in an infinity of instants. Renouvier, a finitist, rejects this argument claiming that, in this case, there would be two infinites to overcome instead of one and that a difficulty is not resolved when one splits it up.[124] Yet boredom's unending lapses of time come to an end: in becoming, we consume the interval, we reach the end of each period. The coextensivity of infinite time with the infinite trajectory expresses the vulnerability of the Infinite to the Infinite; it expresses that movement can gobble up space and that the simplicity of the act triumphs where enumerating dialectics fails. And Pascal for his part takes up an argument that dynamist theories have at all times brought up against atomism: either the "indivisible" already has the power of extension and has parts itself—or it is really inextensive and extension has to emerge from naught.[125]

For that matter, do we not, as Proudhon remarks, negate movement thanks to a movement of the mind? And does not condemning the mobile to immobility condemn progress to become a thinking of paralysis?[126] A long time in passing, quickly past: such is time; such is movement. Aristotle distinguished between the infinity of division or infinite divisibility (*kata diairesis*) and the infinity of magnitude (*tois heskatois* or *kata posos*).[127] To complete an infinitely great trajectory one needs, in truth, an infinitely great lapse of time. But a length that is infinitely divisible is not infinitely long and, to exhaust it, an infinitely divisible but finite duration suffices. Understood this way, movement is no more impossible than the present is, this perpetual miracle, this inconceivable limit of past and future. We might as well say, Mill remarks, that the sunset is impossible: for if it were possible, it would have to take place either while the sun is still on the horizon or when it is below the horizon. But this sunset is nowhere since it is defined precisely as the transition from day to night.[128] To assign a place to change is to suppress it. This refutes the immobilism of the Megarian school.

The study of organic totalities has shown us that every spiritual being is necessarily complete; and what is true of movement or the free act will be equally true of extension and intellection. Movement is no more fabricated from points than extension from recollections or meaning from signs. In the same way, the free act is so to speak perpetually total down to its least elements. Such an "irrational" tension can only be grasped by a method that is close to life and imitates the figure of life. Retrospectively, action crumbles into instants and motives that are multiplied indefinitely to reconstitute its curve; and correlatively, our dialectic exhausts itself in approximations and rough measurements. The critique of the actual infinite, which is the alpha and omega of a finitism à la Renouvier, only expresses the sterility of these retrospective decompositions. Activist and healthy freedom escapes this obsession with an actual infinity realized by dialectics. This invulnerable freedom's lack of concern with the obsessive fears of corrosive scruples is a proof of health in willing and in acting. Powerlessness strikes those who let themselves be broken by interminable doubts. But how would a mind truly contemporaneous with itself, truly immunized against retrospective scruples, how would such a mind waste its time by eternally regretting what is already done? How could it not work the miracle that consists in contracting, in every instant, the infinite richness of its experiences into simple decisions? This sovereign ease of the mind is nothing other than *grace*. Our arts do their best to imitate it but naturally it belongs to life alone.[129] Graceful actions would above all be—and this is no mere wordplay—gratuitous actions, actions whose charm and spontaneity cannot be altered by any retrospective procedure.

Like the rehabilitation of universal time, like the refutation of the Eleatics and of Einstein, Bergson's theory of freedom is thus a tribute to common sense. Movement and action once more become for the philosopher what they never stopped being for everyone else, the clearest and simplest of *facts*. "One only knows how to reply but keeps marching along," Joseph de Maistre says.[130] And it is here that the incomparable originality of Bergson's method comes to the fore. The point of view of common sense is the point of view of the actor while Zeno's point of view represents the fantastic perspective of the spectator who refuses to live duration and participate in the action. For the actor who is personally committed in the drama of freedom, it is of vital interest that movements reach their goals and that acts end with effective conclusions. But for the actor there is, precisely, no doubt: movements come off and actions succeed. The essence of Bergson's philosophy is to affirm that this naive observation, so naive that it barely seems to deserve the honor the philosopher accords it, is the only one to offer a point of view on the absolute. Better still: actors do not even have a "point of view" because they are within the drama and see all its aspects at once since from within they personally play in all its episodes, since they are the drama itself, the whole drama, including the most subtle of details and the most secret of driving forces. Point of view means limitation, and that is why Leibniz's God does not have a point of view, only his monads do. The Eleatics offer a speculative point of view on movement, that is, a perspectival and partial vision that makes our view entirely illusory; we exchange the clear and total evidence of intuition for the mirage of a dialectic dazzled by stage lights and the prestige of distance.

Free acts thus are, like the movements themselves, individual entities that have their "local sign," their own originality. Mathematicians can standardize movements only by neglecting their spiritual essence, by taking their "mobility" lightly, a mobility that is always a particular tendency, a qualitative and oriented alteration.[131] The only form of knowledge that has a grip on the free act, the only form that reaches the haecceity of the free act is intuition. It lies in the nature of intuition to remain general and yet to adjust with precision to individual objects. *Knowledge of life must be an imitation of life.* While the intellect is always dissimilar to its object, there is no essential difference between the movement of intuition and the movement of freedom or of life. Just as, according to Empedocles, like is known only by like,[132] so life can only be penetrated by life.[133]

Plotinus's saying, which Goethe so admired, takes on a new meaning: "No eye ever saw the sun without becoming sun-like."[134] "Let your eye be the thing it looks at," we read in *The Fruits of the Earth*...[135] Let your retina be the skies themselves, let your vision be the fire in person! This is how I interpret the realism of pure perception. Intuition, for its part, is not the speculative assimilation of something that senses and something that is sensed; it is, rather, a drastic coincidence and, to have out with it, a re-creation. To understand, is that not to redo? Does not the interpretative effort demand that the mind, in the presence of problems, place itself in a spiritual atmosphere and *discover* the true meaning by *assuming* it? Intellection thus always consists, ultimately, in assuming that the problem is solved. Yet when it comes to movement, does not assuming the problem to be solved mean to move? And in just the same way, there is only one good way of showing freedom to be possible: it is to will and to act. This activist solution, in which paradox and good sense come together, thus implies at least an arbitrary approach, a kind of initial adventure: one has to "begin," take a risk. Reasoning is always subjected to the preexistence of a given, but action creates itself in its entirety because it only exists as complete and total.[136] Montaigne's pedagogy had well understood this, prescribing before all things an apprenticeship of experience, exercise, and action. It is by speaking that one learns to speak; and it is by walking that children learn to walk. The spontaneity of our initiatives sheds light on the problems around which dialectics roams because it *offers* us a totality instead of bringing the scattered members of this totality together. Action breaks the circle in which justifications confine us. Is action not *causa sui* [its own cause]?

This immanentist conception of freedom does not deprive the decision of its exceptional value as a *beginning*. To bring home to us the solemnity of the *fiat*, Bergson, unlike Renouvier, has no need to make too much of the discontinuity of free acts. "Begin is a great word!" Jules Lequier exclaims in a moving fragment cited by Renouvier.[137] There is no reason to believe that this great word loses any of its dignity in Bergson's free will. Does not Renouvier himself set about differentiating very carefully between freedom and fortuitousness?[138] In a language that could be Bergson's if it were less awkward, he protests against an abstract arithmetic of motives, against the mythological idea of an indifferent and chimerically absolute will. The will is not a passive *hypokeimenon*, a blank slate waiting to be determined by motives coming in from the outside. Renouvier adds the profound insight that determinism and indeterminism share the postulate that *the will is fundamentally and essentially indifferent*.[139] Nothing could be more Bergsonian...

Nikolai Berdyaev, too, refuses the idea of a substantial will that would choose from competing motives juxtaposed to one another or, better still, from a void without all motivation. According to indifferentism, willing is essentially a wish deciding amid nothingness, an *adiaphoron* lacking differences that would determine it. According to determinism, willing accidentally receives an irresistible impulse from certain factors visiting it from the outside. In theory, the will is said to be essentially distinct from these factors, be it considered as active or as passive. Yet we know, on the contrary, that *every motive is already something that is willed*. But is this not to renounce personifying or "reifying" a willing that transcends the person itself? My will is not in me like a stranger or a visitor, no more than my duration designates something really distinct from consciousness itself. Between my will and me there is, on the contrary, an intimate familiarity, a long-standing companionship. This is not an indifferent tête-à-tête between a person purely willing and a person purely willed but a coincidence at every instant. It is true that the act of freedom thereby ceases to be an arbitrary decree, an unheard-of catastrophe. "Am I free to be free?" Renouvier's sense for such radical innovations, such crises of action is well known. "It is a thing strangely singular and apt to frighten a profound gaze, this power to produce an instantaneous, new phenomenon, to produce it, certainly, not without precedents, without roots, but finally without necessary connection with the eternal order of things..."[140]

Meanwhile, as entirely preformed as it is in the tradition that prepares it, in Bergson free action remains no less a surprising action, a true beginning. For us, there is something unforeseen about our initiatives, and the I contains everything that is necessary to transcend its own limits. Creation is everywhere, in us and around us; at every moment in the inner life, there is a Rubicon to cross, a perilous leap to make. This is readily seen in the absurdity of certain sudden decisions that burst forth out of the blue and seem less to follow our tendencies than to precede and to lead them. "Taking place," need we say it again, is not a vain formality, in the life of the soul no more than in nature. Only the event counts. That is to say that the dénouement of the action is in no way a conventional ceremony, a symbolic closing gesture. Far from it. It is the conclusion that counts, it is the conclusion, demanding to be affirmed at all costs, that creates the ceremonies of justifications for its purposes. Everything is thus done for the dénouement. Logic and reason are left to manage as best they can. No one is fooled by the acts they put on, their pretty formulas, all that ritual legalization. Only the dénouement has a price; only it merits that we subordinate everything to it. *Only the dénouement is effective.* And how could a philosophy as concerned with effective realities as Bergson's not place the decisions that create an activist and conquering freedom above everything else?

That said, Bergson allows for innovations but not for radical creation. We shall see why this continuationism of plenitude cannot allow for an absolute beginning: to Bergson's mind, a creative continuation is no more contradictory than a creative evolution! Also: freedom is not a vertiginous option in a void without preferences and preexistence, nor even a power to inflect or arbitrarily suspend the course of representations. Freedom is not a surprising *clinamen*, a fortuitous declination of the future but rather an extreme concentrate of duration. It follows that Bergson, in opposition to Renouvier[141] and Lequier, is careful not to affirm the transcendence of the will; "*in ea vivimus et movemur et sumus* [in it we live and move and have our being]":[142] freedom is its vital milieu. Bergsonian freedom, like Bergsonian memory, is unshakable. As the soul always recollects, so consciousness is free, with a continual freedom and even beyond conflicting duties or great moral options; for this continued option is duration itself. Is the problem not to be oneself, wholly and all the way down, much more than to decide or to choose a side? "Become who you are," whoever you are! Humans are naturally free, even if they do not want to be: the intimism of *Time and Free Will* also pays no heed to the exceptional, intermittent, discontinuous crises that result from obligation and that express, in someone like Renouvier, the importance of moral debate and practical reason. Bergson compares free choice to a biological hatching or to a fruit's organic maturation so often that the *fiat* loses some of its crucial and revolutionary character. A fig, Epictetus already wrote, is not made in an hour; it takes time.[143] Fragrance of a scent, emanation, natural evolution, ripening, flowering and fructification; everything here comes together to engulf the sudden instant in immanence and in the continuity of a *Legato*.[144] *The Two Sources of Morality and Religion* will depict initiative in a much more incisive way! But in *Time and Free Will* freedom evokes less Christian drama than Neoplatonic procession; less élan than effusion.

Freedom is thus a certain tonality of decision or, as Renouvier says, "this character of the human act . . . in which consciousness posits the motive and the motor identified with it as closely united."[145] Of all the works authored by humans, free action is the one that most essentially belongs to them; in free action, they recognize themselves better than artists in their work, better than fathers in their children. It is a more profound paternity, a powerful and intimate sympathy. Freedom *emerges from* the total past; it *expresses* a kind of superior necessity—the determination of the *I* by the *I*; for here, it is the same who is at once cause and effect, form and matter. In matters of life, we are always brought back to life itself as the ultimate authority beyond which there is no appeal: mind presupposes mind, action presupposes action. Inner experience does not allow us to exit this circle. And thus I am wholly implicated [*tout entier en cause*] in each of my actions. As Schopenhauer says, while my responsibility seems to apply to what I do, in reality it applies to what I *am*; I am responsible for my *esse*; I am wrong to be myself.[146] I am wholly in my act, and wholly, too, in the motives that cause it. The free act that emanates from the total person is not the work of a divided soul but of the whole soul. The free human being wills and decides "by the movement of the whole soul," as Plato, quoted by Bergson, puts it.[147] What is *free*, in this sense, is what is *total* and what is *profound*; and the essay on *Laughter* forcefully and succinctly asserts: "All that is serious in life comes from our freedom."[148] The serious, this is it! For if the comical, an effect of mechanics, is a regional or partial incident, the serious is totality.

An act is all the more free the more veridically and more expressively it testifies to the person—not to the oratory and mundane portion of the person we set aside for social exchanges but to my necessary and intimate person, the person for whom I feel responsible and who is truly "myself." A free act is a significant act. The determined act, on the contrary, is the refuge of what is most peripheral and *insignificant* about the person; it is a superficial and local act. Freedom thus conceived would furthermore— as Plato, the Stoics, and Spinoza understood—be an organic necessity that opposes both indifference and determinism. Such is the wise man's freedom. Considered as a demand, freedom implies that we have a duty to remain *contemporaneous with our own actions* as much as possible, to flee neither to the past of efficient causes nor to the future of retrospective justifications. It is the opposite of fiction. It has the hypocrisy of excuses, the pathos of eloquent abstractions against it. Its name thus becomes *sincerity*.

CHAPTER 3

SOUL AND BODY

Often, I have woken up out of the body to my self and have entered
into myself, going out from all other things.—Plotinus

Matter and Memory (1896), perhaps Bergson's most brilliant book, is his
first to study consciousnesses as bound up with an organism on which it
seems to depend and that manifests it on the outside. What exactly is
the nature of this dependence? And what form do the antitheses first
sketched in *Time and Free Will* subsequently assume?

1. *Thought and Brain*

Bergson's theory of how body and mind communicate is directed against
parallelist (epiphenomenalist, realist, idealist) systems that imply an equivalence of the cerebral and the conscious or even consider the facticity of
consciousness to be a vain idea. More or less surreptitiously, all "centripetal" psychologies, all metaphysics that go from the outside to the inside
and from the body to the soul, affirm this equivalence. But our vision of
spiritual things makes this a priori solution very improbable. No material
phenomenon, no cerebral modification whatsoever, can be coextensive
with the infinite immensity of a state of mind. There is nothing in the
anatomy of the nervous system to account for the inexhaustible depth
and richness of the most humble of spiritual realities. Bergson expresses
this fundamental idea in a thousand different ways: memory is infinitely
more extended than the brain, and the self exceeds the body that impris-
ons it in space and in time—in space because our imagination is gifted
with ubiquity and because there are no borders for so agile a being; in
time because the mind remembers and thus always goes beyond itself.[1]

What, then, is the nervous system good for? My body, first of all, is nothing but a center of action. It receives and returns movement. In this center of action, the essential mission of the nervous system is to receive excitations and to extend them into movements. On the level of the spinal cord, the excitation is immediately "reflected" as a motor reaction. Reflex thus essentially constitutes a kind of circuit open only to the outside world: the excitation, making its way from the periphery to the inferior centers (spine, ganglia, medulla), immediately provokes an explosive discharge that does not bring the brain into play.

The presence of the brain in higher vertebrates has the primary effect of postponing or delaying responses. The system of infallible but unilateral and blind adaptations is replaced by a system of slower, less fatal but supple and variegated adaptations. As reflex thus complicates into deliberating volition, the brain's mechanism inserts an increasingly long delay between the two terms of an act, between external solicitation and response. This deferment increases the indetermination of our comportment. Employing Pierre Janet's language, which on this point is quite apposite to shed light on Bergson's point of view, we could say that the main virtue of beings endowed with will and judgment is a virtue of prowling and waiting.[2] What the living being owes to its brain is, above all, the power to *abstain* even more than the power to will.

Yet is abstention not as positive as impulsion? The circuit just mentioned has opened a second time, but on the other side, toward the inside; or, better, cerebration replaces the circular act, infinitely distended by the exterior side's energy reserves, with unforeseeable and increasingly arbitrary acts. The automatic arc, which can no longer contain the spiritual world, shatters into free acts swollen with recollections and images. Circumspect man succeeds spinal man.

The brain with its procrastination mechanisms is thus the organ of choice and abstention. Baltasar Gracián, the theorist of "temporizing" and of precautionary prudence, would have said that its function lies in this delay (*Mora*) and that it is "moratory" by nature.[3] It allows for "intrigue" and changing one's mind, for example, while reflex actions, spinning round between the provocations of the outside and the inferior centers, discharge our impulsive vengeances instead. The possibility of foreseeing the long term thus saves us from the swiftness of surprises and terrifying improvisations. And yet, Bergson insists, there is no essential difference between the functions of the spine and those of the brain.[4] The only difference is that in the brain, one and the same centripetal excitation can be shunted onto an infinity of motor paths, and the range of reactions, too, by far exceeds the range of possible triggers.

The essential homogeneity of spinal and cerebral functions is one of the fundamental principles of Bergson's biology, and contemporary neurologists have fully confirmed it.[5] As we go up from simple irritability to sensibility and to "spontaneous" movement, the disproportion between excitation and reaction increases, as Schopenhauer already remarked;[6] in volition, finally, the centers seem to create the energy that our muscles spend.[7] Articulating the complete action in time, the brain, very simply, stores infinitely the energy supplied by afferent impressions. For us, this disproportion ultimately signifies freedom of choice. But the brain itself is not an absolute cause of movement.

One might want to accuse Bergson of being a "naturalist" since he refuses to grant the labor of the brain this miraculous originality, while the idealist considers it indispensable to confer this originality on the brain in order to preserve the immaculate dignity of the human spirit. Yet we will see that the exact opposite is the case and that by refusing to locate the scission between spinal activity and cerebral activity, Bergson retains the means by which to transfer it, deeper and less surmountable than ever, between the cerebral and the spiritual. He thereby renounces what had been nothing but a surreptitious expedient to extricate thought from nervous modifications. It is quite remarkable that Bergson, in his discussion of the problem of affective intensity, does not hesitate to adopt, as William James does, the centripetal theory of effort and to invert the ideological causality of common sense, which is, as we saw, a victim of the retrospective illusion.[8] And yet we know that he interprets intellection as a central and radiating effort. But it is for the benefit of the mind itself that the reversal takes place. Rather than attribute who knows what power of creative emission to the nervous centers, it is better to keep insisting on the role of peripheral modifications because these could never compete with the spiritual, the unique center of movement and action.

We can thus guess at the role the brain plays in inserting itself between excitations and movements. We have no trouble seeing what is gained by diverting the nervous influx via the brain: we gain time, and here time means freedom. The main business in life's struggles is to be able to postpone one's interventions and to choose one's hour, to keep for oneself a reserve of the possible. Those are strong who foresee far-off challenges and, by temporizing, multiply the reach of their actions and the precision of their calculations. The brain, an instrument of reprieve, is thereby an instrument of freedom. What this freedom is as such, *Time and Free Will* has been telling us all along. But how is it possible now that its fate be tied to a brain?

The brain is a sort of "central telephonic exchange" whose role is to relay a message or to make it wait.[9] It is a commutator capable of sending the movement it receives from one point of the organism into a plethora of possible directions.[10] Even more clear-cut is Bergson's comparison of the brain with an organ of "pantomime."[11] Its role is to mime the life of the spirit, not to engender it. That is to say that there is indeed a certain correspondence, or at the very least a synchronism, between the molecular modifications of the outer layer and the succession of images. How could we be surprised to see a conductor's gestures correspond at every moment to the rhythmical articulations of the symphony when their function, precisely, is to scan them? And yet we know very well that the symphony is neither in the conductor's baton nor on the rostrum and that the gesture of beating time [*battre la mesure*] does not create time. The life of the brain, if we may say so, beats the time of the life of the mind but the life of the mind is not a function of the life of the brain, no more than a play is exhausted by the gesticulations of the actors.

Bergson often makes this point by taking recourse to the notion of *play* [*jeu*], and it may well be said that he has completely renewed it.[12] The relation between what can be played or acted to what is played is more a mimicking than an imitation. It excludes all relations of literal resemblance or transitive causality. The presence of the one only indicates that the other is there. The mental is not a line-by-line translation of the cerebral, which is what the parallelists imply.[13] There is exactly as much in a translation as there is in the original language and, save the difference in language, the transposition neither adds nor subtracts anything. But here, the two versions placed in counterpoint are both infinitely unequal and absolutely heterogeneous in their very nature. There aren't, as Spinoza would have liked, two parallel idioms in which a unique substance articulates itself:[14] there are two qualitatively different orders of reality. Nor is there such a thing as transitive causality. On this point, Bergson readily appropriates Leibniz's criticism of how Descartes solved the problem of the communication of substances; even more precisely, *Creative Evolution* shows how corporeity, far from exercising any effective action on life, plays a primarily negative role.[15] The relation that links thought to the brain is more of a relation of expression, a symbolism.

Signs do not *imitate* the things signified, no more than symbols resemble the things symbolized. They *play* them. This is what Descartes himself, at the beginning of his "Treatise on Light," seems to suppose when, concerned above all with maintaining a dualism as favorable toward the purity of thought as toward the autonomy of science, he insists on the essential dissimilarity of images and sensible objects.[16] Translation creates an internal and total dependence between two things since it founds their similarity on the very parallelism of their contents. Symbolism, on the contrary, is a unilateral and abstract relation that applies to a function of things and not to their morphology. Translation transports the entire thing by merely dressing it up in a new garb whereas symbolism extracts a portion from it in order to stage it. In musical transposition, for example, the melody changes its pitch but not its profile. To raise or lower a tone by the desired interval, all it takes is to modify the key and the tonality or simply to move the notes on the staff.

But the spiritual is not the cerebral transposed, and a simple substitution of an algorithm will never transport us from one notation to another. This is how *Matter and Memory* finds itself elaborating and specifying the role of *symbolism*, which *Time and Free Will* had above all denounced for its negative function, its dryness and opacity. This cerebral symbolism now appears to us above all as a mimicking. Yet in a mimicking there is obviously much less than there is in the feeling mimicked, since what happens of ourselves in our gestures and our movements of expression is only the playable part of our emotions, that is to say, the most summary and skeletal portion of the inner life. Graphology, too, for example, indicates only characterological types but not singular specificities, nor does it indicate the qualitative nuances of such specificities, which are as incomparable as they are inimitable. This is because mimicking and the thing "imitated" belong to two entirely different orders: they are not on the same *level*—and we already know that, in the essential heterogeneity of psychological states, there are differences in levels rather than variations in degrees. Signs and things signified are on two different and superposed levels; translation, on the contrary, is neither on another level than the original nor of a wholly different order.

The cerebral is thus nothing but the staging of the spiritual. There is no common measure between these two levels, and from the outset, Bergson's psychology appears as scrupulously dualistic. The fault shared by all parallelist systems—idealist as well as epiphenomenist—is that they fail to recognize this radical heterogeneity. Cerebral modifications are, so to speak, nothing but themselves, that is, they are a very particular image among thousands of others that constitute the material world. But the perceptions they are supposed to provoke represent precisely this entire universe, including the cerebral phenomena themselves. They are not "on the same level." In its marvelous elasticity, in its aptitude for living up to the entire world, spiritual reality is essentially totality. Yet while two parts, equal or unequal, of a single whole can be compared with one another, the whole itself cannot be compared to one of its parts: the difference is *toto genere*.[17] Nonetheless perception, as a mental reality, *is everything*.[18] Are epiphenomenists not frequently, and rightly, reproached for conceiving, by way of thought, of these cerebral movements as tasked nonetheless with giving rise to thought? The vicious circle Bergson denounces in his criticism of the psychophysiological paralogism (a circle in which Schopenhauer's idealism, for example, moves when it locks the macrocosm into the brain, which is but a detail) has its origin in the priority of thought and in the necessary evidence in which it envelops us. It is a particularity of spiritual life that it thus condemns to a *petitio principii* all peripheral, empirical, or centripetal explanations that claim to generate spiritual life from its own elements.[19] Spiritual life is universal presence and total certainty. This total thought clings to a brain that mimics it as best it can the way a piece of clothing hangs on a nail[20]—but has anybody ever claimed that the nail resembles the piece of clothing? If a nut serves to hold a machine together, would anyone say that the machine as a whole is equivalent to the nut?

Thus vanishes the idol of cerebral localizations that in the last century could pass for the promise of a truly scientific phrenology. As early as 1896, Bergson, in a veritable stroke of genius, outpaces most biologists by delivering a fatal blow to the reigning theories of Eduard Hitzig, Carl Wernicke, and Paul Flechsig.[21] Victor Nodet and, from the first hour, Arnold Pick recognized the value of Bergson's anticipation, and we may say that today, thanks to the work of Pierre Marie and François Moutier, Constantin von Monakow and Raoul Mourgue, no one would seriously go on talking about image centers. The absolute heterogeneity of the cerebral and the mental prohibits us from understanding how images could sleep in the cells of the cortex and, generally, how this entire geography of the soul could make any sense whatsoever.

The study of aphasia confirms this impression. We know that the various disorders provoked by certain lesions of the brain's hemispheres served as the starting point of the cerebral topography Broca established in 1861.

Yet nowhere do we find a necessary connection between these interruptions of the cortex and the disappearance of recollections proper. First of all, if recollections were really lodged in the cells of the cortical substance, then, in the case of aphasia, words would have to disappear mechanically one after the other as the lesion expands.[22] As we know, it is characteristic of material things that they do not imply anything but themselves and exclude one another reciprocally. If, then, recollections or images corresponded point by point to cerebral traces the way tracing paper covers an original, the accidents to which they succumb would have to precisely manifest their mutual exteriority. In fact, however, experience allows us to distinguish between two cases: either it is the function of mental hearing in general that weakens as a whole, disappears as a whole; or words disappear in an invariable order that on the whole obeys the law of regression formulated by Ribot: first proper names, then common nouns, finally verbs.[23] Who would imagine that verbal images are spread across the brain according to their grammatical nature—here the verbs, a little further the adjectives—and that a lesion, thanks to a miraculous change, thus eliminates them turn by turn, always in the same order? It suffices to formulate so laughable a hypothesis to show how strange it is.

For words seem to be afflicted because of their *function*, and not in isolation. The general relationship between the brain and thought gave us a sense that functional relationships like "play" occupy a much more important place in psychology than morphological similarities or structural parallelisms. In truth, forgetting in aphasia affects categories and not words. Yet even if words were preserved singularly in the brain as sound images, classes of words, in turn, are in no way localizable. Classes of words are abstract series whose unity is entirely formal, genera separated by our mind that no sensible experience could have inscribed in the cerebral cortex in zones we could pinpoint. These categories result from thought and are themselves totalities, that is to say they accommodate, from the very beginning, an infinity of real or virtual words. But no nervous tissue is capable of fixing an infinity of thought. A material organ is coextensive with another material existence but not with possible existences or with reactions: substantially defined centers are incapable of marshaling the dynamics of the possible. This puts the advocates of localization in an outrageous position between the terms of a desperate alternative: either admit a center of adverbs and a center of prepositions or abandon, once and for all, a language that is as approximate as it is arbitrary.

More generally still: if memory adhered to the brain, I would have thousands and thousands of discrete images of one and the same word, one and the same object, because each object, each word has come to impress my senses in an infinite number of individual forms, in all sorts of singular circumstances of lighting, place, setting, and intensity.[24] For there is nothing in an "engram" that allows it to go beyond itself, and the brain registers exclusively what sensitive tremors are supposed to inscribe in it. Yet it is nonetheless a fact that I conserve of the same word, and of the same person, one unique, supple, and dynamic image by which I at once go beyond the dust of these discontinuous impressions. The auditory image is a genus and, as Bergson has shown for another problem that opposed him to the associationists,[25] we have to renounce composing genera by way of enumeration. Memory is totality, and the advocates of localization exhaust themselves in trying to reconstruct it with atoms...

In the case of aphasia, this totality, far from crumbling piece by piece, disaggregates simultaneously across its breadth. This is proven by the dissolution of verbal memory: it is afflicted in its entirety from the beginning and more and more deeply. To speak the language of soldiers, forgetting attacks recollections along the entire line, not by punctual undermining: instead of progressively making its way word by word, it digs and penetrates from one level to the next. The disease, which accentuates the structure of beings by dissolving it, in a way acts across the mind's greatest dimension. Yet the mind, as the relation of the sign to the signified proved to us, is organized depthwise, and it is in this respect, therefore, that it is most vulnerable to progressive amnesia. In dissolution "by undermining," forgetting would from the beginning be total depthwise, but be limited in extension. In aphasia, on the contrary, forgetting appears from the first in almost its entire extension; it begins by being superficial and subsequently eats more and more deeply into memory. Parallelism wants pieces of diseased substance in the brain to correspond to pieces of disease, as it were,[26] just as atomistic "expressionism" wants language fragments, nouns, prepositions, conjunctions to respond to fragments of meaning...

Yet meaning, undivided intention, on the whole and after the fact, is inherent to the entirety of the sentence that exhales it like a scent, from which it is released like an incantation. It does not distribute itself among the *disiecta membra* of grammatical morphology such that the words, reassembled, would reconstitute it like a puzzle. Much rather, signification figures entirely in each word... This is how a melody of Fauré's could express in its entirety the poetry of a poem without each of its notes corresponding to each of the details of the text.[27] Meaning is not spelled out word by word, nor is an incantation spelled out note by note... nor are recollections spelled out neuron by neuron. In reality, in Bergson's own expression, "the whole brain is affected, just as a badly tied knot may make the whole rope slack, not just this or that part of it."[28] The disease does not immediately have its final depth, and the direction of contagion is vertical rather than horizontal: it is an increasingly acute penetration of the quick of memory, not an extensive contamination of recollections. Verbs, for example, are more tenacious than nouns because of all words, they are closest to action; they immediately express those aspects of action that can be played and imitated. If, then, they depend on the brain it is not because they are housed there; it is because the brain, organ of pantomime, essentially governs action and because a lesion of the brain entails above all a disease of action. Action is not *in* the brain, and if there is localization, it is in a sense dynamic and not mechanic. The majority of disorders provoked by an interruption of the cortex thus affects the activation of recollections rather than the recollections themselves; it is our aptitude at using them that is diseased. The effect of the lesion is not to *rarify things*, things that are, like all things, impenetrable and finite. It is to *relax a function*, the very function that Bergson calls "attention to life,"[29] a function whose vigilance is blunted by aphasia. That is why, as *Creative Evolution* will point out, the difference between the human brain and the animal brain always resides in a "global" character. The details of structure do not explain anything. Eugène Minkowski, explaining schizophrenia by autism and the loss of "vital contact with reality," supports Bergson's philosophy with his profound clinical experience.[30]

In its very disappearance, language [*langage*], which *Time and Free Will* was content to blame for the sclerosis of mental becoming, thus gives us a better understanding of how the brain stages thought. It is instructive, above all, to find contemporary biology take up Bergson's theory of actualization. Monakow and Mourgue's "chronogeneous localization" has no other meaning.[31] A lesion is in space, but a function is not. A function is *in time*. Does not this necessary distinction result from the irresolvable antithesis that opposes consciousness to space? To operate, a function needs an anatomical substrate in the sense that *without* an organ, no function would be possible. But the function does not reside in the tissue; nor is that necessary condition of thought we call a brain ever a sufficient condition! A function is organized like a melody whose successive moments adopt a rhythm that increases in complexity the more it is concerned with better-integrated tendencies.

And we in fact observe that most of the diseases that were studied so much in the last century, in the age of the "localizers," are characterized by operational disorders, by a panicking and disequilibrium of melody. They are diseases of time—the time that the presence of a brain capable of waiting, of choosing, and of looking to the future inserts into human undertakings. Such is, for example, a melody that becomes incoherent, lacunary, shaky; and in apraxia, the actualization itself is compromised. By the same token, aphasia is an inaptitude at *mobilizing* the internal words such that they flow out successively: inner speech generally remains, but contact is lost between thought and the verbal melody; the dynamic utilization of phonemes and words is affected. The biologists cited here have taken the trouble to classify the various forms of this temporal cacophony: perseveration, duplication, anticipation, confusion, false convergence...[32] The melody is variously crippled or broken; but in all cases, the *figure* [*allure*] is much more important here than the *structure*. A long time ago Ribot, albeit still blinded by the prejudices of "centripetal psychology," already noted the silence of anatomy on the main degradations of the will.[33] Abulia, for example, is characterized by an integrity of the muscular system and of the organs of movement, which remain as intact as intellect and desire; what is blocked is the transition to action. Abulia is thus truly "powerless."[34] It is particularly interesting to compare it to aphasia, because it experiences in our place: abulia isolates the dynamics of volition, the attention to life, respecting all the rest.

In his weakening of the role of incitation, Ribot, to be sure, tends toward giving a peripheral explanation, not seeing either that what is affected is not affective life as such but sensibility as call to action or, as Pierre Janet says, the function of the real.[35] Janet, in whose work the idea of psychological tension plays a role comparable, on the whole, to the role perception plays in Bergson, rightly notes that the function of the real does not only endow the present with stronger intensity. If perception, for example in the madness of doubt, were in effect attacked exclusively in its breadth and sharpness, one could admit that in mental pathology, the essential thing is the anatomical lesion since there would be a clear and intelligible relation between a material interruption of nerve substance and the quantitative gradations of our perception. Yet Charles Renouvier already had noted the spiritual, not anatomical, nature of mental alienation. Psychosis is everywhere and nowhere: linked in general to nervous centers, it is never to be pinpointed there. Between powerlessness and attention to life, the difference is not one of degree but one in nature. Janet has grouped a certain number of mental insufficiencies under the by-now classical name psychasthenia, disorders that essentially affect the transition to action or, as he puts it, "presentification." He reproaches Bergson with seeing in the function of the real only the movements by which our perceptions become active. This reproach is rather surprising coming from a disciple of Ribot's usually put off by the "metaphysics" of *Matter and Memory*: does he not himself recognize that by "movement" Bergson often means "action" in general and that in *Matter and Memory* Bergson is above all concerned with the living dynamics that puts us in contact with the external milieu?

But there would be no end to a list of all the support modern neurology has given to Bergson's anticipations; Henri Delacroix, in his book on language, enumerates a crowd of convincing facts.[36] Neuropathology has to resign itself to the nonexistence of the clinical entities thought up by the classical theory of image centers. The mind has its seat everywhere in the cortex, and nowhere its center. Increasingly, clinicians (Pierre Marie, for example) insist on the general intellectual disorders provoked by aphasia; and intellect here most often means the faculty of forming relations and organizing systems, the symbolic faculty by means of which we rapidly adapt to the present. Aphasics, in Delacroix's terms,[37] are no longer capable of manipulating the temporal and spatial atlas—the temporal above all. Almost always, observers note a significant weakening of memory and of "ultimate intention," a narrowing of past and future, a confusion of the whole chronology of actions. A study of aphasic jargon (Pick's agrammatism, Head's syntactic aphasia) shows that what is in play here is syntax much more than nomenclature: and how could we be surprised since we already know that the totality is older than the simple elements with which we reconstitute it? Aphasia, Jackson already remarked, affects above all propositions. It disorients the propositional movement that carries the successive sounds with it.[38] It is a veritable distress of "grammatism." In "semantic" aphasia, the disease affects the transition from meaning to sign; it affects intellection itself. But in what province of the brain could intellection, the act by which we *understand* signs, reside? One might at a pinch understand that animal images have taken residence in the cortex, Ebbinghaus observes; but where would one then locate the resemblance between two animals, the genus and the species to which they belong?[39] Where, we ask, could the sudden illumination that renders sounds and images significant reside? Words, verbal images might be localized; but who will show us the seat of sentences?

The brain is thus the "organ," in the proper sense of the term, of the soul, the instrument the soul uses to penetrate things. But it is not the "translation" of the soul; it does not justify the soul. And subsequently, our interest moves from cerebro-spinal topography to the avatars of vitality itself. It is no doubt a good idea to renounce metaphorical manners of speech like the "Map of Tendre."[40] Every material thing is simple, poor, and rough; it is incapable of fixing the concrete plenitude of the mind. That is why it is possible to deduce the sign from the meaning but not the meaning from the sign; at most, cerebration from thought, but not thought from cerebration. The continuity of spiritual life carries with it infinitely more subtle and delicate things than a gesture could ever gather together, and in all of the brain's gray substance there is nothing that could account for all these riches. In a state of mind, in turn, if it were to yield its secret, there is much more than we would need to guess at the corresponding molecular movement. By deciphering a spiritual reality, we a fortiori read in its choreography. To transition from one to the other, we do not need to add but subtract. We need to let go of specific difference to be content with the genus. We need to renounce the individuality of the mental state to coerce it into scholastic classifications. We need to sacrifice the innumerable nuances of inner lyricism to the banality of a rubric. In a transposition in which the two melodies run parallel, we pass indifferently from one to the other: it suffices to know the cipher or the "key" to read the first in the second, immediately and note for note.

But we know that the mind is not the brain transposed. The mind, therefore, cannot be deciphered through its symbols, no more than we would be able to go back to a text if we were only given the punctuation marks. It is a problem with too many unknowns. One and the same territory of the brain thus governs a multitude of mental states.[41] It does not determine their "haecceity," so to speak, that by means of which such and such an experience is unique and inimitable. A given "center" commands a whole variety of body movements and postures; the same synergies and the same muscles govern the most varied gestures. The advancements of modern neurology precisely invite us to consider the nervous system as a network, increasingly ramified from bottom to top, all the way to the mental reality that exceeds it in turn. But as we descend toward the periphery, the nervous pathways merge with one another, little by little, and they rarify the moment they surface on the outside. Just as, following Sherrington's observations, there must be "common paths" for several actions since the spectrum of possible gestures infinitely surpasses the number of nervous fibers,[42] so, at the other end, one and the same zone must correspond to an infinity of possible perceptions since the register of emotions and tendencies surpasses any conceivable mechanism.[43] That is why there are many more nuances and tones in human sensibility than there are keys on the keyboard of excitations; and it is also why motor functions infinitely exceed the extent of possible impressions.

In this margin of motor functions, in this *too much*, freedom resides. I have more ways of responding than the outside world has of asking, and that is what makes my conduct less and less foreseeable, my spontaneity more and more aggressive. Because in the moment of the response all I have is an embarrassment of choices, I become so to speak fuller and more diverse than the events to which I respond. But since not all complications of morphology manage to contain this overflowing surplus of action, we have to admit that the multiple qualities and sonorities of our actions do not consist in a few grams of brain matter. The brain thus makes freedom *possible* but, as we foresaw, freedom does not reside in the brain's convolutions. The brain is made to go beyond excitations, but the mind infinitely goes beyond the brain; and the mind in turn tirelessly goes beyond itself because it is infinitely infinite. I am as unforeseen for myself as my initiatives are for the surroundings in which I live; my own will perpetually is a subject of astonishment and fright. This is a great mystery. Life is a perpetual going-beyond-oneself,[44] and when it penetrates, with the fine point of action, into the outside world, it exceeds it to such an extent that it weighs down on it with all its weight.

Above all, Bergson's critique of localization familiarizes us with the profoundly philosophical idea that the mystery is not in space and that it is of *an entirely different order*. Thought is not to be deciphered in the cells of the cortex. Even if we stare indefinitely with eyes wide open, we will not decipher God in the twinkling stars (although the starry sky, in its own way, "tells" of the divine glory). Nor is genius deciphered in writing. Nor do we read death in a dying man's last breath; death itself is neither here nor there. The mystery of vitality, in turn, is not shut up *somewhere* in the core or in the chromosomes' "genes." No, the vitality of life is radically non-ascribable, deceptive, evasive, and it infinitely escapes our pinpointing. The topography of the mystery is as vain as Broca's atlas because it only serves to "fix ideas"—as if ideas needed to be fixed! The mystery is always something else and always somewhere else, *aliud* and *alibi*... The mediation of signs in which meaning is supposed to hide itself is thus a perfectly empty and symbolic mediation, as empty as a cenotaph, a deceptive contemplation that is the very type of false profundity... *Ubique et Nusquam!*[45] This is true not only of God, but also of the incantation and of the soul itself, the soul omnipresent, omniabsent, the soul linked to the body and yet neither to be pinpointed nor localized; the soul that is in the body but also outside of it; the soul that is in the body as the body is in the soul! Is incantation not completely different from the grammatical sentence, something other than the sound and the face in which it yet must become incarnate?

II. *Recollection and Perception*

Bergson's philosophy is an energetic defense of the idea of psychological polarity, and the duality of recollection and perception occupies a central place in *Matter and Memory*. Pure perception, immediately solidary with the action for which it is made and the movements that extend it, and pure recollection, disinterested like the very past whose signature it bears, are distinct in nature, not by degrees. Bergson aims all of his dialectic against those who, openly or covertly, undertake to erase this distinction. The critique of the idea of intensity in *Time and Free Will* already taught us that everywhere, Bergson's naturally dualist philosophy substitutes qualitative heterogeneity for differences of intensity.

Some would willingly turn recollection into a *weakened* perception. Others treat perception like a *strengthened* recollection. Both, concerned as they are above all with systematization and homogeneity, seek the simple element, the primitive fact that, more or less multiplied by itself, would mechanically yield all mental phenomena. The former say that the past is simply a faded or muffled present.[46] But the faded present remains a present; weakened perception will forever be perception, all the way until it disappears. Between the most immaterial pianissimo and the re-memorized melody, there is an absolute difference, an abyss that no decrescendo could ever overcome. To misunderstand the specific pastness of the past is to forbid oneself to understand recognition. Who would take the perception of a light sound to be the recollection of an intense noise? According to Taine, who speaks in the language of Hume and the associationists, true "sensation" differs from the "image" above all by its greater intensity: that is how it is representative of exteriority. But how do they not see that, to pass from recollection, which is nothing but recollection, to perception, which is nothing but perception, there needs to be at a given moment a perilous leap? Those who engender recollection from perception are the same who render action or movement impossible by fabricating it with points. Some revealing lines from *Matter and Memory* betray convincingly the solidarity of the two problems:[47] if the past comes out of the present little by little, by a gradual decrescendo, when do we say that there is no longer any perception but recollection? What intensity must an image possess to become perception once more?

It must well be the case that the transformation takes place at a precise moment—*at one moment rather than at another*, since it is radical and since it must transport me from the present, which is action, to the past, which is speculative, "dated," picturesque but idle. Associationism does not explain this *rather than*, incapable as it is to construct the mind unless it be by accidental and fortuitous complications. We recognize here the quibbles and sorite paradoxes in which intellectualism has at all times attempted to confine movement (to immobilize it) and continuity (to chop it up). But true change, which is adventure, modulation, innovation, does not let itself be caught in a specious net of sophisms nor be disaggregated by aporia. To the sophisms of the New Academy, Cicero, via the mouth of Lucullus, already objected that "there is nothing that cannot be carried over from its own class into another class."[48] That is because intellectual atomism, which renders the metabolism of mutation unintelligible, condemns itself to immobility, to the desperate identification of opposites. But just as the free act cannot be explained without an arbitrary approach, so the relation between two spiritual facts that do not share anything obliges associationist deductions to undergo a sudden metamorphosis. Only the idea of qualitative change can really account for this suddenness. Perception and recollection thus differ in their essence, not their quantity of being.

One would then try, inversely, to deduce perception from recollection. Earlier, recollection was materialized by fabricating it from the perceived; now, the perceived is to be idealized by fabricating it from recollections. This is the most common prejudice, the one that inspires all the sensational formulas used in the last century to designate matter and external reality: true hallucination, coherent lie, well-founded phenomenon. Affections or primitively inextensive ideas were said to associate in order to compose extended perception. In sum, one would obtain exteriority by a gradual projection of affections in images. But, as usual, the genetic explanation runs in a vicious cycle: where does extension emerge if it is made from pure inextensive elements?[49] Like it or not, we must put extension already into recollection, let the ghost take on flesh, if we want to see solid reality come out of it. Extension, like freedom, like mobility, is something original that needs to be acknowledged all at once, in its entirety.[50] By wanting to fabricate extension piece by piece with the primary matter of ideas, atomism condemns itself to inserting it everywhere, even into the ideas to which it claims to reduce it! We may add that the subjectivism of true hallucination is an insult to the real whose dignity proper it refuses to acknowledge. The entire world becomes a dream well put together.

But between the most coherent of dreams and the images of the waking state there is an essential difference. A vigilant and activist image is not a strengthened simulacrum. We may multiply dreams by themselves however much we please, we will never obtain the waking state: these two worlds are not of the same order, they belong to two different *levels*. To leave the realm of powerless shadows, we need, at one time, to pass through the bitterness of "awakening."

The Megarian school's aporias prevent Socrates from trespassing and Achilles from running. But those who have tasted the vertigo of freedom and the anxieties of action know that "one mustn't sleep" and that there is a distance between the most lucid sleep and the most humble action that geneticism cannot overcome. The lack of distinction between dream and reality—is this not the central theme around which Janet's psychasthenics and "hypotended" assemble almost all their testimony? The false idealist, who lacks humility, makes a system of this confusion and renounces taking on the real one-on-one. Only dualism accepts this one-on-one because it has too high an opinion of the real to declare it hallucinatory and because, not having mixed the impurity of recollection in with the givens of perception, it does not, in exchange, expose itself to transporting the spatial given into the interiority of the subject.

The purity of the object and the purity of the subject are thus solidary with one another and Bergson's philosophy would already be beneficial if all it did was show us that true idealism cannot be had without a scrupulous realism. This single fact makes it possible to gauge the ignorance of critics who reproach Bergson for dissolving problems instead of solving them and impute to him a "dilettantism" they claim to be as fatal for action as it would be for theory. The opposite is the case.

Bergson's philosophy puts a high value on the "sense of the real" and truly provides the philosophical justification of realism. In *Matter and Memory* especially, Bergson does not tire of saying that "pure" perception is faithful; that left to itself, it would place us in the things; that it is de jure part of matter; that the external object is perceived there where it is.[51] The problem of its "authenticity" does not even come up. That is a false problem stirred up by subjectivist relativism, which emerges with Hobbes and is connected with what I call *miniature theory*.

Just as, for the parallelist, thought is a simple transcription of cerebral language, so cerebral movements are said to represent in miniature, so to speak, the contemporary events that unfold in external reality. How does this cerebral miniature project itself? On this point, opinions diverge and theories have become more complicated. Since the ancient theory of simulacra, sensible emanation has been subjected to ever more subtle distortions. In the system of "critical idealism," for example, the a priori filters exteriority so perfectly that our mind gathers up simple "phenomena." Perception thus becomes an original *alteration* as the macrocosm is transformed into a "*Gehirnphänomen* [cerebral phenomenon]"; the nervous system, instead of remaining an instrument, the "organ" that puts us in relation with the external world, becomes the screen that isolates us from it. Perception lies, and science is only the well-fabricated system of these lies. This is how cerebral idealism inevitably entails skepticism. At the root of subjectivism, we find another prejudice: that exteriority inscribes itself in reduced form in the brain and that theoretically, one could find the exterior, in very condensed but complete form, in the traces or "engrams" it inscribes there, the way a photographer observes the miniature of a complete landscape in the viewfinder.

But the complete landscape is already thought, it is itself already representation, and we know thanks to the study of localizations that thought does not reside in the cortex.[52] To explain the importation of the macrocosm into the brain, miniature theory thus anticipates subjective elaboration and presupposes thought itself, which, by hypothesis, ought to emerge after the cerebral inscription. At all cost, the engram is to somehow *resemble* the physical agent that determines it because a stubborn anthropomorphism demands that we spiritualize the physical from the outset by materializing the spiritual. Unbeknownst to us, we see in the brain something like a mirror in which the original reflects itself more or less faithfully; and since we have already charged this original with quality, we only have to think of it as shrunk to obtain the corresponding excitation. As long as we do not sufficiently shelter interiority from matter, and unless we acknowledge true dualism, we cannot put enough distance between exteriority and the mind. But the brain, as we saw, is nothing but an organ of reprieve meant to suspend or choose movements and to accumulate reaction energy. In the brain, we find dilatory mechanisms, but nothing that resembles miniatures or vignettes.

There is more. The relation of the engram to the impression, of the cerebral to the mental, is not the relation of model to image. That is why perception is necessarily *veridical*. Where there is imitation, as in miniature theory, there can also be alteration. Counterfeit is given with resemblance when resemblance is subject to as distorting a milieu as the nervous system. If, however, we renounce the ideas of an "afferent influx" or an object's transitive action on a subject, perception is indeed de jure authentic since it is exteriority itself. How could the senses cheat us, they who settle us in the midst of things? Error is possible if the *image* is an *imitation*, a mediate projection of the real archetype because exemplarity is always relative and because, on the discursive trajectory from the paradigm to the image, there is space for the false. The search for an exemplary similarity between the engram and the physical agent thus leaves the mind disarmed before the most suspect of disfigurations. Doubt, here as so often, is the price to be paid for systematic homogeneity. In leaving the brain with a purely instrumental role, meanwhile, we gain the unshakable certainty that the senses do not lie.

Analogous ideas are at the basis of the "intuitivist" gnoseology professed by the Russian philosopher Nikolai Lossky.[53] Like Bergson, Lossky protests against a rough substantialism that irremediably uproots the evidence of perception and of knowledge as a whole. The central, and entirely Bergsonian, idea of Lossky's is that *the given does not go out of its way to penetrate us*. What we subsequently know of the given is not a double (a miniature, phenomenon, or simulacrum) filtered by organic sensoria, it is the *res ipsa*, the "original" itself (*podlinik*). In this sense, there are only "primary" qualities. In this realism of the immediate, we have to recognize a fundamental characteristic of Russian thought, and who knows whether Tolstoy's objectivity is not one of its consequences? But whereas Bergson starts from the idea, precise and well established by neuropathology, that memory is incommensurable with matter and radically expulses perception from interiority, Lossky admits certain metaphysical presuppositions and leaves the two terms in place: the subject immediately "contemplates" the "transsubjective" object, and the ecstatic act of knowing realizes the miracle that has the transcendent original become immanent to the subject without leaving the space in which it subsists. Far from the original projecting into our consciousness an always more or less adulterated reflection of itself, therefore, it is the exemplar itself that, present outside of us, *simultaneously* appears in us, as common sense demands. Classic idealism *absorbs* the object; the new realism leaves it in the universe of knowable things. The interest of this conception lies in weaning us off the idea that knowledge is a progressive assimilation, a digestion of the real, an engulfment of the universe, as intellectualist pride has led us to believe. The cognitive relation or, as Lossky calls it, "gnoseological coordination," is something absolutely original and specific. It is *magic* in the sense that Schelling used the word, a kind of action at a distance that escapes the curse of remoteness and discursion: the object is there and thanks to a spell of knowledge it is instantaneously also in the mind.

Thus the light shines and in so doing lights up what surrounds it without leaving itself and without settling in the things "from without" (*thurathen*). Does not light, which is the very symbol of omnipresence and ubiquity, live both in the flame from which it emanates and in the room in which it radiates? Such is Plotinus's One, which pours itself out into creatures without alienating itself. Realism, discrediting the prejudice of gradual elaboration, thus restores the humility of true knowledge: we do not annex the given but accept it with confidence in an immediate and in a way mystical act. Is not the acceptance of a transrational exteriority the best remedy for psychasthenia?

Meanwhile, we also see that Lossky names the difficulty more than he resolves it. Bergson, for his part, "takes the limit": leaping above all transitions that the dialectics of the homogeneous indefinitely inserts between recollection and image, he drives perception back to the surface of the self. The self would not perceive anything if perception did not put it outside itself, just as Socrates would never trespass if his life did not at one time arbitrarily place itself within death. Yet the mutation succeeds. The mind, robbed of itself, must settle, by way of perception, at the heart of matter if it does not want to condemn itself to solipsism. Solid and real extension cannot be obtained by condensing, little by little, the light phantoms of memory, no more than duration can be constructed from instants.

Others, unable to seriously contest this respect for the given that breaks out on every occasion in Bergson, would rather attack his "confusionism." Skeptics readily reproach the philosophy of intuition with a pernicious dilettantism that destroys all limits drawn by reason.[54] Richard Kroner, for example, accuses this "biologism" of drowning the forms of thought in the becoming of organic life and prefers a criticist philosophy that is inherently attentive to the articulations of the mind (*krisis*).[55]

But Bergson's philosophy is indeed *critical* in this sense. This philosophy is the philosophy of *levels of reality*. Nowhere else has the distinction of superposed "levels" ever played such an important role. Pierre Janet, to be sure, often speaks of a "mental level,"[56] and he explains psychasthenic disorders by the oscillations of this level, i.e. by the variable tension of the mind. Monakow and Mourgue, in turn, borrow from Hughlings Jackson the idea that morbidity can be explained by the superior level's regression to the inferior level. But Bergson is the first to endow this hierarchy of the vital with a qualitative and spiritual meaning.[57] Does the thickness of mental life not result from a continuous sedimentation that is the effect of time and memory? Bergson's philosophy labors at separating these tiered universes by eliminating intermediary and impure forms in them, by dissociating the blend of perception and recollection concrete experience offers us.[58] *Pure* recollection, *pure* perception, which are, as we will see, nothing but limits, betray this natural repugnance on the part of Bergson's criticism to confound the hierarchical and the vertical organization of the spiritual.

Bergson's philosophy, to be sure, leads to an intuition that absorbs its object, to a memory all of whose elements give expressive testimony on my entire person. But to discover this universe of immanence in which the mutual exteriority of things is resorbed, one has to go through the fire of purifying antitheses and acute conflicts.[59] The two levels of memory, for example—the memory of picturesque recollections and the memory of movements or habit—represent two vital "tones" that are to one another as the past is to the present. "Tone" here means both *tonality* and *tension*: these two hemispheres of the mind are as opposed to one another as are two musical "tonalities." Their opposition is produced by the variable "tensions" of the mind, which oscillates between the complete relaxation of dreams and the vigilant tonus of played or "attentive" action. The distance between distracted memory and tonic perception seems insurmountable. But do we not know that spiritual syntheses are built on exasperated multiplicities? Harmony is always born in moments of crisis, that is to say, of the greatest distinction; and this birth is what we now have to explain.

If pure perception in fact places us right in the midst of things, error becomes impossible. Perceptionism did not explain the truth of science, and it turned the success of science into an accident. Now our senses are condemned to always being right; perception is the prisoner of its own evidence. How, then, is our knowledge of things not always true? Error is possible in two ways. (a) Perception, which is made for action and for the satisfaction of our needs, is practically interested in only a small portion of the external world. It deceives us, first of all, not because it adds something of its own to materiality but on the contrary because it takes something away. This is what Lossky, for his part, expresses when he distinguishes between the reality of *objects* and the perception of *contents*.[60] Perception does not capture all of reality. Nevertheless, it very well is what it is, and the partial is not the false. To be able to speak of error, there must be a confusion of part and whole. For every error implies a judgment, an act of discernment or of comparison. (b) It is in fact this contribution of thought that alters the authenticity of the pure given. How are we to understand it?

In practice, Bergson's "nativism" joins the conclusions of subjectivist philosophy. There is an a priori. But the source of error is not perception itself since in pure perception our mind is in a way entirely outside itself. The source of error is memory. Yet it is obviously something entirely different whether one says that there is a "noumenon" of which the subject, however, does not take anything in because it distorts everything it touches—or whether one sets up truth in the mind by driving the principle of illusion back to the heart of recollections. Exteriority is humanized while knowledge is naturalized, and both meet in the native extension of pure perception. But pure perception, which is narrower than matter, is also narrower than memory. Recollections without flesh seek to take on a body and settle on perceptions. Perceptions without soul, for their part, solicit the mind and lose their imperturbable fidelity. Born from this meeting is concrete perception, the only one effectively to exist. The intrusion of memory has altered its testimony on things. And let us not reproach Bergson's dualism with having rendered the cohabitation of recollection and the perceived within a mixed perception impossible in advance. Such an impossibility exists only for intellectualism, for which the intimate and paradoxical nature of change remains impenetrable.

But the mind ignores these contradictions, no, more than that: it feeds on them. All of spiritual life thus appears as a miraculous and continuing victory over contradiction. The incarnation of volatile recollection, the sublimation of the heavy image of extension and matter—such is in fact the miracle that sensation operates at every instant.[61] Besides, is there really a miracle here? Recollection is pure quality; unlike the abstract concept, it does not resist the vivacity of images; its extreme deformation calls forth all figures; its fragile individuality is focused on the solid generalities of perception to settle there. Bergson's philosophy, concerned as it is above all with respecting the depth of the spiritual, is much more attentive to this double vertical movement from top to bottom and from bottom to top than it is to the horizontal movement according to which recollections form chains.[62] It is little interested in the rectilinear association of ideas. The a priori of knowledge thus does not reside in a definitive form that would alter, in advance and irremediably, all of the given. The totality of personal memory colors our experience in diverse ways according to the tonicity of the "*Gemüt*" [mind], and across the fissures of a past that perpetually haunts our action, we see, in clearings, the true nature of things. At the root of knowing, there is no original and fatal sin but only an always progressive labor by which recollection and perception seek to find their way.

We know the role the idea of "emergent action" plays in Bergson.[63] It seems that this expression translates in Bergson's philosophy a perpetual effort to be present at the generation of things, to follow the slow maturation that reconciles opposites, to insinuate itself at the precise point at which recollection becomes movement and at which the disinterestedness of the idea transfigures the utilitarianism of action. The most intimate fusion is thus born from the greatest contrariety. Parallelism turns this symbiosis into a relationship of vicinity forever incomprehensible and fortuitous. But there are no epiphenomena in psychology and in living beings; everything proceeds from an internal and organic necessity.

One could say that concrete perception is the most benign form of *illusion* in the precise sense in which modern psychologists use that word. If we take the external world to be a "true hallucination," it is not the fault of the external world, it is ours. The external world may well coincide with our perception, but from the bottom of memory, our perception draws a throng of "prejudices" in search of matter. For memory is indeed the storehouse of prejudices if by prejudice we understand a certain kind of a priori that is not an intellectual form fixed forever but instead the concrete plenitude of *my* past. In fact, there is no perception that is not *interpreted* since our past follows our action like a shadow. And this is indeed what keeps subjectivists from allowing for a "pure" perception. But the instant the recollections and associations that saturate experience do not necessarily exclude an absolute intuition of matter, Bergson escapes the solipsist "pleonasm" American Neorealism warns us against.[64] The substance of illusion does not belong to the self. Nor is it a truism but, on the contrary, it is a synthetic judgment to affirm the subordination of this core of truth to an illusionist memory that plants its roots at the basis of character.

Bergson's philosophy, therefore, is a bit like Berkeley's nominalism. It is a kind of effort to dissociate the immediate given from the "suggestions" of habit and association. This point is well made, for example, by Berkeley's elegant attempt at explaining optical illusions in his *Essay toward a New Theory of Vision*. Bergson's philosophy is, so to speak, a reversed perceptionism; the sensible "idea" has become a pure outside. But there is, for Bergson no more than for Berkeley, no reason to wonder if, by themselves, sensations lie. Both repudiate the idea of a sensible duplicate—Bergson because he affirms the absolute authenticity of pure perception, Berkeley because he suppresses any archetype external to the mind (but is this not still a way of reserving the monopoly of originality for the act of perception?). One wonders, Berkeley observes, why we see objects in place when they appear on the retina upside down.[65] This question makes no sense at all and comes from our following in our minds, so to speak, the course of refracted light rays from an imaginary archetype to its miniature. The eye that sees does not look at itself as it is seeing, and the refracted image is not upside down except for a second vision that contemplates the first and that sees from the outside what the latter sees from the inside. Everything that does not belong to perception *stricto sensu* is suggested to it by empirical "connections"; and if Berkeley does not go through the trouble of establishing the profound duality of these two series, he nonetheless makes a vigorous effort to isolate from the pure given what one may call the "conditional" elements of experience: has not the patient of Molyneux's problem, in sum, had the experience of pure perception in Bergson's place?[66]

Between mixed perception and pure memory there is thus the difference that separates *implied* illusion from *free* illusion.[67] Free or disincarnate, recollection bears witness to my total person and that is why it carries my illusions with it. Illusion is the daily bread of experience. It fills in the lacunae of the given. It is still speaking when perception has long gone silent. It works where reality stops providing. Mixed perception itself is nothing but the perpetual commentary of our illusion; it owes its soul to illusion as it gives its body to the true things. Illusion is thus not only the evasion of those things just betrayed by the present. It gives us full possession of the perceived. It places us in a universe of familiarity in which nothing remains mute for our experience, indifferent to our memory. Knowledge becomes recognition [*la connaissance devient reconnaissance*]. A network of subtle and marvelous sympathies attaches the mind to the real, and we do not even resist this universal conspiracy of things any longer.

III. *Intellection*

Memory will sometimes voluntarily exercise its spiritual power over the perceived. Above all, the effort to *understand*, which sharpens the power of mutual attraction between recollection and image, highlights the descending movement into which recollection enters.

"Intellection" is the most *intense* attitude of all, the one we adopt when we offensively make our way through the spiritual thick of things.[68] This is the effort Franz Xaver von Baader calls "penetrance" (*Penetranz*), a word that expresses the superimposition of levels and the dimension of depth.[69] For to understand, as Maurice Blondel puts it, is to conquer and enter into meaning, and intellection itself is but a certain convergence of these penetrating intuitions. Yet strictly speaking our intellect has only a choice between two attitudes: the soothing and extensive attitude, thanks to which it so to speak stops at the surface of things, and the intense approach that, on the contrary, makes it pierce this surface with a powerful ray for which everything is diaphanous and permeable. The intellect owes this conquering power to the collaboration of intuition, without which no movement of thought, no progress and thus no intellection is possible. And intuitive vision, ideally perpendicular, if we may say so, to the geometric plane of things, is rightly opposed to an entirely optical vision that spreads across the outer face of the real. The effort to understand is *profound* because it is made to seize life in its voluminous plenitude and in its reliefs, not in a flat actuality. It is to penetrate, no longer to just turn *round about*.[70] But since in intellection, penetrating thought appears in its reflected form, it is possible for us to describe, to live, as it were, the paradoxical orientation of spiritual energy.

The commonplace solution to this problem in fact provides us with a striking example of a retrospective illusion. For conventional wisdom, to understand is essentially to go from the sign to the thing signified, from words to meaning, from imaged perception to abstract relations.[71] This seems quite natural since what is initially given in the labor of interpretation, whether of a written text or of oral statements, are obviously material characters and sounds, and the task, precisely, is to pierce the sonorous shell and graphical envelope to render them significant. Yet intellection has to go from the sign to the significant thing because logically it is the sign that is more *simple* and because the operation that is most agreeable to the mind is the one that consists in fabricating the complex from the simple. Let's suppose we are grappling with translating a difficult text, an obscure Greek one, for example. When the text *is understood*, it seems to us the hermeneutic movement relies on words to then give them a value since initially only words seem to be given immediately: our eyes see signs, not what is significant.

The illusion, as we can see, consists in transporting oneself after the fact, to when the process has unfolded all its psychological episodes, and in confusing the vital order of lived facts with the logical order of reconstructed concepts. This is a clandestine reversal thanks to which signs, this abstract *residue* of thought, are said to become the organic *germ* of thought itself. For *the moment* we seek to understand, i.e. *during the fact*, things take place the other way around. Signs (a bit like sense appearance in Plato's dialectic) simply play an evocative and occasional role: they serve to initiate, trigger, and orient the interpretative current. But the true starting point of the mind is in the signified itself or, better, in a certain preexisting idea that we labor to confront with the signs perceived by our senses. If not, we have to believe that sounds are already significant by themselves and that, similar to the elaborated elements or to the concept-judgments discussed above, they implicitly already contain the meaning to be fabricated. If many small cubes precede the mosaic, the artist's conception in turn precedes the small cubes, governs their size and layout.

In general terms, we recognize here the vicious circle in which the defenders of philosophy have always managed to confine empiricist, sensualist, atomist, and associationist theories. Either the spiritual is born from zero or one has to presuppose on the periphery precisely that which was to be explained by the construction at the center.[72] Either recollections, which so to speak develop in perception, are themselves extended or there is no extension: spiritual totalities are, essentially, complete from the outset and do not emerge, bit by bit, in a composition that agglomerates parts. A *logically* simple sign thus takes the initiative only accidentally; only *organically* simple meaning is a real beginning. In reality, we do *not* go *from sign to meaning* but *from meaning to meaning via signs.*

Matter and Memory expresses this point even more profoundly than *Mind-Energy* by opposing a *linear* conception of interpretation to a *circular* one.[73] The linear conception is that of associationists who think of the interpretive or intellective movement as a procession of the mind in a straight line starting from the alphabet of sensation. I'll add that intellectual atomism, in its concern with savings and didactic clarity, needs generally to provide itself with these purely progressive linear series without turnarounds, without possible inflection: can one imagine the movement of fabrication going backward and, in a sense, curving? The approach of the mind, on the contrary, whether it perceives, recognizes, recalls, understands, or invents, is always a *circuit.* We (accidentally) start from sensations, these syllables of thought. Yet we so to speak immediately reflect ourselves on ourselves, on our personal stock of recollections and accumulated experience that refer us once more to signs. But now, in the wake of this regenerative contact with the self, these signs have become intelligible, expressive, and *significant.* We may say, therefore, that everything is as if the proposition in a way rebounded off our recollections and drew from them, in a flash, a value and a meaning. The self, personalized by the original ensemble of its recollections, in a way acts as a signifying force and a source that goes out everywhere to meet the given in order to understand it.

In every process of interpretation, there are thus two inverse currents: an afferent current that starts from the given and a centrifugal current that proceeds from a spiritual totality.[74] The spiritual totality, whose principle is memory, in a way circularizes the indefinite and rectilinear progress with which associationism hypnotizes itself. It is this totality that closes the circuit; by curving the mind onto the extensive afflux of the given, it spiritualizes the "pure outside" and totalizes the elementary. The self is thus the true revelator of sense images. It is the self that guarantees us, as Le Roy might say, the dynamic "prepossession" of the true.

As we can see, the point of view of the organic method such as the study of intellection imposes on us is a *central* point of view. The chapter in *Mind-Energy* on intellectual effort, written five years after *Matter and Memory*, underscores, perhaps more carefully, the "centrifugal" character of the interpretative movement. Focusing essentially on the most dynamic and most intense aspects of *effort* (recall of recollections, comprehension, creative invention), it retains no longer two but only one current, the efferent current. To be sure, *Matter and Memory*'s emphasis in the "circuit" is already on the reflux, not the afflux.[75] We see with the mind at least as much as we see with the eyes, and in no way is perception for us merely an occasion for actualizing recollections.[76] But *Mind-Energy*, analyzing the kinds of effort that, like the imagination, free themselves almost entirely from all centripetal solicitation, brings out only the efferent approach. That is because the other branch of the circuit is not really an approach: it is a simple suggestion, an instantaneous appeal by what is felt to memory, an appeal the mind takes as a signal to oppose it with a central "dynamic schema."

The dynamic schema, i.e. the "preperception" that seeks to settle on the words we read or hear, is already presented to us as an élan.[77] In this image of élan, does the idea of "departure" not win out over the idea of "contribution"? *Matter and Memory*, unaware of the dynamic schema, already speaks of a certain "tone" or "disposition" of intellectual labor, which is the true starting point of interpretation. Memory in general no longer suffices to orient creative approaches like invention or intellection, which demand a less diffuse and more imperious authority. Such is the "dynamic schema," which is truly a concentrate of memory, an always particular initiative. Henri Bremond speaks of "a vague presentiment, a certain promise of the masterpiece to come, but no clear view of it."[78] Taking a hole and putting something around it—that, according to Claudel, is the miracle of inspiration![79] Bergson, nominalist philosopher that he is, would never have spoken this way, nor would he have admitted, as Proust did, a nothingness from which the poem would spring forth. No! Nothingness, like negative theology's More-than-Nothing, is the possibility of all things: in it, the work will germinate. Sharp and fine like steel, the dynamic schema is the only one to possess the power of the *beginning*. It is in a way the sharp point of the soul, *acumen mentis*. It renders us capable of inaugurating something. In this schema, the self gathers and streamlines for the inspirations of genius. If there is no such thing as clairvoyant vision, there are at least, as Charles Van Lerberghe would have said, glimpses [*entrevisions*].[80]

The principle of Bergson's "centralism" is that there is infinitely more in the meaning than there is in the signs, in thought than in perception. That is because memory infinitely exceeds the brain like the brain in turn exceeds events by potentializing our acts, by liberating the spontaneity of our acts. In relation to the infinity of our recollections, the suggestions of exteriority no longer count. We must not say that sound and words compose meaning since meaning *inspires* sounds and words. The artist's "inspiration" brings spiritual centralism to a head because it implies the idea of an inner forum that would be richer, more fertile, and more intense than nature itself. It is not the things that are "suggestive," that is to say, "bring to us"—suggest—their beauty;[81] it is the self that renders them expressive and imparts its own youth to them. That is why everything is inexpressive to the vulgar mind while everything is new, moving, and significant for the "golden races."[82] But already in the most humble perception, our memory plays this inspiratory role; and the intellect that makes an effort to shed light on problems is an inspired one as well. The *intelligibility* of noetic things derives from the implicit or explicit system that justifies them to reason. Their meaning radiates from the explanation that relates them one to the others.

In the same way, it is not the present that is "evocative"; it is the past that is suggestive. We do not reconstruct the past on the basis of the present, we place ourselves straightaway in the past—this virtual past that is us and that projects us into action, far from letting itself be justified a posteriori. Memory is inspiration, impulsion; it is not retrospective and regressive induction.[83] William James's well-known criticism of Maine de Biran's theory of muscular effort thus does not apply here.[84] To be sure, the resistance of an initially unintelligible given is necessary to trigger the intense labor of the mind. But this labor itself radiates from the inside and expires in the perceived signs that incorporate it. The tragic destiny of spiritual life is that it only fixes itself by perishing and that it must yet fix itself to act. The error of "peripheral" explanations, here as everywhere else, thus consists in placing themselves *after the fact*. We might say the psychologists wait for the effort at the exit, at the moment the effort will fade away and settle in sensations—as if these sensations did anything other than refer our own actions to ourselves. But action properly speaking, *the moment* it penetrates among the images, is something wholly different from an arithmetic result of sensation. It is something simple and voluntary; it is the effort itself. James refutes the rough metaphors that assimilate effort to a substantial "emission." Yet if we dare pick up on the image, we would do better to compare effort to an immaterial radiating in which the radiating source coincides with the light it radiates. The appearance of the "centripetal" is thus nothing but a retroactive effect thanks to which relaxed signs, once understood, turn against the idea that has interpreted them: the centripetal is but a backlash of the centrifugal.

Effort thus in a way *tends toward relaxation*. It is "attentive," and it aspires to deploy itself beyond images. Bergson often speaks of the "verticality" of effort: that is how true it is that "penetrance" is profound and essentially made to seize the spiritual "volume" of things. To understand is not only *intelligere*, to read through the inside, but also *comprehendere*, to embrace in all dimensions, to contract in a simple act of intuition. Intellectual effort moves from top to bottom within the cone imagined in *Matter and Memory*,[85] and its verticality is made necessary by the infinite richness of the mind that, going ahead of things, renders them explicit and eloquent for us. The portion of ourselves interested in this encounter is more or less superficial, depending on whether it concerns perception, mediate recognition, or intellection properly speaking. But as the self is in its entirety in each of its states, it is always our entire past that enters into contact with the given to be interpreted.[86] In the same way, in Leibniz, all monads are immanent to each one of them, even if the "point of view" of a singular monad is more limited than that of the divine monad and its expression of the macrocosm is, in consequence, more local. Spiritual things, we have said here, are always complete and suffice unto themselves: that is why words are solidary with their context. De jure, there are only totalities; but each of them is characterized by dominants, and it is the role of sounds to exaggerate and fix these dominants. And thus memory fades away in the language on which intellection settles it.

To understand is thus not only to spiritualize the perceived, it is also to humble oneself before the given and to experience its resistance. Meaning, projected onto things by our memory, bounces back from the things onto our memory. Those who have said that they understand many things have also had to abandon a lot of themselves along the way. For intellection comes at the price of a narrowing; repeated denials are its ransom. *Intelligere, ignoscere*—to understand is to forgive.[87] But is forgiveness not also the confession that the real is independent of our personal sympathies? And is this not a renunciation of the partiality of distracted totalities?

IV. *Memory and Matter*

Bergson's theory of the relation between the soul and the body raises numerous and severe difficulties generally glossed over by his interpreters. Some of these problems concern the very coherence of Bergson's theory, that is to say, the fidelity of *Matter and Memory* to the conclusion of *Time and Free Will*, while others instead pertain to the idea of dualism. To these latter, Bergson devotes some pages in the fourth chapter of *Matter and Memory* that are among the most obscure and cumbersome passages of his oeuvre. Is it not, to tell the truth, an impossible feat to explain the communication of the body with the soul by irremediably separating the pole of matter and the pole of recollection? I have used the word "miracle" and claimed that the very contradiction, far from blocking unity, invited it. That, after all, is a manner of speaking, and reflecting thought will always have a lot of trouble renouncing the continuity of rational mediations in favor of a mystical attraction. Bergson sensed that it did not suffice to profess the contradiction to disarm those who imputed it to him. In the very chapters in which he pretends to push dualism to ever greater extremes, Bergson instinctively seeks to attenuate its effects.

This is the task, for example, of the ingenious idea of the *motor schema*. The motor schema—whether we define it as a function of "mental photography" or as an internal accompaniment or as a series of instantaneous imitation movements—is above all the meeting of the spiritual and the physical. It is motor first because it resembles perception, and then schema second. Everything that participates in the idea is schema because it has been the object of an attentive analysis followed by a synthesis, and each of its parts virtually contains the organic totality of the schema. When it comes to attentive and no longer just motor recognition, i.e. when the memory of the past intervenes, the motor schema serves as mediator or as shared milieu of images and movements.[88] It is an "attitude," but it is already spiritual because recollections "insert" themselves into it.

Besides, what triggers recognition itself, i.e. the incorporation of recollections? Answers to this question are usually given in metaphors. On the one hand, the past would like to be once again. Dreamed recollections lie in wait for the live givens of perceptions as they pass in order to make them their flesh. There is in pure memory a certain élan toward the present that we discern already in "emergent action."[89] But movements, for their part, solicit memory and offer memory the hospitality of their schemata. In a sense, the present pushes us rather to the future. But it also prepares the actualization of the past by choosing the images to incarnate. Perception testifies to a tendency to be prolonged in attitudes that "photograph" it; and these in turn call up capricious recollections.[90] Is this how we can escape the necessity of invoking a coup de théâtre? "Between presence and absence," Bergson himself writes, "there are no degrees, no intermediate stages."[91] To understand the profound metaphysical solution suggested by the conclusion of *Matter and Memory*, it is indispensable to first survey the headway that has been made since *Time and Free Will*.

Time and Free Will posited only half a problem and posited it in essentially optimistic terms. Its antitheses are not yet critical and vital. Lived duration is entrusted with a true spirituality and the mind has layers of makeup applied to it by language, space, and various social symbolisms. Symbolism thus shows us an entirely different face here than in *Matter and Memory*. It has no function of its own; it serves only to dissimulate the mind. It is a parasitic vegetation it would suffice to trim off to get back to the true self. One might say that spatial concepts and senile conventions are an evil the mind gladly inflicts on itself, out of pleasure, and which it could have spared itself without much damage done.[92] There is no tragedy here. Tragedy is made up of, above all, a necessary contradiction. But for our duration, the contagion of space is not an absolutely inevitable evil. It is possible to meet the mind face to face, which is memory and duration, and to "grasp it firmly with one's hand," as it were,[93] once one has withdrawn it from the coalition of negative forces, e.g. space, language, useful concepts.

In *Matter and Memory*, it is the opposite. Language, which had been denounced as the most dangerous parasite of the mind, now appears in its positive function: as adaptation to the real, as transition to action. Not that cerebral symbolism is henceforth invested with a positive and creative function. The brain, we know, is the necessary but not the sufficient condition of perception. And that is even why its role is manifest above all in phenomena of absence and deficit, in all the negations we call, with privative prefixes, aphasia, alexia, apraxia... There is, meanwhile, a cerebral discipline that, thanks to an internal demand of inner life, imposes itself on the mind from within. Are we not told that pure recollection is a limit case rather than a common fact? Our memory never resists the temptation of matter, which leads it to perception. *Time and Free Will* had told us nothing like it, and this language is quite new. Previously, spatial abstractions were opposed to concrete duration; now we see concretion become the privilege of mixed perception, i.e. of implied recollection in which matter and memory mesh (*concrescunt*). Recollection yields to these renewed invitations. Necessarily unstable and fragile, it finds its balance only in incarnation.

Practically, Bergson thus arrives at formulas that, at least in appearance, lend themselves to a criticist interpretation. Undoubtedly, perception taken absolutely is true. But that does not bring us forward at all since perception is never taken absolutely. Undoubtedly, the "phenomenon" is to the "thing" as the part is to the whole, not as appearance is relative to the archetype.[94] But the fatality of incarnation, the indiscretion of a memory always in search of perceptions to break up, alters its narrowed-down experience no less irremediably. This is what the ingenious discussion to which Bergson subjects Johannes Müller's law shows so well.[95] Bergson avoids idealism only by replacing the hypothesis of a subjective alteration with the hypothesis of an equally fatal choice, a utilitarianism that is just as distorting.

There is more. Memory is the first one to blame for this distortion. Memory has become the great nuisance. Memory, which in *Time and Free Will* was rather the victim of the prestige of space, is now the source, not the dupe, of all delusions. And since memory is essentially the mind or, better still, the mind in the mind, we must think that the mind in the act of knowledge is a nuisance to itself. The person in its wholeness obstructs, by its very presence, the vision of matter that a consciousness entirely divested of itself would contemplate in its nakedness, so to speak. What is tragic, however, is that this vision is necessarily somebody's act. It is the vision of a self that has not been waiting for the present perception to exist and that anticipates this perception with all the weight of its prejudices. Does an intuition of the object exist without a subject, an intuition that would be *no one's* [*de personne*] intuition? That would thereby be the intuition *of all things*? Or would that be a contradiction in terms? In any case, the part of things in perception seems to be all the smaller the greater the part of persons is. The perceiver, who has a past heavy with impure experiences, contaminates the perceived in the very act in which he appropriates it.

Moreover, what is this past that now in turn inflicts on matter the violence that matter, in the philosophy of *Time and Free Will*, inflicted on the mind? The "limit" of the past is pure recollection. Pure recollection is, if I dare say so, the superlative of memory and consequently of the mind. Pure recollections, or recollections that are dreamed, as Bergson also says, would be entirely detached from present action: "Like the Homeric shadows in the land of the Cimmerians, they wander in search of the occasion that will give them warmth and life again."[96] To have out with it, pure memory would be unconscious.[97] The duration of *Time and Free Will* is perfectly continuous, always so full, always present to consciousness; that is even what offers a foothold to the criticism of Rauh, who denies

Bergson the right to speak of past or future if not according to an affirmation transcendent of the given properly speaking.[98] Dreams, on the contrary, are nothing but the blossoming past, the past that, instead of rushing into perceptions, resists their call, comes flooding back into itself and unfurls far from the action. Preformation stops being an implicit and permanent property of duration to become the explicit operation by which recollection joins, at every moment, a matter from which dualism had separated it. *Matter and Memory* thus overcomes the immanence of Bergson's first duration and replaces the picture of a duration suspended unerringly between past and future with the tête-à-tête of a bygone past and a material present that adjust to one another. It is thus this adjustment itself, always in the middle between the two poles, that takes up the transitive dynamism of the first duration. Everything now (at least in the book's first three chapters) happens as if the past abandoned the benefit of its superiority over space to a certain active intuition of matter.

Besides, the antithesis is no longer of present and past, i.e. between two moments of duration where one no longer knows which one takes over the prerogatives of the mind. The effect of dualism was to deprive both of them of the vitality that had been the privilege of complete and organic becoming. We are left to verify that Bergson's philosophy did not stop with this analysis. In the labor with which the differentiated moments seek to join each other again, we will see the indivision and immanence of original duration reappear, and we will see the double transcendence of an unconscious that does not survive—of a pure novelty that did not preexist—little by little resorb itself.

By separating the present and the past, Bergson has not purely and simply split up duration. Matter is now on the level of the present: that means that it, too, has become relatively spiritual. While in perception the mind settles in exteriority itself, exteriority in turn participates in the mind. For the first time, consciousness goes out from itself and discovers the distant kinship that unites it with movement, physical changes, and concrete extension. It learns to no longer confuse true extension with the delusions of a homogeneous space, the tension of real movement with the quantitative schemata that measure it. This sheds light on the penetrating analyses to which *Time and Free Will*, pulled along by the problem of time, subjected the idea of continuity. We could not then understand that mobility was chosen as the "symbol"[99] of a duration that still monopolized the privilege of tension and of quality. We were not told that there was something present to the mind other than the geometers' indifferent space. And besides, we were not aware of what real milieu this space was the imaginary refraction. We now know that even in space, consciousness still feels at home, among the things that vaguely remind it of its own duration. Obviously someone like Rauh, concerned with maintaining the law's intellectual transcendence, would reproach Bergson for confusing change with the perception of change, for identifying space *itself* (*auto*) with a spatial given that, as given, of course resembles the mind. But no matter what it does, intellectualism won't be able to escape the abstract schemata that undergird intuition. Besides, why would real continuity, why would true movement, be distinct from the act by which they are given to us if this act is immediate and truly pure of any memory?

Matter is my present—that means two things: (a) that my present, when it is pure, is extension itself, and that I already find exteriority in myself; but also (b) that matter in turn occupies a place in time. Matter is nothing other than quality in a state of extreme dilution, nothing other than duration in the ultimate degree of relaxation. As for *Time and Free Will*'s homogeneous space, it is something else: it does not exist at all. It is a phantom of the imagination, born from utilitarian needs. In the presence of this idol, there is only one and the same reality, unequally strained and concentrated according to what level one is aiming for: the level of spiritual memory, which is the densest duration, and, at the other end, the level of extension on which duration dissipates and approximates instantaneity. Matter is no longer a hallucination and, meanwhile, dualism is overcome: overcome without our having to attenuate the radical distinction between pure recollection and pure perception.

How are we to interpret these profound metaphysical views? There is a true duration that contracts in memory, and there is an extension that is just as true, whose organ is pure perception. Average or utilitarian perception is situated at the intersection of these two infinities that both exceed it. There thus exists, beyond that shared zone, an intuition of pure mind and an intuition of pure matter. On the one hand, we see that the mind thus isolated shows us a rather new face. Memory, separated from the matter that habitually provides it with a solid foundation, floats in the unconscious of dreams and scatters about a multitude of fragile recollections, each of which has a date in my history. But when Bergson now speaks of intuition, it is usually the other one [i.e. matter] that is at issue.[100] This latter, by contrast, is said to be impersonal, instantaneous; to consist, as Berkeley well saw, in eliminating all the prejudices memory associates with the perceptions; to identify with nature itself, as spiritual intuition does with the mind. The *Laughter* book, in a justly famous chapter, highlights the symmetry of the two intuitions that envelope the mind, so to speak, in a circle of truth.[101]

Where, then, does error reside? Bergson incriminates either the intrusion of affective sensations, in space, or the invasion of recollections, in time. In reality, error has one cause and one cause only. *The cause of error is the confusion of the superposed levels of the mind.* Spiritual life, as we saw, is organized in thickness or polyphonically according to the superposed layers that are stacked up between pure dreaming and the played-out act. Each of these levels is true for itself, provided one sticks with it. The truth, says Brunschvicg, wants to be judged by its peers,[102] and evidence will remain essentially disjointed and sporadic.

The *immediate* will thus flee in two directions, toward the two extreme levels where ambiguity is most completely defeated because here, consciousness is all mind, and there, all matter. Everywhere else, consciousness remains more or less amphibious, more or less incapable of coinciding with the rhythm that belongs to the level it adopts. Bergson's "immediate" has been interpreted in a number of ways.[103] We may perhaps be permitted to say that *the immediate is first and foremost the pure*. Immediate is all thought that, to move on a given level, does not borrow anything from the other levels. Immediate is the thought that thinks the mind only with the mind, matter only with matter. Immediate thought is thereby direct because we do not insert any middle term drawn from different levels between thought and its object. The immediate thus has a relative meaning: it is everywhere where thought stops being muddied and ambiguous, everywhere where it entirely assimilates to the object it contemplates. Such that, as the mystics of all ages have sensed, one truly knows only what one is. "No eye ever saw the sun without becoming sun-like, nor can a soul see beauty without becoming beautiful."[104] This is how, in *Matter and Memory*, extension reconquers the immediacy that *Time and Free Will* reserved for the givens of a consciousness attentive to its own passing flow.[105] The immediate extracts us from that "midway zone" *Laughter* speaks of, the zone to which the mediocre ambiguity of our perceptions relegates us.[106]

For in fact, consciousness is nearly always mixed. It is, Descartes would say, that which prevents us from spontaneously knowing "simple natures."[107] "That is why nearly all philosophers confuse their ideas of things and speak spiritually of corporeal things and corporeally of spiritual ones."[108] It is this constitutive duplicity, Pascal adds, that engenders both the anthropomorphism of physics and the materialism of psychologists. A psychologist in physics scrambles the evidence just as someone who asks, at a performance of Corneille's *Polyeucte*, "What does that prove?" mixes tragedy with geometry.[109]

This inversion allows us to explain all the idols with which pseudo-philosophy is filled. Associationism, for example, is the theory that scrambles all levels of consciousness. In *Time and Free Will*, Bergson himself enumerates the various concepts that emerge from a mutual contamination or, as he calls it, an "endosmosis" of space and mind: such are, precisely, the concepts of simultaneity and of speed.[110] Such is also, according to *Creative Evolution*, the "equivocal" idea of *genus* in which biologists have confused the vital order and the geometric order, either by reducing genera to laws or by reducing laws to genera. Such, finally, is mechanicism in biology, which is wrong to apply the procedures of the intellect to the living.

And yet the intellect is said to be at home in the domain of practice, as speculation is at home in the domain of dreams. Inversely, Bergson does not tire of condemning the hypothesis of a speculative perception because it confuses the level of action with the level of ideas. Not that speculative theory is out of place on the level of memory and pure contemplation. But the idleness of memory must not rub off on action and communicate its disinterest to it, such that true realism is absolutely "objective" in matters of matter and absolutely "subjective" in matters of the soul, oscillating between an intuition of the subject without object and an intuition of the object without subject. Here and there, besides, consciousness would escape the curse of reflexive splitting. Whether it withdraws to the periphery, or whether it collects itself entirely at the center, either way it finds in itself the two poles of reality. It has entirely become its own object.

But the confusion of levels explains above all the existence of the *comical*. Perhaps Bergson's admirable philosophy of laughter comes down to this discovery. The comical is very simply our becoming aware of an awkward confusion of the level of dreams and the level of motor gesticulation. In a dreamed world, dreamers would not be laughable. In an entirely mechanical universe, automata would not be laughable. What is ridiculous is a dreamer lost in our material world, in which human beings live and act in the present. What is comical is an automaton stranded among spiritual creatures who have an original personality, an infinite smoothness in adaptation, and always unforeseeable reactions. Laughter thus always links up with the *relation* of two levels we sense to be scrambled. Yet each level taken by itself cannot but be serious just as it cannot but be true. Philosophers occupied with contemplating the stars would not make their fellow human beings laugh if down here, there were no wells lying in wait for them and none of the thousand other traps the Thracian slaves maliciously put in their way. But we know very well that *at bottom*, these dreamers are touching and sublime—at bottom means: when one has understood that there are two levels opposed to one another and that only the misery of life obliges us to arrange them. In reality, the dreamers are, as *Theaetetus* has it, the true "leaders," the free men par excellence.[111] They are thus thrown among us as the great absentminded, as the somnambulists of life, messengers of a glorious world of whose splendor we have a presentiment, a world that would be pure and immaculate like the fire of the mind. There, they are at ease; among men, they betray the awkwardness of the genius who is ill-adapted both to a world that is too narrow and to a servile consciousness ("that narrow, keen, little legal mind")[112]—and that is what we find funny. Does not Bergson himself connect the comical with the idea of distraction? The subject matter of comedy is this confusion of levels that in life engenders all sorts of entertaining and hilarious failures. But it is also very much an art since it comes from a nostalgia of purity and since all art seeks to dissociate the immediate from the banalities that imprison it. Don Quixote is heroic and absurd; but we know very well that it is not Don Quixote who is wrong but those who laugh at him.

But how is it possible that memory is at present held responsible for these confusions? It is because memory has a double aspect and so to speak denies itself. Bergson is rarely aware of this duplicity, essential though it is in his philosophy.[113] There is a sort of painful irony here that usually does not receive enough attention. It arises because the varied symbolisms to which *Time and Free Will* so eloquently imputes the senile hardening of our life themselves result from a property that all living consciousness has, namely to endure and to perpetuate its past through its present. The forms and schematisms of the intellect themselves issue from the duration that they damage. That is the true "misfortune [*malheur*] of consciousness" that Jean Wahl's beautiful eponymous book discusses in Hegel. The misfortune of consciousness is not that it is split. It lies instead in this malediction, so real and so tragic, that has life carry within itself a germ of death and has it perish precisely by that through which it affirms its vitality.

Let us say for our part that memory can be considered either in the present participle or in the past participle: either as "giving" or as "given." Giving memory makes our life something like a fabric of impalpable traditions that each moment of duration delegates to the following movement such that my present never needs to be explained, as Leibniz would say, with the help of extrinsic denominations. But memory is not only the continuation of the present; it is also, and thereby, the survival of the past—of a past that, as depot and product of becoming, enables itself to escape becoming. For it is a law of all life that the progeny of the mind turn on the mind that gives birth to them.[114]

This ingratitude and this denial, renewing the mishap of the sorcerer's apprentice, do they not favor the illusion of retroactivity? "Constituted" memory[115] is a principle of "prevention": the great rationalists of the eighteenth century stubbornly refused to acknowledge it. The same function that totalizes past and present in a constantly renewed individual experience allows the past tense, when it goes all the way, to detach itself from becoming, like a ripe fruit, and to escape the devouring succession of perceptions. Preterition, mother of pure recollection, is thus trapped from within. When recollection redescends into duration it has a ghostly effect, as the phenomena of recognition so profoundly studied by Bergson show, in which a very ancient past suddenly invades the present. But in general, that kind of memory coagulates definitively in economical signs and symbols that create an impenetrable screen between the I and the self [le moi et le soi]. (Such is the role of the thought Leibniz calls "suppositive.")[116] Memory thus becomes the "historical" function, the organ of erudition and compilation that turns the mind, as Malebranche says, into a "furniture warehouse" or, as La Bruyère says, "the receptacle, register, or storehouse of all the productions of other talents."[117] It is, in a word, the revenge of those who lean on those who understand, the revenge of the pedantic, of the technician, and of all those mocked by Molière, Boileau, Descartes, and Montaigne on the honest man who thinks personally.

Here is what Time and Free Will did not tell us and what the theory of the dream in Matter and Memory now helps us understand: generic signals and concepts whose fatal effects we so legitimately incriminate have the same spiritual origin as our self! A bitter irony and a ridiculous contradiction! In the very act by which it affirms itself, life labors on its own loss. But do we not know that it is accustomed to these paradoxes? Memory, daughter of duration, reacts against duration. Janet very rightly remarks that it serves to neutralize absences just as movement serves to neutralize distance.[118] It is the principle of leisure and thereby fortifies our hold on things. Prying our concepts away from the becoming that carries us off, it transposes the world into nontemporal abstractions that our forecasts and enterprises can grasp onto. But does this "forecast" [*prévision*], which is but a learned prevention, not insult the freshness of true intuition? The freedom of *Time and Free Will* was the way of being of a person capable of sufficient profundity to find all of its past in one of its moments. And now, starting with *Matter and Memory*, a new freedom appears, of which the brain is the organ and which is less purity within than it is mastery without. Such mastery, far from seeking immanence in the labor of a mind always present to itself, brutally fixes the future of things in stationary concepts. It is too afraid that in giving itself over to pure succession it will be surprised by newness. As if, by a cruel irony of destiny, the power of action did not come without a weakness of vision!

The only antidote to this parasitic memory, it seems, would be forgetting—a reasonable and as if concerted forgetting. Does not forgetting momentarily rejuvenate our mind by restituting to us the virginity of perceptions? That, precisely, is what Bergson calls common sense [*bon sens*].[119] "Common sense" is nothing but a controlled and durable forgetting. Common sense, I'll add, is above all the art of liquidating one's past. To have a joyous present one must indeed overcome one's past, must indeed circumscribe things past in order for life not to be encumbered by them. Death does not lie ahead; it rather lies behind, in all the intellectual superstitions that keep us from seeing and understanding. Whoever has well suppressed his past, Schelling says, will have a clear and light future ahead of him. A future thus sheltered from the old spontaneously flowers into joyful actions.

Forgetting rejuvenates not only action but sensibility as well. Those who know to forget find the artistic and naive vision of things that the proliferation of utilitarian prejudices has caused us to lose. They view the world as if they saw it for the first time. They discover in the world treasures of grace and emotion of which we never have the slightest inkling because we live on recollections and heavy conventions that in a way anesthetize our sensibility. That is why artists are characterized by a great power of admiration and wonder, just as the power of indignation is proof of the moral sense. Science is born of wonder because its task is to suppress it. But art is not born from wonder, it is wonder itself, implicit and perpetual. The power to admire abundantly is a precious gift, rare among all gifts; its spontaneity, its freshness is the measure of the sincerity of emotion and of the resources of the mind.

This might be what the mystics mean to say when they preach learned ignorance. Learned ignorance would be nothing but a profound naivety of the mind and of the senses, a tête-à-tête with the immediate. That is what Bergson's philosophy asks of us. No other theory has ever shown more forcefully and more lucidly to what extent this learned simplicity, which separates us from our dear and old superstitions, in reality brings us closer to the center of the mind. Those who recollect too much will always remain ignorant of the innocence of life. But those who know how to renounce their memory will find themselves and, in themselves, reality.

And this is the last question raised by the theory of the soul and the body in Bergson. This cruel rupture with memory, this harrowing sacrifice, is it always indispensable? *Time and Free Will* teaches us that the richest consciousness is the one that is pregnant with all of its past and, far from renouncing the least part of its spiritual capital, in a way fills itself with itself. The difficulty vanishes when we think of the *confusion of levels* in which we denounced the unique cause of the obscurities and lies of experience. Memory is only a nuisance and an intruder when it descends to another level of consciousness, when it meddles, for example, by legislating to plastic sensibility.

Born from this indiscretion is common sense's fundamental prejudice, which Bergson calls the illusion of breaking up [*morcelage*].[120] Breaking up is possible because there are interested and partial memories that congeal intuitions in stationary schemata. But memory here only misleads us by slicing up the universe according to an anthropomorphic plan whose rule is provided by our subjective needs and not by the objective nature of things. It distorts the material universe by applying to the undivided continuity of extension the abbreviating symbols born from human utility and human practice. In other words, memory becomes opaque and deceptive once it confuses levels, once it claims to substitute itself for the disinterested intuition of matter. The degenerate signs of suppositive thought are born from this usurpation: they are ambiguous concepts just as, inversely, those concepts are ambiguous that are born from a contamination of the mind by space—speed, simultaneity, etc. The former originate in the demands of action, of artisanal freedom and of industry; the latter come from the visual and immobile schemata that influence our intellect.

Memory would always be spiritual if it did not go beyond the pure dream that expresses its picturesqueness. Is it thus condemned eternally to go round in circles among the shadows of recollection? Bergson is not dogmatic enough to dare make that claim. In a world of glorious and angelic minds, dreams would become reality itself. That is not the world of *Matter and Memory* and *Laughter*. Not that an eschatological intuition, as it were, did not permit us intermittently, in flashes, to see the splendor of pure minds: art, for its part, has indeed the mission of eternalizing for our eyes the spectacle of pure forms! But for our amphibious minds, those are exceptional escapes. According to *Laughter*, the beauty and elegance of life are entirely expressed in the attentive movement by which memory espouses all the meanderings of experience. This is indeed a way for recollection to go beyond itself and to join the materiality of perceptions on the outside. And we are not told that this incursion impoverishes and devastates the world of extended forms.

For there exists a means for our memory to escape the dream and to adapt to reality without doing violence to it: it is to *understand* reality. The movement of the intellect is the only movement that permits recollection to descend from one level to another without confusing their respective rhythms. Intellection is thus not only the movement that transports us from the recollection to the perceived. For so poor a result, it would not need to call for so intense an effort. Everyone is capable of the mediocre totalizations that abolish the joyful variety of nature and coerce the universe into dreary concepts. All it takes is letting oneself go on the downward slope of memory, which is naturally greedy for matter, naturally oriented toward lazy confusions and facile analogies; what governs these mechanical applications it is the principle of economy...

Intellection is the power of descending from one level to another *and at every instant remaining in accord with the tone of the level on which one is*. Intellection is thus *perpetually on par with things*, no matter what level they belong to.

Prejudiced memory is always ahead or behind, and that is why it scrambles the levels of consciousness. Either it is ahead and thus, obeying its natural inclination, imposes on nature the sordid uniformity of its prejudices without taking the time to observe the capricious diversity of things. Or it is behind because, discouraged by the sight of all this originality springing up, it prefers remaining the prisoner of its dream. Powerlessness or impatience—prejudiced memory never marks the same time as real things do.

Intellectual effort, on the contrary, brings together without confusing. "Intelligent" people are precisely those who, with unflinching cold-bloodedness, "adapt" specially to each new situation and regulate their perspective according to the things, far from bending the things to their perspective. They are always on par with the real; they know to make a distinct effort of readaptation in each distinct case. "They will talk about whatever was being talked about when they came in."[121] They are without stiffness and without fanaticism—since most of the time, intolerance is but an appeal to parsimonious generalization. They willingly place themselves in someone else's point of view, possessing naturally the gift of thinking apart the things that really exist apart,[122] and other people are grateful for their thus understanding so many things. They have a special talent for abstraction, for *abstracting* abstraction and no longer *abstract* abstraction.[123] That is why everyone agrees in praising their "impartiality." *Impartiality* is but the sentimental and lived form of abstraction; it is, if you like, integral abstraction, permanent abstraction, fixed in a habit and a lifestyle. Impartiality is, literally, the quality of someone who does not *participate*, who has no part in something. It implies a certain detachment with respect to superficial associations, a certain restraint in relation to passionate "involvements," a detachment and restraint that are precisely what is called a critical Spirit, the spirit of discernment and intellection.

Intellection is thus perpetually contemporaneous with its objects: perceiving with the perceived, dreaming with the phantoms of dreams, always equally lucid, equally attentive to the given; respectful enough of newness to resist the calls of a partial memory, meanwhile spiritual enough to listen to the invitations of a memory truly sympathetic with the real. That is the road memory has to take if it wants to join the given without its symbols chasing fantasy and the unforeseen out from itself. Above all, Bergson's philosophy teaches us that the mind spontaneously goes out toward the things because all light comes from the mind. But the generous mind does not remain confined in a smug memory. It does not impose a summary reading [*solfège*], which it rejects, on the admirable variety of nature. Going beyond itself, it seeks to encounter something other than its own image because it needs nourishing and truly positive realities. The intellectual effort signifies that we have kept a means of conquering the given by experiencing the originality of things and the resistance of problems, by keeping intact the sensibility toward the unforeseen that knowledge really consists in. A profound science does not come without great innocence.

CHAPTER 4

LIFE

More so than *Matter and Memory*, it seems, *Creative Evolution* takes the conclusions of *Time and Free Will* as its starting point. Discovering the unity of life outside itself, consciousness no longer manages completely to overcome dualism, whose effects were almost avoided in the experience of tension and movement. Moreover, the mind now presented to us is the conquering mind, evolution reaching for the future. The past and the present-future, separated in *Matter and Memory*'s polarizing analysis, now find themselves again in their original immanence but enlarged to the scale of cosmic life. The question is no longer to discover the mind's own excellence in the laziness of dreams; dreams on the contrary manifest our fall into space![1] Where, then, would this life find the leisure to scatter itself in idle recollections, this life which is entirely absorbed in the forceful creations of its genius? The very need for creation will put life in the presence of a matter that is impossible to avoid this time. Before studying the relationship of *matter* and life, we have to show: (1) that biological *finality* renews in living organisms all the paradoxes of duration such as the analysis of freedom or of intellectual effort had us bring out; (2) how the antithesis between *instinct* and intelligence extends, by shedding light on it, the antithesis between memory and perception, between duration and space.

1. *Finality*

In aiming at an end that, as we saw, is in reality preformed in the free action itself, the legislation of actions seems to withdraw our will from determinism. Theories about life bear the mark of this illusion. In fact, biological life, the life of organized beings, fosters the same pretensions and the same demands as the life of acts or of penetrating intuitions. Before Bergson's dialectics finally reveals its secret to us, we have to show that what holds for lived duration within holds equally for duration deployed in tissues and organs. As the critique of *Time and Free Will* places the two adverse unilateralities of determinism and indeterminism back to back, so *Creative Evolution* rises above the traditional conflict of mechanism and finalism. Bergson's philosophy, just like freedom itself, rejects Manichean bifurcations and sharp options, and it refuses the ultimatums that would call on it to choose between extreme dogmatisms. But Bergson's entire originality is concentrated here, in the denunciation of finalism, the insincere defender of life, just as it used to be concentrated in the refutation of indifferentism, the compromising champion of freedom.

The vice radical finalism and mechanism share is that they consider only what I have called the *past participles* of life, and never its *present participle*. The illusion of the *accomplished act* here has its correlate in the illusion of the *evolved*.[2] Finalism in particular, which subjects life to the execution of a transcendent program (under whatever form, incidentally, it conceives of this program), is, like indeterminism, a victim of the myth of "attraction-causality."[3] It exhausts the unforeseeable movement of life in advance, in a fictitious future that is not "to come" (except on paper) and that, mentally, is already past. If life truly realized a preestablished plan, its creative originality would only be a phantom: considering the destiny of spiritual things, attraction and impulsion, albeit mechanically inverse, are completely equivalent. But finality thus understood, precisely— understood as the logic of our actions—is true only in the "future perfect," that is to say, *after the fact*.[4] Vital evolution, therefore, is made such that at each instant it has traced a harmonious and directed curve, and such that *at the moment that* it is tracing, nothing at all can be prejudged. Finality thus appears as a perpetual effect of retroaction thanks to which the imagination, settling in *what ought to be* [*le devant-être*], turns toward *what is making itself* [*le se-faisant*], which thus becomes something *all-accomplished* [*du tout-fait*], and formulates its teleological nature.[5]

The finalists' fictitious evolution, like the indeterminists' fictitious volition, thus corresponds to the false perspective of the accomplished fact. It seems to indicate a direction and describes, basically, a trajectory. It is entirely posterior to the fact. Spinoza already denounced the chronological inversion the finalists committed. In the famous appendix to the first part of the *Ethics*, he shows us men seeking the finality of accomplished things, of "what has been done," and he adds: "For what is really a cause, it considers as an effect, and conversely. What is by nature prior, it makes posterior."[6]

Finalism, this most human of "fictions,"[7] devalorizes causes to the point of turning them into *means*. But by positing the "means," it has surreptitiously posited the end, the way a lawyer's arrangement of an argument surreptitiously prejudges his own conclusion—or else it is necessary to extract the finality of life from nothingness and to invoke a permanent miracle. The means, in fact, like the motives of the justified decision and the signs from which reconstituted intellection starts, are logical junctions, totalities, intentions, in which we already discern the goal: this intentionality is why they exist.

What we said of penetrating thought thus also applies to this biological finality: it is intermediary between the past of impulsion and the future of attraction.[8] That is why Bergson seems to express himself in turns in terms of causality and finality. Now he speaks the determinist language of Eimer;[9] now he formulates the teleological hypothesis that the nervous system is the end of organization.[10] This explains certain equivocal expressions in *Creative Evolution*: "harmony is rather behind us than before. It is due to an identity of impulsion and not to a common aspiration." "The unity is derived from a *vis a tergo* [a force acting from behind], it is given at the start as an impulsion, not placed at the end as an attraction"[11]—an obvious concession to the point of view of impulsion-causality.

Just like the declared causality of the mechanicists, the surreptitious causality of the finalists deprecates in advance the signification of development. What differentiates the impulsion of the cause and the impulsion of the "élan" is that in the first case, the motor principle remains distinct from the movement it imprints, whereas in the second, the productive force coincides with the very act of production. Mechanical causes, while transcending their effects, virtually imply these effects. That is how a shock envelops in advance, in speed and in direction, all the characteristics of the movement it provokes. That is how in the defense plea's thesis, the entirely fictitious actions that will justify it preexist de jure and analytically. But between an organic cause and the growth of which it is the source or the germ, there is no greater local separation than there is between the intention to act and the acting will. The will itself, on the condition of being serious and sincere and impassioned, is already emergent and activist action—does this immediacy not define courage? Nor does any distance insert itself between the inspiration of the genius and the creative labor. In improvisation, the initial incarnation of the schema excludes any middle term. Only the image of an explosion expresses this immanent production of the vital passably well because here, the exteriority of the shock to the thing shocked is no longer perceptible: the central force appears to be the spurting spray itself, projected into a thousand diverging splinters.[12]

The "vital élan" thus conceived is not, no more than the "dynamic schema," a metaphysical person. The "vital élan" is nothing: whereas Schopenhauer's *Wille* is a veritable principle of universal explanation, the Élan— the word is already an indication—only designates a certain direction [*allure*] of evolution, always harmonious, never predestined. In this way, the vital thrust is determined just enough not to progress randomly, without cause and without direction. Its future, far from resulting mechanically from its present, nonetheless innovates on it at each step. By a singular paradox to which the meditation of duration has already accustomed us, the finality of life unites in itself two contradictory properties: *after the fact* evolution appears at every instant as oriented toward a goal; *before the fact* our intellect is never capable of anticipating the event to come. That is what Bergson expresses when he speaks of a retrospective finality. One could in this sense say that the free act, like creative evolution, only retroactively allows for determinism.

What, besides, is this original "unity" that seems to dictate its program to evolution? An "impulsion," a "vis a tergo," a "harmony," a schema, that is to say, something dynamic and motor that, far from imposing the development of an analytical formula, gives free rein to all of the whims of invention. It is thus not a preestablished harmony, and Bergson's synthetic harmony here ceases to resemble the implication of predicates in a subject. Le Roy sheds light on the dynamism of thought with the notion of "limit" such as the mathematicians use it when they talk about irrational numbers, yet the "goal" of evolution would indeed be a limit in this sense.[13] It simply defines the general direction of its path, the internal convergence of its hesitant approximations.

The continuation of life is thus always intermediary between *Unde* and *Quo* [Whence and Whither] or, to speak Schopenhauer's language, always on the path from the *Warum* to the *Wozu* [from the Why to the Wherefore]. If I use Schopenhauer's formula here, I do so not because Bergson historically owes him anything whatsoever but because the same organicist and vitalist theme is present in both.[14] To criticize the physico-theological argument, Schopenhauer uses almost the same language as

Bergson in his refutation of the old anthropocentric teleology. Finality is not, as Leibniz would say, a transitive action, the action of a transcendent intellect on beings. The intellect is not before life, it is after. No discursive art extrinsically preexists a beehive, a termite colony, or a beaver society. Bergson, for his part, would have said that deliberation is an ideological reconstruction made after the fact. True finality is *immanent* and has its source in "Willing." Only Willing is primary. Before Willing, there is still Willing, and always Willing. Far from emerging suddenly to execute the plans of the intellect and to satisfy the needs of the tissues, Willing radiates in tissues, in brain and intellect. Willing is comparable to a magic lantern in which a simple flame makes the most varied images visible. Does this image not recall Neoplatonic Emanatism? Behavior, organs—all of ethology and all of morphology—are thus but an irradiation of willing, which alone is primary and which alone is productive.

But common sense does not see it this way and, when it abandons the myth of a providential wisdom, it wants at all costs to relate vital actions to their proximate causes. Birds fly *because* they have wings; bulls strike *because* they have horns. But in reality, it's the contrary: because they want to strike, bulls have horns; birds *first* wanted to fly, and then they had wings, and they flew. Vital willing engenders, along with structures, the functions adapted to the structures, just as, in the human soul, the will inspires actions at the same time as it engenders the ideological justification of these actions. Schopenhauer thus has us witness once more this reversal of the "because," the inversion of the etiology that Pascal, theoretician of the "heart," had noted. Common sense has difficulty resigning itself to this because common sense only conceives of a type of visual causality. It does not understand anything of an organic causality that would resemble the inspiration of genius and whose principle would be, just like genius, invisible and profound. The sand wasp kills the cuckoo wasp with its sting although it does not eat it and although it is not attacked by it; but the cuckoo wasp lays its eggs in the sand wasp's nest and threatens the sand wasp's posterity.[15] The sand wasp does not *know* anything about this or rather, it knows it with an intimate and central knowledge that is inspired by its very tendency to live and perpetuate itself. This tendency is beyond any end, as it is beyond any cause. It is the only true *Prius* of creative life. Is this not the "finality without an end" (the intuition of which Schopenhauer, according to Léon Brunschvicg, found in Kant's *Critique of Judgment*) that is the hallmark of Romantic voluntarism?[16]

It is true that, after evolution has evolved, life seems to fulfill a program. The judgment of finality is thus indeed a judgment a posteriori. And we will see how, in biology as in physics, the retrospective view replaces the historical order of organization with a mechanical order of fabrication.

This inversion preoccupies both Bergson and Schopenhauer. How close they are is perhaps nowhere more clearly demonstrated than in the convergence between the brilliant and profound last pages of the first chapter of *Creative Evolution* and Schopenhauer's astonishing intuitions. Albert Thibaut, it seems, is the only writer to have signaled this encounter but without, perhaps, sensing its true import.[17] Schopenhauer's vocabulary, even though it is governed by the point of view of Kant's critique, must not confuse us about the profound significance of this coincidence.

The task is to explain *teleological astonishment (teleologisches Erstaunen)*,[18] the admiration the perfection of the works of life excites in us, and which invites us to assign to them a transcendent finality. If the complication of organisms seems marvelous to us and if the all-natural simplicity of their functioning disconcerts us to such a degree, it is because, without noticing it, we imagine them to have been fabricated piece by piece the way we ourselves fabricate our machines (*Machwerke*). Yet, on this account, it is clear that the divine artisan's skill lends itself to confusion. Let us recall the section in the *Monadology* in which Leibniz opposes mechanisms, which are *simply machines*, to organisms, which are *machines to the infinite*.[19] While nature does not proceed differently from artisans, its art is nonetheless infinitely more complicated just as its works are themselves infinitely more complicated. But in thus reducing the operation of nature to a procedure of the mechanical type, our intellect in a way admires itself. It is in fact one of the intellect's most absurd manias to thus create within things a certain complicated order for it to then enjoy the spectacle.[20] It is perpetually lunatic and loses itself in the ridiculous contemplation of its own image.

Our intellect begins by mechanizing life and is then astonished that this mechanism subdivides indefinitely without the simple ever appearing—it is astonished by a miracle of which it alone is the author! The infinite only induces vertigo when we conceptualize it:[21] it is then "indefinite." Once withdrawn from the dissolving and reductive action of concepts, however, it is on the contrary actually and globally infinite. Nonetheless, the common illusion rests on the prejudice that *things have been fabricated discursively and piece by piece as they can now be analyzed before our eyes but in the in-*

verse order, the synthesis by which they have been constructed is said to reproduce, by reversing their order, the successive degrees through which analysis passes to decompose their form into elements. But the analysis to which living beings lend themselves is an analysis without end, and what astonishes us is the inconceivable skill of the artisan who has combined these very parts of which we in vain seek the term. And we do not want to see that we ourselves have created this marvelous thing. Schopenhauer comments on the illusion just described with a troubling comparison taken from the *Critique of the Power of Judgment*. Teleological astonishment resembles the astonishment of the savage before whom a bottle of beer is opened and who, seeing the foam spill over, admits that what he admired most was less that the beer thus escaped the bottle but that *one had been able to confine it there*.[22] This confession lucidly betrays the prejudice of reversibility that falsifies any retrospective view. The order of fabrication is assumed to be literally coextensive with the analysis we practice on the entities all said and done and then assumed to map onto it point by point, piece by piece. Where analysis turns out to be inexhaustive, fabrication must partake of the miraculous. It is as if, Schopenhauer comments elsewhere, we admired that all the multiples of 9 yield 9 when we add the two ciphers that form them: a marvelous coincidence when we want it to have been explicitly combined by the mind—an entirely simple and natural property when we remember that it is already in a way prepared within the decimal system of which it immediately expresses a singularity.[23]

The disastrous effects of this illusion, I believe, extend well beyond the field of the organic. In an example, Schopenhauer himself gives us a glimpse of its permanent intrusion into all operations of the mind. Teleological astonishment can be compared to the wonder that might have gripped Gutenberg's contemporaries when they saw the first printed books, thinking that perhaps their admirably regular characters were the work of a copyist's quill. And in fact, a serious examination of our consciousness reveals the presence of this intellectual fiction in the astonishment every very new invention inspires. When, for example, we admire wireless telegraphy, the telephone, television, or remote control, we in a way surprise ourselves at picturing them in the egocentric categories of common art or manual technology that know only action by contact. If, in general, the miracles of electricity, magnetism, or nuclear disintegration bewitch the imagination to such a degree, that is because our laborious routines, eager for continuity and homogeneity, invite the mind to reconstruct these phenomena patiently from the mediate artifices of fabrication. The speed of light, the smallness of electrons, the remoteness of Sirius would be so many *masterpieces* (in the manual sense of the word), prodigious records measurable on our empirical scales, performances comparable to our discursive operations. The dumbfounded mind likes to stagger about this way by imagining light-years and galaxies, just as it likes to sink into gloom by thinking of nothingness and death...

And, meanwhile, the very enormity of these astronomical and physical givens should represent to the mind a demand for abstraction and habituate us to considering the infinite of nature as something entirely simple, instantaneous, and immediate. We could say that matter, by sometimes offering us the sight of a "fourth dimension," finally demands of us, as life does, to break with the inertia of thinking "from the elements." There is never anything irrational for a thought that does not, in egotistical admiration, stupidly compare printed pages to manuscripts, living beings to "masterpieces," and the depth of the sky to the laborious smallness of our industry, but instead understands the infinite with the "heart," as Pascal says, and settles directly in the center of things. For the one who from the beginning adopts an entirely different scale, who from the outset conceives an entirely different metempirical and supernatural order, stupid *amazement* will no doubt make way for *wonder* and veneration of the sublime thing.

If a world is to exist, this world must, a fortiori, be viable,[24] since a "thing... which is capable of a certain amount as maximum must also be capable of that which lies within it."[25] And in just the same way, life conceals no mystery even though it is itself and in its radical effectiveness a mystery for the intellect: what has been possible must all the more have been natural! For example, it is thanks to an amphiboly that is entirely conceptual that the enormous waste of species sometimes scandalizes and astonishes us so profoundly. The carefree profligacy with which nature abandons animals to their destruction remains impenetrable to us because, without realizing it, we are used to considering the living as a precious masterpiece, and because the disappearance of such a treasure would seem cruel to us if it were the work of our hands. Having condemned in our minds, so to speak, nature and life to forced labor, we make, as if for no reason, the shadows of physical evil ever more threatening. The very excess of finalism and anthropocentrism has rendered our final abdication before Chance, our horror of the mute indifference of nature, even more desperate.

But these very complaints are, at bottom, still teleological. The universe is not "hostile," and living beings are not "precious." Nature has not laboriously fabricated organisms piece by piece, and it costs its generosity as little to destroy them as it does to construct them.[26] The extermination of biological species, just like their production, is thus of another order than the order of masterpieces and values. It escapes, as Schopenhauer says, the scalpel of the intellect[27]—it belongs to the infinite realm of the infinite and the immediate. It is thus in the nature of the vital to reject the jurisdiction of retrospective schemas. We must stop believing that by reversing the analysis to which bodies lend themselves (which, besides, is entirely approximate), we will obtain the *history* of vitality. For that, we would have to resign ourselves to perpetually remaining contemporary with this history. But this, precisely, is what is arduous and painful. Knowledge is only possible because I can be *posterior to the fact*. The tragedy of the mind consists in this, that our knowledge of objects so to speak obstructs our intimate and central understanding of them.[28] Anatomy has taught us too many things about the eye for our notion of vision not to be as if obsessed with fabrication schemes. From all sides, accomplished things and "prejudged" things envelop the mind. But how, short of renouncing the very virtue of Explanation, can we chase away these phantoms?

The finality of life, like movement, like freedom, is thus explained by a centrifugal act that is the very act of organization. This act alone is *decisive*, revealing, all at once, the simple in the infinite. "To create life," Guyau says in some prophetic pages of his *Morale d'Épicure* [*Epicurus' Ethics*], "nature does not proceed artificially by assembling all the parts of a body and joining them."[29] This clears up the disconcerting paradox of organicity that Bergson characterizes in such eloquent formulas. The profound meaning of this paradox, of the contrast between the complication of form and the simplicity of functioning, has not escaped the great organicist philosophers, Leibniz, Bergson,[30] Schopenhauer. The structure of the eye is infinitely complicated, and what is really unheard of is that it is enough for the eye to open for vision to operate just as it is enough for Achilles to dart off for the throng of Zeno's quibbles to dissipate. This is no miracle of ingeniousness: the solution of life is the most naive, the simplest there is—simple not in the sense of that abstract simplicity *Time and Free Will*'s criticism denounces but in the sense of the dense and concrete simplicity that is a privilege of vitality. The intellect sees vision but only *the eyes see*, intransitively. Between the intellect on the one hand and the anatomy and physiology of the eye on the other there is a natural distance that mediates our knowledge of objects, whereas between the eye and the act of seeing there is nothing. Vision is nothing but the extension and as if the blossoming of the visual apparatus. In an adventurous passage of his *Decline of the West*, Oswald Spengler compares the Greek bust and its eyes without irises with the modern portrait illuminated by the life of the *gaze*.[31] Similarly, we might say that science knows the solitary eye, the eye without gaze and without spiritual milieu, while life alone gives a meaning and a spiritual perspective to the depth of the gaze. For life is sympathetic with life, and action sympathetic with action.

Nature realizes organisms without knowing anatomy just as the printer executes typographical masterpieces on the first try without being a calligrapher or, if you prefer, just as snow crystals acquire the perfect symmetry of their shape all at once, without laboriously employing square and compass. And thus it is simplicity that, in vital things, is truly essential and primitive. To take up one of Henri Bergson's most beautiful formulas, all there is in the thing is simplicity, and complication is rather in the hesitant views we take on it, the way the intellect's effort is simple in its movement and infinitely complex in the images this movement solicits.[32] This is still what Schopenhauer expresses when he speaks the strong and moving language of Giordano Bruno: "Art works with foreign material; nature with its own. Art is outside matter; nature is within matter."[33] The sober audacity of this formula is not concealed very well by the Aristotelian terminology. *Art stands outside matter*—Bergson, taking up Plotinus's formulas, will eloquently say that the intellect turns around life.[34] The intellect is a virtuoso in circumlocutions and periphrases; only the vital élan penetrates and settles in the ipseity of the body. This means that our miserable industry, to accomplish its "masterpieces," must impose itself on a matter that inwardly protests against this violence. In the labor of organization, on the contrary, no opaque milieu inserts itself between the work and the worker; or, rather, the operation of life is but one with the work itself.[35]

The distinction between matter and form no longer makes any sense here because matter is already all saturated with form the way form, for its part, is still so to speak entirely carnal. The matter of an organism, Schopenhauer says, is in a way but the "mere visibility of its form," its form incarnate and rendered visible.[36] Reciprocally, the form of an organism is but the dream of its matter, a dream emanating from the center of life. That is what Bergson saw so well, he who gave us to see, across the entire hierarchy of beings from the vegetal to the higher animals, an ever more intimate copenetration of "form" and "function."[37] In a machine, function and matter live side by side, so to speak, without getting along; in organisms, function is an intimate and necessary continuation of the structure. That is why we must say that *a mechanism functions and an organism operates*—hence the spiritual lightness, the inimitable beauty of life and of the works that imitate life. Only organisms, according to Goethe's dictum, seem truly "necessary" and "natural" to us because only they represent the perfect success of the compromise between the inexpressible simplicity of function and the infinite complication of matter. The farcical heaviness of automata derives precisely from the sensation of an implicit disagreement between matter and function, from the feeling that their encounter is "deliberate." The ornament here isolates itself from the thing ornamented and cruelly, outrageously underlines the mechanical rigidity of artificial works. There is, on the contrary, nothing "deliberate" in the works of life, neither ornament nor thing ornamented. The paradoxical combinations life realizes are always the only ones possible because their matter directly expresses the very essence of the living individual.

For the third time, the study of finality has brought out the need for a truly organic method, truly contemporary with life—for a method that would explain the elements by the whole and not the whole by the elements. There is infinitely more in the initial tension of life than there is in the assembly of tissues that embody it, just as there is more in the spiritual "intention" of freedom than there is in the acts in which this intention expires, more in a movement than in the successive stations of which it seems to be composed,[38] and more in the "meaning" than in the interpreted "signs" in which meaning scatters. And yet, *in the moment in which* life deploys itself in species, *in the moment in which* the genius of my freedom inspires me with a given course of action, *in the moment in which* the intellect's effort penetrates mute enigmas, no one can prejudge their inner destiny. That is why reconstitutions have only retrospective value. Nothing is simpler and more natural than the vital movement from the center to the periphery; and meanwhile, nothing is more impenetrable than fabricatory logic. Nature, Schopenhauer says, is naive like genius.[39] But we have unlearned the language of nature because we have become too learned to understand it.

II. *Instinct and Intellect*

The philosophy that refers evolution back to fabrication generally implies the ideas of perfection along a scale and of an indefinitely rectilinear progress toward the future. Mechanism and finalism are quite content with a linear evolution. They enjoy the pleasant sight of a resto-ration of comprehensive repose that, of course, regularly attains its goal because it walks in the footsteps of an inverse analysis that one pretends not to talk about. Just as associationists directly deduce ideas and clusters of ideas from sensory shocks,[40] so pseudo-evolutionism loves arranging living beings end to end along a great unilinear series the way one strings together the beads of a necklace. In its schematic form, this represen-tation is clear and soothing for the mind because it enrolls all beings under one and the same law of generation, which aligns them horizon-tally in duration. Within this immense filiation, species and individuals tend only to conserve a certain ordinal value. They would be as so many numbers arranged in increasing progression along a homogenous series.

Bergson, on the contrary, is very much concerned to specify that cre-ative evolution is pluri-dimensional.[41] It has, as one would say in the lan-guage of counterpoint, several "voices." Like all true polyphony, it offers a certain thickness that evolutionism would very much like to neglect. It is a rich, varied, and unforeseen becoming in which we recognize the same superposed levels, the same depth-wise organization as in the intel-lectual effort. Life generally goes from the narrow to the wide, from the enveloped to the blossomed, from the possible to the real. The movement it accomplishes is centrifugal and radiating. The relationship among species is defined not as a morose longitudinal filiation but rather as a cousinhood. The process of deployment or of "development" that charac-terizes the *evolution*, in the proper sense, of the individual organism thus also serves to define the germination and maturation of the macrocosmic organism.

This vision of becoming has two distinct advantages: first, it alone accounts for the basic diversity of species. Bergson, like all philosophers who are attentive to the pure given, never misses an occasion to under-line the plurality of the real. We have seen what importance *Time and Free Will* attributed to the heterogeneity of states of consciousness and how the continuity of becoming was, in sum, made up of nothing but resorbed originalities. What does the idea of quality do but respond to this concern with diversity? For if there is one quality, there are several qualities, there is an infinity of qualities, each defining itself in relation to others. The given is truly plural and defends itself, with its irreducible variety, against the enterprises of an intellect that would contemplate itself only in the monotony of measurable magnitudes. Life offers us the sight of the same resistances, and the language of the learned shows us that the pluralists' humility is, in certain respects, an eminently scientific attitude.[42]

Yet the centralist and radiating intuition of becoming also explains the gaping discontinuities and hiatuses of evolution—or, in Louis Vialleton's felicitous phrase, the "bursts" of mutations that one after the other renew the living world—much better than an insipid progress can. For the spectacle of species presents us with more *aberrant* characters than it does with *transitions*. All Darwinian genealogies won't keep human nature and animal nature from irremediably diverging. There is divergence between the animal world and the world of plants, too. Within the animal series itself, the same irreconcilable divorce is reproduced between vertebrates and arthropods, especially between Man and Insects (Hymenoptera). Evolutionism, instead of showing us the generations that make up the chain that would transmit one and the same biological tradition, a single genetic heritage from one generation to the other, ought to instead tell us how one species after the other turned its back on the others in order, each apart, to try its luck in the world. Evolution is just the history of these repeated divergences.

Dare we say that Bergson himself has, on this point, been a little too severe with Aristotle,[43] who had so lively a sense of the discontinuities of nature because he, too, started with the experience of life, not with mathematics? Mathematics sets out to impose silence on the cumbersome originalities that trouble our dear habits of uniformity. But the admirable diversity of the living won't stand for it. The same caprice of nature that withdrew the antithesis of recollection and perception from sensualist or idealist leveling, or the fantastic heterogeneity of feelings from Fechner's logarithms, here shelters biological dualisms from any endeavor to unify them. *Creative Evolution* has refuted some of these endeavors. Such would be, for example, the idea in Darwin's selection hypothesis that insensible variations could little by little compose structures by adding small accidental differences.[44] Instinct, to be more precise, is said to be progressively fabricated by summing up lucky differences that one would in a way see settling little by little around a primitive habit or a simple reflex to make these differences grow and turn them into a complete instinct.[45] In these attempts we recognize the same idol that lies at the basis of all associationist geneticism: one looks for the primary matter of the vital, the simple element that, indefinitely multiplied by itself, would provide the will with all living structures. Is the essence of measurement not to quantify quality, which in all things represents the contesting and recalcitrant principle, to retain of individuals only that which they have in common, namely the homogenous unity of magnitude that lets us measure them? "Atomism" indeed counts on none of the antitheses of life being able to resist its miraculous panacea. Antagonisms melt away and, at their head, the gravest of them all, the one that encompasses all the others, the antagonism of the vital and the geometrical. In this happy system, from which concepts have chased all fantasy, apes and human beings, instinct and intellect, memory and matter don the same uniform.

Bergson's criticism cannot bear such lazy confusions. Between diverging species, the gulf grows bigger because there is no longer any immediate consanguinity, transitive filiation, actual "descent" between them. Instead there is, if we may say so, a preestablished disharmony between them that continues to aggravate. To find their kinship, we have to go back all the way to the branch they once shared, to where the bifurcation took place. Organization is inseparable from these multiplied splits. Here Bergson for his part takes up Plotinus's image of the cosmic tree. Above all, however, he employs a battery of metaphors of deflagration that suggest the idea of a centrifugal élan (*explosion, shell, sheaf, fireworks, cluster*).[46] We may in fact say that the "sheaf" or, as Vialleton has it, the "bushy growth [*buissonnement*]"[47] is the characteristic symbol of vital movement. This divergence, as Bergson will say later, obeys a law of "frenzy."[48] *Matter and Memory* was indeed concerned with a deployment across a spectrum or with a cone whose base was formed by dreamed recollections. There, this image, to be sure, had no temporal significance. And yet it already expressed a distinctive tendency of life and of mind: the mind, left to itself, blossoms spontaneously into capricious and picturesque recollections just as life explodes, so to speak, into more and more original individualities. Now, dissociated species and individuals in a way represent the dream of the vital élan. Only that here, in *Creative Evolution*, what had been the effect of a distraction on the contrary results from an irresistible push.

Individuals, moreover, are more the plaything than the source of this push. They have no need to be particularly "attentive to life" to let themselves go with the imperious élan that develops in them a single tendency and closes all other paths to them. It is rather with a view to combating this dispersion that individuals need to pay special attention. The effort of spiritual intention that is intuitive thought in effect neutralizes the consequences of biological "distraction" by contracting the dissociated tendencies. It is thus possible to go on speaking of distraction provided we understand by this a violent dispersion (*distrahere*) of the virtualities of life, a veritable rending of the possible. Imagine, therefore, the cone of *Matter and Memory* with its basis turned to the future, that is to say, in the direction of the greatest expansion, substituting static perception, which had formed the tip, with something explosive and impatient, the compressed germ from which the manifold of species will spring forth. For all possibles must happen.

On the other hand, the idea of an arborescent evolution also explains the profound kinship of species. As we know, the paradox that we must exalt the qualitative heterogeneity of states of consciousness to honor, finally, their unbreakable continuity, is very instructive. In a singular irony, atomism, which begins by fabricating all beings from uniformity, no longer finds the reason for their inner affinities. That is because life ignores the dilemma of the Same and the Other.[49] Instead of monism condemning itself to an arbitrary apportionment for having ignored the natural originalities of becoming, an apportionment that would be all the more irremediable for its being more arbitrary, the acute alterity of feelings and of individuals makes veritable sympathies possible. Things that have been separated will no longer rejoin because they have become indifferent and average.[50]

And this is how the superstition of a breaking up is born, which is nothing but the preference given to artificial—and therefore desperate—discontinuities over the organic discontinuities of a nature articulated and harmonious as a whole. Separated tendencies may in effect have diverged more and more; they have nonetheless remained complementary. They have maintained, as Schopenhauer says, a certain family resemblance that betrays their common origin.[51] Complementary here means both distinct and harmonious: divergent tendencies remain complementary like the organs of the same body or like the different individuals of an animal colony.[52]

Unity here is thus not a promise but rather a reminiscence. What the spectacle of life points out to us is its survival, not its arrival. Species, left to themselves, do not tend to reunite but, on the contrary, to widen the gaps between them even more. In each of them, meanwhile, the primitive totality subsists like a living reproach, like a perpetual invitation to overcome the exile of dispersion. It is a sort of paradise lost. But Bergson's philosophy, which is a futuristic philosophy, does not kindle in us a nostalgia for the past. Creative evolution will not spontaneously restore the lost unity. Diaspora is the opposite of a curse: evolution is indeed progressive, as science claims, and not cyclical. Unity is reestablished by strokes that follow a personal and painful effort of intuitive thought. Nothing could less resemble the mystics' gracious transfiguration.

This explains the reciprocal immanence of separated tendencies. The different species, Schopenhauer says, are like so many variations on the theme of the thing itself.[53] Yet in each variation, the theme is present in its entirety: only the perspective changes, Leibniz would say. Something like the hope for animal motility sleeps in plants, for example, but the accent is on vegetative life; something like a recollection of vegetative life subsists in animals, but the accent is on sensibility and consciousness. The victorious tendency represses the enemy forces, which pass into latency and survive like a silent remorse, waiting for their eventual liberation. The intellect envelops something like a nostalgia for instinct; at the heart of instinct live promises of the intellect that demand only to be realized. The vital always appears complete in each species; in each species it envelops a clear zone of consciousness and a variable fringe of insinuations that represents the repressed principle. But just as choice does not abolish the possibility of the excluded alternative, so the species that has decided on separation does not escape being haunted by repressed powers. "Thus everything now is Dionysus."[54]

The main difference between evolution in bursts and rectilinear evolution is that in the former, there is something to explain both newness and immanence. Rectilinear evolution, in turn, inscribes itself in the schemas of a finalist or mechanicist dogmatism and does not even make up for the unforeseeability that is lost in the mutual copenetration of its moments. Innovation has become entirely fictitious, although it is not for all that possible to speak of a reciprocal implication of tendencies. In this sense, the philosophy of becoming is truly the meeting of reconciled contradictions: as alterity is reconciled with the continuous, so is newness with immanence. Immanence first—since unity stands at the beginning, like a golden age of which only ruins remain among the scattered species. Then innovation—for there is between the germ of life and the adolescence of life as much of a distance as between the possible and the real. Germination is the springing forth of a being that absolutely did not *exist*, even if, ultimately, the mature organism is implied in the virtual organism and is not born by spontaneous generation from a radical nothing-at-all. Yet declared existence has an incomparable superiority over the mere possible, and the discussion of solipsistic theories that reduce perception to recollection has already shown us the value that Bergson's philosophy attributes to actual reality.

As for rectilinear becoming, it ought to at least bring out the conservation of vital "themes" since its progress, decidedly, is a simulacrum of progress, since fabrication simply redoes what an anterior dismantling has undone. Not at all! The words "preformation," "survival," "immanence" only make sense where there is duration on the one hand and, on the other, a real plurality of living forces that by turns make their way into the light, repressing the others in a provisional unconscious in which they keep their autonomy and vitality. But in this linear progressivism, we are no longer dealing with anything but a single type gradually complicated by a juxtaposition of exterior characters. There is no longer a victorious ("dominant") principle, nor a vanquished principle, nor a hierarchy, nor gradations. To say immanence is to say superposed levels. But here, everything is on the same level, such that one can say, at will, either that the theme does not vary at all or that it disappears completely in each of the successive ornaments, in each of the embellishments in which one dresses it up.

In this theory, each species resembles a superficial and entirely pure sound in which none of the harmonies that constitute its entire flavor vibrate. But what good is it to express that something conserves itself if the dominant lives indifferently alongside its variants, if one substitutes an inert gradation for the vicissitudes of a becoming rich in conflicts?! The continuity of a musical development is not made up of the pure and simple conservation of some fundamental theme but of the resistances this theme encounters on its path, the embroideries that would suffocate it if the musician were not able to make them transparent, of the hostile ideals against which it has to defend itself and that inflect it in their own direction. This subtle discourse, made up of mutual concessions, of defeats and of revenge, is the very image of life. But what is left of all of this in an insipid dialectic that reduces becoming to a collection of inert imprints deposited around the type of the species?

Expansion is thus the law of life.[55] But in this movement, there are two particularly important paths: the one that leads up to Instinct and the one that leads up to the Intellect. Of intellect and instinct, it is instinct that is closer to life; better yet, instinct is the vital élan itself, captured in brief clearings of matter. That is why it is said that instinctive activity extends the labor of organization itself. The most essential instinct of all, for example, the maternal instinct, is so to speak the transition site of a unique impulsion that carries the current generation toward the future,[56] just as the sexual instinct, for Schopenhauer, expresses the foresight of Willing-to-Live, which is always oriented toward the metaphysical interest of the species.[57]

Besides, is it not remarkable that Schopenhauer and Bergson both looked at love in the dimension of time, as the vehicle of an effort reaching for the conquest of the future, while a sociologist like Guyau instead considers love in the actuality of space, as the perfect agreement of consenting individualities?[58] It is in this sense that instinct can pass for sympathy. In Bergson, "sympathy" is not, as it is in Guyau, an affectual communion, a unison of consciousnesses. It is penetrating rather than loving, and it is not for nothing that Bergson speaks of *élan*, Guyau of *vital expansion*. If we knew how to read animal instinct, we would no doubt find there the depth and the stratifications of the intellectual effort, for the intellectual effort is but an intuitive and intense form of instinct. It goes, like instinct, in the very direction of life. Guyau's sympathy spreads in the collectivity of consciousnesses, in concentric layers of devotion and generosity. Bergson's sympathy would be, among others, that of the digger wasp for the cricket it will kill: this "sympathy" can be aggressive and murderous! Just like intellection, it is a conquest more than it is altruism; it settles in the object, it takes possession of it, far from letting itself be invaded by love of the neighbor. To use Max Scheler's vocabulary here, there is as much distance between Bergson's devouring sympathy and Guyau's self-denial as there is between "emotional identification" and "fellow-feeling" or between *coincidence* and *coexistence*.[59] That is because for Guyau, the most intensive life is also the most extensive: hence this theory's warm but also somewhat limp optimism. In Bergson, on the contrary, there is an antinomy between individual duration and social space: a life that spreads is a life that loses density and wastes its dynamism.

Evolution, we said, is radiation. Yet it does not dilate in all directions: the vital élan pushes it above all along the dimension of time, in an attack on the future. The self, instead of sacrificing its ambitions to the harmony of social consonances, exalts itself, all the while assimilating itself to the object. What is understanding if not gaining ground among the things? This jealous intuition demands that the mind violently seize itself and twist back on itself. In Guyau, on the contrary, the vital expansion results from a spontaneous blossoming of the most natural of our tendencies. What Guyau lacks is a sense, so acute in Bergson, of the resistances and antitheses that make the crisis of intuition inevitable. Just like intellection, just like pure perception—which, as we know, is intuitive as well since it is the immediate vision of a presence—instinct is an *ecstasy* in the Plotinian sense. In instinctive knowledge, the mind is entirely taken from itself, *extroversus*. That is why Bergson could speak of its unconscious; unconsciousness is the state of an ecstatic thought. But does not the very term *ekstasis* (lit. displacement, *isstuplenye* in Russian) indicate that the individual, far from passively waiting for the grace of compassionate love, goes out from itself?

This explains the infallibility of instinct. Instinct is life itself; in its own sphere, therefore, it is an absolute knowledge and a manner of gnosis. The biologists, it is true, have a tendency to react against the mysticism of instinct implied in the metaphysics of someone like Schopenhauer or Driesch.[60] Yet they have not upset the idea, the only one essential to Bergson's philosophy, that instinctive knowledge is a specific, absolutely original knowledge that is metaphysically distinct from intellectual knowledge. Certainly, instinct does not enjoy supernatural immunity. It is at the mercy of accidents that would derail it,[61] just as pure perception is at the mercy of an indiscreet memory that has prejudices to place. Nonetheless, instinct is said to be infallible de jure the way naked perception is said to be spontaneously veridical. From the fact that the intervention of consciousness is able to trouble the reflex mechanisms of respiration, will we conclude that these mechanisms are not perfectly adapted?[62]

The finality of instinct offers the same character of vital simplicity as does the free act. It must thus be admitted in its entirety all at once, instantaneously. Having wanted to engender it with intellectual elements, the Lamarckians condemn themselves to invoking a perpetually renewed miracle,[63] since the property of peripheral explanations is to exhaust themselves in reconstructing an infinite that is globally, naively given in life. The "prodigies" of instinct are thus as naturally explained as is the complication of organic structures, as is the continuity of movement. It has sufficiently been shown that prodigies exist above all for an intellect eager to bend everything to its norms, an intellect innocently astonished by the resistances life puts up against it. But since it has only a single type of explanation at its disposal, since it has refused to give itself the sovereign simplicity of vital intention from the outset and, as Plotinus would have said, "globally,"[64] it has to complicate its schemas indefinitely to contain within them the vitality that troubles and frightens it. For a mind capable of admitting several types of operation unrelated to the familiar procedures of our intellect, a good number of mysteries would no doubt disappear, in particular those that surround eschatology. The act of understanding, which ceaselessly readapts the mind to the successive levels of the real, is at bottom nothing but the meaning of this metaphysical diversity.

Yet the intellect, precisely, does not want to "understand" instinct because to do so, it would need to renounce leveling the real and settling the reassuring mediocrity of concepts in the world. Instinct, Bergson says so well, is a veritable view at a distance,[65] that is to say that to know, instinct does not need, as the intellect does, hesitant and discursive approximations. Our mechanicist intellect understands very well only what it touches. Where things are too far away to be touched, it throws a bridge of middle terms across the void (such would be, in Descartes's physics, for example, the mediating function of "subtle matter").[66] Against logical Distance, the distance that separates concepts, the mind uses syllogisms. But instinct escapes the malediction of discourse. The study of perception has already shown us, in what I have here called *miniature theory*, an effort to explain how the paradigm projects a subjective duplicate into the brain. We do not easily rid ourselves of the idea that perception is the (more or less disguised) "transport" of something into the mind because the idea of transport, which is the idea of a continuous discursion in which we seize all intermediaries, passes for a clear and calming idea. But we have seen that perception is the object itself in the mind, that there is no mediation but rather "magic," if we call magical, in the proper sense of the term, the influence a being exercises on another by the sole fact of its presence, without any contract, without any transitive operation. Instinct would well be magical in this sense and that is why it cannot in the end be wrong.

This theoretical infallibility shocks scholars[67] only because they obstinately seek to turn instinct into a second-rate intellect, the way idealism turns perception into a branch of memory, and because the law of the intellect is discursion the way the law of recollection is relativity. Meanwhile, if the bird had mediately chosen the materials with which it builds its nest, its industry would multiply the miracles. In reality, though, it has achieved its work because it was undertaken by *this* bird, because it was *this* bird's industry. It turns out that here, the only explanation that does not add to the mystery is the mystical explanation because it admits the relation of the animal to its work as a primary, original, and irreducible fact instead of reducing it to some type of mechanical causality.

This conception, so simple and so natural, did not escape the Romantics of the Philosophy of Nature who had, in a way, a panbiotic sense of living reality. Schopenhauer himself cites passages from Karl Friedrich Burdach's *Physiology* that associate instinct with sympathy.[68] Sympathy or, as they call it, the "sympathetic" phenomenon, occupies an immense place in the dynamist systems of thinkers like Friedrich Hufeland, Dietrich Georg von Kieser, or Johann Carl Passavant.[69] It is true that in Bergson this sympathy above all manifests the presence of a vital élan oriented in duration toward the future of species, whereas in the Romantics it only expressed the actual unity of the macrocosmic organism and the tendency of all living activity to cross the visible borders the body imposes on it. For them, one seeks the symptoms of sympathy not only in instinct but also in "animal magnetism," in sexual generation, in phenomena of infectious contagion, and even in gravity or magnetic affinity. But in von Kieser, Hufeland, or Gotthilf Heinrich von Schubert, we also find an entirely realist theory of instinctive "clairvoyance" that, despite some mystical formulas, closely resembles Bergson's. All agree in thinking that, in order to know, instinct has no need to touch, that it does without the rational schemas of mechanism. It is a telepathy, really, a prophetic delirium.

Hence the so remarkable anticipations of animal instinct: birds build nests for the young they do not yet have, spiders set traps for future prey. Animals act by inspiration, not deliberately. Instinctive prophetism, unlike astronomers' foresight, is thus not the pure and simple elimination of time. It is instead the divination of a future that keeps its value as future, its absolute posterity. Foresight, because it is intellectual, really affects the future. It denies tomorrow as a real tomorrow and purely and simply annuls creative duration. But prophetism, far from denying duration, espouses its movement, and that is why it operates at a distance, without contact, crossing the thickness of becoming in one fell swoop.

Thus the essence of artistic inspiration is to anticipate the schema, never existence. It is a presentiment that does not exclude the randomness of creation, one that has to reckon with the reality of time. That is why Bergson is right to say that duration is essential to invention,[70] just as it is essential to intellection and instinct. That, precisely, is the function of the dynamic schema. The musician always knows in what direction he will find the poem he meditates and whose themes already float in his imagination, but he himself does not suspect all the encounters he will have along the way, the marvelous and charming adventures his own genius is preparing for him. The essence of *improvisation* consists precisely in giving oneself over without reservation to these adventures of musical creation. The improviser sets out on the discovery of himself and for that he gives credit to the unforeseen resources, to the miraculous surprises that our mind inexhaustibly reserves for us. What can one not expect from oneself?

But then, it will be objected, how does instinct differ from philosophical intuition? And what does it lack to be the very contemplation of the absolute? It is, precisely, that one cannot expect everything of instinct. Better not to run any risks with instinct. For instinct does not improvise. Instinct is not of itself prodigious. Instinct never commits the generous imprudence of forgetting the theme that inspires it. It is not only prophecy but reminiscence; stretched toward the future, it remains riveted to the past. In instinct we find side by side the Epimethean principle and the Promethean principle, as Carl Gustav Carus would say. This inferiority is due to a singular fatality of evolution. Evolution, as we saw, is increasing divergence. A being can thus not unite in itself all excellences; perfections are incompatible and must separate.[71]

The opposition of instinct and intelligence did not go unnoticed by the Romantics. Von Kieser's curious *tellurism* theory already provides a glimpse.[72] "Telluric" thought, as opposed to "solar," diurnal, or vigilant thought, is characterized by the predominance of the soul's nocturnal and demonic forces. Its seat is the ganglionic system whereas the seat of sensibility is the brain. The biologist Treviranus, even more neatly, opposes mediate, abstract, and reflective thought to immediate thought. The first, working with symbols, is fallible but infinite and competent everywhere. The second, unconscious like a dream, always applies to particular cases; it is limited but infallible; it depends neither on the senses nor on their exercise.[73] Be the judge whether Treviranus's Bergsonism can go far![74] For von Schubert, the separation of the ganglionic and cerebral systems was a consequence of the Fall; for Bergson, the duality of intellect and instinct is the natural result of a dissociation of tendencies. Evolution has presented all beings with an analogous dilemma. We cannot have everything at once, and it is one of life's great laws that every superiority is bought at the price of some sacrifice. The progress of human memory, as we saw, drags behind it its own punishment. The intellect's conquest is paid for by renouncing instinctive clairvoyance. And the ransom of instinct is the sacrifice of intellectual vigilance.

Instinct, left to itself, is blind. Since Burdach, much ink has been spilled over the unilaterality of instinct, and today, zoologists give us a mass of very curious examples.[75] These examples in no way destabilize the theoretical infallibility of instinct. On the contrary. Instinct, if we may say so, is sometimes wrong only *because it is too right*.[76] In just this way, many dementia patients lapse not at all by a lack of logic but on the contrary because their logic is ridiculously logical, because their reasoning is too obstinate: they are wrong for being inexorably right. Is not the true logic, according to Russell, the art of deduction?[77] It is not skill that instincts lack: they are precise and certain like a sleepwalker's perilous acrobatics. But the moment the slightest obstacle arises, they remain mute because they are not made to resolve any but one single kind of problem. Instinct is prophetic but not foreseeing. Intelligence is foreseeing; that is to say that, possessing a limited penetration yet armed with reasoning and calculation, it in turn has the means to face an infinity of possible circumstances. It compensates for the myopia of its gaze with the circular extension of its vision. It is shortsighted but at the same time, with memory, it looks back and, with inference, it looks ahead. Reciprocally, instinct has a piercing but narrow vision; it is, if we may say so, blindly lucid. This is what Bergson expresses in a striking formula that deserves being famous: "There are things that intelligence alone is able to seek, but which, by itself, it will never find. These things instinct alone could find; but it will never seek them."[78] We thus acquire intellectual foresight only by losing the acuity and certainty of instinctive vision. Instinct, absolute and entirely completed knowledge, imperturbably knows what it knows. But it knows nothing else. If all situations were simple and immutable, as it is itself, it would be truly gnostic and could be compared to the mystics' learned ignorance. Instinct is infinitely learned in matters it is made for, and marvelously ignorant since it looks neither right nor left, since it is prisoner of its rigid excellence, since it ignores all things except one single thing that it knows with the certainty of unconsciousness.

The hives of bees, Pascal says, are made up of hexagons that were as perfect a thousand years ago as they are today.[79] The instinct's technique is always equal to itself in its narrow perfection. Instinct is to the intellect a bit like reflex is to volition or as habit-memory is to pure memory.[80] The voluntary act gives us freedom and an infinity of choice only by renouncing the blind certainty of reflex. Choice means hesitation, and there is no hesitation without the possibility of error. And in just the same way, the ransom of conscious memory is the disappearance of the happy mechanisms that Samuel Butler associates with the reign of "grace" or unconscious beatitude.[81] Pure memory is as capricious as habit is faithful.

Human beings know that they can absolutely count only on automatisms, and, by means of the gymnastics of apprenticeship, they seek to automate as great a share of their motor activity as possible.

That might be why the yoke of freedom is so heavy on their shoulders. There is in spontaneity, especially when it appears in its moral form and puts our responsibility into question, a mystery that deeply troubles us; for we adore our chains. No one wants to be delivered, Paul Dukas says with the lyrical drama *Ariadne and Bluebeard* in mind: the women do not want to follow the well-meaning Ariadne toward the light just as, in Plato, the prisoners in the cave did not want to follow the philosopher toward the sun of truth.[82] Only those who sidestep the risks of free initiative have never been wrong. Glorious errors are not part of their calling. They keep to the prudent certainty of a glorified automatism.

This alternative gives us a strong sense of the basic opposition of instinct and intellect. Instinct is irremediably limited because it does not *know* itself to know. We may well say that it is *in itself* but not yet *for itself*. The intellect, on the contrary, capable as it is of fabricating "tools to make tools," by nature possesses an infinite power of splitting that allows it to reflect on itself. And in language, it finds a means for definitively separating itself from its objects.[83] Instinct is ecstatic, that is to say, unconscious, since it has not projected a problematic object distinct from itself outside of itself, into the universe of abstractions.[84] In turn, in immediately extending organization, instinct always applies to particular realities, as Burdach and Treviranus saw very well. It is "categorical" whereas the intellect is "hypothetical."

The bitterness of deliverance consists precisely in this, that to dominate things and to act on them one must renounce knowing them singularly. Working with memory (the one I have called *constituted memory*), the intellect inserts between thoughts and things the distance without which there can be no leisure and thus no foresight. In a given landscape, for example, a geographer will show us a certain physical configuration, a soldier will show us a "ground" more or less easily defended, an agronomist a given "soil" with its own cultures: only the artist sets out to adhere to the landscape itself and to find, if we may say so, its haecceity, the original and truly unique physiognomy. For beyond the abstract sketches that the engineer, the tactician, or the geographer superimpose on it from their respective points of view, there is still something inimitable that makes it such that one landscape never resembles another, and it finds itself absolutely defined when its individuality has been expressed. At bottom, the intellect is above all the organ of the "average" [*quelconque*], and it is understandable why a nominalist like Bergson is inclined to underline its powerlessness. The last two chapters of *Creative Evolution* establish with marvelous lucidity that the triumph of modern science lies in the advent of relations, that is to say, of laws, and more specially, in its aptitude for considering *no matter what* moment of time.[85] One may in fact very well say (and on this point, Bergson could have invoked the example of logistics) that thought tends to render itself *indifferent* to its matter as much as possible.[86] Concerned above all with foresight and economy, it seeks to get as much as possible from as little as possible and sets out to bring to reason the recalcitrant givens that still refuse to be absorbed by our laws. Nothing, in fact, distresses the scholar as much as the necessity to admit a qualitative given that must be thought apart.

This is how it seems that quality is "irrational." But we could just as calmly decree that all existence is irrational. Is not our dearest ambition to act as if nothing existed? For we are very much resolved to not be burdened by singularities too original. Perhaps the single fact of existing by itself is already a primordial originality, a kind of radical contingency whose mystery we would rather not go into more deeply, since formal and hypothetical understanding has no means to account for the quoddity or effectiveness of being. In any case, we understand very well that nothing intervenes to trouble the marvelous universe in which one knows even before knowing, in which everything is foreseen in some relation ready to receive no matter what content, in which truth would really, literally be indifferent to its effective realization. All there would be left to do would be to replace letters with their variable values and to "effectuate," the mind limiting all its expense to a few conventional definitions. These savings are greatly favored by language. Words exempt us from relying on effective things, the way money exempts us from relying on natural goods, and the way checks exempt us from too often cashing out money still judged to be too concrete. One takes oneself to be pushing back infinitely the— nonetheless ineluctable—moment in which effective existence will reassert its rights and sanction the abstract algebra that thought to have made it useless. Unlucky speculators know very well that ruin is the revenge of facts on the game of quantitative relations. Such revenge is the most real thing in the world. Yet what is it but the means of convincing the intellect that its enterprise resembles an unfortunate speculation?

Such is no doubt the reason for which mathematicians substitute their reversible series and reciprocal relations for the irreversible order of life. A reversible series is a series that can be taken up at *no matter what* end because all of its terms are interchangeable, equivalent, and homogenous. The irreversible order of life, on the contrary, from the outset opposes us with a certain absolute and something like an elementary constant, namely its orientation: for life *has a direction* [*a un sens*], a single and obligatory direction. There is a right way of taking it and a way of taking it in reverse. We are no longer entirely free to begin wherever we would like. Life in effect comprehends events that are absolutely anterior and others that are absolutely posterior, the way Aristotle's universe comprehends a top and a bottom. This hierarchy is an arbitrary given to which we have to resign ourselves.

The biographer, the novelist, the musician, who possess the experience of narration, know that vital succession is a fact whose "term" cannot be pushed back. The artist pays cash and that is why he deals only with effective realities. Thus, for having wanted to know everything, the intellect will never know anything. It plays with promises of existence that it cannot keep without losing some of its universality—but its universality is but an inhuman neutrality, a refusal to take sides, and the famished mind has to turn elsewhere to encounter a nourishing reality. It will turn, for example, to art. Where the intellect offers us nothing but symbols, that is to say, signals that do not have their end in themselves, the artist discovers beings that have a value of their own, their autonomy, and their dignity. No longer is there behind the visible things an essence that they would allegorize and whose realization would be indefinitely postponed. There is nothing but existences taken in their own direction that lead to nothing but themselves. To speak in Schelling's terms, we would say that beauty is "tautegorical." Art is disinterested—that means first of all: art does not reduce the universe to the miserable and instrumental function imposed on it by the ulterior motives of a utilitarian intellect always absorbed in its concern with savings. The artist does not skimp on the real and that is why theorists of play have rightly made leisure a condition of aesthetic activity. The universe is enriched by all things that are good for nothing, things whose natural powers we can then discover.

A new duality thus adds to the list of Bergson's antitheses. Bergson's philosophy rejects both an anthropomorphic zoology that projects the procedures of our intellect into the instincts of industry and a naturalism that, explaining superstructures "from the bottom up," turns the intellect into a complication of animal behaviors. The antithesis of intellect and instinct can no more be reduced to the difference between more and less than the antithesis of perception and recollection could. Monism, as Vialleton profoundly remarks, is absorbed by the search for transitions and intermediaries, such as, for example, the mechanicists' mania of "plugging holes," filling in the gaps of the given. Nothing embarrasses us: where the void persists, we will invent some transitional fiction destined to complete the mediation.[87] Yet nature is far from furnishing us with all the middle terms we would need to impose silence on newness. The philosopher is surrounded by diversities he does not easily get rid of.

Nevertheless, we cannot without reservations affirm a parallelism between the antitheses of *Matter and Memory* and *Creative Evolution*. There is certainly a sense in which we can say that instinct occupies the place of the Mind since it goes in the same direction as vitality. The intellect would then represent the pole of matter, since it is toward matter that it naturally lets itself fall. That is what I expressed in the language of the Philosophy of Nature, by comparing instinct to a dream: is not the dream the limit toward which an increasingly disinterested memory spontaneously tends? But on the other hand, instinct manifests an incuriosity so remarkable that "disinterestedness" is, in certain respects, the prerogative of the intellect instead.[88] It is easier for the moon to rise in the west, Carus says, than it is for the bee to fabricate round instead of hexagonal cells or for the spider to weave a square web.[89] While instinct in its blind virtuosity appears incorrigible, the intellect derives from our wanting the gift of research and adaptation that is a privilege of freedom. The intellect, which descends toward matter, meanwhile, is made to know form. In reality, the intellect is anti-vital only to the extent that it scrambles the levels. In a philosophy as scrupulously nominalist as Bergson's, every error derives from the *confusion of levels*.

In *Matter and Memory*, the antithesis, in my view, is less between pure recollection and pure perception than it is between these two "pure" knowledges [*savoirs*] and an "impure" knowledge [*connaissance*]: the latter is now mixed perception, to which memory is added, now recollection, bastardized by perception. There is an intuition of matter that is as immediate and absolute as spiritual intuition, and instinct can therefore resemble pure perception without running the risk of being confused with the phantoms of space. Bergson does not tire of repeating that the intellect is quite at home in the world of geometrical solids and that if it limited its ambition at this point, it would go from one success to another.[90] A critical intellect, that is to say an intellect attentive to the "level" for which it is granted, would always be right. But the muddled intellect is hounded by the demon of error. Tempted by the gift of reflection and infinite splitting that singularizes it, it begins by invading the mind itself, which is in no way made for understanding. It takes recourse to language, the instrument and summary of all impurities, of all usurpations, of the crudest approximations. Is equivocity not formed in paronymy? Language is tuned to the same tone as concepts are. But it has nothing with which to express states of consciousness. It is on another level. A disinterested intellectual knowledge is thus perfectly possible.[91] It suffices that our intellect renounces, for once, the ambiguity of its natural approach, that it ceases to think the moving with immobile, the vital with the mechanic, that it, finally, ceases to perceive in order to act.

But the intellect never tires of "imitating." There is in Bergson an entire theory of *imitation*,[92] a sort of mimetics that does not oppose, as in Plato, an archetype to its image but two distinct realities of which the one usurps the face of the other. This imposture, and it alone, makes up all the illegitimacy of intellectualist counterfeits. Besides, it is in the nature of the intellect to seek to annex this foreign land that is the mind. It imitates duration, movement, instinct. It is mediately and by artifice what intuition is immediately. This virtuoso of combination fabricates machines and automata that have nothing spontaneous about them but an equivocal appearance of spontaneity. Armed with its symbols, strengthened by the breaking up it practices on the universe, the intellect laboriously fashions substitutes in which the freshness of the living no longer recognizes itself.

Only the native freshness of intuition has kept the secret. Intuition is the antidote of imposture. It is always without admixture and unalloyed, not having had, like the symbolic intellect, to traverse the thickness of conventions to get back in touch with life. It will never substitute the dismal artifices of chemistry for the gracious and ingenious progeny of vitality. In Stravinsky's 1914 opera, *The Nightingale*, the Japanese emperor's artificial bird cannot rival the living nightingale. Why would life imitate when it can find the original? Intuition takes us back to the lost paradise of the mind in which complementary superiorities do not exclude each other. No more incompatible perfections: the virtuosity of instinct allies itself with the unbounded curiosity of the intellect; we escape, for an instant, the fatality of the alternative evolution confronts us with. If instinct finds without being able to seek anything else, and if the intellect can seek no matter what without ever being assured of finding, only intuition can both find and seek, and very often, it only seeks because it has already found... Intuition no longer needs to choose: it momentarily overcomes the misery of life, transcends the law of last resort Leibniz speaks of that in the universe places the Best where one would have expected absolute excellence.[93] But intuition also hesitates to annex the real violently. That is why it deserves, like instinct, that we call it by the name of ecstasy. The intellect, barded with prejudices, melancholically drags its armor of concepts and schemas among the things. It does not condescend to the given and remains deaf to the unforeseen and the non-understood. It is up to things to arrange themselves as best they can such that they fit somewhere into a compartment of our system, which, moreover, asks no more than to house them: for everything has been foreseen. Intuition renounces these childish satisfactions. It is not only assimilation *of* the given but also, and above all, assimilation *to* the given. It rejects the layer of prejudices. Instead of attracting reality toward itself, it goes to find reality where it lives, on the level that belongs to it.

But ecstasy has a surprise in store for us: in the most acute objectivity, the self experiences the fervent and passionate intensification of its own powers. Intuition, which is as lucid as instinct, is as unconscious as the intellect. We owe it the acute consciousness of ourselves and not, as frivolous minds have written, the torpor of the senses. In rapture, mystics experience the paradoxical exaltation of their self, in the unifying extroversion, they experience the heat of contemplation. In a singular derision, the intellect, which would devour the whole universe if it could, only manages to wear out our person little by little. Yet the mind that condescends to the given and deepens it by forgetting its self will find itself: it will be altogether face to face with itself and one on one with the object, altogether alone and, as Plotinus says, "alone with the alone" (*monous pros monon*).[94]

III. *Matter and Life*

This life and this instinct are not alone in the world. They are in the presence of a matter with which they do not do as they wish, and Bergson is too much of a realist not to take this into account. This is the other side of the coin. Real organisms thus result from a compromise that life, willing or not, has had to accept. *Matter and Memory* described a psychological aspect of this compromise: the relation of the brain to thought. We learned then that between body and soul, no intelligible relation of causation exists, no transitive communication or, as Leibniz would say, no real "influence." The brain is, in the sense proper, the organ or instrument of recollections, that is to say that it is at their service and does not contain them. The brain serves to activate memory, it allows memory to convert into movements, perceptions and action—that's all.

The analysis of biological finality authorizes us to be even more categorical. Life is infinitely rich and profound. It has nothing to gain from linking its destiny to a matter incapable of expressing all of its nuances. The organizing élan explains, all the more so, the "miracles of the organism." The prodigiously complicated structures of living beings are not to be admired; for a "thing . . . which is capable of a certain amount as maximum must," *a fortiori*, "also be capable of that which lies within it."[95] Behind these astonishing forms, there is the vital élan that could still do a lot more and whose works do not exhaust the inexhaustibly varied resources of its genius.

At bottom, teleological astonishment derives from a kind of unconscious materialism that is explained by the usual approach of our intellect, always avid as it is to assemble elements to compose totalities. The least details of an organism are said to represent so many positive conquests, as if, by themselves, they had a value and a meaning. One is thus only interested in the "optical" or morphological reality of a thing, the only one to occupy a place in space, the only one that exists for the eye, the only one that seems to be captured from nothingness. But the idea that this visual complication could be explained by an entirely different principle significantly diminishes our admiration for the machine itself. In fact, the body represents less a set of means employed than a set of obstacles avoided.[96] Language, similarly, is less an instrument than an impediment. Language dissimulates and distorts as much as it expresses. Language betrays, in the two senses of the verb "to betray": it reveals and it repudiates. The supreme derision: it only reveals by repudiating!

Such is the ironical contradiction of the organ-obstacle: it is the *quamvis* [although] that is the *quia* [because]... The body in general is thus an impediment as much as it is an instrument; the body screens perception and *in so doing* renders it possible! Its very resistance and inertia are paradoxically a stimulant for vitality... The body expresses what life has had to overcome and also what it has had to abandon of itself in order to render itself visible. In this sense one could say, without vain paradoxology, that the animal sees *despite* its eyes rather than by means of them.[97] There is no idea more profound and more fertile in Bergson's philosophy. Bodies, we may add, far from being the cause or even the simple translation of the spiritual, on the contrary represent everything the soul has had to vanquish to live alongside a matter that seems to do violence to it and in which it believes itself to be boxed in. The soul cannot be without a body and yet it is not made for the body either: everything tells us that. It protests, rightly or wrongly, its incomparable dignity and its sublime vocation. The value and the beauty of the body do not at all reside in the things the body succeeds in expressing but, on the contrary, in those that we guess at and which it will never express, in the mute protestation of innuendos. The perfections of the body are but a derisory allusion to this unexpressed beyond. The mind argues against the heaviness of the flesh that insulates it and divides it against itself, and that is where all the metaphysical misunderstandings of knowledge are born. All the same, the Pythagoreans' *sōma sema*[98] lacked the dialectical complication and the paradox of the organ-obstacle: for the prisoner needs his prison, he is the little that he is only in this prison and thanks to it! The heaviness of the flesh is the very condition of his personal existence. Nonetheless, it remains true that the vinculum [chains *or* fetters] have something gratuitous and contingent about them. Speaking of the plurality of inhabited worlds, does Bergson not suggest that in unknown galaxies, life may take on the most unsuspected forms?

We see, therefore, what we have to think of the relation of matter to life.[99] Matter does not favor life any more than the mountain causes the tunnel. Obviously, if there were no mountain, there would be no tunnel. But if tunnels themselves were useless, who would dream of complaining about it? The tunnel simply represents the best one could do on a planet where there are mountains and a thousand other difficulties that keep roads from passing through. But the tunnel itself is nothing: it only represents vanquished mountain, the same way each of our organs represents a defeat of matter. The body is thus there only to be vanquished. Life does not need the body; on the contrary, it would very much like to be alone and go straight to its goal without having to pierce through mountains. But the body is there. It has had to be bypassed, eluded, sublimated by all kinds of learned ruses. To really understand this operation, we would need to invert from top to bottom the favorite order of our mechanicist intellect. We would then see that the only positive and truly primary reality is the very effort of life to ennoble and spiritualize the matter that resists it. Such is the inversion of the facts that Bergson's philosophy suggests: the epitome of positivity is not what is obvious and spatial, tangible and visible. The body represents a partial interruption of life, the way the idea is a negation of thought and rest a negation of movement. We have trouble getting used to the idea that concepts, instants, and bodies express a loss, not at all a gain. Meanwhile, the concept is a fracture of thought, a thought suspended. We could say that the concept and the word, like matter, are "obstacles avoided" and that they draw all their value from the spiritual energy that fights them.

We easily see how, beyond *Matter and Memory*, *Creative Evolution* seems to link up with the conclusions of *Time and Free Will*. Matter no longer appears so neatly in its positive function, which is to activate the past. It is above all a *necessary evil*, which amounts to saying that it is a last resort life has had to accept. Life does its best, and it exerts itself to accomplish masterpieces with these wretched materials. There is no more ingenious adaptation to ill fortune, nor a more elegant solution to what Aristotle would have called the lesser evil (*meion kakon*).[100] If life did not have to reckon with this yoke, what miracles would it not accomplish! But at each step, it runs deadly risks. Matter cruelly has life pay for its undertakings. Bergson calls this return action, by which matter destroys the work of the vital élan, "fascination."[101] Already at a time when he rather insisted on the positive function of cerebration, Bergson often speaks of the attraction that the present exercises on recollections without flesh.[102] Now, speaking once more the intransigent language of *Time and Free Will*, he underlines above all the perfidy of its seduction and he does it in terms that recall certain formulas in Plotinus: at every moment, the body bewitches the soul with its charlatan's glamour and threatens it with stiffness.[103] In certain animal (Foraminifera, Lingula) or plant (fungi) species, life has thus let itself be hypnotized or stupefied by matter. Evolution has stopped short while the vital élan succumbed to the invading torpor. But what is important to understand here is that precisely in adversity, the mind remains its own victim. Life falls into its own trap, and the forms that it imprudently tries to master turn against it.

Much of the function of comedy is to make these offensive returns of matter visible for us.[104] The accident must not, of course, reach the center or the totality of our destiny, for the comical would thereby become serious again. If the slip costs us our life, it becomes tragic. But if it is a simple, passing, superficial, and local revenge of gravity on a being whose calling is levitation and grace, it makes us want to laugh. We are entertained by the anodyne defeats of the "distracted," in whom caricature exaggerates this fascinating action of the body even more. Thus a *lapsus* makes us laugh because it is a fortuitous victory of weightiness, a minuscule lapse of vital attention, because, like an ill-timed yawn, it is the distraction-flash of our vigilance and of our freedom. Like all carelessness, this imperceptible relaxation pertains to corporal inertia... Life is grappling with a barbarous principle with which it does not do as it pleases and that easily revolts. The history of species is full of such revolts and such defeats.

Are we thus to regard matter as a kind of deplorable luxury that nature gladly afforded itself, a luxury that has no other effect than to delay the advent of freedom? If that were the case, the fourth chapter of *Matter and Memory* would really have been for nothing and the study of the conditions of life would reestablish the dualism that an attentive meditation of perception had overcome. Yet what I called the dialectic of the organ-obstacle already establishes the necessity of incarnation. There are no souls in pain. Several times, we are given to understand that matter is not only an *impedimentum*: it is also, on one side, life's essential collaborator.

(1) And first of all, in becoming, cosmic matter has not lost the role it played in its opposition to individual memory. While it often weighs heavily on life, it must also be said that *Creative Evolution*'s point of view is no longer psychological and that the role of the body is here taken up by matter. Matter is not, like the body, already touched by the spirit but represents the absolute limit of pure perception, the philosopher's *terra ignota*. And yet this radical outside is not even absolutely anti-spiritual. It helps the vital élan to become conscious of itself. It makes it such that life is "for itself" and not only "in itself."

In 1911, in one of his English lectures, Bergson attributed two main functions to matter: first it *divides and specifies*, then it *provokes an effort*.[105] Not that matter possessed anything resembling a power of individuation: for all "haecceity" comes from the mind. But matter alone is capable, by *narrowing* life, to render it present to itself. After all, the organism is *ōrismenon kai teleion*, perfect and divided! Like the Absolute, the organism is a closed masterpiece, a monadic totality, and a microcosm. The fundamental utility of perception consists, as we saw, in narrowing consciousness. Our memory is infinitely vast; but who knows whether infinity does not sometimes mean powerlessness? An outsized memory does not ordinarily help us at all to confront the urgent problems of existence, and there is no creative effort without a systematic narrowing of knowledge. "Wisdom knows the proper limits of things," Seneca says.[106] In a curious reversal, Bergson even ends up treating dreams, with their jumble of useless recollections, as the irruption of veritable materiality in the mind.[107] By itself, life tends to occupy as much space as possible. But what good does that do us if it thereby loses all efficacy, all serious influence on the destinies of the universe?

Fortunately, matter is there, which filters the vital current across divergent individualities the way discourse filters thought into discrete concepts. The sole goal of the nervous system, as we saw, is to specify and channel a diffuse energy.[108] It thus intensifies our action on things. And more generally, the function of matter, in all living beings, plant and animal, is to accumulate a potential energy that life then spends freely. Matter thus serves to concentrate life, to make it attentive and vigilant, at the same time as it serves to separate consciousnesses. Like practical perception, instinct, which is life itself, bears the constraining charitableness of this narrowness. Not that it depends, as perception does, on the brain's policing. The limitation of instinct, necessitated by matter in general, is not as distorting as that of utilitarian perception; it is only restrictive. Narrowed down to itself, it acquires lucidity and precision. It gathers itself and makes the operation of life visible to us. Narrowness, condition of all revelation: was this not already the central idea of Böhme's philosophy?[109]

On the other hand, matter "provokes effort." Not only does it represent at every moment the resistance against which life has to affirm itself; it is originarily the trampoline whose spring has projected the vital élan onto the increasingly ramified paths of evolution.[110] This is expressed by the image itself of élan or growth [*essor*]: an élan presupposes a solid fulcrum, a trampoline that furnishes life with the initial impulse, the way an explosion presupposes an obstacle against which expansive forces revolt. It is on a trampoline that the *Republic*'s dialectics and the *Symposium*'s erotics receive their élan to leap, the one toward the Good, the other toward the Beautiful. In Plato, "steps" (*epibaseis*) give rapid movements (*hormai*) their spring.[111] Is there not something Platonic about Mourgue's *Hormé*?

It is likely that if there were no matter, there would still be life, but not the vital élan. Evolution properly so called would lose its *raison d'être*, which is the growing prevalence of freedom. The mind, desperately solitary in a desert-like world, would have forgotten both the joy and the anxiety of danger. For joy is in victory. "All great joy has a triumphant note. . . . Wherever there is joy, there is creation."[112] That is our true greatness, and our very defeats are glorious, since they manifest the dignity of the mind. Life thus demands an alterity that is relative to life because it owes its spring, its internal convergence and, to have out with it, its finality to it. Often, Bergson even ventures to treat the two forces as necessarily complementary.[113] Because matter resists our freedom, the mind henceforth has a vocation in this world: across successive species, it prepares the apotheosis of freedom.

But perhaps that is but a manner of speaking after all. What do we care that matter collaborates, in its very hostility, in the edification of freedom if in itself it remains an autonomous and indocile given? Reduce it, in thought, to almost nothing: it must nonetheless still be there for evolution to begin. Organization, which is opposed to fabrication,[114] starts from an *almost* mathematical point, from a *minimum* of matter. But a minimum is not nothing: matter is already there, and this second principle seems to be independent of the first. Life, furthermore, enters space only with regrets, but in the end, like it or not, it enters it, and space seems entirely to wait for it to furnish it with food for exciting negations. It is true that elsewhere[115] (for the question is certainly one of Bergson's philosophy's most complex) the monist affirmation prevails: the things themselves endure and matter is still relatively spiritual, different from the mind only in its greater indulgence for the inertia of space. Be that as it may: the problem raised by matter will now pose itself concerning space. It suffices that there be two limits, two theoretically conceivable absolutes that are beyond matter as they are beyond consciousness. No doubt, we are promised, twice,[116] that their shared origin will be demonstrated. But what follows proves that matter endures only thanks to its solidarity with life, that everything positive about matter belongs to the life in which it participates to a still very weak degree.[117] Certainly, life resembles that which in matter is vital: yet this vitality is but the accident of a principle dominated by materializing forces.

The truth is that in Bergson's philosophy there are not as much two opposed "principles" as two inverse movements: one ascending, the other descending. This is what our earlier remarks on the "confusion of levels" now makes easier to understand. From consciousness to matter there is at bottom but a single scale of less and less dense realities. But we can take this scale either in one direction or in the other; either right side up or the other way around. Matter, in sum, is nothing, and the contrariety is rather between directions than between *things*, one absolutely positive, the other absolutely negative. Just the same way, 'nothingness-in-itself'—which, in Plotinus, is paradoxically the principle of evil—is always already beyond, always lower than the Low. Does absolute nonbeing not, in sum, coincide with the intention of descending taken to its limit? Instinct, intuition, intellection go in the same direction as life. Like the *nisus formativus*,[118] that is to say, the labor of organization, they are centrifugal. And even if they are inspired by a dynamic, or seminal, totality, they are really innovative because they unrelentingly go from the

possible to action. In the opposite direction, we find the fabricatory intellect, ambiguous perception, constituted memory that, instead of remaining
contemporary with life, delay its movement by transporting their ready-
made symbols onto other levels.

The coefficients "more" and "less" thus affect two *tendencies* and not at
all two *substances*. Bergson's philosophy appears to us as a *monism* of substance, a *dualism* of tendency. There is no absolute reality but life. Space itself exists only by means of the contraband vitality it has managed to steal
or to counterfeit, and which it uses, after a fashion, to delude us. Without
this filching, without the pastiches of mechanism, it would be nothing.
Space is nothing; but the anti-vital tendency that arrives at this nothing is truly something. In a dynamist theory that only admits oriented
tendencies, the "polarity" of principles has a very clear and, we might say,
experimental psychological sense: matter represents everything that goes
against the course of life, everything that reverses a naturally irreversible
order, everything that resists the effort of consciousness.

Not that the seriousness of the conflict is in any way attenuated by
this. Now that consciousness has recognized an obstacle to its growth
not in a substance but in a tendency, its destiny is still more critical. Of
this tendency, it is itself the seat—for tendencies only exist through a will
that is their source. We would almost hope for a malicious entity named
matter, space, or whatever you like: an entity from which one can turn
away, the way Ulysses steers his galley away from the Sirens who mean to
wreck it. Plotinus, too, sets about proving that evil does not derive from
intentional malice (something the Stoics had an inkling of) but from an
inverted hypostasis. We would very much like to circumscribe evil outside ourselves, and we would even do the impossible to avoid such bad
company. Yet evil is in us. We would prefer the demon provided it could
be localized and found. But how does one exorcize oneself? Evil is not
an entity, it is an intention, an evil will, and consciousness does not easily
purge it. Consciousness shelters its own enemy. The worm is in the apple.
Does not the philosophy of *Laughter* itself contain an imperceptible dose
of bitterness?[119] First of all, mechanist science—which apprehends of life
only the aspect of destruction or "catagenesis"—shows us that there are,
present one to the other, one *in* the other, two inverse movements.[120] The
evil tendency attaches itself to the progress of the positive tendency. It is
the evil tendency that at every moment converts evolution into a circular
process.[121] Just as gravitation results from two divergent forces that join

one another, so the stagnation of stationary species is but the compromise reached between levitation and geotropism, between life that wants to rise and the anti-spiritual inclination that wants to descend, between the inertia of weightiness and the vocation of progress, or, as Bergson would later say, between pressure and aspiration. Consciousness, torn against itself, adopts a mean and spins in place.

When we analyze this transactional solution that Bergson only points to, it reveals the cruel antagonism of tendencies: the living no longer advances and its immobility represents a victory of the regressive force. But this immobility is not a rest pure and simple, since in the universe, there is no rest pure and simple, there are only tendencies that accidentally immobilize each other when their forces are equal and inverse. If matter prevailed absolutely, it would provoke a dissolution, that is to say, another movement. Aristotle already said that "there is not only an activity of movement but an activity of immobility," or again: "Not everything that is not in motion can be said to be at rest."[122] For there is, according to Kierkegaard, an active immobility in which the intense energy of rest and the positivity of negation dissimulate.[123] And Mikhail Lermontov, too, speaks of this tranquility in passions, which is a sign of secret force, of plenitude and depth. The immobility of the living must thus hide an internal effervescence, and that is what the image of rotation expresses: the positive forces have not entirely succumbed because the living subsists and defends at least the ground gained. Hence the profound impatience of the immobilized mind: life remains active in inaction and refuses to disappear.

But what is most tragic is that the deadly tendency lives at the heart of vitality itself. In order to affirm itself, life, in a singular derision, needs the matter that kills it. In life, there is a rift that emerges and is resolved in the continued movement of becoming. It explains both the utility and the malice of the spatial principle. The same irony that makes memory contradictory to itself condemns life to perish at the hands of life.[124] This is the ransom paid in this world for any kind of superiority. Constituted memory, we said, repudiates and denies constitutive memory of which it is nonetheless the necessary blossoming. According to *The Two Sources of Morality and Religion*, the intellect turns against the life it had been destined to serve. Freedom expires in the choice that nonetheless manifests it. "The faculty of choosing cannot be read in the choice we make by virtue of it," *Duration and Simultaneity* will admit, and in *Creative*

Evolution we read: "The act by which life goes forward to the creation of a new form, and the act by which this form is shaped, are two different and often antagonistic movements."[125]

What we have here is a kind of spiritual parricide that is the law of life itself. The individual thus realizes itself completely only in its descendants, and yet we know that progeny is naturally ungrateful and willingly forgets the maternal sacrifice. The individual realizes itself completely only in society, and most often, society is deadly for the originalities submitted to its law. As the individual perishes at the hands of species and of the group that ought to exalt it, the species in duration, the group in space, so life itself perishes at the hands of the individual and more generally at the hands of the organic forms that, by making it visible, repudiate it. At each instant, creative improvisation is thus in mortal danger; at every step, the genius of innovation is threatened by drivel, watering down, and faltering. In this respect, musical creation is perhaps the most disappointing of all. Musicians relentlessly experience the antagonism between the two inverse movements, one constraining and holding back the other. Inspiration has barely taken on flesh and already it succumbs to the conventional developments that come in from all sides to meet it. The least of melodic idea attracts a crowd of ready-made formulas toward which any sensibility that is a little complacent will willingly let itself slide. The beginning has no sooner begun than it already sets about continuing, that is to say, to keep harping on. Such slackening ambushes the inventor like a curse. The veritable creator refuses to be carried off by clichés. This is a fight at every instant, since we feel in ourselves the fatal downward slope on which the genius sets foot by the very fact of ending his abstinence. At each point of the creative labor, we must thus turn a deaf ear to the thousands of good formulas that offer to help us to get out of our predicament.

We now understand better in which sense matter is distinct from the mind and in which sense it is akin to it. The invitations of matter are certainly fatal for life; but what makes them particularly insidious is that they emanate from life itself. Unless life braces itself against itself, the same demand that carries it toward a complete liberation will also imprison it in forms without soul. The most subtle of all temptations is the one that comes from the mind, speaks in the name of the mind, pretends to lead us to spirituality. We do not voluntarily dissipate this ambivalence. We continue to regard the forms without soul as a gain and a success of life when in fact they announce a decadence. But what is paradoxical is that we are not entirely wrong since life must take that path and since its very decadence prepares its apotheosis. This excuses at once the gross blunders and cunning tricks of the intellect.[126] I say excuse, by no means justify. The intellect is the purgatory of intuition. It is a necessary evil. Life could not gratuitously inflict on itself the yoke of a materiality that might crush it at any moment. Everything life touches must have an internal and organic signification. Death, Bergson says, "retain[s] for a time the features of the living."[127] Would one dedicate an entire book to the mechanisms that draw the mind from its dreams if these mechanisms were just a vain and expensive fantasy of nature, if they did not themselves bear the signature of the mind?

Life will not elevate itself too much above this cruel reality. How would it volatilize matter since matter is the result of a tendency it carries within itself? It cannot therefore be ignorant of its enemy. Besides— and Bergson often repeats this with great clarity[128]—the force of life is a limited force, not an all-powerful one. It will thus maneuver with *ruses*, in small and humble ways at first. Life's *tour de force* was to make matter serve its designs by cleverly adopting its inclinations in order to then capture matter and vanquish necessity.[129]

What results from this subterfuge is the *modus vivendi* we call the brain. The metaphysics of matter retrospectively sheds new light on the function of the nervous system. The brain, as we know, is neither the cause nor the seat of thought (for these words make no sense), and corporality simply represents an interruption of the vital élan. How are we to understand this? Life accepts matter as it is, but, like a good diplomat, it divides in order to reign: the brain, precisely, serves it to "divide automatism against itself," for bringing action into conflict with action.[130] The function of the brain is to indefinitely create new habits capable of neutralizing old ones. Directly, the brain can create only mechanisms, that is to say, something spatial. But the mechanisms reciprocally annul each other, and consciousness takes advantage of this annulment to escape matter. Even the worst turns to our advantage. Like clever engineers, we oblige hostile forces to work for us, we employ nature to vanquish nature. Life will thus calmly let the automatisms devour each other and, during this civil war of motor habits, it will establish our freedom on an unshakable foundation. Can we dream of a more elegant, a more economical solution? The automatisms themselves take care of their own expulsion!

Life only takes the pain of *triggering* our definitive liberation.[131] Of course it sometimes happens that it lets itself be caught in its own trap. Life then plays a game analogous to the one Schelling imputes to the Creator and that he calls *universio*.[132] There, God pretends to admit the universe, which is suspended divinity, and in the same way, the mind, the better to realize its designs, tolerates materiality, which is reversed mind. That is only a feint, and the materialists let themselves be thoughtlessly taken in by it because they only retain the letter of things. They take the subterfuge of the mind at its word, and the irony of the body remains as impenetrable to them as the irony of the world.

Cunning as they might be, the ruses of life express nonetheless the misery of a consciousness reduced to prevaricating with adversity. Matter, no doubt, is but an "inversion" and nothing more. No doubt, it only has reality thanks to the positive tendency of which it is the reversal: given no matter what movement, one can always conceive of the inverse movement. But why did this temptation have to slumber at the very heart of life? It could, it ought not to have existed. The relation of life to matter is not without analogy with the attitude of Leibniz's God in the presence of evil. Evil, the *Theodicy* says, finds in God its "deficient" cause and by no means its "efficient" cause.[133] God has not committed evil but simply allowed evil. He has taken the oblique path that was, relatively, the shortest. Not because the straight line would have been absolutely preferable. Transposing Bergson's philosophy into Leibnizian language, we would say: the vital élan wills mind and freedom with an *antecedent will*; with a *consequent* will, it wills active and mobile bodies with a brain capable of accumulating potential energy. This body equipped with a nervous system is but the result of antagonistic forces life has had to reckon with, just as the Best results from the pact the incompatible perfections have had to agree on among themselves. Sins thus turn to the glory of God, and in the same way, life draws good from evil. What is deplorable is not the heaviness of matter but the humiliating fatality that obliges us to compose with this matter.

This, in fact, is the great novelty of *Creative Evolution*: in *Matter and Memory*, the mind, without the body, dissipates in dreamy and powerless recollections. But we now know that life without matter would be the absolute itself in its omnipotence. Not that matter is radically unusable. Since it is there, one must come up with a reason for why it is there. But if it did not exist, we know that instinct would not have been obliged to separate from the intellect, that life would not have divided up complementary functions among the animal and the plant kingdoms, that organized beings would not have to perpetually choose between incompatible perfections. Bergson has thus not stopped believing ever more firmly in the basic independence of the spiritual principle, capable of vanquishing all obstacles, "perhaps even death"![134]

In his *Mind-Energy* lectures, he insists even more this idea.[135] That is because the ripening of his intuitionist metaphysics henceforth allowed him confidently to glimpse an eschatological future, to perceive "the joyous song of the future,"[136] to hope, finally, for the definitive victory of freedom and the sublimation of the spatial principle. The insertion of freedom into necessity, besides, demands a violent effort that strikingly manifests the resistance of matter. While pure perception and pure recollection are "limits," intuition is a fact: a rare fact, but a fact nonetheless. Yet if life is the unique absolute, there is no veritable intuition but that of pure life. The opposition, as we know, is less between two things than it is between two movements of which one is positive, the other negative. And thus all knowledge that espouses the positive movement, the very effort to understand matter will be to some degree intuitive. There is a way of thinking matter materially that would lead us to the heart of the absolute: that is how life itself proceeds when it adopts the descending movement of mechanisms; for that it suffices to place oneself *from the outset*[137] on the level of the object studied. But symbolic knowledge will never resign itself to this because its aversion against life condemns it to scrambling all the levels and to turning its back on the movement of intuition.[138] There is only one unequally dense reality that can become, on all levels, the object of a veridical intuition—provided that the rhythm of the subject coincide with the rhythm of the object, provided that we renounce the symbols that erase natural and necessary distinctions.

And yet it would be a mistake to believe that all these intuitions have equal dignity. The only one that can vanquish death, the only one that allows life to blossom is the intuition of the pure mind. This intuition would no longer be insinuating, it would be triumphant. It looks down on the pitiful ingenuity of an intuition that spends all its skill on being welcomed by matter. It no longer has to laboriously measure out its own content to coincide with diversely equivocal and unequally impure realities. It leaves us one-on-one with complete reality. This reality we are now surprised to find in ourselves.[139] And we admire how much the absolute is close to us, how much it resembles us. That is perhaps where we would least think of looking for it. For the right path, and the most welcoming one, is always the last one we see. The absolute is a mystery that realizes itself at every moment in each of us, in life and through life. We must, in Goethe's words, *learn to believe in simplicity.*[140] When the far-off is in us, we must renounce the idol of a far-off absolute and no longer look for complications where there are none.

CHAPTER 5

HEROISM AND SAINTLINESS

After the fact, it seems to us that Bergson's philosophy could not have concluded otherwise than it did. And yet no one could have predicted what was to arrive. I do not yet know, "but I foresee that I am going to have known it,"[1] is how Bergson himself talks about phenomena of false recognition. For my part, I suggest the formula that the future is foreseeable only in the *future perfect*.[2] "If I knew what was to be the great dramatic work of the future, I should be writing it," Bergson writes in "The Possible and the Real."[3] And Proust's Bergotte, for his part, says that a creator never does what his imitators would have done in his place.[4] Bergson's goal was not at all to write something "Bergsonian," just as Fauré's goal was not at all to write something "Fauréan." Now that this book of ethics has been written, we think we recognize it, and it seems to us we have always foreseen it. Such is the finality of life, always surprising, but always reasonable, such is the expected unexpected Alain speaks of:[5] at every moment, we are able to anticipate the future although the future is always a novelty. Does not effectiveness—be it Vermeer's blue or listening to Fauré's *Ballade* in F-sharp Major—always add some je ne sais quoi that is new and unsuspected to the most expected of performances? A genius in becoming authorizes only prophecies! And when, by bad luck, the work of the genius is cut short, no one can write the finale of the "unfinished symphony" in her place: whatever the imagined finale might be, we sense that she would have written something else entirely, something of which we have no idea; after the fact, this thing would have been as simple as ABC... But one had to have thought of it. Irritating secret of the *almost* foreseeable unforeseeable, always just about to be guessed at, always mysterious! The ethics of *The Two Sources of Morality and Religion* is not the ethics a contemporary of *Time and Free Will* and of *Matter and Memory*, who knew nothing of *Creative Evolution*, could have foreseen. Now that Bergson's philosophy has come and gone and we are posterior to it, the "finality" of the doctrine appears to us entirely natural and almost organic. Skeptics challenged Bergson's philosophy for never ending up in wisdom: they should resign themselves. Achilles once played on them the trick of catching up with the tortoise. In the same way, Bergson's ethics, which they had already condemned as a kind of inconsequential dilettantism, eludes all their forecasts and culminates in a call for heroism without otherwise being bothered with aporias.

There is now in Bergson's philosophy one more antithesis—that of two moralities and two religions. Like many great philosophies, like that of Descartes, like that of Kant, Bergson's approach could be called a *Critique*, that is to say, a separation. Is not to have a "critical" mind to possess a certain gift of discernment that allows us to dissociate where common sense confuses? Is it not to seek beings that are only themselves, that is to say, without admixture of any other? Thus Descartes, with his method of clear and distinct ideas, dissociates the impure and murky alloys of Aristotelian physics. Like Pascal, Bergson turns against those who "speak spiritually of corporeal things and corporeally of spiritual ones."[6] Like Descartes, Bergson is looking for simple natures, opposing space and duration in *Time and Free Will*, pure perception and pure recollection in *Matter and Memory*, intelligence and instinct in *Creative Evolution*. If we want to elude Einstein's phantasms as well as Zeno's aporias, Fechner's logarithms as well as the bastard concepts of associationism, then quantity must be thought quantitatively and quality qualitatively. Chemistry may well teach me to consider the air that I breathe to be a crude mixture: I nonetheless do not breathe oxygen separately, nor do I breathe nitrogen separately. And in the same way, recollection and sensation indissolubly associate in perception. Having separated the two moralities and the two religions, Bergson will thus have to show how mysticism is embodied in a confessional dogma, how social obligation evaporates into charity and love.

I. *Suddenness*

This is the theme of Bergson's ethics: between "static" morality, which is the morality of the city, and "dynamic" morality, there can be no pact, no transaction. Common sense, which likes nice regular gradations, would very much like to extract step-by-step the love of humanity from the love of family and from patriotism, just as it would like, when it is idealist, to extract perception from recollection, and, when it is materialist, to see recollection emerge from an increasing extenuation of perception. Nothing would come in to interrupt this exemplary crescendo at the end of which we find all the fine virtues of human consciousness—dedication, charity, and heroism. That is a geneticist illusion, the illusion of a mechanicist and manufacturer who toys with constructing the entire universe from a simple element more or less multiplied by itself—transformed sensation, "nervous shock," or enlightened self-interest. It is easy to criticize a prejudice of this kind in unilinear evolutionism and in all ideas of rectilinear perfection.

In ethics, such a symmetry would not only be economical, it would also be reassuring; to enlarge domestic and corporative solidarity in small doses and to obtain, at the end of this magnificent widening... charity: what a godsend for egoism! Virtue and group interest would finally be reconciled. As for collective interest, the utilitarians, by way of all kinds of hypotheses of substitution and transfer, set out to prove that it coincides with personal interest. We need not be afraid to add the following postscriptum to Bergson's critique: if the good citizen learns to love humanity in the family, or if he goes seamlessly from tribe to country,[7] why would he not, in loving himself, learn to love his family? At the center of all these nested circles, there is obviously the self that is an infinitely small circle, almost a point—and charity will appear as the superlative of egoism!

There is something tiresome and disquieting about differences in nature, something that prevents the surveyor from measuring things according to a common scale.[8] The surveyor also has an aversion to "qualitative leaps" that interrupt the nice progressive lines of concepts. The taste for simplistic gradations is developed and maintained by two illusions that I have called, one, Illusion of retrospectivity, and two, Confusion of the state of mind with its object.

I have insisted on the first and we must note that here, for the first time, Bergson becomes aware of the role it plays in his own theory.[9] The root of this illusion is the retroactive power of the present over the past. We place ourselves in the "future perfect" to reconstitute, backward, the possible by means of a kind of retrospective forecast. The intellect gives itself an exemplary image of movement, of justice, of volition, and of the real eating away at the ideal, after the fact, bit by bit,[10] or, as Bergson also says, of the real chasing after the Idea.[11] We also find this reconstruction starting from elements in the atomistic and pointillist mania of scaled gradations. Retrospectively, everything has an explanation, and patriotism must lead the ego-altruist to total devotion just as well-being puts us on the path of luxury. Love of self is thus a love in miniature. This links up effortlessly with Aristotelian substantialism, which turns the friend into an *allos autos*, an *other myself*.[12] The logic of this other self has driven out all supernaturalness.

On the other hand, this mania rests on the confusion of a state of mind with its physical support.[13] From a growing excitation, Fechner concluded that sensation, too, must be growing. Because wave physics describes wavelengths, Taine and Spencer have no regrets about neglecting the discontinuity, the fundamental heterogeneity, the irreducibility of sensible qualities. Because the nation resembles a big family we are to treat humanity like the biggest possible nation... It is the cosmopolitan, therefore, who will beat all patriotism records. Yet who does not see that human "society" is not a society like the others? The relationship between humanity and the various national and domestic groupings is the same as the one between part and whole. A part is comparable to another part, but not to the whole; yet humanity, by definition, is a whole. To love humanity, to go "to the limit," there must thus be a sudden decision, a conversion, a "metabole." Family and States posit themselves by opposing one another, because they are finite societies that reject each other. Yet what would humanity, which is infinite, oppose itself to? There certainly is love in closed communities, nation or family: nonetheless, loving against someone, loving by excluding enemies, is not yet loving with that infinite love that is charity. The veritable break is thus not between family and city, which are, all in all, two groupings of the same type, but between the city and humankind.[14]

For there is a break. More than ever, Bergson's philosophy remains a philosophy of the élan, of metamorphoses and great enthusiasms. It is not by intensely loving ourselves, by deepening our egoism that we will encounter the pure charity that is entirely positive and loves without ulterior motives. Likewise: subtilize your pleasure as much as you like, scratch and dig—you will obtain nothing but pleasure. It is with love as it is with movement: to find it, it must first be given, and *all at once*.[15] Rest is not a lesser movement. Movement is not the height of rest. That is true of all things and, for example, of the love of women. Love is not a consequence of esteem. Love does not begin with friendship but with itself. "Now or never!" Friendship and love correspond to two entirely different vocations that diverge more and more. The manufacturers of complexes, however, in their logical inanity, pretend to believe that love builds up little by little from feelings of friendship and that one becomes a lover by being a friend. They want nothing to do with discontinuities and leaps that make becoming become and the future happen.[16] And yet, the distance between the language of friendship and the language of love is insurmountable. We try to fill it in with imperceptible transitions or artificial devices analogous to Darwinism's "little differences." Since one can go from concept to reasoning via judgment, and from sensation to recollection via perception, why would there not also be a continuous genealogy of feelings? Alas! The one who settles first in friendship will only ever find friendship...

To go from static morality to dynamic morality, we also need, not a "multiplication," but a conversion; we need, as I say elsewhere, to be able to *modulate*. Perhaps more directly than in any of his previous books, Bergson here signals the source of these heterogeneities.[17] At every moment of becoming, we only find perfect combinations, complete organisms or, better yet, totalities. Like Minerva, feelings, for example, are born adults. The relation of static morality to dynamic morality is the same as that of the closed to the open, of pressure to attraction or aspiration. To convert to the dynamic, that is to say, to movement, there is an adventurous mutation to go through. This mutation, this opening and mobilization of the soul has taken place, according to Bergson, thanks to the Prophets first, then with Christianity.

This, then, is how open ethics lodges a challenge against the mania of the common denominator that enlists all beings in the same uniform, subsumes all individuals in the same genus, makes every specific experience a particular case of a single law, and claims to classify events in categories. Where "continuism" and "continuationism" multiply gradations and imperceptible transitions (between life and death, between human and God), the philosophy of the vital élan seems attached to the idea of the discontinuous leap and perilous jump. Never has Bergson's continuity been so close to Kierkegaard's discontinuity. We also see better now how James could reconcile the flux and the *fiat*, the transitive and the "substantive," affection for Bergson and loyalty to Renouvier. Whereas *Time and Free Will* and "The Perception of Change" reflect above all on the interval and on indivisible blocks of duration, on the mnemic past and on the anticipated future that, according to the *Philebus*, thicken the indivisible limits of the present and radiate around the momentary *Nun*,[18] *The Two Sources of Morality and Religion* is above all a meditation on the punctual instant and on emergence, the principle of ingenious newness. As Kierkegaard rejects Hegel's logical immanentism, so Bergson provides us with an antidote to Megarian sophisms and the cumulative sorites paradox that conjures the mystery of the start and of *the first time*. The suddenness of events, the flagrancy of the *Kairos*, demand henceforth to be surprised in the act.

II. *The Open and the Closed*

If dynamic intention arises all of a sudden, how do static morality and religion constitute themselves? Let us note that here, the philosopher's analysis remains largely introspective. Bergson always refuses to admit the heredity of acquired characteristics.[19] It obviously hurts our pride as civilized people to admit our fundamental identity with the primitive. And yet this elementary consciousness, whose evolution we seek to trace, is a fact we find within ourselves, pushed back by a whole moral and social police. The subordination of the individual to the species, be it in a bee-hive or an anthill, is automatically guaranteed by instinct. To obey "duty," we only need to let ourselves go. By blindly devoting itself to the group, the individual thus follows the line of least resistance; it is disinterested out of laziness. In the same way, in closed societies, the easy thing is to do one's duty. The difficult and courageous thing is to evade it. But, out of curiosity and indiscretion, intelligence does not wait for long to disturb the comfort of the species. By developing in the civilized an apprehension of death, by favoring the egotism of the individual, by sponsoring homicidal technologies, by its very fallibility, finally, and its infinite apti-tude for posing problems, the intellect dialectically turns against the life it was to serve. The individual will thus resist its duty.

To resist this resistance, human beings have invented Moral Obliga-tion. Obligation—"closed" obligation—suppresses what had been sup-pressing. In Hegelian language, we might call it the negation of a nega-tion. Obligation thus undoes what the intellect has done; via a detour it restores a cohesion that instinct should have sufficed to guarantee. It is a kind of "reversal of the for into the against." In closed obligation, however bitter it may be, there is also a principle of bourgeois punctuality that is rather reassuring. Negation here has nothing violent or adventurous about it. It allows the calm virtues of the civil servant and of the good citizen to prosper among us. Is it necessary to recall here how matter itself, accord-ing to Bergson, reduces itself to an annulled consciousness in which all antagonisms are neutralized? How our brain, opposing habits to habits, ultimately serves to liberate us?[20] This is what our closed morality does as well, by instituting a kind of civil war between a rebellious intelligence and our duty. Under the mask of bourgeois zeal, closed morality is conducive to our rest, our escape, our comfort. It offers us an ideal of arithmetic justice founded on the law of the "tit for tat." It surrounds itself, finally, with a retinue of timid and provincial perfections, average virtues that it makes accessible to everyone of good will.

Closed religion emerges in a very similar manner—as a reaction against the indiscrete curiosity of the intellect. Not only does the intellect, thanks to its egotistical reflections, compromise the cohesion of the group, it also shakes both our confidence in life, by representing to us the necessity of death, and our faith in action, by separating more and more the initiative of our undertakings from their outcome. Against this double danger, nature must defend itself: it calls up rituals and myths that, just like moral obligation, are substitutes for instinct. The beginning of wisdom is to overcome instinct thanks to the intellect. But the end of wisdom is to come back to instinct and to negate what negated it—either, like static morality, by creating a habit of duty that is, so to speak, the imitation of instinct by intelligence, or, like static religion, by calling up a labor of fabulation. But what is most curious is that the remedy comes from the very intellect whose turbulence is to be stifled: it is intelligence that imitates the social instinct, and it is the intellect, too, that imitates the devastating experience in its superstitions. Hence an entire system of fictions that counterfeits true perception and has its internal logic.[21] Mythology, like the dream, like instinct, like dementia, by nature possesses a certain logical ferocity, a kind of coherence in its absurdity that favors the proliferation of phantasms. This absurd logic (which, by the way, is not a "primitive mentality" since it is ours still) substitutes imaginary facts, hallucinatory representations, for the facts perceived.

The idea we need to start with is that nothing prevails against a fact: only what is perceived or perceptible exists, only what is given in a real or possible experience exists.[22] Bergson is the very first to put this superior positivism into practice when, in order to know something about God, he consults the mystics who have experienced his presence. Does he not himself often say, and almost in the same terms as Tolstoy: we must consider what humans do, not what they say?[23] Experience alone is a sincere witness; experience alone is *effective*. Where it falls silent, we manage to have an imaginary experience that makes up for the gaps in our perception.

We thus surround ourselves with an illusory and excessively prolific universe thanks to which consciousness escapes from this prosaic world.

For example: the image of survival, with its corollary, *Animism*, opposes the unbearable idea of death like an antidote.[24] To neutralize the vagaries of a too-intelligent intellect, humans offer themselves a mystical counterfeit of mechanism, namely *Magic*. The intellect likes danger: it builds machines that are more and more complicated, ventures into far-flung projects it will never see the end of. It takes the field, but we do not know if it will ever arrive... jack of all trades, master of none. It thinks big, but it is as fallible as it is infinite: to the extent that the itinerary of the discourse and the mediation stretch further, the chances of getting lost on the way increase! Let us recall that Descartes's intuition is tasked precisely with shortening this intellectual itinerary, with sidestepping the traps of memory and the voids of discourse... The primitive intellect, which has gotten lost thanks to its perspicacity, will thus call for help from certain magical powers thanks to which it will easily fill in the gap, demolish the interval that separates it from the goal. This is how, bit by bit, personal gods are outlined in human beings' imagination in neatly traced forms. The first magical powers whose assistance is called on are neither thing nor person, yet mythology soon replaces these equivocal representations, these "efficacious presences" with mobile figures that have a name, a body, attributes. Static religion is born.

Open morality and open religion have an entirely different vocation. Until now, we have not come across anything that would resemble charity, heroism, or love, nor any of those absurd and useless virtues without which life would lose all its value. Closed morality, founded on an entirely mercantile idea of equilibrium and reciprocity, stays in place, spinning madly. Bergson has shown elsewhere how this dizzying rotation results from two inverse movements joining up: taken up between the élan that carried it forward and the matter that weighs it down at any moment, the species adopts a middle position and turns around and around [*tourne en rond*].[25] In circular morality there is thus a principle of progress, but this principle is immobilized, blocked, and in every instant the élan of our heart stops short [*tourne court*]. In each instant, the circle that has been opened up by isolated enthusiasms closes again.

The circle of closed morality is burst open by Christianity the way the circuit of reflexes is broken by cerebration, which inserts the infinity of our freedom. Dynamic morality no longer orders us to obey a predetermined form because it relentlessly overcomes itself, because it is beyond all forms, because its infinite unrest carries it further than all laws. Do not ask it, then, *what* is to be done: it would be just as well to ask at which point of a movement mobility is to be found! "Virtue is in the action,"[26] like mobility or like freedom. Is charity not a "good movement" that is often a *first movement*, an élan of the heart? This is what Bergson shows magnificently in a passage that is perhaps the apex of his book: the paradoxes and contradictions of dynamic morality disappear when we consider the *intention* of its maxims, which is to "induce a disposition of the soul." "It is not for the sake of the poor, but for his own sake, that the rich man should give up his riches: blessed are the poor 'in spirit'!"[27]

Thus the Eleatic aporias are resolved for anyone who does not confuse movement with the stops it passes through. The *good movement* is not reducible to a series of stops any more than movement is. Open religion is very similar: the true mystic can be recognized by his not granting his own ecstasies more than a provisional and in a way symbolic value. For him, rapture is not, as it is for the Greeks, an endpoint but a transition, something to be overcome. Let us here complete Bergson's philosophy by pointing out that Plato, and Diotima of Mantinea, and Plotinus, just like Saint John of the Cross, have always had the élan to leap further, higher, beyond. Dynamic morality and religion will give us not well-being but joy; not the egotistical and cozy comfort that benumbs us in the security of our bourgeois virtues but the mystics' adventurous enthusiasm.

III. *Bergson's Maximalism*

It does seem that beyond *Creative Evolution*, *Two Sources* in a sense picks up on *Time and Free Will*. Not that Bergson's biology has given the lie to Bergson's psychology. It has, meanwhile, given us the cosmic scale of a becoming that *Time and Free Will*'s "dilettante" had found inside himself. It is true that the vital élan is not, like Schopenhauer's Will, the "genius of the species," that is to say a metaphysical character. Evolution, meanwhile, is large-format duration, the metaphysical duration of the species. The individual is limited to transmitting an impulse that it receives from the distant past: across the succession of generations, the vital élan mediates in each of us its secular designs.

Let's say it clearly (since, besides, there is no contradiction here): there is something that has changed in *Two Sources*. How else to explain the rather unexpected role Bergson attributes to great individuals, the "superhumans [*surhommes*]," the heroes and the saints in the bursting of circular morality? Just as in *Matter and Memory*, pure recollections are dated, picturesque, and individual, so the mysticism of *Two Sources* admits the person. And inversely, static obligation is impersonal just like habit-memory. *Time and Free Will* and *Laughter* considered society only to impute to it the idols of grammar and space that deprive us of our living self. Bergson's philosophy in *Two Sources* ignores neither society nor even sociology.[28] Yet it attributes to them such importance in the genesis of moral obligation only in order to deprive them of heroism and love, just as *Matter and Memory* substitutes the biological point of view for the intellectualist point of view only in order to emancipate thought from the brain. Never before has Bergson thought so highly of these geniuses who by themselves, as Kierkegaard says in *The Concept of Anxiety*,[29] represent a new species, who upset and distort social routines. Hence the increasingly dramatic, "personalist," and voluntarily anthropomorphic character of Bergson's evolution. Certainly, we long suspected the role that discontinuous mutations play in it, but we did not know to what extent these mutations depend on individual initiatives.

Without catastrophes, without "metaboles," and without adventures, no veritable change: for at what moment would newness declare itself? And why at this moment *rather than* at another?[30] Like Leibniz's finalism, Bergson wants to explain the *potius quam*, the sufficient reason for which the mechanicists and atomists can furnish only by allowing for a large number of fortuitous coincidences. To what point of your "imperceptible transitions" are you going to assign the threshold of change? Yet there are no decisive changes but those where a will assumes the initiative by supposing the impossible to be resolved.[31] Mysticism would not exist without the warmth and radiance of a great individual example: heroism calls forth heroism. There is a kind of magnetism and mystical "aura" that surrounds superhumans and imperiously solicits admiration. The contagion of love spreads from these superhumans like an entirely moral electricity.

And not only the single person merits being loved or imitated but many human feelings, too, have at their source an individual invention. They are born on this or that day, in this or that book, in one of those creators that once a century renew the sensibility of human beings by enriching it with precious emotions, by discovering, like Debussy, invisible harmonies and unheard chords, by capturing, finally, all these mysterious waves that run through the ether of the soul. There is nothing great, efficacious, and exalting that was not found by *somebody*: Debussy's whole tone scale and parallel sevenths and ninths, Fauré's modulations are not collective phenomena but inventions that appeared one fine day[32]—a happy day on which all sorts of new joys began to exist for the ear and for the mind! Bergson would no doubt have refused to admit that an epic, a collection of fables necessarily have collective and anonymous origins. For we must not be ashamed of being too "humanist" when it comes to explaining the mystery of individual wills.

A humanist theory, Bergson's theory could be said to be "emotional-ist," and it is perhaps not a distortion to compare it to Newman's fideism. How can a pure idea ever yield action? How can we draw from a concept anything but more concepts? Your abstractions will never by themselves sprout into movement unless movement is already contained in them—but then you are cheating, and it is not astonishing that after having fertil-ized the intellect with emotion, you draw emotion from the intellect. You will find only what you put in. Bergson would certainly object to intellec-tualism what Schelling objects to Hegel: those who, from the first, place themselves in the "notional" may well monstrously stretch and inflate it; they will only ever find the notional. And then let us recall the distinction *Creative Evolution* makes between intellect and instinct: the intellect is "hypothetical" and specializes in establishing *relations*. What no intellect in the world will ever explain is what we may call, in a word, Preference, put differently, the *effective* election of a possible chosen and collected among other possibles. Why does this possibility, as Leibniz says, exist "preferably to the others"? Without emotion, neither finality nor "sufficient reason." Without emotion, all possibles are indifferent. Emotion is what makes our ideas want to *exist*.

And this, once again, is what resolutely distinguishes Bergson's axiology from his biology. Between the antitheses of *Two Sources* and those of *Cre-ative Evolution*, there is a displacement analogous to that which, in *Matter and Memory*, drives back into the past a spirituality that *Time and Free Will* reserved for the present. In *Creative Evolution*, instinct is closer to life than the intellect. To be sure, instinct is not intuition; infallible but narrow, it does not have the infinite competence of our intellectual organ; and the intellect, on the other hand, is the obligatory prelude of all intuition. De-spite everything, among these two, the one that most resembles intuition is ecstatic, penetrating, immediate instinct. Instinct coincides with the dyna-mism of Organization or, better, it is the vital élan itself captured live, across the clearings of matter. In *The Two Sources of Morality and Religion*, on the contrary, instinct presents itself to us rather in its conservative, cyclical, and family aspect. Does not life itself appear to us now as nourishing, now as conquering, according to whether our biology is more economist or more Nietzschean? *Two Sources*'s instinct automatically ensures the cohesion of the hive. It makes itself visible in the swirling of the species rather than in the élan of the person. Intellect, on the contrary, is all curiosity, inventiveness, risk-taking; the intellect loves adventures. Not that the Bergson of *Two Sources* has an unexpected soft spot for "intellectualism,"[33] but he does indicate, more clearly than elsewhere, the intermediary nature of the intellect, always in the middle between pressure and aspiration. There is in the intellect a principle of restlessness and an as if infinite itch that announces the freedom and impatience of the Mind. But, on the other hand, this instability, this fidgeting of our soul, does it not make us run the worst dangers? The intellect is a killjoy; in itching for adventure, it ends up compromising the very comfort and security of the closed society. This merits explanation.

The intellect was not made to get in the way of the designs of nature but to support them, to render them more efficacious—and here it turns against this nature. The intellect, which was to place itself at the service of life, wanted to know everything, even that which it had every interest in ignoring. It got mixed up in solving insolvable problems, the mystery of death and all the most secret things. And now the angel punishes it for its accursed curiosity! This is a paradox that usually does not receive enough attention and that, following Simmel, I would call the *Tragedy of consciousness*: the élan of life leads to structures that deceive life; freedom leads to a definitive choice in which it manages to make itself unrecognizable; the species in duration and the group in space hurt the individual who, in a derisive contradiction, needs the group and the species to affirm all its powers; "constitutive" memory, finally, expires in "constituted" memory, which nonetheless extends it. It is with the intellect as it is with the species, as it is with the accomplished act: life trusted the intellect in order to fully realize itself, but the intellect betrayed the hope of life.[34]

We are now in a better position than ever to respond to the stupid reproach, often repeated, that Bergson is a dualist. *It is the same life that yields the intellect and mystical intuition,*[35] just as it is the same élan that, turning on itself, topples circular societies and, tearing the enchanted circle of the species asunder, gives birth to heroism. There are not two substances but one single life that, being movement and tendency, can take itself the right way or the inverse. "Evil" is thus but a certain immanent direction of life, a temptation to draw back. We now understand what Bergson means by "dichotomy": there is no *duality* but *divergence*. The image of divergence marks out exactly what we intend to retain from dualism since it implies, on the one hand, community of origin and, on the other, progressive scission or, as Bergson says, "double frenzy."[36] Instinct and intellect are like two cousins who no longer know each other: the further they go, the more they separate. And yet they develop, each in his language, the same heredity, the same biological theme.

This theme of the Élan is still perceptible in closed morality. *Everything positive in instinct comes from life.* That is why mysticism already haunts magic, why in social obligation we already have a sense of charity. Nobody would believe in this bourgeois virtue if it did not vaguely resemble love, just like nobody would believe in the time of the mathematicians if there weren't in it a lingering allusion to pure duration. Profound irony of life! Closed morality needs to pass itself off as mysticism to inspire trust, and while the inclination to materialize survives even in mysticism, mysticism and dynamism, for their part, are one of the last chances for saving swirling morality. Up to this point, I have pointed above all to the negative and deceptive role of *imitation* in Bergson: the intellect counterfeits movement, duration, and life, and in the same way, enlightened self-interest is dying to resemble devotion. Do we have to recall how the intellect builds up the morality of the city by imitating instinct with habits, and static religion by imitating perception with phantasms? This mimetic is not a simple fraud, as *Creative Evolution* led us to believe. It testifies instead that the intellect and the very artifices of the intellect do not escape their spiritual heredity. Such are the clocks of the *Heure espagnole* or the crinoline dolls of the *Valses nobles et sentimentales*, in which Maurice Ravel succeeds in making a tenderly human heart beat. Steel and porcelain spectaculars! Everywhere a kind of illusory humanity awakens that is not absolutely mechanical. In this respect, Philistine morality, which is a kind of intellectual substitute, resembles the musician's automata: it owes its living and its being believed to its usurpation. It is the little that it is exclusively thanks to love; without love, it would be nothing. That is the good of evil, the positive of the negative.

That said, Bergson's philosophy will happen to speak in terms of dualist philosophy, just as we, even after Copernicus, happen to speak of the sun setting although it is the earth that turns. With implacable lucidity, Bergson detects the alloys or, as he says, the exchanges that take place among contrary realities; but the peculiarity of Bergson's philosophy is that it never loses sight of the amalgam being an amalgam, of the Concrete also being the Impure. Never before has a thinker captured with such marvelous subtlety the imperceptible effects of contamination and spiritual osmosis, these "ricochets" that allow social obligation to usurp the face of love, allow habit to imitate memory.[37]

We could show, on the topic of the "psycho-physiological paralogism," what acute virtuosity Bergson's dialectics deploys in the dosage of these Mixtures. That is a special talent of Bergson's he exercises on every occasion: he excels, for example, in finding the bastard divinities that are neither personal nor impersonal,[38] the equivocal concepts that are always undecided between obligation and necessity, between the law that commands and the law that expresses, between the social and the individual, between soul and mind, between pressure and aspiration.[39] Thus the religion of love needs an ecclesiastical skeleton to make itself visible and dogma, vice versa, would have no punch if it were not inhabited by love. Bergson never gets lost in these admixtures, he never takes the complex to be simple, he never confuses the original and the derivative. For example: justice benefits from a certain kind of charity to which it owes its drive, its warmth, its sparkle; vanity is completely filled with sympathy;[40] and sociability still rubs off on egotism and on desire [*envie*], which is not to say that desire is generous nor that sordid equality replaces love.

And it even seems to me that in Bergson's ethics, the "extreme cases" no longer appear under as theoretical an aspect as they do in *Matter and Memory*, for example. Thus mysticism stops being a pure limit, like pure recollection. Mysticism has realized itself somewhere in certain predestined souls who, bearers of a supernatural message, had almost found the center of the creative impulse. Nowhere more than in *Two Sources* does the Mind [*Esprit*] seem capable of making the flesh so transparent, glorious, and useless. The *principle of frenzy* certainly corresponds to this change of perspective. Unknown before the eschatology of the *Two Sources of Morality and Religion*, it expresses that every tendency will go to the very end of its possibilities. That, perhaps, is the reason for this new accent, for this tone of predication and even of utopia that Bergson courageously adopts in *Two Sources*. How else would we explain this call to simplicity that, in some ways, recalls Jules Michelet, Charles Fourier, and Jean-Jacques Rousseau? A third simplicity is added to the "two simplicities" of *Time and Free Will*, the simplicity of morals: for asceticism is to life what intuition is to organic and spiritual realities. As intuition at one fell swoop dissipates the undefined complications of mechanism, so asceticism strangles luxury, which is born from a too-civilized mechanism. Are not intellectual pseudo-problems the luxury of the mind? Perhaps there is even only one Simplicity, or rather one single spirit of simplicity, at once contemptuous of material riches and attentive to the true richness of the soul. There is thus no difference whatsoever between the pure movement that at once swallows up all of Zeno's aporias and the ascetic who leaps over the exuberant multiplicities of well-being in a single jump. For intuition is the asceticism of the mind; and asceticism, in turn, is nothing but intuition become the diet, catastasis, and permanent exercise of our soul.

Bergson's ethics is thus not for the lukewarm. "You are neither cold nor hot," says the book of Revelation. "So, because you are neither cold nor hot, I am about to spit you out of my mouth."[41] The cult of the inner life that filled *Time and Free Will* makes way for heroism. The activist and futurist progressivism of 1930 has supplanted the backward-looking solipsism and intimist introspection of 1890. In "The Perception of Change," Bergson still invites us to let ourselves be cradled and "lulled" by the melody of the inner life.[42] And alas! It is a cradle indeed in the age of big industry, of violence, and of urgent options! The intransigence in *Two Sources* thus reaches the acute limit of extremism, of radicalism, and of purism; Bergson visibly forever revokes the concessions that *Creative Evolution*, at certain moments, seemed to make. *All or nothing* seems definitely to be the motto of a philosophy that never admits degrees of intensity. Thus the nuance of finalism seems much more accentuated in *Two Sources* than it is in *Creative Evolution*. Never before had Bergson underlined the "intentions of nature," the utility of instinct and the intellect for life in such deliberately anthropomorphic language. *Matter and Memory*, certainly, knows of something like a finality of perception; but Bergson does not yet dare write what the messianism of *Two Sources* will later make him say: that the human being is the true "raison d'être" of creative evolution.[43] And let's not pretend that that, like the "sunset," is simply a manner of speaking, that things happen "as if" the human being were the goal of evolution. In reality, this teleology, like the principle of frenzy or the call for simplicity, is explained by Bergson's maximalism. As evolution progresses, the end of evolution appears more and more clearly. The intuition of *Creative Evolution* is but an instantaneous flash that now and then tears through the night of our conventional existence. In *The Two Sources of Morality and Religion*, the life of the saints has fixed, embodied, and perpetuated these victories of the mind. They are no longer intermittent victories. A hero represents a jump ahead in creative evolution. It is death in him that is dead. There is no longer so much intuition as revelation, apparition, or visitation. Just as prodigious precursors multiply as a great event approaches, so heroes undoubtedly announce to us the future age of the Mind. This age is already here as it would be if the body no longer weighed us down; that is what the men's choir proclaims at the end of Liszt's *Faust Symphony*: "What no-one could describe is here accomplished."[44]

CHAPTER 6

THE NOTHINGNESS OF CONCEPTS
AND THE PLENITUDE OF SPIRIT

For certainly, my friend, the attempt to separate all
existences from one another is a barbarism and utterly unworthy
of an educated or philosophical mind.—Plato

The critique of the ideas of disorder and nothingness is the key to Bergson's philosophy. Bergson has devoted some admirable pages to this problem, pages that might be among the most troubling ever written by a philosopher.[1] We have always had to read this critique between the lines. Bergson's speculation in its entirety lets us anticipate this critique, which shines through all of it. Life, we said, transcends finality because attraction, the mental equivalent of the impulse, would abolish the unforeseeability of evolutionary movement. And yet, life is pushed from behind, by a kind of organic cause. The free act is all creation and all geniality. And yet there is at its source a certain intentional state that orients it and inspires it. Intellection, finally, is indeed search, tension, and inventiveness. And yet it presupposes a "dynamic schema" that precedes it. And already we guess that the law of the things of the soul is, in a word, preexistence, that the mind is, so to speak, always anterior to the mind. Why, put off by the transcendence of causes that anticipate their effects, by the substantial priority of theses that prejudge of their conclusions, does spiritual life always demand a preexistence? And how does it nonetheless remain innovative, hostile despite everything to the economical mechanisms of doctrinal thought?

1. *Fabrication and Organization: The Demiurgic Prejudice*

Fabricating thought, which goes (in appearance) from less to more and from part to whole, needs a void to operate. The void is its natural environment, and that is why it tacitly presupposes the impossible possibility of nothingness. Where there was nothing, fabricating thought puts something. Out of little it makes a lot. With elements it composes totalities. And it hardly matters that the physical principle of conservation theoretically denies all creative power. In fact, and for the eye, fabrication is an increase in volume, it fills empty places. In Aristotle's list of movements, it would belong to the genus of growth and diminution.

As Bergson saw so well, this is no doubt due to practical preoccupations and notably to a representation of productivity and labor in terms of scale.[2] The more masons work, the higher the building rises. The more copyists copy, the longer their copy becomes. Fabricating labor is the only labor in which the amplification of the product is quantitatively, spatially proportional to the progress of action. A large share of Greek philosophy has lived on the sculptor's and architect's idea that there is a form that little by little smoothes brute matter, marble, granite, or wood, and confers an increasingly determinate existence on it. "What shall it be, a god, a table, or a basin?"[3] A technician's and artisan's thought willingly concentrates on this demiurgic elaboration of the indeterminate. It gladly presents itself with the spectacle of a "masterpiece" or, in the sense proper, of a *work* [*ouvrage*] progressively extracted from chaos by human industry. Is *hyle*, or matter, not originally the word for a rough tree trunk? What interests an instinctively artisanal, artful, and artistic mind the most in the world is the transition from a minimum of being to a maximum of being, from the *apeiron* to the *peperasmenon*, or from chaos to cosmos. Where there had been almost nothing, if not a neutral support without qualities, we witness the birth of a complete order, armed to the teeth with all predicates of existence. In Hesiod, Nyx (Night) and Erebus (Darkness) give birth to Aether (Brightness) and Hemera (Day),[4] that is to say, indeterminate night brings forth the bright day. Chaos is older than the Earth, the Earth than the Ocean, and the Ocean than the Sky. Hesiod's genealogy thus proceeds from the unformed and nebulous to the most luminous and most plastic beings. Creation is represented as a fabrication. As far as specious clarity and simplicity is concerned, this so-called creative fabrication also wins out over the idea of *transformation*. When it first appeared, the physical law of conservation did not state a spontaneous thought but responded to a demand of scientific reflection.

Chance [*Hasard*] is even more mythological and theological than the idea of a Cause. This is because the principle of causality, as Lachelier and Meyerson saw, is a principle of preexistence,[5] and because preexistence is not seen, it is inferred. What is seen are appearances and disappearances, novelties, catastrophes. At first, the permanence of matter, the continuity of natural metamorphoses, shock the mind, which is in the habit of considering the spectacle of the world as a drama in which accidents burst forth, in which capricious wills perpetually make and unmake things. But the creationist idea has taken refuge in metaphysics and theology. In this form, it has resisted better than the belief in spontaneous generations or in perpetual movement because it in fact poses the true metempirical problem. The human being is the only being that is astonished that it exists, Schopenhauer says in moving terms.[6] This is indeed the fundamental metaphysical need: radical contingency gathers up what the secondary contingencies tracked by science have lost. The first randomness is obviously that of existence in general. While we no longer ask in how many days and in what order God fabricated the world, we hope at least to shed light on the mystery of Being by deploying a sort of metaphysical void that would let us witness its gradual generation. The mind thus tends, as much as it can, to convert "substitution" either into creation or into annihilation;[7] or, if again you prefer Aristotle's formulas, "alteration" is more tiring for the mind than growth and diminution, more nuanced than generation and corruption. Only movements that start from nothingness... or lead back to it can be measured on a scale and translated into concepts. Let us show that fabricating geneticism, if it really started *from Nothing* [*Rien*] would never lead *to anything* [*rien*]. Does it not in fact lead to something because it furtively inserts something into its nothingness? What am I saying? It has already stowed away in the initial nonbeing everything that was, precisely, to be engendered. Is not this vicious circle the great sleight of hand of demiurgic philosophy?

(1) Already the critique of the notion of *intensity* in *Time and Free Will* is very enlightening on this point. Mechanicist common sense claims that a pain that "intensifies" really goes from less to more and from a little to a lot. It so to speak inflates or contracts in space. Psychological analysis, on the contrary, shows that our sensations do not transform quantitatively but qualitatively. They modulate without changing in magnitude. Where fabricating illusion dissolves "intensification" into an—always finite—multitude of fundamentally homogenous impressions (homogenous because they are only gradual, that is to say, they differ only in degree), the philosophy of qualitative plenitude treats intensification as a continuous movement in the course of which one and the same sensation successively reincarnates in an infinity of different forms.[8] Put differently, quantitative movements like growth and diminution are at once discontinuous and

uniform; qualitative changes, that is to say, mutation or alteration, impose a supple and dynamic unity on heterogeneous contents. Prejudices and theories have got us used to considering black an absence of color or a minimum of light,[9] and the various colors of the spectrum are said to arise from this minimum in a regular growth. But for a naive consciousness, which puts itself in the presence of immediate givens, black is a color like all the others, and its claim to existence is as founded psychologically as are the claims of the so-called positive colors. Yet we want colors at all costs to spread out along nice straight lines whose successive gradation would in a way give rhythm to the growth of a single colorless sensation. Black and white would be the two ends of this crescendo, the two extremes of this polarity. To this Manicheanism of black and white, Bergson opposes the thousand nuances of impressionism, the multicolored palette of hues and qualities. Black is neither a lesser white, as the quantitative philosophy of gradations would have it, nor its nocturnal antithesis, as the dualist and dramatic system of polarity would have it: it is a qualitative specificity as original as the others.

The demiurgic prejudice is the basis of the theories that consider muscle effort to be the emission of a certain substantial force preexistent in consciousness in lesser volume and so to speak in compressed form.[10] But above all, the critique of the idea of nothingness animates, invisibly and tacitly, all of *Matter and Memory*'s dualist argumentation. Why does idealism confuse perception and recollection?[11] Why does it not recognize the radical distinction between the extended and the unextended, between motor memory and pure memory?[12] Why if not because it, like all technicist thought, unconsciously obeys the absurd mania of fabrication? Extensive perception must constitute itself little by little in the growth of unextended sensations[13] just as the absence of color, by progressive and continuous inflation, would little by little become colored impression, or as instinct is gradually fabricated from accidental variations.[14] One would, for example, have a learned lesson be a sort of composite image arising from the superposition of successive readings that little by little, by repeating themselves, fabricate a certain motor habit. Between the complete habit and each of the readings that enter into its composition there would thus be the simple difference of the whole to the parts or of more to less. But who does not see that each reading already by itself constitutes a complete recollection? Recollection, far from resulting from an artificial apprenticeship, is given all at once in intuition. Recollection is not "learned." As the organism is born small but complete, in the manner of monads, so pure recollection surges up at a single stroke and entirely whole. In the same way, meaning is regenerated complete in each word; in the same way, the equation of the curve figures complete in each infinitesimal fragment of this curve. But the fabricating mania is tenacious. One claims that from representation to sensation, from image to idea, there is a whole range of imperceptible transitions. In the same way, attention in these theories results from a single movement of growth,[15] affection becomes extended by diminishing in intensity, perception becomes affective by strengthening itself.

Yet what non-prejudiced experience painfully reveals to us is something positive, original, and active, by no means a modality of representation. And likewise, attention appears as an "attitude" that is as original, as "indeductible" in its kind, as is the perception of the real as opposed to recollection or intelligent interpretation as opposed to raw sensation. Although Bergson does not do so in these terms, one could no doubt apply what I have earlier called *miniature theory*. One draws a great straight line between object and subject and gives oneself the satisfaction of following the rectilinear path from excitation to the moment in which it becomes representation. But all we can say is that the series begins with an excitation, ends with a representation, and that there is a moment in which the representation replaces the excitation without our being able to say with precision when that has happened.[16] This way, the Sorite's paradox of the Megarian school, worthy as it is of the Eleatic sophisms, is completely naturally conjured. Mutation is mobilized, repaired, freed from its curse; it starts up again and reaches its end.

Some crucial lines in *Creative Evolution* fully bring out the meaning of this criticism.[17] Fabricating illusion rests essentially on the prejudice that *only one part* of living bodies, free actions, or states of mind could have been realized, that their complete realization is "a kind of grace." This means precisely that the things of life are outside the category of growth and diminution, that they are not susceptible to more and less but only to "modifications." That is even why natural destructions, following Schopenhauer's remark, terrify the mind by their magnitude.[18] The discursive procedures of fabrication have got us used to a laborious movement of growth in the course of which things pass through all possible volumes one after the other, and we mentally scrutinize [*détailler*] these great catastrophes the way we scrutinize the appearance of beings.

But life, in this sense, is incorruptible and unengendered, and nowhere in the plenitude of the mind does the intellect find the fault into which it could insinuate itself to describe its genesis. The spiritual world is thick everywhere, just as in each of the circuits of recollection, memory, according to Bergson, is always wholly present.[19] Inequalities are purely qualitative and concern only the density of the milieu, never its visible thickness.

Would we say that disease sometimes causes breaches in this invulnerable plenitude? Not even that. Its diminution, if diminution there is, affects the *weight* rather than the number of states of consciousness.[20] The study of aphasia has proven the point: all of consciousness is affected, in its "attention to life" or in the vitality of its sensorimotor functions. Recollections lose their weight, the "sense of the real" declines, there is a functional weakening of all of memory. The dynamic equilibrium and the apt insertion of the mind into the things are, as we know, the most characteristic signs of mental health; when this health declines, all of our states are thus more or less affected. Could we even say that the pathological represents any "lessening" of the normal at all? Bergson's philosophy is original in showing that, on the contrary, disorders like hallucination, delirium, idée fixe are "presences" rather than absences or negations.[21] Mourgue and Monakow remark that classical neuropathology, that of the "localizers," treats nervous disorders as simple deficit phenomena, as "degenerations."[22] The very names it gives them express this negativity in their privative prefixes (aphasia, alexia, apraxia, agraphia...). Yet how can one nonetheless allow such a purely destructive lesion to entail such a series of positive symptoms?

There is a logic of insanity[23] the same way that there is a logic of dreams, of the imagination, and of the comical.[24] All these para-intellectual logics differ from normal logic, not at all by defects or rarefaction, but, on the contrary, by their deplorable exuberance. Between dream and waking state, it is certainly the dream that is more diffuse and, if we may say so, more fertile. In a sense, dreams are more "natural,"[25] and ordinarily, the waking state, as the phenomena of false recognition show, is but a narrowing of this disastrous vitality, a repression of frenzied forces always ready to deceive the vigilance of the mind. By thus affirming the positive character of morbidity, Bergson joins not only modern biology but also certain medical views of Schelling's and Baader's.[26] Life's pathological or teratological manifestations represent an "ataxic" order, an inflammation or disturbance of order, and by no means a rarified order. Temperance [*Temperatur*] becomes excited and turns into distemperance [*Distemperatur*]. Sick consciousness is not a lesser consciousness but rather a frantic or unleashed consciousness. It is no closer to nothingness in sickness than it is in health. Its vitality is unsettled but not lessened.

That is what I, for my part, expressed when I spoke of the *autarky* of organisms. Everything that is organic is perfectly and necessarily complete.[27] If we know how to take apart a machine, Leibniz says, it will yield real partial parts (even if here, too, a halo of intellectuality surrounds the simple and pure element). But we will never meet with one "half" of an organism, nor with a "quarter" or a "thousandth." Organicity is always present in its entirety, and it follows us into the infinite smallness of tissues and cells. There is never any quantitative decrease that would allow us to insert ourselves between two "fractions" and to seize the point starting from which life has fabricated itself. The same goes for individuals, the same goes for the least of mental contents. We may very well say (to take up Leibniz's formulas again) that the "point of view" of our various inner states is always of equal extent. What varies instead is the more or less profound manner in which the whole person finds itself expressed in them; what varies is *the spiritual weight of our emotions and not their volume.*

Bergson's critique of intensity already proves that the thought of nothingness is a nothingness of thought. Where there is more and less, zero is equally possible. Yet it is an entirely abstract fiction and an absurd fiction that has us consider "zero" to be a number—the smallest of numbers and a little also the source of numbers.[28] That is why children sometimes think that, because four times one makes four, four times zero must also make something, just a lot less. They do not see that zero is as heterogeneous to the order of quantities or magnitudes as nothing is heterogeneous to something. Between nullity and the most mediocre fraction of a unity, there is a metaphysical abyss that the regular succession of numbers and our mind's fabricating instinct invite us to cross. All our errors rest on the temptation to hypostasize the Nothing and presuppose the absurd idea *that the Nothing is the smallest conceivable Existence, that Nothingness is the limit of the infinitesimal, and that by dint of rarifying themselves presences become absences.* But the mind is not fabricated from atoms of spirituality, from absences of mind, no more than perception is fabricated from recollections, movement from *kinēmata*,[29] duration from instants, and action from rest. That is what we first had proven to us by the study of *intellection.*

(2) Bergson's theory of intellectual effort means that if one starts with nothing, one understands nothing, and that thought is so to speak the prisoner of its own plenitude. Thought only breathes in an a priori of positivity

and signification. There is no interpretation, no thought in general without a spiritual preexistence.[30] This is what Claude Bernard, for example, already observed when he brought out the ideality of experimental induction: "Just as man goes forward, in the natural movement of his body, only by putting one foot in front of the other, so in the natural movement of his mind, man goes forward only by putting one idea in front of the other. In other words, the mind, like the body, needs a primary point of support. The body's point of support is the ground which the foot feels; the mind's point of support is the known, that is, a truth or a principle of which the mind is aware. Man can learn nothing except by going from the known to the unknown."[31] This primary point of support—the physiologist's "idea a priori"—is already a little bit the dynamic schema that gives meaning to mute signs. And thus, not only do sensations and emotions resist all fabricating synthesis, but the very products of abstract reflection, such as concepts, these "indivisibles" of thought, are still totalities rich in meaning and quality. All of modern gnoseology invites us to see in thought in general a relation that subsists only by way of this very plenitude. A concept is not "an entity or a genus."[32] A concept, says Goblot, is virtually attributed in an infinity of judgments.[33]

There is no "pure attribute." Every attribute is part of a certain utterance that is the attribution and whose role it is to attribute it to a subject. Adjectives seem to represent the type of a pure predicate, but their purity is strictly grammatical and morphological. Adjectives are made for nouns to participate in their essence. Adjectives are made to qualify beings but, taken absolutely, they *are* not beings. Adjectives are abstract generalities, and a being is always a particular subject. Every attribute that is really thought, that is to say, every attribute that is not a simple formal paradigm, a sonorous sample, implies a determinate relation.

It is impossible to think of an absolute existence to which such and such a relation would not by virtue of that fact be immanent. The absolute concept is neither true nor false; it is that of which I affirm nothing, that which is indifferent and without relation to my mind; it is a suspended thought. Victor Brochard has brought to light the solidarity that ties error to judgment, and Bergson for his part insists on the spiritual plenitude of negation.[34] Their analyses show that a kind of melodic idea always circulates within reflective thought, and more specifically still, within the deficient relation where it seemed to us at first that it rarified itself: in the act of negation and in false belief. Just as language, according to Montaigne, "is made up of affirmative propositions,"[35] so thought, according to Bergson, only thinks by affirming. Whether it affirms or denies, thought is condemned to affirmation. The mind is never more totally present to itself than where the void seems to spread within it, when it denies and when it is wrong. That is why Socrates says to Theaetetus that those who speak about nothingness say nothing at all.[36] And the Eleatic stranger in the *Sophist* says that those who speak of nonbeing say nothing. Nothingness is strictly speaking "unthinkable, unutterable, unspeakable, indescribable."[37] We must neither define it nor name it. And as Plato denounced the contradictions into which nonbeing drives anyone who claims to speak of it, so Bergson does not tire of repeating that the idea of an abolition of everything implies a contradiction and a vicious circle "since the operation consists in destroying the very condition that makes the operation possible."[38] "By means of the observation itself, the observer must introduce the conditions whose absence he tries to observe."[39] We find the same idea expressed in exactly the same terms in the Romantic Carus: the idea of a positive Nothing is an idea as absurd (an *Unding*) as that of a square circle.[40] We may thus very well say, in the language of the *Sophist*, that negation expresses an alterity but by no means a nothingness: "When we speak of not-being, we speak . . . not of something opposed to being, but only different."[41] In Hesiod, the Chaos thanks to which theogony begins is a Gaping [*Béant*] rather than a Nothingness [*Néant*]. Even the abyss that, in Genesis, precedes the six days of cosmogonic creation, this abyss is not nothing since God's breath floats above the dark waters.[42] Plenitude can thus not be turned into nothing: we have to take its side lest we perpetually deny ourselves.

(3) Fabricating logic, which wants to build up thought from concepts ideally neutral between the true and the false, claims to construct free action from *indifferent* states. One operates with a *zero* of decision, as earlier with a *zero* of thought. The indeterminists imagine the deliberating person in a sort of spiritual void analogous to the one in which theologians place the Creator when they endeavor to explain radical Contingency. At first there was nothing, as in Hesiod's theogony; then the self came along; something built up—motives, motivations—which led to action. The hesitating will, pronouncing the words of decision in a nothingness of inner life and within a kind of vacuum chamber, would truly, literally be creative. It is thus supposed to be absolutely independent of the person as of all influence and all circumstance. It ignores everything I have experienced, everything that belongs to me, that I cherish or loathe, all of my past, my raison d'être, ignores, in the end: me. It is indifference. Indifferentist indeterminism has thus cleared the ground: only the desert and silence

and solitude, and the present totally oblivious of all preexistence, and the blackness totally devoid of all coexistence, and abstract adiaphoria, and pure ideal innocence could verify the exercise of an absolute freedom.

But who does not see that such a fiction is not only absurd but contradictory in itself? If the two branches of an alternative are not already rendered unequal by a differential and preferential qualification, a decision is inconceivable just as intellection is inconceivable when we refuse to presuppose the signification of the enigmas to be interpreted. The deciding *fiat*, the adventure of choice, are possible in their dynamic activism only because the indifferent hesitation that prepares them was at bottom already qualified and oriented. And the hesitating will takes this qualification from the self itself, from the integral, preexisting self, and it is there with all its capital of accumulated experiences, of tendencies, of needs, and of emotions. This is the price at which the will overcomes the dissolving and paralyzing abulia that is the ransom of an extreme freedom. For what is an extreme freedom if not an extreme servitude? The indifference hypothesis rests on the idea that the self can in a way preexist its own actions. Locked into an inhuman abstention, the will would be a spectator of the splitting of alternatives fate offers it; it would so to speak live twice at the same time.[43] But one only lives twice on the condition that one cut oneself off from any particular and actual experience. Past and future are still (or already) a qualified present. And in the same way: *I am the only one to be me.* If I consult my real present and not a phantomlike possible, it appears that *at the moment at which* I want, I only want one thing in each instant. In each instant, a preference, however subtle, orients the apparent confusion of our hesitation. No matter how hard we try, this is a debate in which we are always one of the parties. The belief that we have touched on the ideal impartiality of an indifferent referee is a vain belief: on the point of reaching it, we surprise ourselves in the act of expressing in our indifference a kind of preference in the second degree, a preference with exponent, the way we find our thought to be entirely whole at the moment of its annihilation. That is because I am always there, I who choose and who decree, and for me to reach this chimerical impassiveness, I would precisely have to suppress myself, my self, and my past. The self did not wait for the present situation to exist, and it is thanks to it that the voluntary act is not only a piece of eloquence but a drastic solution. We are ourselves much older and much more venerable than our actions: that is all our dignity, and we are deprived of it when one would have us decide without reason.

We do not decide, as Leibniz says, without rhyme or reason.[44] The absence of reasons is still a reason, the pleasure of acting without reasons being already a reason to act; or, as Friedrich Schlegel writes, the refusal to choose is itself a choice...[45] In this case, we can repeat with Pascal: those who are not with me are against me.[46] In other words: between *Against* and *For*, there is no neutral zone, just as between Good and Evil there is no median zone, no intermediary realm, no buffer state that would be neither the one nor the other. Everyone is tied in, everyone bets, and the very ones who think they can escape the dilemma have already implicitly bet, and those who have chosen to remain on shore have, in their way and even more so than the others, set off on the adventure. Everyone knows it, those who abstain vote, too, without knowing it! Lamennais, denouncing the impossibility of indifference, and Lev Karsavin, pleading against impartiality, have each in his way oriented this critique of the tabula rasa in the direction of a pathos-laden philosophy.[47] It is Leibniz, once again, who says, in a letter to Clarke: we want what we find good according to our taste, be it out of caprice or a spirit of contrariety, be it to prove our freedom.[48] The formula, in the *Meno*, according to which "desiring the good" is, so to speak, a pleonasm of, simply, "desiring,"[49] expresses this preferential plenitude of any free decision in optimistic terms. We "prefer" more or less covertly, and it is a non-sense to say that we make decisions in any absolute manner *whatsoever*. Buridan's aporia, just like the Eleatics' aporias, consist in fabricating the free act ex nihilo, and of course our sophists condemn free will to starve to death the way Zeno condemned the arrow to immobility. And yet the arrow reaches its target, and Achilles arrives first, and human beings eat their fill even though their contrary motives theoretically cancel each other out. These successes could not be explained if deliberation, far from being a pure dialectic debate, were not a prophecy. Deliberation prophesizes and anticipates the choice and prejudges it, which is why, strictly speaking, there are never either imponderable motives or indifferent alternatives. In Leibniz's moralism, intelligibility justified the universal indulgence of the wise who "despises almost nothing."[50] In DSRM, on the contrary, universal qualitative plenitude would justify an extremism of passion that, following the example of Revelation, spits out the lukewarm and the neutral.

"It is only order that is real."[51] This amounts to saying that I always find, in the infinite plenitude of my past, something to upset the balance of a neutral deliberation, something to take sides when everything is all the same to me. Leibniz observes that between points in "disorder," no matter how incoherently and fortuitously they are grouped together, it is always possible to trace a curve, find an order, a more or less complex equation and something like a rhythm or a formula whose latent regularity will be underlined by some kind of figure.[52] Astronomers have drawn constellations into stardust. And in the chaos of indeterminate whims we equally discern spiritual *constellations* that reveal to us, underneath the anarchy of indifference, an interested and oriented consciousness. To those who can see, does not wild nature offer the spectacle of a profound and vital order, of a "beautiful disorder," of which the English garden, for example, is the first stylization, while the "constellations" of parks *à la française* trace the symmetries of classical architecture? Eugenio d'Ors has brilliantly shown how the Baroque, despite its extravagances, its carnivals, and its paradoxology, obeys a law—this law is eccentric, but it is a law! The Baroque is not a pathological phenomenon, or, rather, the Baroque is a normal disease.

The most arbitrary of our acts appear to resemble somewhat what grammarians call *exceptions*. By definition, the "exception" denies the rule. Indirectly, however, the rule also sanctions the exception because it has its "exceptional" value only in relation to a necessary system to which it is attached by an intelligible link of kinship. With rebellious exceptions, our grammars draw "constellations" that bring out, within a primitive system, a relatively rational secondary system. Spiritual life is thus slave to its own coherence. Just as our reason, in the very act in which it attempts to localize the fortuitous, implies its virtual intelligibility, so the indeterminists can no sooner conceive absolute indifference than they restore a relative coherence to it of which they then vainly try to lighten the yoke. The human being, Schopenhauer said in criticizing optimistic pedagogy, is not a "moral zero."[53]

Nor are humans mental zeroes. Their liberty is not made from an illusory void that would set itself up between present and future. It is made, on the contrary, from plenitude and continuity. It is not a substantial and arbitrary creation. And nonetheless it is a renewal. For just as the number of lived experiences on which it draws is infinite, the combinations it imagines, the arabesques it unfolds, become radically unforeseeable. The most brilliant musician uses, in chords, intervals, groupings, and figures, a sonorous matter that existed before him. What will always be new is the order he introduces among these elements. "For even when painters try to create sirens and satyrs with the most extraordinary bodies," Descartes writes in the first of his *Meditations*, "they cannot give them natures which are new in all respects; they simply jumble up the limbs of different animals."[54] In fact, Bergson's creation is neither a creation ex nihilo nor a mechanical rearrangement of old elements[55] but, in contradictory fashion, it is a continually inventive immanence, an always-beginning improvisation among the innumerable plenitude of preexistences. There is no more a "great year" of spiritual combinations than there is one of musical combinations. And the very possibility of inexhaustibly reducing them to constellations testifies to their incorruptible youth.

More than that: Chance, insofar as it is the absolute limit of disorder beyond all conceivable order, is humanized, finalized, rendered intelligible in turn.[56] And correlatively, Despair, which is the radical impossibility of integrating tragic evil, in turn regenerates as hope. Just as the absurd is, in infinity, normalized in the positivity of becoming, so sorrow is, in infinity, digested, transfigured by the mediating power of futurition. There is thus nothing astonishing about Bergson's hero being not only optimistic, like Leibniz's sage, but first and above all joyous.

II. *On the Possible*

"It is only order that is real." Thus dissipate all the desperate problems that the illusion of nothingness allowed to surge up, at the head of which is the problem of radical contingency that occupies so important a place in the speculations of someone like Schelling, a problem that Leibniz's moralism had so ingeniously evaded. In a little known and marvelously lucid passage, Bergson shows the solidarity that unites this illusion with the prejudice of the *possible*.[57] Things, it is said, are possible before they are real, and they are more in their actual existence than in their possible existence. That is why one tries at all cost to have no voluntary decision without a deliberation in due form that precedes it. That is why our grammars go from the alphabet to syntax; our logics, from concept to judgment; and our psychology textbooks, from sensation to recollection. Experience can protest all it likes that concepts are virtual judgments, that words are implied sentences, and that sensations are emerging recollections: it seems reasonable, precisely, for things to follow this rectilinear progression and to exist "a little," that is to say potentially, before they exist actually, that is to say, "a lot." Our mind is unwittingly obsessed by the idea of perfection—in the metaphysical sense, that is to say by the image of a *quantity of being*. As if this quantity could vary! As if Being taken in its entirety changed in any other way than in quality! Never mind—one wants the dose of being in the will that deliberates to be lower than the dose of being in the will that decides, and one imagines the free will to stand at the crossroads of virtual actions the way Leibniz's God chooses between possibles...

Nonetheless, can we say that Bergson does not admit the Possible in any way? To answer this question, we need to distinguish between logical possibility and organic possibility. With respect to logical possibility, we can indeed say that it is nothing, that it makes no sense whatsoever because by definition it is not the object of any actual and particular experience. *Duration and Simultaneity*, for example, constantly opposes the possible to the real the way the fictitious is opposed to the perceived. Times are more or less dilated, dislocations of simultaneities and contractions of lengths are phantomlike virtualities that physicists pretend to take literally. In the same way, instants are only virtually stops, that is to say, they are actually nothing but could be realized if by some artifice I artificially immobilized time somewhere. Mathematics has specialized in determining these possibilities, which it can choose no matter where and no matter when. In the same way, finally, the indeterminists' possible act is not anything I have done but simply something I could have done.[58] The possible is an ambiguous being that in a way sits astride the Nothing and the Something. But in logical possibility, it is Nothing that prevails. *The possible is something that is nothing.* The idea of possibility only expresses that this nothing could exist, that no logical or theoretical obstacle opposes its existence. That, however, is a permission, not a promise.

Organic possibility, on the contrary, is a positive promise of reality, a hope.[59] It does not resemble Hegel's desertlike Nothing but Schelling's and Kierkegaard's attractive Nothingness.[60] This nothingness is now an élan toward the concrete and a *nisus formativus*, now a mystical indetermination, rich and profound and sonorous like the silence of the night. Possibility is nothing now but it will be, we are sure of it, and each of us, on the threshold of the real, experiences the certainty of our far-off future. Possibility expresses itself in futurity, not in potentiality. It is not a Platonic declaration but a genuine commitment that life enters into with itself. Not only does the germ (for that is its real name) promise where logical possibility permits but, starting right now, it keeps its promise. Can we in fact say that it is itself a zero of existence? On the contrary, the possible here is already something but it also represents, in a compressed state, an existence that will freely flower in the adult. The dynamic schema is not the complete work but neither is it nothing. The proof is that it does not prophesize just anything but only this determinate work. It is a particular, precise, and sharp possibility. Nor does anything less resemble an abstraction or a genus than the vital élan, this primitive unity in which all hopes for the future already slumber. And the same can be said of all the "emerging states" at whose description Bergson's philosophy excels: such is, for example, our primitive character that is in a way our emerging self and where Bergson, with marvelous delicacy, tracks down "all that we began to be ... all that we might have become."[61] An acute consciousness emerges from the extreme density of possibles without reality.[62] We might even say that the childhood of action is even richer than the adolescence of action, the way hope is wider than the future itself.

One will wonder how Bergson's philosophy, a nominalist and actualist philosophy, could make so much room for schemas, élans, virtual actions, and all the forms of embryonic or emerging thought that seem to shy away from immediate perception. We now see that organic possibility *is a thing that exists*, possessing the seminal powers of the complete adult. Moreover, intuition, to be actually and to be the immediate cognition [*science*] par excellence is no less infinitely wide. We may say: instinct is exclusively cognition of the *actual*. The intellect captures only the *possible* and does not wonder what possibles will exist. Only intuition is made to know the possibles that will be actual. Only intuition surprises the virtual at the precise moment of its passage to action. Intuition is thus indeed the cognition of immediate and particular things. It does not, however, limit itself to the narrow and bright zone of the accomplished given. It is competent wherever there is impulse, élan, tendency. Tendency is an appetite for reality; it is still present and given. Intuition thus does apply, if you like, to the possible, yet this possible, like youth, contains the impatience and enthusiasm of life.

Bergson's philosophy is thus a nominalism of the virtual, a paradoxical nominalism according to which duration, movement, tendency can be the object of particular albeit extralogical knowledge. On the other hand, the germ's richness and vitality do not depreciate the raison d'être and value of evolution. Evolution, let's not forget, is a "creative" evolution, and if Bergson destroys the demiurgic prejudice, which is founded on the idolatry of Nothingness, he does so to honor true creation. In the same way, we saw, he discredited the time of Spencer and the free will of the indeterminists only in order to raise pure duration and true freedom even higher. Creationism becomes the truth when we stop representing creation on the model of the artifices of human industry. Instead, creation in this sense is the very law of duration, the gushing forth of an always complete and always new existence. Fabrication is not creation, and there is something divine in the constant innovations of duration that in vain we would seek in the servile fabrications of an anthropomorphic intellect. The germ certainly contains everything that is necessary for the adult. But that is not enough. The germ expresses these preformed things in an entirely different language: in the language of reciprocal implication and of involution. Yet nobody would be happy with so elliptic, so concise a language. "To take place," we have often said, is not a vain formality; the real is incomparably superior to the possible in that it exists explicitly and openly.

What Bergson instinctively seeks to justify are the crises, the great adventures that allow becoming to modulate and progress, that make it such that action always innovates over against its antecedents, "being an advance upon them such as the fruit is upon the flower."[63] Truth be told, our immanentist vision of continuity does not make things easy for us— after all, nothing is less unforeseeable than fructification! But that may be so just in appearance. There is a theory for which change and creation remain forever impenetrable and that has already proven it to us by giving a childish explanation of the fact of volition: the philosophy of growth and diminution. Going from idea to act, where would we say that the idea ends, the action begins?[64] The sophism of the destruction of the heap (*acervus ruens*) naturally comes to mind.[65] In the philosophy of duration, on the contrary, change stops being an incomprehensible miracle. There is no longer any need to wonder how many "imperceptible variations" need to accumulate for us to be able to say: this is a new structure. Growth is continuous but all change is sudden. Retrospectively, this explains how Bergson, at the end of *Matter and Memory*, could discover the distant kinship between memory and perception without betraying the initial dualism. Each of my feelings is a microcosm, a sort of insular and autonomous empire; yet my duration works the miracle of continuing all these sentiments one into the other. How could creative evolution not accomplish what my personal duration accomplishes? And why would the qualitative difference of superposed levels keep us from going from one to the other without noticing, in a continuous development?

Besides, it is difficult to see why it would be impossible to tear apart the envelope of memory and immanence that grips our thought. From time to time, as the aesthetics of *Laughter* testifies, an intuition of matter in itself, a pure perception, settles in a consciousness devoid of prejudices and importunate recollections. This is a new youth, a beginning anew of all things and of ourselves. Just now, the mind suffocated, full of its own memory: in the restful silence of recollections, in the relative nothingness of our self, sensation will gush forth more vividly and more freshly. There is thus space for newness in the plenitude of the mind.

And thus the real is much better than the possible. Evolution is not useless because it says something the germ kept silent about. The great task, Schelling says, is to abstain. What, on the contrary, is essential, says the philosophy of creative evolution, is to be all one can be. This creative progress, down here, has a destination, a mission. Bergson, who discredits teleology and the idol of nothingness, does not, however, reject all polarity of values. There is still a good and an evil in Bergson's philosophy. There is, opposed and hostile to the ascent of life, a certain "negative" of which Bergson does not shy away from saying that it is an "inversion of the true positivity" and even a "suppression" or "diminution of positive reality."[66] Matter is interruption, absence rather than presence. It is true that this negation is not pure and simple nothingness. On three occasions in *Matter and Memory* and in terms that could appear slightly enigmatic at the time, Bergson announces that matter is a kind of annulled consciousness, "a consciousness where everything balances and compensates and neutralizes everything else." In material nature, actions and reactions, being always equal to each other, "hinder each other from standing out," and they keep each other in check.[67] We may easily compare the nullity of matter to the weight of the air: equal forces, exerted in all directions at once, mutually annul each other.

But there is a great difference between this latent gravity and the imponderable absolute. We now know that the least disequilibrium can manifest the heaviness and positivity of matter, the way the vacuum of the barometric chamber reveals the weight of the air. In the same way, *Creative Evolution* was later to say that consciousness surges up from the unconscious by virtue of a disequilibrium or an inequality between representation and action.[68] The unconscious is more an "annulled" consciousness than it is a "null" consciousness. It is a zero, if you like, but that is not nothing. This is all too obvious only on the day that a gap of any kind upsets this equilibrium. On the day our brain no longer opposes habits to habits and mechanisms to mechanisms, materiality's own tendencies free themselves and carry us away,[69] since the role of cerebration would be, precisely, to retain matter in this happy nullity, so favorable to the blossoming of the mind. But people get it wrong and mistake this nullity for an eternal zero, this *akinēsis energeia* [active inaction] for a pure and simple Nothing. The cruel revenge of matter is there to remind them of their error: "Not everything that is not in motion can be said to be at rest."[70] We can therefore affirm without reservation the absolute negativity of the anti-vital principle. Nonetheless, Bergson says somewhere that all that is positive about matter comes from the intellect, which reflects itself in matter as in its own work and results, therefore, from a mirage effect; here, it is nothingness that becomes the true.

In reality, I think, Bergson's matter is *negation* but in no way *nothingness*. Nothingness = non-sense, as we know. But negation is not nothingness. It is a movement that annuls another movement, a tendency that neutralizes another tendency, an active resistance. Negation itself is no longer negative. It becomes a refusal, a positive force. No doubt this explains the role, so useful and so affirmative, this resistance plays in the differentiation of species. Yet matter is indeed an inversion of life. This formula expresses—to use the language of physics here—that Bergson's philosophy has adopted a system of reference. Bergson's philosophy ultimately places itself in the point of view of life. From then on, it is matter that will be life reversed; it is matter that will undo what life does. In *Matter and Memory*, where this absolutism is not yet so declared, one could say at will that dreams are the diminution of something (when we place ourselves in the point of view of perception) or indeed that matter is the privation and degradation of a duration (when we place ourselves in the point of view of memory). Now we have taken sides: we are on the side of biological order, against the mechanical order. Once more, there is an order and a disorder. Finality will be even more passionate in *The Two Sources of Morality and Religion*.

What is to be rejected is finalist idolatry, and it alone. Evolution finds its veritable destination and yet we are not to look for what progress *wants*. There is no more a gaping void between the means and the end than there is between cause and effects. Like the will, creative evolution and open ethics operate in full plenitude! Here, Bergson's philosophy links up with Spinoza. Albert Thibaudet, in one of the most penetrating chapters of his description of Bergson's philosophy, did not get it wrong,[71] and I dare say that on this point, Bergson himself did not always do justice to Spinoza's intuitions. Everything that is, Spinoza says, is in virtue of an eternal necessity. It is as absurd to ask when nature has begun to exist as it would be inept to look for the origin and end of the equality of sides in an equilateral triangle. Things are more or less perfect in relation to our human needs (*usus hominum*). Absolutely speaking, the perfection of nature cannot be denied because it is identified with its power or virtue, which is necessary and infinite.[72] Spinoza, to be sure, is not concerned with duration or life but with mathematics, with a "mathematics, which is concerned not with ends, but only with the essences and properties of figures."[73] But who does not see that Spinoza's *mathesis* is destined, precisely, to chase out the throng of dialectical problems that a sincere mediation of the things of the soul would suffice to dissipate? What geometrical beings prepare us to understand is, in Léon Brunschvicg's expression, "the universe of a science that refuses to be carried away into the shades of virtuality, that brings everything into the light and into action..."[74] Equations and figures, we may add, oppose to us, like life does, an infinite plenitude. Nowhere does logic discover the least void, the least rarefaction of existence, or any gradations in "perfection" or quantity of being that could enable our corrosive aporias.

Nonetheless, pseudo-philosophers need a void of this kind to endow the superstition of finality with credibility. And, if we believe Spinoza, it is the same way for all prejudices concerning Good and Evil, the Beautiful and Ugly, Order and Disorder, Virtue and Sin, for all our complaints, our recriminations, our praises and our blames. That is why we admire like fools or detest with extravagance; that is why we madly hail things as miracles and invoke supernatural Art the moment we go more deeply into the "factory of the human body." This blissful astonishment (*stupor*)—Schopenhauer's "teleological astonishment"—has its source in our imagination. It is entirely subject to the disorders of the brain and by this very fact subjected to the anthropocentric point of view of discontinuity and oratory antinomies. Before the philosopher of intuition, the philosopher of geometrical order has underlined the relativity of the *ordo–confusio* opposition. Both thinkers agree in relating the idea of order to the peripheral parts of our mind—the imagination in Spinoza, the utilitarian intellect in Bergson. The imagination, fascinated by the schematism of language, articulates the unique phenomenon that is the history of the world in dramatic and discontinuous events. It dreads the plenitude of the mind and airs it out with voids and breaks. It assigns a *beginning* and an *end* to all things. It is creationist and finalist. There is, on the contrary, but one transposition to make to go from Spinoza's impassible universe to Bergson's qualified universe. The one like the other turns away from the nothingness of concepts and toward the plenitude of the mind. The one like the other invites us, "like an educated man, to understand, not to wonder, like a fool."[75]

And yet life has a vocation in this world. Its mission is to insert freedom into matter, to prepare the advent of the mind.[76] The idea of this vocation opposes Bergson's oriented evolution to Spinoza's philosophy. It is a history fertile in surprises, and it cannot be assigned any end that it does not immediately go beyond. Barely have we begun to enframe it in the clear limits of a program: it is already beyond them. As in Ludwig Tieck and Friedrich Schlegel, irrational forces burst open the rational forms that tried to curb the Dionysian élan of life.[77] But would it not still be a "program," this will to reject programs, this effort to break all frames? Let us recall that there is no pure caprice and that the ear will still find a harmonious order in even the most unheard-of dissonances. The contingency of evolution does not escape this inexorable law of intelligibility. While life does not remain within the forms of rigorous necessity, its unforeseeability, at least, is foreseeable. Thus we know that the eye goes for vision, the mind tends to elude, to dissimulate the very heavy body alongside which it must live. The existence of the body and of the brain make the prodigies of evolution and the destinies of the mind perceptible to us. It even appears that the mind could have ensured its liberation by entirely other paths.[78] Visibly, there is a higher end that alone counts and to which everything else must be sacrificed. It was not necessary that life had to contend with a matter that, as far as life is concerned, is good for nothing and that puts it in mortal danger at every step. Matter could, should not even exist. What sin has brought this metaphysical punishment on us? There is a radical contingency here that opposes Bergson's sense for mystery to Spinoza's philosophy. Creative evolution is the detour that a vitality weighed down by matter had to take. Evolution serves to heal us of our bodies. Amidst these obstacles, it restores the free mind whose advent is constantly delayed by the absurd presence of matter. Matter cannot be humanly explained. Afflicted by this burden, life spends an incredible ingenuity to lighten it. Our acts, by virtue of embellishing it, end up making us believe that it is the very organ of the mind. But why was it that so much skill had to vanquish so many obstacles? That is a question philosophy can no longer answer: eschatology will answer in its place, and, along with eschatology, the emotion and the prayer this eschatology excites. That is why Bergson's philosophy is not, like Spinoza's, accomplished in an intellectual love of God but in a mad and fervent hope.

When we penetrate, as Bergson managed to do, the operation of life, this is what we find: life appears as plenitude itself, as a continuous totality in which neither novelties that come from the senses nor our own creative acts can settle without blending in with the rest of our spiritual existence. That is to say not only that the adventitious given is never entirely transcendent to the mind because for us disorder exists only in a relatively ordered way, because words do not fabricate thought if they are not already hypothetically meaningful; I, too, am never entirely transcendent to myself, so to speak, because my will lives only on the sap of my past, because the free act is the one that I want with "all of my soul." The mental fiction that Bergson attempts to realize in order to prove the nothingness of nothingness[79] is the exact reversal of the fabricating myths geneticist philosophy spread in the eighteenth century—the philosophy of the clean slate, of Condillac's "statue,"[80] of the innocent savage, of the born blind. Bergson foils the ridiculous artifice of robinsonades, demonstrates the powerlessness of the conjurer to really write a first sign on his white page, to really populate his desert island. The philosophy of Plenitude lodges a challenge against moral nudism. Necessity, in Bergson as in Spinoza, means plenitude, and freedom is nothing but the central destiny of a self imprisoned by its own riches. To be sure, Bergson, like all nominalist philosophers, presupposes that each thought is present and particular. But thought is given to us precisely as the aptitude to conceive what one cannot perceive, to conceive the absolute, the entirely different order, the limit case at the point of contact between experience and the metempirical and, in the end, nothingness. But in truth, does not Bergson himself admit, with intuition, the possibility of a great breakthrough through which the human being pierces the ceiling of its finitude? And does not heroic sacrifice take the superhuman off the hinges of his or her being? In the end, Bergson has had only one enemy all his life: it is called Kantian Apriorism. No, the author of the "Introduction to Metaphysics" has not remained a captive of "psychologism"!

Along with the eristic pseudo-problems, the very possibility of skepticism vanishes. The philosophy of life is surrounded by certainties. As Friedrich Schlegel well saw, the philosophy of life is at the very center of what is evident. From the moment that the shadow of the possible invades the universe, giving rise to the illusory perspective of finality, disorder, and indifference, we get the idea that perhaps things could have been otherwise than they are. We even wonder, as metaphysics no doubt has the right to do, why there is Being rather than nothing. Contingency, and with contingency, doubt, are given at the same time as the false perspective of fabrication: for if being is susceptible to more and less, it is clear that it is also susceptible to zero. That, no doubt, is because the problem of quoddity was posed in terms of fabrication when it only lends itself to an instantaneous glimpse. The philosopher of geometrical order, too, had understood that skepticism always accompanies finalism and that, entirely to the contrary, the truth of an idea is but the very positivity of its existence when we think it in all its actual plenitude. That is why Spinoza considers the absolute faculties we call Will, Desire, Love, Regret to be "complete fictions, Metaphysical beings, universal notions," faculties that generate uncertainties and run false ideas into positive beings.[81] Descartes himself had the intellectual experience of the mental contradiction inherent to nothingness. More than that, his very approach manages to gauge the depth of this paradox of Bergson's, that negation is in many respects richer and fuller than affirmation.[82] The first certainty—the intimacy of a thought truly contemporaneous with itself—gushes forth precisely from radical doubt. In the same way, Socrates's ignorance is a positive knowledge, and Kierkegaard's irony refers to one of the most serious systems of reference. Once again, Bergson's philosophy brings out the vicious circle of radical skepticism and the kind of generous egoism that, linking up life with life, immerses my mind amidst obvious facts.

For we cannot get out of order.[83] This, in a way, is the counterpart of the Megarian aporias. Immersed in visible realities, all we have to do is open our eyes. But we have to open them. The mind, to take up an admirable phrase from Plotinus, "is always present to itself."[84] The philosophy of life would thus be an "actualist" philosophy. The kinship that makes Bergson's thought close to that of someone like Berkeley has long been noticed, as has the way in which the two philosophers, equally nominalist, equally hostile to unconscious abstractions, agree in purifying the immediately lived from the superstructures that encumber it. We remember an absence. But we perceive only presences.[85] Every idea is thus necessarily existent and present to consciousness. Bergson's philosophy is also naturally affirmative: forgetting raises doubts, recollection goes without saying. Presuming an immortal soul, the negator of nothingness liked to say: the onus of proof is on those who say no.[86] A single positive experience is infinitely more convincing than innumerable negations.

But a singular fatality has it that, in the very act in which its greatness affirms itself, the mind labors restlessly at its own destruction. Evolution sums up this tragedy. Life must come out of the possible to be complete, for there is nothing like the real. And yet it has everything to lose in running these risks. It will divide into species, deny itself at every step, give in to the temptations of matter. In the same way memory, which liberates our consciousness, is always about to deny it. Memory is naturally and constitutively retrospective. And the supreme irony is that without this retrospectivity, there is no representation, no knowledge, and no science. Memory excavates around consciousness a gaping void, the problematic void that is the first condition of objectivity—for objects are always projected at a certain distance from our present. But as it is the organ of leisure and of foresight, so it is also the source of vain regrets. Memory only liberates us by perpetually lagging behind life.

Is there an appeal against this supreme irony of culture? The function of the mind is not to elude contradiction but, on the contrary, to accept it wholeheartedly to resolve it. Between the obsession of the past and the chances of the future, there is space for a thought always contemporaneous with itself. This thought would like to be wrong about not being able to be wrong: it is obligatory truth. Around us and in us there are only pure facts. True, the pure fact is a mystery. But if mysticism is above all the acknowledgment of the pure fact, we can affirm that Bergson's philosophy is a mystical philosophy in the experiential sense of the word. Mysticism in this sense would be nothing but realism, that is to say, the humiliation of the understanding before the fact. In *Two Sources*, Bergson turns to Saint Theresa the way he turns to clinical practitioners in *Matter and Memory*, to biologists in *Creative Evolution*. Does not intuition demand from us the kind of intellectual humility that alone allows us to condescend to the existent and to the pure given? Movement, quality, the free act are no longer accountable to reason. As in "commonsense" philosophy, they are immediate and irreducible givens, pure and original facts that justify themselves by their mere presence, without waiting for consecration from our proofs.

The difficult thing is no longer to justify the given (the philosopher accepts it without asking for its credentials) but to find it. In the act of knowing, the mind perpetually gets in its own way. It would need to know how to remember, and also know how to forget, in order to coincide with itself. Forgetting is rejuvenation. It is forgetting that makes decisions more solemn, colors more vivid, and melodies more moving. If we knew how to forget and to gain deeper knowledge of ourselves, we would not judge works according to what we already know about their author, and our clear vision of things would not be obfuscated by insincere justifications. But this art of forgetting is the trickiest of all because "all that is beautiful is difficult."[87] We live amidst accomplished things that offer us the restful pleasure of reconstitutions. We do not resist the temptation of fabrication. We gather up words to make thoughts, motives and motivations to make acts, anatomical elements to make life. Alas, all that is missing, as Mephistopheles tells the student, is the *spiritual bond* "that made the parts a whole."[88]

CHAPTER 7

SIMPLICITY... AND JOY

O, how amiable this simplicity is!
Who will give it to me?

1. *On Simplicity*

It is not too surprising to see Bergson return to Simplicity in *The Two Sources of Morality and Religion*, a return he propounds in the register of prophets and preachers. At the same time as it urges us to step back and collect ourselves, all of the nominalism of plenitude urges us to this great and purifying simplification that makes the phantasms of pseudo-philosophy vanish. *Time and Free Will* distinguishes between two kinds of simplicity that oppose one another like fact and law[1]—one that is primary by nature, *protera tē physei*, and last by right and the other that is last in fact and first ideally. A logic that runs through the genealogical order backward reconstructs this order, lived in its place by consciousness, in reverse. Once it has been lived, the chronology such as it is yields to the deduction such as it should be. The first come last, the effects becomes causes, and what is derivative becomes primitive. The relationship between what is original historically and what is first ideally is the same relationship as that between germ and principle, between organic possibility and negative or abstract possibility. The simplest is thus not what you think.

Simplicity is of two kinds, now elementary and abstract, now concrete—and that is the source of the misunderstanding that troubles almost all disputes about priority in psychology. On the one hand, the simplicity of simplicism, by multiplying and combining with itself, builds up heavy structures of *complication*.[2] On the other hand, the simple is immediately given as intrinsic *complexity*. For "complex" and "complicated" are two different things: polyhedra of polyhedra, the macromolecules of organic chemistry, the composite structures of atomism are complicated. A lie, which is a consciousness of consciousness and, doubling itself, is also a consciousness of this consciousness, and on to infinity, is complicated; the relations of relations, mediations, relations and correlations in the second degree assumed by a *logos* that has become a *logismos*, finally, are complicated.

The complex simplicity that Henri Bergson in all circumstances demands we take as our starting point brings together the contradictory predicates of the one and the many.[3] Even better: it is beyond all categories and can be defined only by an apophatic description. Even more so than unity, one would call it a totality because, like the organism, it refers to particularities and because it presupposes, along with the harmony of antagonistic forces, all the rich connotations of synthesis. To compose it, the immanence of coexistence—the whole that comes alive in each part—has collaborated with the immanence of succession that makes the past survive in the present by means of memory and the present anticipate the future by means of preformation. And just as it explains our continuous duration, this system of mutual implication also explains the creative and unforeseeable newness of any free decision.

Here, then, we have face-to-face the indivisible simplicity of the *element* and the complex simplicity of the *total part*, indivisible thanks to the very infinity of the possible divisions to which it lends itself. The total part is simple in its inexhaustible comprehension, and the element is simple like "simple natures," insofar as it is pure and unalloyed. Of the element, we may say that it is negative, being the terminus ad quem or goal of a simplifying abstraction that step-by-step strips it of all its qualities to turn it into an insipid *stoikheion* [element], colorless and odorless like pure water. Whereas the other simplicity, the total part, is *ante rem*; like the dynamic schema,[4] the matrix of difference, it is all aflicker, fluttering, and aglitter with virtual qualities. It has not "become" simple by impoverishing itself and returning to the homogeneous. It is simple from the outset of the entire variegation of heterogeneous elements that interpenetrate underneath this unified face. Thus Plotinus is right: simplicity is always at the origin, and the principle (*arkhè*) is always the simplest (*haploustaton*): "for all that is not primal is not simple."[5] But this simplicity is not the major nudity—the primordial white, Rameau's "tyrant C"—from out of which the composite will come, not at all the transcendent presupposition of the multiple, but the plural itself in its greatest density.

The logical series thus starts where the lived order ends, and the alpha of the one hooks onto the omega of the other. In going back up the irreversible order of life, against the flow, logic strives to cover it with a superposable fabrication schema. But it manages neither to enumerate the innumerable nor to exhaust the inexhaustible, nor to reconstitute after the fact the infinitesimal movements of duration. Simple things must be done simply, which means: done like duration, which, by the miracle of futurition, effortlessly propels the teeming continuity of instants. To understand movement, for example, is to imitate and to go along with it. Diogenes, the simple man from Sinope, Diogenes, our eternal common sense, will always silence the cruel Zeno who is in each and every man. Did Eugenio d'Ors not rank the man from Elea among the "accursed philosophers"?[6] "One only knows how to reply but keeps marching along," says Joseph de Maistre. "Whither does it lead? Do not ask, go," Nietzsche cries out in the third *Untimely Meditation*.[7] Yet while the Eleatics and the scribes still wonder how movement is possible and get stuck in their aporias, Achilles catches up with the tortoise, then passes it. Does not Bergson also suggest we turn to Achilles: Achilles must know what he's doing, no?[8] Consult Achilles, listen to the melody, choose for yourselves!

Jacques Maritain would say that that is not an answer, and that knowing is thinking, not at all doing. In truth, it is not about "doing" but about redoing, in the sense in which Max Scheler says of sympathy that it is "reproduction."[9] In the sense, too, in which Philippe Fauré-Fremiet speaks of re-creation:[10] here every iteration is re-creative, that is to say creative, and the second time is as initial as the first. Yet in matters of movement we are all inventors. It is a thing in which everyone is competent, original, and *conditor alter* [second founder]. Thus, for example, the love I experience—Diotima's *Eros*[11]—is old newness, eternally young, fresh, and matinal by the grace of a repetition that is continuous beginning. Reliving is here a drastic realization in which secondariness and primariness are but one.

Besides, the facts are there: movements reach their goal, revolutions come about, and the consternated idealist, stopwatch in hand, is always lagging behind the event, still has not understood why Achilles makes short work of notional speculations. Effective change takes over, and Vadius,[12] getting bogged down in his hypothetical, quidditative, and rhetorical concepts, is still "studying his lexicon to find out the meanings of *scab* and of *arse*."[13] Idealism is a lack of courage.

Let us finally understand that the simplicity of movement and free action becomes intelligible for another kind of simplicity that would be coextensive with it: that flight of the mind, the entirely gnostic and drastic *sophia* that Bergson calls intuition. The infinite, if it is not absurd and contradictory, wants to be judged by its peers. That is why Henri Bremond says that poetic experience is to be interpreted *by redoing it*, by taking up oneself, as Claudel would say, the role of cause or *poiētēs* [maker]. And when Alain speaks of the profession, he confirms Bremond's poetics: "we learn *by trying*, not by thinking we're trying."[14]

This might explain in what respect intellection is at once efferent and afferent: we do not understand by starting with naked signs unless they already have a meaning (but then intellection is already presupposed). Nor do we understand starting with an unexpressed meaning, a broken-down meaning that would secondarily incarnate in words to make them significant... Starting from nothing, it is true, one understands nothing. But Bergson no less renounces the hegemonic precedence of a thought for which language would simply be a tool, a servant, or a vehicle. The imperious and ideological precedence of thought always has something mythological about it. Intellectualism holds to this logistical etiology and declares that one must conceive before one speaks, deliberate before one decides. And Bergson, for his part, would readily have admitted that form and content, essence and existence, possibility and reality surge up together in incarnation. Backward causality, thanks to which the effect is the cause of its own cause, is no less real than descending causality, and James's peripheral theory is no less right than intellectualism. Thus one can think *in* speaking, deliberate *in* choosing, or, like the poet, create the poem *in* making it and in having made it! The poetic act is not a unilateral relation but a mutuality of correlation. In the poetic act, expression and counter-expression, direct wave and induced wave, interfere. Is this coincidence of the centrifugal élan and its repercussion, of the élan and the countershock, not improvisation?

Aristotle, so attentive to the irrationality of practice, already knew that habit (*ethos*) gives rise to disposition (*hexis*) and that disposition, in turn, is the form of this matter and the condition for its exercise.[15] One must behave well to become good, but one must already be good to have good behavior. And in the same way, it is both true that I am fleeing because I am afraid and that I am afraid because I'm fleeing. It is *by playing the lyre* that one becomes a lyrist, and yet one must already be more or less a lyrist to play the lyre...[16] While one must seek to find, one must already have found to be able to seek! Pascal, speaking for those who seek anxiously, considered the search itself to be a first indication of the find. And Lequier, in search of freedom, also thought that the search is already a discovery...[17]

In truth, the precedence of totality, in intellection and in action, has already resolved the vicious circle: beyond the intellect that seeks without finding as well as beyond the instinct that finds without ever seeking any other thing, intuition is the miraculous coincidence of the worried search and the joyous find. One can desire what one has, just as one can learn what one knows. Militant activism breaks the circle, being at the same time the search and the first solution.[18] It is thus a matter of beginning— and the technical recipes that hold for the continuation apply neither to the beginning, the great word Beginning Jules Lequier speaks of, nor to the prime will. For one does not learn to begin... Alain, too, affirms that one must begin by ending...[19]

How do we go about wanting? Ask the scrupulous who have lost the function of taking action. To want, my God, you have to want it, the same way you need to create to create. This is a circle, though not at all a vicious one: a virtuous one, a healthy tautology, and the "beautiful danger" (*kalos kindunos*)[20] par excellence. The *causa sui* posits itself in the decree of a circular Because: one cannot answer but with the question! The way the *petitio principii* is resolved in the movement that makes this petition, so certainty, according to Renouvier, ripens in the free option itself, that is to say in the exercise of a thought in action. And in just the same way, movement, too, goes from the problem supposed to have initially been resolved to its explicit solution and heals the disease of Eleatic doubt.[21] It jumps into the water without waiting for the dialectic to have demonstrated movement to be possible—for once it is effective, the fact will a fortiori have been possible.

"Freedom is affirmed by an act of freedom," says Jules Lequier[22]— Lequier, who is looking for freedom, has also already found it! Liberty is proven only by a militant act of freedom. Freedom begins with itself. It freely chooses itself by betting on freedom, by adventurously preferring to be free! Freedom is a brilliant improvisation the way movement is a miraculous solution, and if it is true that genius is creative freedom par excellence, the role *Two Sources* assigns to the hero and to great innovators is no longer that astonishing. Just as Bergson's philosophy in general is to be thought in Bergsonian terms, and just as one demonstrates movement by moving, so freedom is proven by being tested, that is to say, by deciding, without translations or transpositions of any kind. Action, expressing itself in its own language, always presupposes freedom. In the same way that intuition captures time *temporally*, so it is in the gratuitous option that the will proves to be "automotive." The Gordian aporias and Zeno's scruples are decided from the outset by the anticipating spontaneity of a bet that itself is freedom. Instead of indirectly proving a problematic free will, Bergson, from the beginning, simply and without any precondition whatsoever, settles in the immediate evidence of freedom.

But simplicity is a grace that excludes all apprenticeship: "It would be necessary to have that grace to be able only to speak of it."[23] That is why it is so easy, when one has been converted to good will, to will absolutely, to will purely and simply. In the simplicity of the Will *tout court*, all the innumerable splits of wanting to will diminish. Passionate intention, exposing the vicious circle, puts an end to the never-ending prevarications of the *Velle*, that is, that hypocritical "will to will" that is but an alibi for vague desires and unwillingness or, more simply, nonwill [*nolonté*]. For one wills by willing, ipso facto!

The start and success of movement is resolved by routine before it is explained by dialectics—what could be simpler and clearer? What is simple where our action is concerned is no less simple where the operations of life are concerned. Here, the teleological astonishment that admires the infinite complication, the marvelous finality of organisms corresponds to Zeno's abulia, which constantly gets bogged down in scruples and hesitations. As incomprehensible as the fabrication of an eye seems when it is represented working from its elements the way a puzzle works, this "masterpiece" of nature becomes so economical and simple when we place ourselves from the outset in the "entirely different order." The coppersmith who has worked and forged the metal has not made all the grains of the piece with his two hands, but the piece has made itself all by itself in the flame. The photographer has not literally executed all the lifelike details of a scene because once the setting and the lighting had been chosen, he only had to develop the negative. Even the pastry cook who has baked the cake has not made the infinite pattern of the dough with his hands, but the heat of the fire has worked for him. The artisan, trusting the demiurgic spontaneity of his technique, intervenes manually only from time to time, to guide the automatism of material forces. Intention, which is creative only once at the beginning, simply triggers the physical operation and then finds itself immensely surpassed by it. What is true of mechanical work, despite the minimum of artificial manipulation it presupposes, is true all the more of an organism. It takes all our intellect's anthropomorphism to claim that nature has proportioned, in space, the fabulous, unimaginable, and unsettling complication of its industry to the infinitely small parts of anatomy and the complexity of physiology. And no more is there a juxtalinear correspondence between the neurons of the gray cortex and recollections than one can read the formative élan of life in the juxtaposition of assembled cells: they are two texts inadequate to one another. Who can claim to decipher word for word in the autonomous offspring the maternal impulsion from whence it came? Here as in the thing that has been wrought, the author is an author only at the beginning, to engender it. He is a thaumaturge who is himself astonished by the miracle he has caused. The human being decides, and then time rolls on by itself. The one who descends from the organizing intention to matter and from the center to the periphery will understand that the body represents an obstacle that has been evaded but not the means that has been employed: such is language, which dissimulates more than it expresses; such is thought, which has to make itself understood not thanks to words but despite them and by making them more transparent; such is all the acrobatics of "style."

Everything becomes simple[24] and natural when we think the living vitally [*penser vitalement le vivant*], when we follow the vital movement that goes from the totality to the elements *for stronger reasons*. But the marvelously viable structures of vitality become chancy and hesitant when we reconstruct *from weaker reasons* and by combining the parts... and not only the vital structures but the symmetries of crystals, the graceful arabesques of snow, and the decorative figures of the kaleidoscope, too. We might as well calculate the age of the captain when all we know is the speed of the ship.[25] That is why Bergson speaks so often about prodigies as entirely simple and natural things: telepathy, the survival of the soul, and the plurality of worlds no longer make us dizzy. And the thaumaturgies of nature, in turn, no longer strike the imagination so forcefully!

In springtime, nature does not wake up the daisies in the field one by one, nor does it hang the blossoms on the trees one by one. Nature can spare a blossom. It is the misers who, getting the scale wrong, do the inventory and dress the list of blossoms the way they count their pennies. In this respect, the indivisible élan of generosity has something of spring about it: the heroic sacrifice, like the élan of the vital charge or the progress toward vision, is the simplest action in the world. For an upside-down philosophy, it's like emptying the ocean with a spoon. But for a philosophy right side up, which goes in the same direction as life and starts from the center by going a fortiori from vision to the eye, the difficulties no longer exist. The continuity of innumerable instants, which the maniac spelled out one by one, leads entirely naturally to the mutation.

That's not all. There is in the intellect a principle of frenetic inflation and indefinite exaggeration that stems from the downward slope of consciousness itself. Consciousness, once it has split itself, when the smooth brow of its innocence has begun to furrow, no longer resists the proliferating madness. Taken with dizziness, consciousness finds no arbitrary reason within itself to stop... This is the logos of fugues and counterpoint that does not stop thickening its polyphony, the baroquish imbroglio that complicates its puzzles as it pleases, makes its labyrinths more intricate, and gets tangled up in all the inextricable it has fabricated. From exponent to exponent, and given the dialectical speed of complication, God knows how far megalomaniac consciousness will go! While around it, the proliferation of luxuries becomes heavier, consciousness makes itself more and more subtle and becomes imponderable, aerial, and super-ironic. Out with excess, records, arms races, and ornaments, in with rarefaction and extreme preciousness. Is this contrast of a tropical technique and a meager consciousness occupied with nitpicking not the very definition of decadence?

Before this monstrous skyscraper collapses, before the catastrophe that will make this windbag with its swollen body and this pea-sized soul die of indigestion, Henri Bergson announces that wisdom is the spirit of simplicity.[26] Like Leo Tolstoy, Bergson invites us to penitence and austerity. We must expiate the luxury born from technology, and impose on ourselves, in a spirit of renunciation, the purgative path of poverty and sobriety... The automatism of concepts and the polluting embellishments of civilizations are two forms of pleonastic profusion. Sophism, in this respect, is not the anti-logos but, as the sorite paradox shows, a plethoric logos, linear reasoning pushed to the point of frenzy or, in the language of Pascal, geometrical deduction. Did not *Mind-Energy* and *Laughter* describe an exuberant logic of madness, dreaming, or the comic? The tower of Babel and Zeno's paradoxes—two forms of the unsolvable that stem from a lack of understanding the instant, uninhibited movement, sudden conversion. And watch how our classics purge consciousness of the mannerism of rhetoric, which encumbered it with frills, eccentricities, and curiosa, to convert it to sober modesty. Bergson is this classic, the enemy of trinkets, calligrams, and twisted problems, the enemy, finally, of charlatans and jugglers.

The jugglers, who know their conjuring tricks, have nonetheless reproached him with volatilizing "problems" instead of solving them. The intellect does not easily renounce its enigmas and great riddles—evil, nothingness, free will... The intellect is angry with Bergson for thwarting its pseudo-problems.[27] But it is typical of cheaters to hide the real problem by inventing an artificial problem to take its place. "We first raise a dust and then complain we cannot see."[28] Hence Zeno's sophisms, and Paul Langevin's projectile, and so many other relativist paradoxes, so many hyperbolical utopias and "impossible suppositions" compared to which the Eleatic and Megarian aporias are inoffensive games. Consciousness enjoys getting dizzy from these absurdities. And Bergson, for his part, simply says that when the problem does not exist, it is not to be raised.

"All these monsters aren't real at all," writes Fénelon. "To make them disappear, all you have to do is not look at or listen to them willingly. Just let them vanish: simple nonresistance will dissipate them."[29] This is not, as it is in Tolstoy, about disarming evil with the supernatural injustice of forgiveness (because evil is inexistent), nor even, as according to the Gospel's precept, about loving one's enemies (because there is no enemy), nor, finally, about evading the obstacle by persuasion (because there is no obstacle): it is only about untangling the complex by analysis. This is what Socrates's irony did, dissipating rhetorical and sophistical phantasms. Who knows? When Bergson takes over Christ's invitation to scandalously turn the other cheek,[30] he does so not only in the name of open charity but perhaps also because malice is but a misunderstanding, because the malicious are simply sulkers. Is a "fuss" not about confusion as much as it is about enmity? Just as one keeps a temptation at bay not by a tension or pathetic contraction of all muscles but, instead, by gently refusing to consent to it any longer, so it is not necessary to exorcize the demons that twist me up and to brace myself against their resistance...[31] Instead it takes, as Fénelon thinks, a certain abandon, "something flexible and indifferent that succeeds without our thinking of it."[32] No, becoming tense does not do any good and neither is contracture really effort. One might perhaps rail against Bergson's alleged counseling of laziness and resignation; and one does not see that it is precisely this facility that is difficult; and one feigns ignorance of this violent inversion of all habits, this radical reform that is at the basis of Bergson's catharsis.[33]

Simplicity is not simplicism. In the same way we might say that the depth of memory raises no fewer problems than the virginity of sensation. The difficult thing is not to interpret the percept by dint of associations and recollections but to recover a fresh, ingenious, juvenile vision of the given. *Haplōsis* [simplification] has no more a historical sense than the sense with which Rousseau endows the return to an idyllics and to original innocence. It is less about phylogenesis than about personal ascetics, less about lightening up or cutting down on the excesses of luxury than about obtaining an intimate and qualitative conversion of consciousness as a whole, to inflect its direction itself. That is the true *haplōsis*, the one that is not negative even if it is a purging of the soul. Let us be clear: Bergson does not claim that all problems stem from misunderstandings—as if, for example, we would just have to sit down at the piano with simplicity in order to play with virtuosity and in order for the imaginary problems of technique to melt away. It is not enough in order for the fiery tongues of the Spirit to rest on men, for mute tongues to become untied or for the gift of languages and polyglot garrulousness to suddenly animate the nations... Let's not count on magic, nor on thaumaturgy, but instead on labor—for nobody escapes the irreplaceable Event. Achilles dashes off... and the problem no longer exists. No doubt. But he still needs to dash off and not in a dream but in truth, that is to say, effectively. He needs to dash off himself and in person.

To make a long story short: it is not necessary to clench our teeth, knit our brows, and sweat (because one can sweat and have one's head empty) but we must nonetheless *will*, and nobody can will in my place. Will, and not break off the fight in any way. Good will, which neither resigns itself nor convulses, begins painfully and from the outset with the decisive *fiat* as intellection begins with the totality, then lets itself flow gently toward the evidence of movement. Thus, in the transition from waking to sleeping, where all that is lacking is the first decision, the soul falls asleep because it stops bracing itself in order to sleep, because it consents to dreams. And in the effort of recall, the fleeting word presents itself gently to a spontaneity that renounces to force it with violence and constraint and that, being its own mnemotechnique onto itself, begins by ending! Is willing to will not simpler than breathing, falling asleep, or existing?

Now we can say: we should have thought of that! But to think, one precisely had to already have found, such that the solution was in the question itself, the way the "purloined letter," in Edgar Allan Poe, was not in a deep hiding place but on the table. And one wonders why we could look in such remote places for the key to an enigma that is no more secret than the midday sun. How did we not think of it sooner? The quarry was at our feet, and we did not see it, says Plato about justice.[34] And Pierre Bezukhov, musing over life: "How simple and good it is . . . How could I not have known before?" And Ivan Ilyich thinks on his deathbed: "'How right and how simple'. . . In place of death there was light."[35] Say that we complicate so many problems with our lack of simplicity, of naturalness, and trust! And that an imperceptible mutation of the will is enough not to resolve but to dissolve at one fell swoop the aporias arising from scruples! It is easy to say, for example, that saints and heroes treat obstacles with disdain or act as if they did not exist: saints and heroes deny that there is a problem.[36] Difficulties? They do not even see them. Suffering, enemies, death, even? None of that any longer exists for them... Whereas dosed, gradated, and rationed devotion is a laborious duty; infinite sacrifice and total abnegation, going to the limit, no longer cost anything. Dying for others becomes as simple as ABC.

Yes, the mystic sees simply. And for the simple, everything is simple. The alternatives and contradictions that exist only for a retrospective vision of the mind melt away as if by magic. Our embarrassment instantaneously turns into certainty, and your obstacles become my reasons: this is the liquidation or liquefaction of pseudo-difficulties, the great thawing of our soul and, in a way, the first springtime warmth that wakes up and mobilizes our will, imprisoned in its Eleatic ice shelf. Achilles, Buridan's ass, stiffened consciousness—look at them all stretching their legs, shaking off the indifference that paralyzed them—conjuring, finally, Diodorus's old curses: it is divine matinal simplicity that loosens their limbs and gives back the easy, natural, infallible gait we see in them. Jesus says to the paralytic in Capernaum, "stand up and walk,"[37] and the paralytic, miraculously healed, that is to say, freed from his spell, becomes as mobile as Achilles... Who knows? Maybe it was an Eleatic sophism that nailed him to his modest bedstead! In getting up with simplicity, he decrees his disease to be inexistent. Jesus resuscitates the dead as if death itself were a misunderstanding, a belief, the product of an imaginary suggestion, and he commands the strips of cloth that shackle Lazarus's arms and legs to unbind him.[38]

We have to understand that the grace of movement and simplicity suddenly mobilizes the man knotted and tied up in his complications. In the blink of an eye, consciousness has surveyed all the thickness of the sky that separates Defiance and Love. The lie, from its first degree onward and to the infinite, will multiply its malice, folds, and frauds. In this reflective regression, its head is spinning; it becomes maniacal and impalpable like scruples. Watch how Bergson speaks of the doubter panicked by the same vertigo of reduction as the liar: he closes the door, then verifies that it has been closed, then immediately checks his verification.[39] He hesitates indefinitely only because he wants to be absolutely sure and because he has no absolute certainty if not in the spontaneity of a first movement accorded to the present. Plotinus is on the verge of admitting, beyond the first "it thinks," a second "it thinks" tasked with thinking the first, and, one thing leading to the next, a third for thinking that thought ("it thinks that it thinks that it thinks" and so on "to infinity"). Yet, facing absurdity, he catches himself and compresses the double thought, the one that thinks itself and the one that thinks the intelligible, into a single intuition ("a single application of the mind").[40]

Above all, gnostic love, and it alone, would have this simple, direct, and absolutely human figure that ironical consciousness imitates in vain. For the inspirations of love are eloquent. If one had to find through study and courtesy what love knows from the first thanks to an omniscient gnosis, it would be, as Leibniz says, like having "the ocean to drink." One might as well reconstruct, in a Darwinian manner, instinct with some pretty marquetry work. Love knows in all cases what it has to do. There is no need to tell it because before we even open our mouths, it has already done it. This is—is it not?—the immense and refreshing simplicity, the one that unties the Gordian knot of complexities as if it were child's play. Ariadne's thread, which leads Theseus through the convoluted meanderings of the Labyrinth built by the ingenious Daedalus, is love. That was the miraculous find: love, the infallible guide, unravels all complication. And it gets better: Daedalus, lost in his own labyrinth, fabricates wings for himself and flies off into the air, under the very nose of the stunned monsters. He simply flies over the artificial problem he has himself fabricated; he suppresses, with a kind of "Gordian" solution, the imbroglio he has himself complicated. Is that not the straight and narrow path par excellence? The path of rectitude and simplicity? The "follow your heart" can do what the learned could not, and perhaps it is time to give it its true name, which is Innocence.

"In this point is something simple, infinitely simple, so extraordinarily simple that the philosopher has never succeeded in saying it."[41] This simplest of simplicities invites us first to *Seriousness* and then to *Joy*.

To seriousness because simplification is above all other things "essentialization" or reduction to what is essential. Life is short and wisdom has no time for trinkets and periphrase. Only the essential! Bergson would take Socrates's side against Gorgias's verbosity, or Molière's against the rhetoricians' exordia, ceremonies, and circumlocutions, against *Homo loquax*, as he says.[42] Against the spirit of redundancy, he represents beautiful aridity. Bergson wanted to cleanse life of the formal bombast and the grammatical categories that muddy it to obtain, by distillation, the concentrated alcohol of duration. Such is the instinct that goes straight for its target, without preambles or putting on airs, and no longer looks for complications where there are none... Bergson's philosophy is the search for the *immediate* given. "Let us go directly to movement and examine it without any interposed concept."[43] One would think it was Fénelon speaking: "Carry on then . . . Carry on regardless . . . We must quite simply go our way. Everything extra you put there is too much and forms a cloud between God and you."[44] This is the regime of severe nudity, the philosophical poverty *Two Sources* induces us to. Is this not the ideal of frugality that Erik Satie and Charles Koechlin and the very asceticism of Fauré are striving for? "Semplice" (simply) is Fauré's advice in his last works:[45] for, like the operation of nature, the masterpiece is "made from nothing." We might call music without notes, something like the song of the soul, what is softly, in its sovereign poverty, sung by the Capriccio of the *Pièces brèves*, in which there is nothing but the life of the everyday and the miracle of divine poetry.

As we will have to show in conclusion, this extreme sobriety, this asceticism without matter, is the state most favorable to the radiating of Joy. Thus come together, in the pacific ocean of simplicity, Bergson's joy, Fénelon's pure love, and Gabriel Fauré's immense nocturnal peace, the peace that rises from the *Requiem*, the *Treize Nocturnes*, and the *Chanson d'Ève* like a sky from the origin of time. There are thus not two simplicities but a single simplicity that is poverty of diet and innocence of knowledge together. This double simplicity is but another name for joy, since in it, feeling and acting have stopped being inversely proportionate to one another. The philosophy we want would give us both, since in the end the two are but one—doing with knowing, the effective with the ideal or, as Plotinus says, "simplicity of character along with purity of thinking."[46]

II. *Bergson's Optimism*

Bergson dared call himself an optimist,[47] and perhaps it is this basic optimism that explains the disaffection toward the greatest philosopher of the twentieth century that today reigns among the frivolous and the violent. Perhaps for the first time in the history of doctrines, mobilism no longer explains the unhappy condition of the creature. So much had an immemorial prejudice, shared by Plato, Plotinus, Christian theology, and nineteenth-century pessimism, linked beatitude to thoughts of stability and hieratic immobility that becoming weighed down on the human being like a curse. The philosophy of *Creative Evolution* reverses the traditional relationships consecrated by perennial statism and puts a philosophy that had been walking upside down back in its place. No longer is movement the wait before a goal; now it is stopping that is an interrupted process, and the concept that is a suspended thought. Time is no longer a moving image and a degradation of eternity; on the contrary, the eternal is a phantasm and an immobile image of time. Time is no longer a negation or dilution of eternity: time is instead the affirmative positivity par excellence of which eternity is a privation. Time does not derive from anything else either by relaxation or degradation but is an absolutely original and irreducible specificity. As a result, the human being does not save himself by escaping into some unrepresentable eternity but, on the contrary, by planting roots in temporal existence. "I am of those whose desires are on earth," says a poet set to music by Fauré.[48]

Pessimism was but a disappointed contemplationism. There is one point at least on which Schopenhauer agrees with Clement of Alexandra, with the *Phaedo*, and even with Aristotle: the vocation of the creature is unchangeable. *To flee*[49]—that is therefore the only remedy this metaphysics of chimerical transcendence and of desertion can offer. Yet languor turns into joy when the creature ceases to regard itself an exile in the midst of Heraclitian becoming, and instead recognizes in change its true homeland and its very substance. Those who pity Bergson's "mobilism" are thus Eleatics, and they are more to be pitied than Bergson! The man of time does not have to expiate his temporality as if it were a sin. Whereas a Catharist consciousness glimpses beatitude only as a nostalgic past or a supernatural future, that is to say only as that unhappy hope promised to uprooted souls, the man of duration, for his part, finds joy on the spot, in the very immanence and fascinating present of his historical *Down-here*. The man of duration is no longer a pilgrim on earth, nor is the duration of man a vain detour devoid of meaning. As long as becoming was a futile circuit and a tedious circumlocution, a periphrase of the eternal, history appeared either as a punishment or a boring wait for the final judgment. Bergson recuperates all this lost time. And he thus gives a new intensity to this *vitae meditatio* [meditation of life] that Spinoza, already, wanted to substitute for the *Phaedo*'s thanatological wisdom. Becoming is not dying on a low flame or moping by doing crosswords while waiting for the end. It is realizing oneself to infinity.

(1) In the perfectly present, always lived and particular plenitude of becoming, there is no place for the idols of unhappy metaphysics: nothingness, negation, chaos, the possible, the void, evil, the *beneplacitum indifferens* [pleasure of the undifferentiated] and so on. For negation is still a positing and even a double positing, and nothingness is something, and the void a plenitude, and disorder an unexpected order, and the possible, in its way, an actual experience. Scaled gradations are reduced to verbal myths invented for the needs of fabrication. Like Chance or Evil, Despair is an unreal limit. Despair, as the absolute impossibility of coming to terms with misfortune, is no doubt a bogeyman. Does the despair that emerges from the Tragic not stem from a confusion between the infinite chances of futurition and the objective crescendo of a danger? Day after day, the affirmative and mediating positivity of becoming normalizes the absurd; our dignity adopts a modus vivendi with shame, and our everyday optimism reconstitutes itself around bad luck and pain. It is a digestion and a continual transfiguration of misfortune and an indefatigable regeneration of hope! The vital order is no sooner disturbed by disease than consciousness already finds a fallback position in a more subtle order. The opening through which "the joyous song of the future" reaches us reconstitutes itself at every moment and to the infinite.[50] That is how, by opposite means, by way of the experience of duration and by way of the super-rational vision of the eternal-necessary, Bergson's nominalism and Spinoza's actualism end in the same wisdom, the same meditation of life. This wisdom chases away the black butterflies of metaphysical anxiety. The champions of modern anxiety and modern defeatism were angry at it for thus frivolizing their precious "problematic," as those say today who speak German in French.[51] They reproach it for the "psychologistic," subjectivist and even anthropological optimism of its critique. False problems, they protest—that is quickly said! Things must not sort themselves out too well, too quickly, too simply. Fénelon, let us recall, had already answered them: "All these monsters aren't real at all..."[52] But the friends of the insoluble do not willingly part with their black butterflies. They do not understand that in opposing the experience of nothingness as a nothingness of experience, Bergson's presentism has managed to exclusively refute a literary cheat that sets up the nothing, the amorphous, and nonbeing as positive objects of experience. No need to be tragic, being serious is enough. The

miraculous simplicity of intuition, in which the phantasms of retrospection dissipate, the scrupulous aporias of the Eleatics get resolved, and all misunderstandings are explained, this simplicity is at once an effective experience of everyday empiricity and an instantaneous relationship of the creature with the metempirical. In regard to gnostic love, how could the great *haplōsis* to which we are invited not be a purification?

(2) Bergson did not believe that a tragic antagonism lived at that heart of being, that the vinculum or symbiosis of soul and body was at once paradoxically impossible and necessary. He often said that the eye is both the organ of and an obstacle to vision; that the brain is both instrument of and impediment to memory; that language, finally, only expresses thought by preventing and distorting it. Yet the contradiction of *Quia* and *Quamvis* in no way gives rise to an unsolvable tension, and the last word incontestably belongs to the *Quamvis*. There is thus no torn-apart consciousness, and no more is there a dialectical debate between contradictories: the contradiction in the end leads to viable and stable structures. Thus for Bergson the tragic conflict Julius Bahnsen discovered at the heart of the real does not exist.[53] Georg Simmel has held it against Bergson (the obstacle, precisely, being the means) that he fails to recognize the tragic of our mysterious condition.[54] That is because for Bergson's philosophy, the amphiboly is destined to resolve itself. His reflections on telepathy also led him to grant plausibility to the hypothesis of a soul *haneu orgnanon* [entirely an instrument] that would not be a lost soul. And we know that in the immensity of memory, in the brain's overflowing with the infinite mass of recollections, Bergson saw a presumption in favor of the independence of the spiritual principle and, therefore, in favor of an afterlife. This ending, as happy as it is easy, sometimes appeared on the horizon of a mad eschatological hope... For immortality is perhaps but the limit of the positive plenitude discovered in the becoming of ipseity. Recall *Creative Evolution* and the epic end of its third chapter, where humanity is compared to "one immense army" at a gallop, whose "overwhelming charge" can "clear the most formidable obstacles, *perhaps even death*"![55] What if by chance death, that is to say nothingness par excellence, were itself but the pseudo-problem par excellence, something like a Zenoian hyper-aporia, engendered by an ignorance of mutation and by the absence of simplicity? What if death were but a misunderstanding? And since vital becoming, which is all plenitude, already implies a continual transubstantiation, that is to say, a continuity of radical mutations, why would the lethal mutation, which is the radical mutation par excellence, not take place in full plenitude?

Rather than the transition *from everything to nothing*, why would death not be the change *of everything to everything*? The impossible-necessary par excellence, the one that seals forever the absurdity of our condition, the impossible-necessary is perhaps itself not all that ineluctable, so inevitable, so metaphysically invincible! Have chimerism and utopism ever pushed the hyperbole as far as this empiricist attached to facts? The vital élan is stronger than death. Freedom kills death in the divine folly of the sacrifice for others. And to announce the death of death—"death will be no more"[56]—Bergson goes back to the accent of the Prophets and of Revelation. The deification of the human being—is that not, in the end, the last word of *Two Sources* and as if the testament of an "atragic" philosophy that, as part of personal duration, has rediscovered the vocation of history and of cosmic evolution?

(3) The death of death and the nothingness of nothingness mean, to be frank, the failure of failure and the defeat of defeatism. Intuition bears witness that the common creature, forsaking the stamp of its commonness, can break the finitude of its amphibious nature, coincide with the real, outside of the gnoseological categories and outside of the relativity the vinculum imposes on it, and finally get back in touch with the original sources of being and the generative *arkhē* of life. Intuition means that the *natured* creature is not entirely cut off from naturing nature. Is not Bergson's "realism" a victory over pessimism? Just as at one point—in the evolution of the human—the vital élan strides across the barrier, so the empirical creature at certain points and at certain instants succeeds in breaking through to the metempirical. Like the vital élan, intuition bursts through the ceiling of the A priori. The vocation of the vital élan, *hormē*, is the triumph of freedom, and in fact it inserts into matter a dose of increasing indetermination: progress definitively has the last word. In Bergson's philosophy, there is thus no place for the complexes of failure, impasse, and deception, nor for the convicts of Schopenhauer's Non-sense, Ixion and Sisyphus.[57] The knights of the Absurd won't have an ally in Bergson.

The symptom of these triumphs is *Joy*: not Leibniz's *Gaudium*, which is good cheer, good conscience, and good digestion, but Spinoza's *Laetitia* instead, which is the passage *ad majorem perfectionem* [to greater perfection]. And it is not even *Laetitia*, which is an affection and whose opposite is sadness, but Spinoza's Beatitude in person, which is beyond pleasure and pain and which transcends all disjunctions and all dichotomies the way pure light without admixtures transcends the antithesis of fire and shadows.[58] But in Bergson, it is the very act of transcending and it is the very act of victory that make the triumphant stroke of lightning shine. There is contentment in continuing, that is to say in remaining or keeping, in staying, imitating, or conserving, but there is joy in beginning and creating. Euphoria and well-being emerge from the equilibrium of duty fulfilled, which is the passive past participle of possession. But joy emerges from the effort to be fulfilled. While *Gaudium* results from a mediocre pragmatist success, the philosophy of the Vital Élan paradoxically links up with Spinoza's *Generositas*.[59] Generosity is the last word of *Creative Mind*. The human being, joyous not to have but to give, nor to hoard treasure but to spend, nor to spare but to sacrifice itself, that human being is very precisely *mad* with joy because this rejoicing is a folly, a wise folly, much wiser, certainly, than the mad rational wisdom of the principle of economy and conservation. Satisfaction says, *Satis!* That's enough! It aspires only to conserve *the same*, whereas joy, in this resembling love, says: Never too much! Always more! Joy is thus indeed the symptom of a More. Joy is very precisely the state of grace, that is to say, purely creative efference without counterstrikes or ulterior motives or returns of reflection. Gabriel Marcel says that it is the very gushing forth of being and the plenitude of this being. Yes, Bergson is an optimist but not at all in the Leibnizian, bourgeois, and satisfied sense of the superlative Optimum. The sage who has lunched well is *quite happy* to inhabit this good and decent universe where there are so many liars and sharks but which (it being understood that not everything is possible for God) is still the best of possible worlds. This is the landlords' way of being "optimistic" or "maximalist." Whereas *anagkē stēnai* [lit., "the force to stand"] summed up the metaphysics of a common wisdom that tends constantly to close up, *dei anabēnai* ["there are many reasons for going higher"] would be the motto of an open metaphysics.[60] For an omnipotent freedom that remains open to the infinite, there is neither an optimum nor a maximum in action since it is stronger than death, since it kills death in the mad hyperbole of sacrifice. This freedom can precisely do everything! The alternative of instinct and intellect is paradoxically transcended: with a single sudden élan consciousness leaps into the beyond of all antitheses. But we must realize that if eudemonia continues all along the interval, joy for its part is entirely gathered up in the *Fiat* or the *Fit* of the luminal instant. While *Time and Free Will* still accommodates the well-being of an immanent continuity lived "as it comes," *Two Sources* detaches in the heart of the discontinuous protuberances that are the mystery of mutation and adventurous thaumaturgy and the point of contact of the empirical with the absolute. It is in the lightning stroke of the instant that joy declares itself.

And yet this burning joy, of which Pascal's *Memorial* speaks and that is the symptom of great certainties, in Bergson leads to equanimity. *Laetitia*, violent and incandescent, painfully born in the passion of victory, is the very opposite of an ambition. That is why serenity and joy seem so much like siblings. The jubilation and exultation of joy becomes possible for a consciousness relieved of the worries of scruple and the returns of reflection, that is to say for a pure heart. Gracious joy, to which a simple heart also disposes us, is not so much Dionysian as it is quietist. Change is the very substance of being, and the philosophy of becoming leads those who follow along in the direction of duration not to mobilism but to tranquility of soul. For *Laetitia* is quietude. Not at all static like Epicurus's *galēnē* [calm], and yet calm and without impatience. Joy and philosophy, Epicurus says, are daughters of the same instant...[61] Is not this instant, which appears to us as a fine point, decidedly a kind of eternal present? Not at all, certainly, an intemporal eternity, but an eternity in full becoming, an eternity of life!

Bergson's oeuvre is thus the opposite of a "treatise on despair." And yet it does not contradict Kierkegaard's oeuvre, as one might think. Kierkegaard and Bergson represent two inverse and complementary aspects of one and the same modernity. To unhappy modernity's tragic *saltus* [leap] responds Bergson's joyous instant, which is, at the summit of the soul, the calm and entirely gracious intuition of an absolute. Intuition, like pure love and like the heroic effort, only endures for the Almost-nothing of an instant, which is to say, it does not endure—but this *Quasi nihil* is already like eternity when compared to the absurd *Nihil* of despair. Not that Bergson was completely unfamiliar with this "tragic sense of life" that was so profoundly sincere in Unamuno and in the philosophy, full of pathos, of Lev Shestov. But he did protest against the absurd and refused to yield to anxiety. Intuition finds the Absolute by surprise, but it finds it... An infinite hope, a powerful élan propels both creative evolution and open ethics. Vital Energy, Spiritual Élan! Those who were young during the other postwar period will no doubt melancholically compare the *disperato* in fashion today with the rejoicing of those years when, after crushing the cannibals, everything seemed possible. "We will live!" Penelope and Ulysses echo one another at the end of the third act of Fauré's *Pénélope*. Bergson's Joy, the music of light by Darius Milhaud, Charles Koechlin, Federico Mompou, and Maurice Ravel ("I drink to joy!"),[62] the tide of hope that lifts the last pieces of Fauré's up toward a "chimeric horizon" were phenomena of the same order. Bergson was simple and cheerful. Bergson, like Fauré's *Pénélope*, was confident. For what better response to cruel Zeno and to Mephistophelian sophisms than confidence? A kind of springtime rejoicing animates Bergson's last works. It is also not only for the sake of the beyond but for this world itself, in which it is our destiny to live, that the philosophy of freedom offers us liberation and emergence into the light. *Libera me de morte aeterna* [Deliver me from death eternal]. And who does not in fact think of the liturgical prose of the Requiem from which Fauré has drawn so sublime an entreaty? To the deceased that we all are, to the automata fascinated by the dark lake, to the living dead of daily defeat, render the exercise of liberty. Grant us that we may not fall back into the deep shadows. Grant us both the quietude of becoming and the drunkenness of freedom, the wise duration and the happy minute, this evening's peace and this morning's joy.

APPENDICES

BERGSON AND JUDAISM

The problem of the relationship between Bergson and Judaism lies entirely in the conjunction "and." Moreover, for our problem to be clear in itself, Judaism would need to have a univocal meaning. But this religion seems to be at the same time and paradoxically traditionalist and messianic, formalist in some respects, emotionalist in others. Judaism is the Law, but it is also Prophecy, and within the Law itself there is both a juridical and a mystical aspect. Judaism is Talmudism, but it is also the Hasidic spiritualism so profoundly examined by Martin Buber. To the problem of evil, for example, Judaism provides contradictory responses, the rationalists treating it as privative, some Kabbalists, in contrast, acknowledging a form of positivity in it. This contradiction is not for that matter absent from Bergsonism itself, which oscillates between two contradictory definitions of evil, and there is also a Bergson who is turned toward the past, in *Time and Free Will*, for example, and a Bergson who, in *Creative Evolution* and *Two Sources*, looks rather toward the future.

If there are several Judaisms and if Bergsonism itself is a complex philosophy, able to justify both a conservative attachment to the past and a form of futurism, both tradition and messianism, our comparison is in danger of becoming quite confused. Moreover, certain themes in Bergson that effectively appear to be biblical, such as the idea of creation or the idea of freedom, can just as well be derived from his reading of the Christian mystics.[1] Conversely, to the extent that the doctrine of creative evolution excludes traditional dogmatism and the idea of the transcendent Creator, Bergson is no less opposed to Christianity than to Judaism. We are thus on an uncomfortable footing in a difficult subject area.

Before discovering the deep affinities, if there are any, let's define what, at first glance, opposes Bergson to Judaism. Those who deny any creative talent in the dilettante of duration and the inner melody accuse Bergson of dragging substance into the flux of becoming. Becoming, the solvent of being, would prevent Bergson from building a genuine architectonic system. We can recognize the same inability to provide grounds for the Absolute in two other great theories contemporary with Bergson's: Einstein's physical relativism and Georg Simmel's philosophical relativism, which alike dismiss any system of reference, would effectively fall victim to the same reproach. We should firstly respond to this that while Georg Simmel, in *The View on Life*, was in effect influenced by Bergson, Bergson by contrast, in *Duration and Simultaneity*, conducted a lively polemic against Einstein in the name of the duration of common sense.

But even if we suppose Bergson to be a relativist, are we to think that renouncing a system of reference, mobilizing substance, involving the observer and instruments of measure in movement are symptoms of Judaism? In that case there would be nothing Jewish about Hebrew monotheism and Spinoza, who subtracts substance from time and gives reason the privilege of being able to consider things "under a certain aspect of eternity"; Spinoza, who affirms everything that Bergson denies, would be the opposite of a Jew. It will be said that Spinoza was precisely excluded from the synagogue. But it wasn't for his eternitarian and static monism that he was excommunicated! And for that matter, Bergson, who professes diametrically opposed ideas, went right to the very edge of apostasy. In fact we don't see why "Heraclitism" would be, rather than Eleatism, a Jewish specialty: if that were the case we would have to believe that all of the dynamism, historicism, and evolutionism of the nineteenth century was a product of Judaism. The incoherent, arbitrary, and contradictory nature of these reproaches and journalistic generalizations is thus glaringly obvious.

ha!

There is a form of temporalism in the Bible that, at first glance, may appear specious. *Creative Evolution*, for the first time, reversed the immemorial pronouncement of Plato's *Timaeus*, taken up again by Plotinus: "time is a moving image of eternity,"[2] a pronouncement according to which eternity is the model and time is the inconsistent and quasi-nonexistent image. André Neher radically opposes Hebrew historicism or temporalism and Greek eternalism: the Bible presents itself as a story—first of all the six days of Creation, a series of grandiose events staggered over a week, then the event of sin and finally the historical chronicles. These are three distinct forms of temporality:

1. The *fiat* of the absolute Beginning and the nameless cosmogonic events that follow it are gathered together in a nicely filled Hexameron. These catastrophes, cataclysms, and cataboles, hanging on an initiative more radical than any "clinamen," are expressed in the Scripture in a tense that would be our *passé simple* (simple past or preterite): "Dieu dit" [God said], "Dieu fit l'espace" [God made space], "Il fut soir, il fut matin" [There was evening, there was morning].[3] The perfective or semelfactive form of the preterite tense is applied to events that happen once. Is there not as great a distance between the story of Genesis and the Greek cosmogonies,[4] as between the Creator and the Demiurge, between the God of Abraham and the "author of mathematical truths" or "of the order of the elements"?[5] The high temporal drama of Genesis is no less distinct from the "eternal events" and monstrous ahistorical convulsions recounted in Hesiod's *Theogony*, and it is quite the opposite of a "procession," because what is more opposed to an intemporal Emanation than a succession of decrees?

2. Creation is the absolutely radical origin of all created things, but the free sin of the creature is the relatively radical origin of history. After the cosmogonic ephemerides, the moral event called sin—a sin of disobedience, betrayal, and curiosity—is an accident that is if not absolutely primordial then at least relatively so, occurring at a given moment not at the heart of nonbeing, like the original being, but during the intemporal existence of an already-created creature. This contingent fault disturbs the eternal, ahistorical paradise that was supposed to be established in the Garden of Eden. The evil suggestion of the snake, the temptation of woman, and the sin of man are the three moral events of this ill-fated series. If Adam hadn't given in to his companion and she to the snake, if the keeper of the Garden of Felicity had not partaken of the forbidden fruit, there would be no reason for anything ever to come to pass—because bliss has no history. Just as if the atoms had fallen through the Epicurean void in a perpetual free fall, if the minimal event required for there to be a world had never happened, namely the arbitrary deviation of an atom, the physical universe in its various arrangements, its aggregates of all kinds and its bodies of many shapes, could not have formed: the monotonous fall would have continued *usque ad saecula saeculorum* [continually for all eternity] without anything ever coming to pass. Everything became possible from

the moment a single atom, for no reason, veered off its course. You have to start somewhere! Give me this bare minimum that is the clinamen, and I will give you the whole of nature with its minerals, its rocks, its mountain ranges. Give me the first sin of the first man, and I will give you the whole of history with its curious tales and its massacres. Adam's sin is the first crazy idea, the first inflection or deviation of a free will that suddenly stops willing with God, and just as the clinamen produces ricochets and collisions, so the guilty decision engenders the lumps and nodules that result in the tumultuous conflicts of History.

The initial alteration called sin gets historical time under way: the sinner instigates history and with history are unleashed the vicissitudes, ups and downs, mishaps, eras and episodes that diversify this great adventure. The first complication, which is to say the first kink in the undisturbed eternity of Edenic bliss, will effectively make all the subsequent complications easier; the first free step (the first step is the only one that counts) will produce, in a sort of dizzying bidding war, a string of disasters, a cascade of misfortunes, a cataract of cataclysms: "And the Lord saw the sin of man multiplied over the earth."[6] After the expulsion from Paradise we have the crime of Cain, then the Flood and the confusion of Babel. The sins become more and more serious: Cain's fratricide ups the ante on Adam's disobedience; acts of violence and murders multiply with the speed of an avalanche. The hurried pace of the genealogies goes hand in hand with the frantically accelerated tempo of the chronology. This deterioration constitutes the very historicity of the drama whose sequence was set in motion by the first man, thereby inaugurating a becoming.

3. After the cosmogonic chronicle and the ante-historical, immemorial act of sin, there is the historical record proper, in this case the annals and *res gestae* of the Israelite nation. It is true that this nation is a privileged people, that its story is a "holy" one, and that the vicissitudes of this supernatural destiny shed light on human destiny in general. And yet a fallen humanity can't skip any steps, miss any stations, or skimp on the successive moments in the theological drama of its destiny; this duration cannot be compressed. "A whole world born in a day!" exclaims the prophet Isaiah,[7] because only an unprecedented miracle can save us from proceeding *per gradus debitos*; no magic can reduce to a durationless instant the biological time of gestation. Just as Bergson must wait for the sugar to melt in his glass[8] (because no one can compress the time of fusion, nor in general the duration of changes in state, and physical time is as incompressible as the biological time of a fever), so Israel must await the coming

of its Messiah. Let us give up, with the *Philebus*, the adialectical *euthus* ("immediately") of the impatient.

The temporality that comes to light in the cosmogonic Hexameron, in this initial contingency that is the *parégklisis* ("summons" or "exhortation") of the first will and in the annals of the people of Israel, is it a time in the Bergsonian sense of the word? At first glance one is tempted to say no.

1. Time begins with the fall: history is the child of shame, since it is the child of sin; theologically it is akin to the reflection, shadow, and lesser being, like the Platonic time the *Timaeus* called a moving image of eternity. This explains the shifting transience and artificial character of becoming. In Ecclesiastes the pathos of disillusionment further accentuates the depreciation of time: historical time is a lost time and the vainest of vanities, sterile and monotonous, a perpetual and pointless repetition where beginning and end meet. The curse cast by the Lord on the first offender— you shall return to the earth from whence you came, dust you were, to dust you shall return[9]—weighs heavily on the accursed of Ecclesiastes: it is written in the arc of the sun, in the course of the wind, and the cycle of water. But what is a movement where the end point is the starting point, where the *quo* and *unde* coincide, if not an infernal wheel and a Sisyphean torture? What is a time where what will be is what was and what is already done, where the future leads to the past and the omega to the alpha, where the future is a past in reverse, if not a bewitched time, a cursed time? Death acts as a counterweight to birth, war to peace, "catagenesis" to "anagenesis" and every positive action (building, planting, finding, keeping, loving, and so on) has its symmetrical negative one (destruction, uprooting, losing, dissipation, hating) that balances and cancels it out; the Deed finds its heartbreaking counterpart in the Undoing, "There is nothing new under the sun." What could be more opposed to a "creative evolution"? The time of Ecclesiastes is not the fertile, irreversible, progressive time of ripening and gestation but a stationary or circular time and an absurd detour. "What's the use?" asks Ecclesiastes.[10] How better to question the purpose of a becoming that becomes nothing and consequently contradicts its vocation as becoming and gives the lie to its promises. It is a form of alteration that instead of engendering the other, instead of placing its temporal stress on the other, amounts to the same thing and goes round in circles—that is the monster of cursed time!

This circle excludes not only innovation but memory: the past of *Time and Free Will* is as foreign to it as the future of *Creative Evolution*.

It is not a dimension where treasures can be acquired and piled up, where property can be capitalized, where the fruits of one's labor are amassed and one's works preserved over time but rather the realm of oblivion and dissipation. It is neither conservation nor permanence but rather waste, sterile loss, and pure insubstantiality. Here we think less of a Sisyphus without a future than of the wastefulness of the Danaides. "Our days on earth are like a shadow," we read in the book of Job, and in the Chronicles man is only a guest here below.[11] This image of an image, reflection of a reflection, obviously looks less like Bergson's duration than Plato's *eicon kinēstē* ("moving image") or even Heraclitus's *potmou roē* ("river flow"). Is not man's volatility, the disavowals of a creature unfaithful to the Covenant and the legacy handed down to him, the natural consequence of this lack of substance?

2. Biblical time resembles a large-scale fresco or a long tapestry fully laid out along a wall: its moments are, so to speak, given in space. Bergson would no doubt have said that this time is not evolution in the making but an already-evolved and thus spatialized evolution. Edmond Fleg notes that for many Talmudists the moments of this time could be reversed and that their chronology is ultimately an indifferent matter. The holy story is like a text where you can dip into any section at will, reverse the order, retrospectively freeze an episode, recapitulate its development. An already-developed development, an already-elapsed becoming, biblical time is the opposite of the Bergsonian "in-the-making." Biblical time is not the time of its own contemporaries, a time lived as it unfolds, but rather the panoramic and posthumous time of a theological history where the theologian is both a super-consciousness and a retro-consciousness: an "over-consciousness" looking down on Israel's trajectory and the historical field of its destiny, a retrospective consciousness comparing the different events of this trajectory after the fact. The spectacular and terrible events that punctuate the career of the chosen people, while not eternal events like those of the *Theogony*, are nevertheless normative and somewhat detemporalized: the crossing of the Red Sea, the breaking of the Tablets of Stone, the victory of David over the Amalekites, resemble in this respect the events of Christ's life, whose anniversaries we commemorate with holidays. These events, immortalized in painting and poetry, celebrated on fixed dates of the calendar, periodically recur according to a uniform rhythm, and have thus lost any unpredictable character.

3. History is not only a fallen, stretched out, degenerate form of eternity, or a fully elapsed duration: its outcome also seems to be stripped

of any element of chance. The result doesn't seem to be subject to any doubt, and we can place our bets safely: the direction of human destiny is as predictable as that of a metaphysical drama whose successive stages we know in advance. In this case biblical time would be lacking the only feature that, according to Bergson, can temporalize time: unpredictability. Unpredictability is the untamed and intractable element, disturbing and exciting, the random element, in a word, that constitutes the risk of temporal being. When we do not know what tomorrow will bring, it is time to tremble and the heart beats faster. In the vast panorama of the holy story the element of adventure and risk of the gamble seem reduced to a minimum. This story that excludes the novelty inherent to a genuine "futurition" seems rather an easy adventure. The protagonist of this chanceless adventure may not experience the hope that an open future inspires in man, and which is danger's reward, but he does have trust and patience. Even the aimless becoming of Ecclesiastes, though it implies discouragement and pessimism, seems to exclude any genuine anxiety. The trust of the faithful must find a counterpart in the promise of the prophets. "Yes, there is hope for your future," says the Lord to Israel, speaking through Jeremiah.[12] By a sort of unspoken contract, the prophetic words act as a guarantee to the people that, certain conditions being met, certain commitments will be fulfilled: provided that Israel makes good use of its freedom, the salvation of each shall be assured.

Prophecy appears in this respect as a moral and relatively reasonable form of assurance against the evil genius of time, namely the unexpected in time that could be lying in wait in the moment to come and that makes any "advent" an adventure and turns any imminent transformation into a risk of death. The prophetic word dispels this wariness; it soothes and consoles: "Every valley shall be exalted, every mountain lowered, the crooked paths will be straightened," Isaiah promises to his people, "I shall convert the darkness into light and the rough terrain into smooth," And Jeremiah: "I will turn their mourning into gladness and consolation, I will give them comfort and joy instead of sorrow . . . for your work will be rewarded."[13] This prophesied future is the security offered by a providential finality that keeps history on the right track. But for *Creative Evolution*, the prophetic teleology would instead be proof of the predestined or predetermined nature of this time: everything is said, everything is done, everything is already played out!

The prophets, as we know, speak in the future tense: the Lord will ride on a cloud, the rivers will dry up, the nations will tremble, and so on.

Certainly there is a world of difference between the prophet and the seer; and in fact the Law itself justifies this opposition indirectly by accusing divination of imposture. Leviticus and Deuteronomy[14] effectively condemn as pagans those who consult magicians in order to know the secrets of the future. It is the soothsayer, not the prophet, who neutralizes time and annuls futurity by removing the future's exciting and adventurous uncertainty. It is the oracle and soothsayer who see the future using foresight, who have foreknowledge of the future, read the future in advance, and detemporalize time by treating tomorrow as today. The Bergsonian critique of spatialized time doesn't affect Jewish prophecy but rather the pagan seer and, behind the seer, the eternalism of the Greeks. This vision of a future given in advance, this prereading that reads before the fact, this foreknowledge that knows ahead of time effectively annuls the historicity of history and substitutes what is becoming with what has become. The impostor who foresees and predicts the future in a timeless way turns this future into a present and abolishes time with a magical flourish.

The prophet who has a premonition of the future, on the other hand, does not annul time but on the contrary passes through all of its thickness in full flight. He senses the future within duration and coincides with it in an act that is quite similar to Bergsonian intuition, but what duration gradually discloses in a process of unveiling, prophecy, a concentrated form of duration, discloses all at once in an instantaneous revelation. The professional oracle claims to literally know God, but the prophet, for his part, glimpses a pneumatic mystery: this mystery appears to him in an ambiguous and even contradictory form, and this is why he expresses himself, like Ezekiel, in parables, figures, and allegories. Prophetic amphiboly, it should be noted, is not at all like the prudence of those charlatans who use equivocal formulas to avoid committing themselves; it is rather the esoteric and ineffable nature of the message that makes metaphors and myths necessary. The prophet himself does not have a clear grasp of the situation: something is expressed within him; he does not himself to know what or why. Prophecy, in this way, is more like the poetic inspiration discussed in Plato's *Ion*, or the mystical enthusiasm, the "divine madness" in the *Phaedrus*, than pagan divination properly speaking. The distance between the foresight or clairvoyance of visionaries and the half-sight or glimpse [*entrevision*] of the inspired is as wide as between earth and heaven. The opposite of any "grammatic" or literal anticipation, isn't the glimpse of the prophet a vision across time?

It remains that the prophet, while not annulling futurity, nevertheless foretells the future and, in a certain way, renders it less adventurous: the surprise of novelty is thereby forestalled. And what does it matter if this spokesman of God suffers with his brothers, lives the drama of history alongside them! Time momentarily ceases to be an obstacle for the one God speaks to. "New things I declare; before they spring into being I announce them to you," says the book of Isaiah.[15] Not that the prophet knows the future in advance, but prophetic time is nevertheless deprived of the irreducible element of its temporality: there is no more emergence. The messianic promise has suppressed the disturbing and unpredictable upsurge of novelty.

We cannot therefore identify Bergsonian time with biblical time. But another divergence, more serious perhaps, seems to separate Bergson (or at least the first Bergsonism) from messianic prophecy. What apparently makes Bergson's philosophy of experience the antipodes of Judaism is its decided rejection of any reflections on the beginning and the end, any speculation on the two extreme terms. Bergsonism is, at least initially, a philosophy of empirical fullness and continuity: in agreement with Spinoza, with English empiricism, and (on this point only) with criticism, Bergson refrained for a very long time from asking any questions concerning the first beginning or final end: "I, the Eternal, am the first and last."[16] The first and the last! Bergsonian empiricism would have considered this protology and this eschatology to be pseudo-problems and rejected, in the name of perceived or perceptible facts, any metaphysical or apocalyptic speculation about the Alpha and the Omega. God "has nothing of the already made," the Absolute "endures"[17]—we know what a scandal *Creative Evolution* provoked among the dogmatic Christian theologians with these assertions. Bergson was naturally suspected of pantheism. Did Bergson mean that God is cause of himself, in the sense of Jacob Böhme and mystics? The Bergsonian God is not *causa sui* in this sense, but it is all activity and continual outpouring: the divine is the actual continuation of the élan that causes the spread of organisms and species to blossom before our eyes.

The problem of the radical origin would thus have been for Bergson an ideological mirage and delusional representation: the idea of a creator God positing heaven and earth in the void of all preexistence is for *Creative Evolution* as unintelligible as, for *Time and Free Will*, the myth of a freedom of indifference at the fork between two paths, where the decision of how to proceed is made in a vacuum of any determination. And just as free will is the will of a consciousness supported by its deep past, a psyche pushed by its personal traditions and by the lessons of experience, so the divine act is a creation in the midst of continuation. God no more operates in the spiritual bell jar of absolute nonbeing than free will does. The nominalist philosophy of plenitude, criticizing the ideas of disorder and nothingness, depreciates both the yawning chaos of Hesiod's *Theogony* and the nothingness of creation ex nihilo. Nothingness is a frightening representation the mind uses to scare itself, to make itself dizzy and play at teetering over the abyss. Just as we like to skirt along the edge of a precipice, and especially when there is a parapet, so the metaphysician gives himself the thrill of skirting the precipice of the abyssal nihil from which the first being would emerge. So it is that Leibniz takes his turn at examining the void by writing his treatise on the *The Radical Origin of Things* and for a few moments savors the delicious vertigo, but he quickly fills in the abyss and shows that ultimately God does everything in a very reasonable way and that eternal truths preexisted his benevolent will. There is thus a parapet that prevents the mind from falling into the precipice. The author of *Creative Evolution* could not understand this beginning of all beginnings, this radical Bereshit that, in the first verse of the first chapter of Genesis, remains enveloped in an ineffable mystery, because absolutely nothing existed before the benevolent act that creates heaven and earth, and the fiat lux itself comes after this first making of being.

The philosophy of temporal positivity is, in this sense at least, resolutely anticreationist. Over the absolute nothingness, Bergson would no doubt have preferred the mystical nothingness of the Kabbalah and Dionysius the Areopagite, because that nothingness is richness and plenitude, inexhaustible infinity (*En-Soph*) or, as Angelus Silesius says, "Super-Nothing";[18] that nothingness is not the void where the spectacular magic of creation is wrought in a coup de théâtre, but rather like the dynamic schema that is the germ of poetic improvisation: it is the unfathomable abyss and fertile night referred to in negative theology. If creation is an event that happened all at once at the beginning of time, Bergson is indeed an anticreationist, but on the other hand he is a creationist and more than a creationist if it is true that for him continuation is itself creation, continual and temporal creation. Is this not precisely the paradox of a "creative" evolution, which begins by continuing?

Just as Bergson rejects the problem of the radical origin, he also rejects the insoluble aporia concerning "ultimacy" and dismisses any eschatology. The anguish of the Last Judgment, the millenarian speculations about the End of History, the end of the world, the "end times" do not exist for him. Duration will never stop enduring—because it is spirituality itself. The idea of a time that is fully achieved, unfurled, unwound, is an absurd fantasy, one that generates imaginary problems, maddening aporia, and metaphysical phobias. Time, for this philosophy that is both creationist and "continuationist," is not a finite quantum that would gradually run out until the fifty-ninth minute of its eleventh hour, using up moments until the penultimate one, and finally stopping like an unwound clock when the last stroke of its last hour has struck, and similarly the history of the world does not culminate in a general conflagration when humanity has reached the end of its rope. Humanity, on the way to salvation, does not have a finite gap to fill in, a certain discrepancy to compensate, a certain distance to catch up. These anthropomorphic myths are only metaphysical by pretention, because time, like duty itself, is inexhaustible. The bogeyman of "chiliasm" is thus as foreign to *Creative Evolution* as the vertigo of the Beginning. If nothingness is a false problem, the annihilation that would result in this nothingness, the extermination that makes possible this annihilation, are also concepts made for the empirical world of quantity. *In nihilum* is as empty, as "verbal" a phrase, as *Ex nihilo*.

We can thus understand the infinite precautions Bergson takes when approaching the problem of transcendence: the pluralist immanentism of *Matter and Memory* and *Creative Evolution* doesn't lend itself well to the idea of a monotheistic transcendence. Transcendence effectively leaves gaping a vertiginous hiatus between the Creature and the Absolute: this yawning void is, for a philosopher of plenitude, the fantasy of fantasies. Bergson's distaste for the void that opens up between God and man in creationism could have very easily pushed the doctrine of *Creative Evolution* toward pantheism. We know how Rauh, relaunching against Bergson the objections raised in the *Theaetetus* to the mobilism of Heraclitus and Cratylus, regrets the absence of a transcendent consciousness of becoming that would have allowed Bergson to distinguish past and future.[19]

Does a doctrine that is temporalist, continuationist, immanentist, and on top of all that pluralist have anything in common with Hebrew monotheism? The reason for these fundamental differences between Bergsonism and Judaism, some concerning time and others concerning eschatology and transcendence, lies in the fact that Bergsonism was not at the outset a philosophy with ethical aspirations. It is the moral agent who has a relationship with a transcendent Absolute; it is the bearer of values who feels ruled by a transcendent Good, who is drawn to a transcendent duty, and who wills across the void. The great moral philosophies, like those of Renouvier and Lequier, were both arguments for free will and defenses of divine transcendence and divine unity. In *Time and Free Will*, by contrast, freedom is not so much a practical responsibility and an opportunity to do this or that as a demand for depth: it is about being wholly oneself, not at all about achieving a transcendent ideal. What do the Decalogue and the Tables of the Law have to say to us? At the time of *Time and Free Will*, the Bergsonian individual has nothing special to do: to act freely means to act deeply, which is to say, sincerely. Bergson does not tell us what man's task is, he tells us rather: be yourself, put yourself wholly into your actions, become what you already are,[20] whoever you are. This is what we could call immanence: to ask a will to put itself wholly into its decision, to become deeper, to totalize itself, is not telling it what to do. The Bergsonian problem, at this time, is thus an aesthetic problem concerning personal development and inner life: man acts in the fullness of duration, human freedom is a freedom within immanence and plenitude, and the only real imperative is that of private reflection and energy! Freedom is not the arbitrary, autocratic, unpredictable decree that decides or initiates, but rather it is the expression of a personality. It does not introduce a revolutionary discontinuity in our personal biography but rather emanates from the past like a perfume. The lived duration of *Time and Free Will*, strongly imbued with emotional and descriptive experiences where the body, as in Maine de Biran, plays a large role, appears to be a vehicle for content that is too involved and too concrete and whose pathic mood is too strong for the problem of transcendence to establish itself there: qualitative subjectivism seems, in this period, to prevail over ethics! It has to be said: the writer who recognized freedom in the way of breathing the perfume of a rose[21] was more closely related to Marcel Proust than the prophet Isaiah.

Bergson, for that matter, unlike the prophets, neither thunders nor castigates. The mystical and passionate indignation of Isaiah and Jeremiah are foreign to him, since there is no ethico-religious contract between man and Creator, and Bergsonism is not a philosophy of salvation. It is with *Two Sources of Morality and Religion* that Bergsonian freedom rediscovers a calling.

II.

In fact it is paradoxically in plenitude and positivity that we will recognize Bergsonism's most deeply biblical trait. This plenitude is not, as in Spinoza, the plenitude of being but the plenitude of becoming. For just as Spinoza turned around the Platonic meditation on death into a meditation on life, so Bergson intentionally reverses Spinoza's *sub specie aeternitatis* into a *sub specie durationis*.[22] It is the opposite and perhaps the same thing! The eternity of life, which is an infinite becoming, supplants the eternity of death, which is timeless negativity. Hellenism (and Aristotle is in agreement with Plato on this point) was in the habit of considering becoming as a lesser perfection, as an insubstantial form of being riddled with nonbeing. Bergson, reversing the accepted wisdom, dethrones eternity from its hegemonic precedence and paradoxically recognizes being as a deficit of becoming, stillness as a privation of movement: the negative and the positive terms exchange their signs. Bergson, who establishes us firmly within the immanence of becoming, thereby roots us in our condition here below. Is not this unhesitating implantation a profound trait of the Jewish soul? Becoming is no longer the vale of tears from which man, the perpetual pilgrim, thinks only of escaping; man is no longer in exile here below.

In the first Oxford lecture on "The Perception of Change,"[23] Bergson, accusing Plotinus of preferring contemplation to action, denounces the pathos of flight and desertion that not only fills the Catharism of the *Phaedo* but all of Neoplatonism and up to modern romanticism: let us flee from here, flee toward heavenly Jerusalem, to the holy city of Jerusalem, let us flee to our dear homeland.[24] Flee, always flee! And why, if you please, would our homeland not be here below? Why would our holy Jerusalem not be the Jerusalem here below? The Jerusalem of this world? In his affirmative attitude toward human actions, and even in his marked preference for the activist mystics, Bergson is connected to the ethics of the prophets, even to that of the Law. What contemplationist metaphysics considered to be pure negativity is on the contrary the height of positivity; pessimism is thus turned into optimism. It is because he considered becoming as an imperfect mode of being that Schopenhauer spoke of the misery of existence—man is under house arrest within becoming, man is the slave of the forced labor of temporality—it is thus our eternitarian and ontological prejudices that are the reason for our nostalgia and our languor. On the other hand distress turns to joy if being is a negation of becoming, if there is no other way of being for man than becoming. Becoming, namely being while not being, or not being while being, both being and not being (is this not the way it is conceived in Aristotle's *Physics*?)—this is the only way man has of being a being! Man, turning his gaze away from the mirage of the timeless, put down roots in the joyful plenitude. Is not this idea of an earthly or intraworldly beatitude shared by Bergson and Tolstoy?

There is thus no place in Bergsonian duration for the tragic and intractable conflicts so beloved of modern philosophers, popular in particular with philosophers who have never experienced our tragedies: is this not one of the reasons why the pseudo-tragic youth of today show no interest in Bergsonism? Because the absurd, in Bergson, is still an instrument of progress; the obstacle itself, in *Creative Evolution*, is still an organ! Thus it is that the presence of matter, although unexplained in its radical origin, does indeed seem to come from the same source as life and mind. What, in one sense, weighs down and hypnotizes this mind, brings down and slows the élan of this life, in another sense is the instrument of its positive achievements. Matter is necessary to life as the springboard for the élan: the divine élan, however divine, needs something as leverage. Matter is thus a blessing and not a curse; the reverse tendency of the *élan vital* provides the necessary counterbalance to the upward tendency of life.

Nor is there any room in Bergson for that extra element in the general economy of being, that absolutely irreducible element that must be considered separately, in short for that irrational element that doesn't fit into any category and is called Evil. No theodicy is necessary therefore in order to justify something that is neither a principle nor a moment, and that is not in any way a substance (hypostasis) or a demon. If Bergson had posed such a problem, it would no doubt have been in the spirit of Spinoza, in order to recognize evil as a Manichean fantasy, a myth,[25] analogous to nothingness, a mirage comparable to chaos, the pseudo-problem par excellence. But while the hypostatized nothing (void or tabula rasa) is a myth invented by our fabricating intelligence in order to explain creation and knowledge, evil is rather an anthropomorphic myth of symmetry, originating in what we would like to call the obsession of the "garniture de cheminée."[26] From time immemorial it has been necessary, says the *Theaetetus*, for evil to be the counterpart of the good, to act as a foil to the good. The pairs of opposites in dramatic dualism, the hypostatized zero in the doctrines of nothingness, are verbal abstractions. Just as space and time are in no way parallel, just as the future is in no sense the past turned around the other way, so evil is not an upside-down good: for everything is right way up to a philosophy of the irreversible.

Matter is a not a real obstacle, nor is evil a real principle, and likewise death doesn't have, for Bergson, any tragic significance. In this respect Bergson is very far removed from the Russian Lev Shestov, who reflected on Tolstoy's anguish and had a particularly acute and profound sense of death and the revelations of death. Even more, Bergson was not even obliged, as Tolstoy's pantheism was, to drive back a constantly reemerging anxiety. At the end of the third chapter of *Creative Evolution*, Bergson offers us a hyperbolic, progressive, apocalyptic hope of victory over death. Is not Bergson's immortalization of the death of death already announced by Isaiah?[27] "Death will die," Edmond Fleg has Bergson say. Foreign to any form of tragic pathos, Bergson does not see in death the absurdity of nonbeing to which the individual ipseity is incomprehensibly doomed; death is not an encounter between a supernatural destiny and a trivial physical contingency that abruptly ends our career. Death is nonbeing, and the philosophy of plenitude, extinguishing this nothing like it extinguishes the Eleatic aporia, shows in its own way that death is *ouden pros hēmas* ("nothing to us").[28] Bergsonian thought is certainly without any blend of necromania or necrophilia: the love of death, the taste for the cadaverous, thanatophilia, the morbid attraction of the funereal, all of these complexes whose formation at the dawn of modern times have been described in such depth by Huizinga,[29] all those as well that developed in the Romantic period, these are all pessimistic and ambivalent complexes where an indulgent attitude toward death is bizarrely combined with anguish about death. These very modern complexes are as far removed from Bergson's spirit as the taste for nothingness. "Love," says the Song of Songs, "is as strong as death."[30] But life, for its part, is infinitely stronger than the nothing of death! It is not much to say that life is the set of forces that resist death, given that being is in general the continuing victory over nonbeing, namely negation denied, just as movement is at all times the refusal of immobility, immobility mobilized, resuscitated. Resurrection or rebirth is not only the springtime miracle that happens once a year in the season of renewal but the continuing miracle of each moment; for each instant is spring-like in its way. One could say, in this sense, that duration is a continuous springtime. Maybe we should understand in this way the living God of Psalms, Isaiah, and Exodus, that is to say, the idea of a God that is perpetual spring and renewal. Is not the Bergsonian god itself the élan of a continuous creation, the wonder of every minute?[31] Blessed be the God who allows each minute to follow the preceding one! Blessed be the God who allows the systole to follow the diastole and the diastole the systole! Who allows each beat of my pulse to follow the preceding one! Blessed be the God who allowed me to see this new dawn and this new spring! But the annual renewal and the renewal of each morning are no more miraculous than the infinitesimal recommencement of a duration that continues from moment to moment: our trust in the perpetuation of each moment, justified by the affirmative God of David and Abraham, chases away the bogeyman of the evil genius, just as it dispels the scruples of Zeno. The doubts, nightmares, and trembling are no more. Does not the Hasidic prayer thank God for the inexhaustible grace of each dawn? The *élan vital* is this grace itself, this perpetual blessing. God is life, the supreme positivity, the vital Yes, and, in this sense, as Edmond Fleg recalls in relation to Moses Maimonides, God is indeed the negation of negation.

And not only is the God of Abraham, Isaac, and Jacob the living God, this God is moreover the God for the living, as Jesus himself says, recalling the appearance of the burning bush.[32] "The living, the living," cries Isaiah, "they praise you!"[33] And in the book of Wisdom we read this: "Stop seeking death so keenly in the errors of life!" And a little further on: "for God made not death . . . he created all things, that they might have their being."[34] The ascetic radicalism of a Saint Bernard, nihilistic spirituality, and necrophilia all seem to be condemned in advance here. There will be no sleeplessness or anxiety, "your sleep will be sweet," King Solomon promises us.[35] And Isaiah's God: "Do not be afraid, for I am with you."[36] Let us not be afraid of anything, because even the most atrocious humiliations, even the undeserved sufferings, are just a test, and the unjust trials of Job in turn stop at the edge of the absurd and on this side of absurdity. The tempted man is stretched *usque ad mortem*, to the point of death, excluding death. Abraham as well was tested to the limit: at the next to the last instant of the final moment, at the penultimate second of the final minute, the angel stops the arm of Abraham before it accomplishes the irreparable absurdity of hypothysia and the rights of reason and goodness are restored. But we were afraid! In the end the impossible supposition was not realized, and the hyperbolic evil of the demon, at the last moment, is driven back in its nothingness in extremis. Thus injustice will have had only the next to the last word, for if all is lost at the next to the last moment, all is saved at the last one. So it is that God exterminates all mankind except Noah, which is to say God safeguards the minimum necessary for the continuation of being. Here again our trust remains justified! At the extreme point of tension and at the moment when everything is about to split apart, everything returns to order; all is lost, all is saved.

Just as Hebrew monotheism can be reconciled with an intraworldly ethics, so Bergsonian mysticism embeds humanity in the world here below, in this earthly world where our work as humans lies. Bergsonian mysticism was born in 1888 in the private reflection of inner life and meditation on personal becoming, personal development, and personal depth, but it doesn't remain cloistered, as Marcel Proust's will, in the intimacy and solipsism of the secret. It shows a more and more definite orientation toward action and accepts that our freedom is magnetically charged with values. Bergsonian quality looks less and less like the Verlainian nuance, the muted shades of Proust, the pianissimo of Debussy. In *Two Sources* Bergson always gives his preference to mystics who were not contemplatives but individuals of action and initiative, pioneers, benefactors, organizers: Saint Paul the propagandist and Saint Teresa, founder of monasteries struggling with secular problems. It is not the time to listen to one's heart beat, smell the roses, or appreciate the taste of a madeleine dipped in tea, when war and the industrial age pose so many urgent problems! Man is thus not an outlaw on earth, and Bergson rejects everything that would devalue man's duration. "By wisdom the Lord laid the earth's foundations," say the Proverbs of Solomon.[37] The wisdom of man, a reflection of this foundational and edifying wisdom, is not a form of impressionism busy inhaling perfumes, sounding the vital heartbeat of becoming, or being lulled by the "melody" of inner life. The sage has other concerns than the passions and vicissitudes of their emotional life: the sage makes an effort to transform the human condition. Jewish mysticism, says Albert Lewkowitz,[38] has no desire to overlook social relations but rather wishes to sanctify them: it is therefore compatible with militant action.

Two Sources goes no further than the somewhat simplified symmetry, the exemplary diptych, of the two Testaments, the Old and New, which it opposes to one another. To help us understand the dynamism of the mystical élan, the Bergsonian dichotomy opposes open religion to closed religion, open morality to closed morality. If the Gospel represents for Bergson the regime of open consciousness and the Law the regime of closed consciousness, we have to believe (but Bergson does not put it in these terms) that the prophets represent, halfway between the closed consciousness and the open consciousness, something like a religion that's "ajar [*entr'ouverte*]"—a "half-open [*entr'ouverture*]" religion. "An eye for an eye . . . burn for burn," says the justice of retaliation,[39] just as the justice of bartering, when trading, says "an ox for an ox" or "a sheep for a sheep." This is the Pythagorean justice of *antipeponthos* ("mutual influence" or "reciprocity"), like the reciprocity of Rhadamanthus! Thus after the closure of the Law comes the half-opening of the prophets, then in the New Covenant, the openness of evangelical love.

In fact the moment of opening is already given in the Law itself. It is true that Jesus declares he has come to fulfill, namely to perfect the Law and complete the work of the prophets. What does this mean? And should we understand this *pleroma* or fulfillment as the addition of a supplement that would allow us to totalize the finite but incomplete sum of the truth? Bergson seems to believe that the New Covenant, miraculous and revolutionary in this respect, adds an essential piece to the Law that it was missing: the Law was not full to the brim, Jesus completed it by adding the missing part, "love is the fullness of the law."[40] The *pleroma* of the Law is agape; love is the complementary piece thanks to which the partial Law becomes the Law in full, the Law in its plenitude. But the missing piece was not really missing! Christ himself, responding to the Pharisees who want to embarrass him, sums up the quintessence of his own message in two precepts of the Law, one commanding us to love God with all our heart, the second to love our neighbor as ourselves.[41] Fulfillment here doesn't consist in simply carrying out but in extracting from the multiple prescriptions of the Law the central or pneumatic precept that brings all the others to life and animates their letter, because without the general idea of love, without the invigorating idea of living love, the detail of the prescriptions is simply a dead letter.

This is what happens when there is no heart in it, and this is what Paul means. Christ, himself more modest than some Christians, implies here that the New Covenant exists in embryo in the old one and is therefore not entirely without precedents. It is more like a new form of illumination; it makes explicit a great discovery that could have gone unnoticed in the dense scrub of observances. Thus the abrupt transformation that the Sermon on the Mount represents for Bergson was already anticipated, as Loisy and Guignebert have already suggested,[42] in the prophecy and in the Law. Jesus came, it is said, to open wide onto the infinite a window that was just ajar. A window is either open or closed! But we are precisely able to further specify, and in Bergson's own language, that the only thing that counts is the moment of opening: the moment of opening, namely the qualitative intention, which is an infinite movement and does not depend on the angle of the aperture. Similarly, it is the act of giving that is the conversion to the wholly other order of love, and it is this conversion, this good movement, this intentional dynamism, regardless of the quantitative magnitude of the donation, because the intention to give is not proportional to the size of the contribution! In this paradoxical arithmetic the pauper's penny has the same supernatural value as the banker's check.

Paulinian intentionalism itself thus helps us to understand why all the essentials of Christian "openness" are already implied in the "half"-opening of the prophets. However little the window is opened, everything is already fulfilled! Because from the moment the window is no longer closed, it is already open; consciousness is connected to the infinite plains of the universe and the infinite beaches of heaven, with the ocean air, with the wind that brings messages from the distant horizon, with the smells of the outside world, and for that it is not necessary for the window to be wide open. Wide open or half-open is a matter of numbers and degrees, in other words of more or less, but it is not the big qualitative question of all or nothing. Just as the most fleeting indulgence of temptation is already a great sin, so the infinite movement of love is already wholly given in the moment of the first half-opening. A fledgling love, that of a consciousness that is just starting to open, is immediately an infinite love. The good news of the Gospel is, like Bergsonian novelty in general, a novelty that is already prepared and prefigured in the already wholly positive plenitude of the Law. Is not the Old Covenant itself this continual "plerosis"? Thus in the Proverbs of Solomon, the infinity of forgiveness and the supernatural asymmetry of grace shatter the cycle of vindictive expiation: the unjust love that paradoxically commands us to return good for evil,[43] and to turn the other cheek, transcends the *anti* ("in return for") of the *antipaskhein* ("suffer in return [for an offence]"). *Vulnus pro vulneris* ("a wound for a wound"): this is what was required in the leveling of action with reaction, the neutralization of the flux of activity with the reflux of passivity. The movement of love, going straight away to the limit, clears away these compensatory reflexes and breaks in one stroke the accursed cycle of retaliation.

Biblical consciousness is already this infinite opening, in space on the one hand and in time on the other, but first in extension. It is certainly not the propagation of a faith that constitutes its universality, and this one was always limited in its spread. But neither is it correct to say that the God of Hebrew monotheism is the God of a single privileged nation and shows a jealous exclusivity. Isaiah speaks for the federation of all humankind, and the peace he heralds is an ecumenical peace.[44] The chosen people themselves are chosen only as a mouthpiece of an eternally and universally human truth, as scapegoats or carriers of the great human suffering. God does not reserve any special favors for them. Noé Gottlieb even ventures to say that the "catholicity" of Judaism is even more open than that of Roman Catholicism, as it attaches no denominational conditions to salvation, no specific creed: the Talmud and Maimonides specify that obeying the moral principles contained in the Law is enough to ensure eternal life even to the Gentiles. Judaism only becomes denominational when it imitates Catholicism and closes in on itself in opposition to other faiths. Isaiah is addressed to all men, whatever their language;[45] its message, like that of the Stoics, is a universalist one: philanthropic and philadelphic. But Stoic cosmopolitanism is the rational humanitarianism of a sage who feels sure of their place on earth and in heaven and remains concerned about personal self-sufficiency, whereas prophetic supernationalism is that of an impassioned and ecstatic genius, paradoxically and supernaturally open to all their brothers. The God of Deuteronomy[46] is no respecter of nationality, nor of "person," that is to say, this God has no regard for the contingent distinguishing marks that differentiate the individual from the human being. The Talmud affirms the universal nature of this fraternity, founded on the resemblance between God and his creature and on the divine origin of all humans.[47]

The old Law insists at several points, and with a particular care, on the obligation to treat the stranger as a brother.[48] The argument it uses resembles the "as yourself," the Golden Rule of Leviticus, namely, aiming at the ordinary man, it pulls on the strings of self-interest to turn egoism toward altruism: you yourselves were strangers in Egypt, you know what it is like. Remember then the analogy between the situations and treat the stranger as you would have wished to be treated. This xenophilia, however indirect, is a natural form of universalism in a people whose enemies have always accused it of cosmopolitanism and which itself had an immemorial experience of banishment. The people of the great historical exiles—captivity in Egypt, captivity in Babylon, diaspora, expulsion from Spain, deportations—this people so well specialized in a rootless existence seems condemned to wander among the nations. How could Israel not have a universal vocation? Loving its enemies,[49] the universal people learns the lesson of selflessness twice over: for it loves those who do not love it back, and it loves those who are not worthy of being loved.

After the opening onto space comes the opening onto time and the distant future. Edmond Fleg, a poet of hope, compares in an admirable work the religion of the already come Messiah[50]—where the essential event, despite the anticipation of another order, is in the past—and the religion of the coming Messiah, of the Messiah not yet come and ever awaited, the religion where the essential event and focus are in the future: it is the latter religion that is literally messianic. Certainly every possible shade exists in this regard within Christianity itself: Orthodox Christianity, for example, more infused with apocalyptic hope, more eschatological than Catholicism, attaches quite special importance to the return of Christ and the "second coming,"[51] honoring the God who comes; the sublime legend of the Invisible City of Kitezh is testimony to this. But already in the biblical prophecy consciousness was passionately open to the hope of the future Jerusalem.

In Bergson himself the interval between *Time and Free Will* and *Two Sources* represents the distance between the past and the future. The duration of *Time and Free Will* is above all conservative and past-focused [*passéiste*], its function being to capitalize on memories and build up the past in the present: the weight is on the back foot, and preterition, the laying down of events in the past, prevails over futurition, positing them in the future. In *Matter and Memory* as well, duration snowballs and has the function of accumulating the past in the present. No doubt *Matter and Memory* is oriented toward action. But *Time and Free Will*, in agreement with Marcel Proust's *In Search of Lost Time*, instigates a cult of the past that implies, if not the retrospection of all memories, then at least their retroversion and retrieval. *Creative Evolution* and especially *Two Sources* look to the future. Is not becoming, which brings about the future, a continual "advent"? Is not becoming to become something else by a constant process of alteration? The focus of becoming—*le devenir*—is no longer recollection—*le souvenir*—but the future—*l'avenir*. The "survenir"—what comes up—definitively supplants the "subvenir"—what has gone under the bridge.[52] Becoming rediscovers its true vocation, whose name is futurition or innovation. A vocation is something we feel called by, whereas tradition is something we feel the pressure of. We could say, applying to the past what *Two Sources* says about closed morality, that the emphasis in *Time and Free Will* is still on this pressure, although there is nothing social about this pressure. It is in *Two Sources* that man, responding to the call of dynamic morality, at the same time responds to the lure of the future, which is not a *vis a tergo* but an ideal located ahead. Levitation wins over gravitation. Man thus has a duty, and this duty delimits the scope of things to be done or, more precisely, the region of the things to come that depend on our work: that part of what should be that will be only if we will it. Duty is a future that is incumbent upon me. Duration is no longer the amassing of memories, or the stockpiling of capital; it is not so much the accumulation of wealth as creation and aspiration, not so much progress as conquest. The stampedes, cavalry charges, and conquering adventures in *Creative Evolution* depreciate the mental nest egg of the solitary consciousness, the very idea of the élan creates the possibility of a heroic wisdom!

Thus in the Bible the breach in time cut open by infinite futurity dispels the curse of a circuit that loops back on itself; the Elpidian principle banishes despair. In the Book of Wisdom, as opposed to Ecclesiastes and Job,[53] where time is a shadow, an impasse, a dead end, this pessimism is attributed to the wicked. It is the wicked and the pleasure seekers who, in order to smell the roses and take their voluptuous pleasure from day to day, living from minute to minute, who, in order to enjoy each instant totally carefree, claim that duration has no power and that becoming is not polarized toward the future. "Vanity of vanities!" For the rational optimism of Proverbs and Wisdom, the deep depression of Ecclesiastes looks a little bit like an excuse, a Machiavellian sophism of bad faith, a pretext for ill will, the nihilistic alibi of the perverse. The person who does not intend to work or do anything would like to believe that becoming is the vanity of vanities and absurdity of absurdities, that there is no open futurition but only a closed and cyclical duration, that the end brings us back to the beginning and that all effort is fruitless. Man is not a being born by chance, irreversibly doomed to nothingness and oblivion, a being indistinguishable from nonbeing and who will one day be as if he never were. A world full of meaning and overflowing with intelligibility, a creative wisdom and constructive prudence—this double positivity, cosmological and prudential, is represented in the Bible! Creaturely time is thus valorized as much as it will be in Bergson. In effect, Bergsonian freedom, while it is not, as for Lequier, a dizzying and arbitrary indifference, an initiative without precedents or antecedents, it is also not an aestheticizing totalization or a self-centered deepening of one's personal life. It is not an unprecedented fiat pronounced in a vacuum but neither is it an aimless sincerity. Freedom has a sense (sens), which is to say both a meaning and a direction. It is, in a world of plenitude, a serious freedom with the responsibility of transcendent and joyful tasks, the very opposite of an absurd and gratuitous game. "The heavens will be new and new the earth," says Isaiah, therefore do not dwell therefore on things of the past.[54] Just as love breaks open the closure of "a tooth for a tooth," so freedom cures the "vanity of vanities" of the past future and old novelty.

In the Bible as in Bergson the relation of man to time is an affirmative one. Humanity says yes to nature and society, yes to the physical world, yes to brother and sister creatures. This perhaps explains the sacramental spirit of the Psalms; these inspired verses are a hymn of thanksgiving that the psalmist, accompanied on the harp, sings tirelessly to the glory of the Creator and His works. The glory of the Creator is written over all creation—yes, everything speaks of this divine glory, both on earth and in heaven; the splendor of the sun and the trajectory of the stars and the path of the comets all write their praises to the Lord in letters of fire: "Hallelujah! Praise the Lord from the heavens . . . praise the Lord over the whole earth."[55] Humanity says yes to everything seen, to the daisy in the fields, to the blossoming cherry trees, and also celebrates the wonders of the night.

The glorification of the psalms is not, like the theodicy, a laborious justification of the harmony that exists overall: the theodicy of the theologian is the not very convincing pleading of a not very convinced advocate, with little spontaneity. Leibniz reasons too much to truly believe that our world is the best of all possible worlds: his optimism provides us with a scrap of consolation rather than expressing an enthusiastic endorsement of the thing created. David, for his part, needs no indirect arguments, or cosmological proofs, or secondary reasons for believing. God, the splendor that shines, is wholly present in the splendor shined upon; it is thus with an unmediated vision that we can read the glory of God in the visibility of light. The wonderment of the creature before the sacred wonders of creation is above all an expression of trust and gratitude. I bless you, forests, valleys, cornfields, says the poet A. K. Tolstoy. And Psalm 19: "The heavens declare the glory of God and the skies proclaim the work of his hands. The day tells the story to the day, the night passes it on to the night."

Man says yes not only to the universe but to humanity in general. The universal rehabilitation of one's neighbor, the support for one's neighbor, are essentially biblical ideas. Even in the Pentateuch the Law already opens its arms to all the most humble creatures: the long procession of the injured and humiliated—the widow, the orphan, the poor laborer—files through the books of the Law even before the Gospel has announced its Good News. The Good News is announced in the Old Testament, and this news is the general promotion of those who are afflicted in some way. The words "compassion," "mercy," "forgiveness," "pity" appear in every line of the Law. Dare we say that the Torah is "evangelical" in this respect? "I am kind and compassionate," says the Lord in Exodus,[56] for all those who are humiliated and injured, according to the prophet Isaiah, are God's friends. The God of Job protects the weak against the strong and the poor against the rich.[57] Edmond Fleg has made the observation that love and justice, separate in the modern mind, are merged together in the Bible: "Love thy neighbor as thyself," says Leviticus, as the Apostles will also say.[58] Not love thyself in thy friend, nor love thy friend as an extension of thyself—because such is the language of Aristotle, namely the philosopher of the "other self" or the alter ego, in that specious form of altruism that is simply a roundabout form of selfishness. The substantial and annexationist ego is given first, and others revolve around this nuclear ego like satellites, added on like annexes or outbuildings rounding out its property—a friend in bronze, a stuffed friend, a piece of furniture or a vase would do just as well. The as yourself of Leviticus is not "physicalist" but rather "ecstatic" and properly miraculous. It is *allos autos* (other self) in reverse! "Love your friend as you would your own self" means: I have no other self but my friend; the self has no other self than its loved other—because it is my neighbor who is my own self! Thus the self loves his brother as if he, the lover, did not exist; the self becomes his other in person. The ego is thus in a way enucleated of its egoism; completely dislocated, extroverted into its friend, the self has no more selfhood; the neighbor of the Bible is no longer the "other self" of a shameful form of philautia that dares not speak its name, rather it is really the other than myself.

What is Bergsonian is not so much open morality as the spirit of openness, because a completely open morality is already closed up again due to the fact that once morality is opened, if we do not continue to open and reopen it ceaselessly, it goes back to being closed morality. It is the intention to open that matters, which is always *in motu* (in motion). The prophets struggle tirelessly against the complacency of the professionally well-intentioned, the *belles âmes*, and the self-satisfied good conscience, happy to bloom like the rose or parade like the peacock. Strutting about is not to open oneself up, it is rather to wallow in the excellence of a privileged and satisfied self. Could this refusal of any "strutting about," this profound irony with regard to any good conscience by chance be what is called Bergsonian "mobilism"? There is no holiness in the realm of actuality, and human effort is something always to be renewed: on this point Simmel's relativism, Einstein's nonconformism and Bergson's temporalism would be in agreement.

Men, says Jeremiah, have abandoned the spring of living water to hollow out broken tanks for themselves. And in the same way they abandon the living waters of the living God for ridiculous idols, statues of gold and silver, images carved in stone. The unprecedented, inexplicable, unrelenting dedication with which the prophets and patriarchs track down the ever reemerging temptation of idolatry is proportionate to the irrepressible and protean nature of that idolomania itself. Men, as soon as they are left alone, set about stupidly adoring their cast-iron calves and their golden asses, their crude fetishes, their dolls, and their totems. The temptation of idolatry is the stupid man's permanent tendency on the one hand to fall back into the cult of superficial appearances, on the other to allow himself to be tempted by the fragmentation of plurality and finally to accept the relapse into the inertia of death. The lazy man, for want of élan, no longer follows the movement of life, no longer seeks the unity of essence, no longer penetrates the invisible depths; he thus becomes triply frivolous. If, on the other hand, the specific character of stupidity without any *hormē* is to stop halfway and wallow blissfully on the landing already reached, we can say that the temptation of smiling appearances, the temptation of plurality, and the temptation of immobility are the three principal forms not only of human futility but above all of human foolishness; the overgrown child smiling at a dappled surface. This is our "stupidity," and it is our psychasthenia, therefore our weakness, which explains the immobilization and fragmentation of the divine and the fascinated attraction to the most peripheral layer. At every moment the living waters tend to get lost in the swamp of stale and stagnant waters. Or if you prefer another image: the living water of faith tends to congeal into idolatry. Idolatry is the name of the eternal human frivolity, the one that makes us take a smile for a virtue, the smell of a rose for a truth, and a wooden beam for a God, the one that makes the superstitious bow down before beasts barely more stupid than them.

In the *Symposium* and the sixth book of the *Republic*, Platonic dialogue also electrified the naïf always ready to interrupt his climb, to fall asleep on the landing, to stop at appearances, to let himself be dazzled by shiny icons and tempted by what the Meno calls the "swarm," namely by plurality. Socrates is the vigilant principle that keeps the lazy awake so they go higher, further, always beyond the visible, and without yielding to the temptation of the multiple or appearance. The "Multiple" that Plato warns us against however is not a polytheistic plurality, and as a result indulgence of this plurality, however treacherous its seduction may be, is not strictly speaking a sin. What is condemned in the Bible is the sacrilegious and pagan worship of images: the one who kneels down in front of statuettes or in front of a joist lacerates the divine; he is not only outside of truth but outside of religion.

According to *Creative Evolution* as well, life is tempted at every step to whirl around on the spot: Bergson shows it to be fascinated by the organisms, the masterpieces it succeeds in creating—it asks only to be able to stop at these masterpieces and go no further, only humankind has been able to get over this barrier and sustain the creative élan within itself. Let us say for our part that the temptation to eddy about on the spot is, in its own way, a kind of idolatry and pagan indulgence that hinders the perpetual mobilization of vitality. Man, says Jeremiah, loves stone and wood as if they had given him life;[59] man, succumbing to middle-class complacency, abandons the spirit for the letter and the elusive model for its static image. Even King Solomon, having become too rich and too powerful, falls into polygamy and polytheism; King Solomon becomes middle class and as stupid as an idolator: the wisdom of Solomon, having lost touch with the movement of life, renounces the infinite restlessness of spirit, turns on the spot, and becomes self-satisfied.

The prophets remained ruthlessly faithful to this exhausting imperative of spirit. Isaiah, before the apostle Paul, contrasts the mouth and the heart and subordinates the ritualism of observances to pneumatic pity.[60] The call to a simplicity, a nakedness of spirit, a stripping away, which will find such a moving echo in *Two Sources*, is the constant demand of Proverbs and the Book of Job. Before the Stoic or Cynical sages, the prophets lambast the pleonexia that exponentially develops the hypertrophy of possessions and adds weight to the excess baggage of luxury. The proprietor, stripped of his possessions, relieved of any inessential or parasitic affiliations, is summoned to deeper things; the frivolous forgets his jewels, his gold plate and luxury silverware to listen to the deeper and more austere voice of his inner core; this voice of a simple heart,[61] detached and essentialized, speaks to us of the invisible unity and divine mystery hidden beneath the multicolored appearances. It warns us against the disappointment of which Solomon, victim of precious stones and power, is in some ways the symbol.

WITH THE WHOLE SOUL

I

In the discussion of organisms, I said that there are only totalities. Everything that is is complete, perfectly viable and global, and suffices unto itself. And yet, plenitude fails to be always equally dense: the frivolous and mean, petty and superficial human being fails constantly to totalize itself. It is in the free act, and when the entire soul gathers in each motive [*motif*], that we become translucid again. It is freedom, therefore, not the regional act, that responds to the vocation of life. It is freedom that allows for regeneration. In speaking of freedom, which demands seriousness, sincerity, and profundity, that is to say, the totalization of being, Bergson cites the famous formula from Book VII of the *Republic*: we must convert to the Good "with the entire soul."[1] The captives locked up at the bottom of the cave have to turn not only their head but their entire body to the light. Then they must not turn a little bit, a few degrees or at an acute angle but do an about-face or about-turn and turn around entirely. Finally, they must not simply turn and remain immobile, they must go and effectively exit the cave, and go up for good toward the light of the sun. And in the same way, converting to truth in a true conversion (*epistrophē* or *peristrophē*) in Plato's and Plotinus's sense is not converting with one little corner of the soul, it is to convert with the whole soul. Nor is it going in a different direction but, in a radical inversion, to go in the diametrically opposed direction. Nor is it saying that one will go, cry "Well done!" and after thus taking one's hat off to the immortal truths, remain planted like a fence post, it is to get up and walk.

Jesus himself, responding to the Pharisees, confirms the words spoken so often in Deuteronomy, words he considers to be the first commandment of all of the Law: "You shall love the LORD your God with all your heart, and with all your soul."[2] God is not a being with whom one can have just a unilateral and partitive relationship, nor is he an object one could touch with a little part of one's mind, with knowledge, say, or a fortiori with a tiny little portion of that portion, like reasoning. God demands that we sacrifice our whole life to him and all the fibers of our sensibility, all the forces of our power, all the tension of our willing, all the extent of our knowledge. God does not want to be loved with a corner of the soul, with a superficial part of the mind, or, for example, for ideological reasons. He, the infinitely demanding one, wants us to love him with all our being, he wants us to love him with all our heart and not with a quarter heart, a single auricle, or a single ventricle. He, the Only one, wants to be loved without sharing, as intensely and as enduringly as possible,[3] and with a literally extreme love: not once a week, as well-meaning hypocrisy and ceremonial bigotry pretend, but if possible at all moments of our life; not with reservations but all the way and without measure. God wants to be loved *passionately*. He wants us to remain in his service to the last breath, to the last drop of our blood, and to the last globule of this last drop.

It is thus no surprise that the theoretician of pure love goes back to the language of Isaiah and Deuteronomy when he speaks of pure hearts, hearts, that is, that are not divided and are absolutely disinterested... This was, to be sure, the language of Aristotle and even of Cicero: In the *Nicomachean Ethics*, is the "serious man" (*spoudaios*) not the one who desires "with all his soul" (*kata pasan tēn psychēn*)?[4] For that is how Fénelon pictures to himself the simplicity of a soul that is whole and not divided. The simple, that is to say, the serious and sincere soul resembles a transparent block of crystal in which light reigns without reservations or restrictions. How could a conversion from the whole to the whole, how could a decision that commits *the whole to the whole*, that plays *all or nothing* with our destiny, how could such a conversion not respond to an absolute and categorical imperative? No more half-measures, compromises, or casuistic distinctions! Passionate commitment has only one degree: the superlative; one magnitude: the maximum; one philosophy: extremism or maximalism. Martin Buber very much insists on this recuperation of the whole being's entire powers that characterizes Hasidic saintliness...

In Bergson's wisdom, in fact, profound and passionate conversion, sometimes experienced as "the will twisting on itself," is the prelude to a total internal reform. Bergson always said that the philosophical act is not a rearrangement of already known concepts;[5] nor is it an *ars combinatoria* disposing of old elements in a new order. Just as time is a radical renewal thanks to which the total being becomes an other, so the philosophical approach is a *serious* action and a sweeping conversion of the whole person, a conversion that implies a reversal of all our habits, of all our associations, of all our reflexes.

Let us call an optimistic theory the theory according to which those who are themselves all the way down cannot be bad. Yet does this very immanence of the personal idea not contain a certain danger of solitude? To conclude, we must verify that the realism of the immediate endows this immanent totalization with an intention oriented toward others.

II

This totalization is not only *serious*; it is also *innocent*. Bergson spent the greater part of his life seeking direct contact with the immediate given, hunting down the protocolary middle terms that mediate our relationship with the real, denouncing the mirages of *transposition* and *interposition*. His philosophy is literally a return to the things *themselves*. Is pure perception not *datum ipsum*, the ipseity of the given in person? Do artists, according to *Laughter* and *Matter and Memory*, beyond associations and recollections, not aim at something like the original ingenuity of pure form?

In this respect, Bergson links up not only with Anglo-American neo-realism but also with Russian realism, which in a way is an autodidactic philosophy and a new innocence. Bergson would have recognized himself in Lossky's realism, in Frank's immediate, and even in Tolstoy's objectivity. Reality "up close that is what I'm aiming for!" writes Modest Mussorgsky to Vladimir Stasov. The musician welcomes the noise of the fair and the song of the nurse such as they are. Such as they are—that is to say, without that idealist *distance*, which is the principle of stylization... and of lying, a principle that sweetens the rude flavor of things.

Entering into the matter right away, the sworn enemy of Criticism wants immediate proximity: does not the praise of simplicity and even of vegetarianism,[6] by any chance, have its origin in a phobia of intermediaries? This philosophy without gnoseology and prefaces is devoted to directly lived events: emotion, in *Two Sources*, and, above all, intuition take place *in the person*. Intuition is knowledge but also fruitful union and lived sympathy. It is a glimpse of the truth but also enjoyment and joy. It is not only a gnosis; it is vital diet and a way of being. Plato, speaking of the philosopher's true pleasures, is not afraid of writing the word "to enjoy," *karpousthai*. And the Psalmist says, "O taste and see that the LORD is good."[7]

The absolute is not simply an object for knowledge. It is also food and a divine "meat" that the mind assimilates or something the mind itself becomes, without interposed mediator, in an intimate transmutation and transubstantiation. There is as much distance between purely cognitive intuition and "homeosis" [assimilation of essences] as there is between gnostic vision and ontic participation! Is this not what Christianity calls the *imitation* of Jesus Christ—an imitation that does not consist in miming or aping but in oneself ecstatically becoming the object? Bergson, who condemns the kind of imitation that is mechanical iteration, that is opposed to initiative, on the contrary preaches the identification of essence. Here, no more mimetism, as in dogmatic exemplarism, but total coincidence with the beloved.

There's more. Bergson shows that the insoluble pseudo-problems of pseudo-philosophy and the source of maddening phantasms and vertiginous sophisms lies in a split [*dédoublement*]. The spectator's retrospective perspective splits from the actor's obvious present.[8] Conception, which is perception to the power of two, hypothetical intellect, which fabricates tools to make tools, negation, which is the affirmation of an affirmation, are all stricken with the same exponent and the same secondariness. The subject that, instead of seeing, claims to see seeing, and looks at itself seeing and substitutes the vision of vision for, simply, vision, and stops being internal to the miraculous and entirely simple operation of which it is the first person, and thinks itself as at the same time as I and as He, this subject fabricates absurd aporias that would be to Zeno's taste. The free human being who adopts the spectator's external and perspectival view on his own freedom renders this freedom incomprehensible. The dilemma of necessity and indifference belongs to a speculative and in a way contemplationist point of view on what is making itself. In fact, the human being is freedom itself, just as it is time in person: *tempus ipsum, libertas ipsa*. This is how the innocent, in Tolstoy, do not know the truth because they are the truth *itself*, which has entirely become innocence! In Leibniz, wisdom is the synoptic "view" [*"scopie"*] of the universal theater: in Bergson, it is more of a lived participation...

In Bergson, the absence of any methodology or propaedeutics translates this need for immediate commitment. Becoming begins right away, without prelude or prolegomena. That is why Bergson delayed posing the moral problem as a separate problem for so long. He first looked for freedom by delving into the internal rather than looking for it in the human being's other-oriented relation to an ideal; freedom, meanwhile, proves itself *in doing*. Joy thus follows the moroseness of abstract splitting. In joy, acting and feeling are paradoxically in direct proportion to one another.

This paradox defines wisdom in its entirety, of which Bergson once said that it consisted in acting like a thinking man and in thinking like a man of action. At once gnostic and drastic, wisdom, like poetry, unites in itself knowing and doing. May the philosopher thus not be the spectator of a spectacle but an actor in a drama or, better, the agent of an action in the making! We may say that Bergson's philosophy as a whole is indeed the point of view of the actor, that is to say of creation, and that it invites us to accomplish along with it the efferent movement of poetry. Is comprehension not itself creation? Is it not *poiesis* and, in this case, re-creation? Does understanding not amount to redoing?

Understanding is not the reverse [*sens inverse*] of creation, walking in its footsteps, but goes in the same direction: signification is thus not its destination but its starting point. Is there not a "creative interpretation"?[9] Let's say it again: the symmetry of the centrifugal and the centripetal is an illusion... And since beginning again and beginning go in the same direction [*sens*], philosophy in its entirety becomes for us an act that each of us must redo for himself and before himself, respectively and on his own account, as if he were the first or, better, as if he were alone. That is the example Descartes gave. And in this way, being Bergsonian would not be to repeat *what* Bergson said but to do *as* Bergson did, in solitude and in all innocence. Those who *re*think the great truths are like those who love: they love as if it were the first time that anyone had ever been in love, as if this spring were the first spring of the world. They no longer have a *perspective* but a *destiny*.

Just as intuition and emotion, which come to us in vivo, annul a stylizing distance, so action reunites these two disjointed perspectives. Distancing and splitting, which are two forms of exile, yield to the grace of the immediate. Platonic conversion, we said, is the conversion of the entire soul, a complete turn-about, and an effective approach, for the obligation to *do* is a question of effectiveness. The important thing is neither promising that one will leave the cave nor applauding those who do leave it, but leaving it oneself, at once: the important thing is not saying it but doing it. Our words are not just a derisory and miserably partial commitment of the person, a commitment with the tip of the tongue, nor are they simply a bastardized and degenerate form of action, an elliptic, symbolic, and metaphorical expression. Language is above all an action on actions, an action with an *exponent*, a *secondary* and therefore ineffective and notional action, an action for the one Bergson calls *Homo loquax*, verbose, wordy, moronic man.[10]

Making a commitment [*s'engager*] is not conjugating the verb "to commit oneself," the way fashionable jokers do in their lectures on commitment, nor is it committing oneself to committing oneself, the way famous authors do, but committing oneself *for good*, in an immediate and prior act, in an effective and drastic act I call the decision's *quoddity*. Don't listen to what they *say*, look at what they *do*, Bergson often says.[11] Doing as one says—and better still, doing without saying: that was Tolstoy's constant concern; the sage of Yasnaya Polyana, apostle and hagiographer in one, did he not strive to live the total evangelism he professed? Don't listen, therefore, to what Zeno is saying, which is not that serious: look instead at what Achilles is doing! There is no absolutely total and sincere testimony of intention but testimony by actions. Action, Aristotle says, is more eloquent and more convincing than words: Eudoxus of Cnidus was a hedonist in theory, but temperate in his habits.[12] Better to be an austere hedonist than a saucy rigorist. Better to *be* and never talk about it than not be and constantly talk about it!

There are, therefore, things that are not made to be talked about but made to be done; these things, in whose proximity our words, aborted and atrophied expressions, laughable expressions, seem so miserably fictitious, these things are the most precious and the most important things in life—for their name is: Love, Poetry, Music, Freedom. The nightingale does not give lectures on arpeggios but makes the arpeggio possible *by singing it...* The distance between the nightingale and the lecturer is as great as the distance between Poetry and the various poetics: Poetry is a direct "doing" without exponent, whereas poetics are a doing about doing, doing to the power of two or in the second degree.

Nor do heroes give lectures on heroism. Saints and heroes act on those around them not by what they write, as men of letters do, nor even by what they say, as orators do. They act on them by what they do and even more by what they are; by their song and by their charm, like the Poet who is a "doer" and uses words not to talk but to captivate; by the example of their life and the poetic radiance of their presence, for the being of the human is wholly act and operation. While eloquent preachers, in Balzac's expression, make us change our opinions but not our behavior,[13] that is to say, they convince without persuading, only the one who *does*, the hero, saint, or poet, gives us the desire to emulate. Generosity is not obtained by preaching! For by preaching, one obtains only polite assent. And that is why propaganda is so unconvincing... The sacrifice of the martyr is no propaganda: for the martyr was passionate unto his death, and the exalting virtues of his example are infinite.

Bergson's saint, who is himself an exhortation to movement and conjures the Eleatics' Gorgon, resembles the Russian *starets*. Between the *starets* and the dignitaries of the Eastern Orthodox monastic hierarchy, there is as much difference as between the radiating personality of a Tzadik and a doctor of the Law. The Russian *starets*, the Hasidic Tzadik, Bergson's saint, transform those around them not by their writings, nor by their words, nor by their knowledge, nor by their ideology, but by their being. The person is the message and the call and the lesson of heroism, which is the generous effusion and the inexhaustible profusion of benedictions. From here on out, wisdom is no longer distinct from heroism—for it is heroically wise!

The philosophy of the immediate is, in the literal sense, a *positive* philosophy, that is to say, a philosophy that says yes, yes to life, to being, and to God. It is the Yes that goes by itself! Also, a single yes wins out over an infinity of negative experiences. *Creative Evolution* revealed to us that in negation, there is a second movement that is a judgment on a judgment, as it were. And *Two Sources* adds that it is the intellect that changes its mind, and says no to devotion, and refuses to join the group. If all-efferent joy is the symptom of a More, and if it expresses the pure positivity of the creative élan, it is natural that philosophy be a return to the sources of joy. For the same reason and because pain, according to *Matter and Memory*, is a kind of movement that flows back in the form of sensation, Bergson's activist wisdom will be a victory over suffering, over bad conscience, and over all varieties of failure.

And in this, affirmative philosophy is a philosophy right side up. Its inversions of the obvious, the paradoxical reversals it presents us with, only put back into place what had been upside down. Above all, it is the irreversibility of time that points us in the right direction. There, in fact, everything is in place, including the retrograde movement that thinks it is going backward, including the recollections that seem to go against the grain of becoming: yes, everything is going, *volens nolens*, in the direction of becoming, of creation, and of poetry. Does not the Gospel according to Luke condemn the one who "looks back"?[14] The one who has recognized the true sense of vocation, the one in place, the one who has been put back on his feet looks ahead of himself once more, just as his eyes invite him to, instead of squinting backward, as negations whisper to him. He proceeds freely where his legs are carrying him instead of remaining in one spot. Whereas Megarian necessitarianism prevents the future from coming, the way Eleatic immobilism prevents movement from succeeding, philosophy right side up repairs both futurition and locomotion. Once the malediction of immobility is cast out, once the curses of retrospectivity and retrogradation are exorcized, Achilles not only faces forward once more but faces the future. He rejects the remedies of reminiscence and overcomes the negativism of death.

The philosophy of the Yes thus finds its way back to the *via recta*, the path that is entirely straight and direct: it leads, on the one hand, to the future and, on the other, it links the I to the You and the first to the second person without intermediary. To those who aspire to presentify absence and to concretize far-off abstraction, isn't the second person the immediate and close one par excellence? Had Orpheus not yielded to the mirage of retrospection, he would have kept his beloved close to him. Inversely, it is the beloved woman, the correlate of the immediate relationship, who reveals to Theseus the *via recta* right in the labyrinth. In love, that is to say, in the transitive and direct relationship of the I with its Other, intuition and action are finally synthesized.

Let me show, to come to an end, that care for the other is included in every passionate intention, that intuition is no longer distinct from helpful sympathy, that efficacy is the necessary consequence of effectiveness. Since consciousness, according to *Creative Evolution*, is wholly freedom, we have to recognize in the radiating of this freedom the heroic or genial presence described by *The Two Sources of Morality and Religion*. For freedom has a vocation, and this vocation is to free the serfs that surround it. The one who lives next to a free man wants to be free, like the one who lives within the radiating of a generous man becomes generous in turn. There is something like a contagion of generosity and freedom. Freedom, like a wildfire, lights up all the seats of freedom around it. It is a veritable chain reaction, like the magnetic chain Plato's *Ion* describes.[15] Freedom does not confer this or that, does not do this or that, but it makes us want to be free: generous freedom, heroic freedom awakens freedom in others! Freedom gifts others with freedom, that is to say, with itself, but not at all by way of an external donation or by being poured from one into the other... No! The creative initiative immediately, magically, telepathically induces re-creative initiatives one in the other—for initiative is contagious. *Creative Evolution* said that the vocation of freedom is to introduce indeterminacy into matter, and *Two Sources* would add, without saying so explicitly, that it also inserts indeterminacy into souls... The free man is so free, he would liberate even stones! Isn't there freedom for everyone?

Freedom is not only free, it is liberating. Freedom is a deliverance. Even those of Bluebeard's women who did not listen to Ariadne, who did not follow free Ariadne to the light of day, who were not convinced by this freedom, who preferred the underground of the sad castle, perhaps they were secretly touched by the grace of the new life that Ariadne's message brought them. The one who has had, if only for a second, a foretaste of springtime, will no longer bear the season of meagerness. Freedom is not free to remain quietly in itself, to exercise its profession of freedom in bourgeois fashion. It is free, and at the same time it liberates. When I say that freedom is all operation, that means: freedom is nothing in itself, *freedom is all liberation*, the way movement is also mobilization and life is also animation. God himself "create[s] creators"[16] in a mysterious transfusion of his divinity. Who knows? Perhaps God, for us, is only this continuous deification...

It is a cornucopia of inexhaustible abundance: freedom does not stop giving and being lavish, resuscitating corpses, electrifying the sleepy, provoking the revolt of the oppressed and the generous anger of the prophets. "[T]he gates of the future open wide; freedom is offered an unlimited field,"[17] just as in the Russian fairy tale about Kashchey the Immortal, set to music by Rimsky-Korsakov, the Storm-Bogatyr opens the doors of springtime, of light, and of freedom to Ivan Korolevich. Here, time is the mobilizing principle of the inert universe. Is not freedom a duration condensed in the instant of genius? Is not the free man an embodied becoming that makes the immobile become? Achilles, preaching by example, darts forward and catches up with the tortoise and laughs at the Eleatic aporias. The knights of verbal and notional commitment will be unmasked. This is the routing of the hypnotizers. The entire world released from the curse sings and smiles at us. The paralytic begins to walk and to dance; exultation and lightness seize all men released from their chains. Isaiah pays homage to this rebirth of the human even before Plato does in the *Republic*: the captive, repudiating his mole- and louse-like life forever leaves the cave of servitude.[18] The human is in complete agreement with futurition, which is the normal direction of progress, time in situ,[19] and hears the "joyous song of the future."[20] For the word "Joy" is as important in Bergson as it is in the Prophets. The joy that makes men dance, the joy of a glorious tomorrow, does it not above all belong to deliverance, that is to say, to the operation of freedom?

This deliverance is infinite, the way the liberating war that we use to conquer and constantly reconquer our always-threatened freedom is permanent. The deliverance of the empirical human being will thus never come to an end; incapable of delighting in the interval of a freedom in action, the human will be fighting until the end of times, and its liberation will never come to an end.

That is because the Jerusalem of light, the Russian legend's Invisible City, the celestial Kitezh of our hopes,[21] is a great mystery from which death irreversibly separates us and that we cannot know in this world. And yet the invisible city must flourish and flourish again beginning down here, in our hearts, the invisible city in which men are neither hungry nor thirsty, no longer shiver with misery and cold, and no longer suffer at each others' hands. Then, perhaps, will we hear in the silence the angels of the night that speak to us of the far-away Kitezh and whisper unsayable things into our ears.

PREFACE TO THE FIRST EDITION
OF HENRI BERGSON (1930)

This book originated in an article that appeared in the *Revue de Mé-taphysique et de Morale* in 1928 entitled, "Prolegomena to Bergson's Philosophy."[1] It sought less to give an exposition of Bergson's philosophy than to make it understandable. There is no lack of faithful and solid expositions, and it would have seemed useless to me to repeat once more what Mr. Bergson has said with such admirable clarity in books that are accessible to everyone. I decided that the study of a contemporary theory, and one so profoundly engaged in the intellectual life of our country, did not call for as "historical" a method as the study of ancient theories. Treating of a writer in our language, still mixed up in current philosophical developments, there is no special merit in clearly exposing ideas everyone is familiar with: there are no sources to be discovered here, no philological problems to be discussed. It will come as no surprise, then, that in this book, commentary and critical interpretation take up a scandalous amount of space. Besides, every time citation turns into commentary, the reader is warned of the shift and cannot be mistaken.

To conclude, I have to say that despite appearances, this book is not an "apology" of Bergson's philosophy. Our happy age does not lack strong minds. The salons have become very anti-Bergsonian, and the Prophets that abound among us have proclaimed the bankruptcy of "intuitionism." But that is quickly said. The scrupulous reader, the one truly vaccinated against intellectual trifling, disregards these prophets and their exorcisms. What am I to do about it? It's not my fault if greater familiarity with Bergson's philosophy multiplies the reasons one has for admiring it.

Paris, April 1930

LETTERS TO VLADIMIR JANKÉLÉVITCH
BY HENRI BERGSON

12 May 1924[1]

Dear Sir,

I thank you for giving me occasion to reread the incisive study you were so kind as to dedicate to me.[2] I have already told you all the good I think of it: I am happy to tell you again. Unless I'm very much mistaken, this first one announces works that will be an important contribution to philosophical thought.

With kind regards to you,
Sincerely,

H. BERGSON

27 May 1929

Dear Sir,

I must tell you with what interest and what pleasure I read your new article, "Bergson's Philosophy and Biology."[3] You do my writings much honor, and you render them a real service by showing how they have been able to anticipate certain results of positive science. Truth be told, philosophy and science have met here because they both decided to discard preconceived notions and place themselves once more in the presence of facts.

As I just wrote to Xavier Léon,[4] who sent me the proofs, I admire how you are always at ease and always feel at home in the great variety of subjects treated. You have managed quite a feat in summarizing a book that is itself already a condensation and in bringing out what is essential in a way that will singularly facilitate the reading of the book.

With kind regards to you,
Sincerely,

H. BERGSON

6 August 1930[5]

Dear Sir,

You have done me the honor of dedicating a work to the whole of my writings. I have read it closely, and I want you to know the interest I took in reading it and the delight it has given me. Not only is your account exact and precise; not only is it informed by such a complete and extended textual study that the citations seem to answer, all by themselves, the call of ideas; above all, it also demonstrates a remarkable deepening of the theory and an intellectual sympathy that led you to discover the stages I went through, the paths I followed, and sometimes the terms I would have used had I expounded what remained implicit. I add that this work of analysis goes hand in hand with a singularly interesting effort of synthesis: often my point of arrival was for you a point of departure for original speculations of your own.

Allow me to send my compliments and thanks for this penetrating study, and please trust, dear Sir, in my highest regard.

H. BERGSON

3 March 1938

Dear colleague and friend,

I'm quite late in thanking you for the kindness of sending me your book, *The Alternative*.[6] But I read it right away, and with extreme pleasure. But illness takes up so great a part of my day that only very few instants remain to write: I have had to stop all truly interesting correspondence. *The Alternative* is one of the most multifaceted [*touffu*] books I know—full of ideas, some developed, some left in the state of suggestion. It seems to me your method consists in delimiting a certain *field of thought* and to gather up everything you find there, everything you see or imagine there, obliging us, thanks to your graphic expression, to imagine and to see like you. The difficulty of this method is obviously to delimit the field of thought in such a way that the form of the terrain has nothing artificial about it, that it seems to have been traced by nature itself. It seems to me you've succeeded in doing so and that the three concepts Alternative, Economy, and Boredom, such as you present them, indeed correspond to realities. All three are important, yet there is good reason for the first to lend its name for the title of the book. Alternative, such as you understand it, is a veritable conception of life.

I have long expressed my wish for a study on boredom. You provide us with such a study, and in a singularly captivating way. It interests and instructs me in a special way because boredom is a feeling I have never experienced. Or perhaps I experienced it without being able to name it? I rather think that it never found anywhere in me where it could lodge itself, never having had enough time to do what I had to do. I thought of all of this as I was reading you.

> Congratulations on this book,
> Ever yours,
> H. BERGSON

10 September 1939

Dear friend,

I am deeply touched by your letter, which I have just received. So you have been called to fight for France: that I could do the same! All my life, I have wondered how I could give back to the country some of what I owe it, for I owe everything to France. I had the privilege to serve abroad during the last war; today, old and ill, I can only encourage the efforts of others. How sad!

When you come back for good and, before then, when you have a few days of freedom, come chat with me. I will tell you with what interest I've read your study, as original as it is incisive, of Ravel's music.[7] A long time ago, I was one of the first, if not the first, to foretell you a bright philosophical future. I was not wrong.

> I am, dear friend,
> very affectionately yours,
> H. BERGSON

LETTER TO LOUIS BEAUDUC
ON FIRST MEETING BERGSON (1923)

Paris, Wednesday, 26 December 1923
53 rue de Rennes

My dear friend,

As promised, I'm writing before New Year's to give you Bréhier's address. So: Emile Bréhier,[1] Professor in the Faculty of Letters, lives at *40 rue de l'Yvette*, in the XVIth district; an eminently philosophical district, as you can see, which already counts [Léon] Brunschvicg and Bergson among its children (so to speak).

Speaking of Bergson: last Sunday, I finally saw the great man at his home; we chatted for a good hour and a half. His is a charming simplicity, and I beg you to believe that one feels much more at ease with him—

great man that he is—than with that fussy B[réhier]. Picture a little bony fellow (and I imagined him to be tall) whose 65 years show, with very round blue eyes that seem to latch onto something in the distance when he speaks. His speech is slow (an academic's deformation!) but very simple and without affectation, despite some surprising images that, bursting into the conversation with abrupt impertinence, remind the listener that it is Bergson he's listening to. A detail to which I was particularly sensitive is that Bergson met Simmel in Florence in 1911, an encounter of which he has kept an unforgettable memory. What is truly touching and divine in these two extraordinary men is the reciprocal admiration they inspired in one another and the emotion with which they speak of each other.

You'll believe me when I tell you that Bergson also told me a thousand interesting things, an account of which perhaps deserves better than a letter card. Yet I'm committed not to transcend this narrow frame (for once!!); I'll leave you with this, then, hoping that you'll have the time to send Bréhier all the wishes of prosperity he is worthy of and which your friend hereby sends you with all his heart,

VL. JANKÉLÉVITCH

WHAT IS THE VALUE OF BERGSON'S THOUGHT? INTERVIEW WITH FRANÇOISE REISS (1959)

F. REISS: What remains of Bergson's ideas?

V. JANKÉLÉVITCH: Above all, temporality; an eminently contemporary idea, it remains Bergson's great discovery. And not only the idea of time: Bergson's time is a time that is identical with the very essence of being because it is the very person, the whole person, who is time. The human being is a time on two legs who comes and goes, an ambulatory becoming. Time is not the secondary or pellicular characteristic of a being that would primarily be and secondarily change. Instead, time affects the very essence of being. It is not modal but essential. This is the idea developed especially in the Oxford lectures collected in *The Creative Mind*.

Many young people are doing Bergson without knowing it, and attribute his thought to some fashionable philosopher. An example: "The human being is what it is not and it is not what it is... and perpetually an other than itself." That is a Bergsonian idea articulated in *Time and Free Will*.

Another very modern and at the same time very Bergsonian idea is that of differences in kind and of discontinuities. Qualities are not generated from other ideas. They are not like different degrees of one and the same reality that would increase or diminish on the model of temperatures: they are not "scalar" magnitudes but specific and original qualities. We pass from one to the next by means of mutation or modulation, the way music does. There are many more affinities between Bergson and Kierkegaard than one might think, and one cannot oppose Bergson's continuity to Kierkegaard's discontinuity.

Bergson's continuity is discontinuity to infinity. Kierkegaard's discontinuous qualitative leap is thus also a Bergsonian idea. In Bergson, there is an entire philosophy of the instant even if, at the time of "The Perception of Change,"[1] he only seemed to allow for blocks of duration and intervals. In reality, the instant is everywhere, in decision, in conversion, in modulation, in fits of recollection as in Proust or in the resurgence of the past. This instant then melts into duration but nonetheless appears as a rupture, a discontinuity.

Temperature, the instant, discontinuous mutations... Bergson held that qualities are specific, and he thought that each mental essence must be studied for itself, as if it were alone; such is pure perception, separated from the association of ideas or of memory, such is the artist's originary vision of a quality, independently of recollections or ideology that may distort it. This is in *Laughter*, in *Matter and Memory*, and it is as Husserlian as it is Bergsonian.

F. R.: To what do you attribute the discredit that has marked the reception of Bergson's oeuvre among younger readers these last few years?

V. J.: The main gift the Liberation from Nazism has bestowed on France was, alas! German metaphysics. Yet younger readers are probably unaware that the most recent German philosophy was itself influenced by Bergson. Max Scheler, whom I met at Léon Brunschvicg's, was very interested in Bergson and frequently cited him. Another German philosopher, Simmel, was a friend of Bergson's and very much influenced by him. They had met in Florence. Bergson was as existential as the existentialists. As for Husserl's works, although they only started to be known in France from 1945 on, they for the larger part predate Bergson's works.

But the trend of German philosophy after the last war has contributed to spreading among our younger readers a caricature in which Bergson appears as a distinguished spiritualist, a little master of philosophy who sounds out anterior duration and does not go beyond qualitative and psychological notation. Nothing could be more wrong. Bergson's philosophy is a philosophy of the avant-garde, as we just saw.

Bergson is often accused of not having "committed" himself sufficiently. Those citizens who today talk most about commitment [*engagement*] are not necessarily those who, during the Résistance, were themselves the most committed. During the war of 1914–18, Bergson openly and emphatically took sides against Germany. And for that, the Germanophiles were angry with him for a long time. He committed himself in words and in actions. He completed missions in Spain and in the United States, twice, where he had important conversations with President Wilson. Julien Cain has reminded us of his actions on the *Conseil suprême de l'instruction publique* [Supreme Council for Public Education], on which he served from 1919 to 1925, and of his role at the helm of the International Committee on Intellectual Cooperation, which was created by the League of Nations Assembly and whose principle was taken up in 1946, in the form of UNESCO. In 1925, Bergson secured the creation of a permanent branch of the Commission in Paris: the International Institute of Intellectual Cooperation.

Bergson's philosophy is, after all, a conception of life that calls for an internal reform. An entirely new method, that is what the demanding philosophical intuition is. Bergson always said that philosophy is not an ordering of concepts but an original intuition. What is at stake is the function of the philosophical act. To the extent that it demands an internal renovation, Bergson's philosophy is a kind of wisdom, a conception of life. Intuition is not only a new mode of knowledge but a new mode of being and of essential union with other beings. It gives answers to the questions asked in life.

SOLEMN HOMAGE TO
HENRI BERGSON (1959)

I am particular moved to be speaking in the presence of Bergson's daughter. I accepted to play a role tonight, despite my dislike of the spotlight, out of veneration for the memory of your father—and also because of the friendly insistence of Gaston Berger, whose esteem I cherish and whose trust has touched me very much.

We know that at the end of his life, Bergson preached the return to simplicity. One may wonder whether what we're doing here tonight is very Bergsonian. One may wonder whether it is very Bergsonian, generally, to commemorate Bergson.

There are two ways not to be Bergsonian. The first is to be Bergsonian only on anniversaries, as if that exempted us from being Bergsonian all the other days, as if we had to square accounts once and for all. On that account, we may say, we might be better off being anti-Bergsonian. This anniversary must not resemble the all soul's days that the living invented in order to think of their dead only once a year and then to think of them no more. I hope, therefore, that it is about a renewal of Bergson's thought and that we won't wait for the second centenary to talk about it again. The second way not to be Bergsonian is to treat Bergson like a historical sample, to repeat what he said instead of acting the way he did, or to "situate" Bergson's philosophy instead of rethinking Bergson the way Bergson wanted to be rethought. These two pseudo-Bergsonisms, that of the anniversary Bergsonians and that of the historians, bring me to the two main points of this speech.

Above all: the necessity to think Bergson in a Bergsonian way [*bergsoniennement*], as I think he would have wanted. Bergson's philosophy is a maximalist philosophy that demands a total adherence of heart and mind. For Bergson, there are only complete totalities, organic totalities. There is no void to rarify the positive plenitude in which we live. All that is is complete, viable, and suffices unto itself. Yet these totalities are far from equal in dignity. They differ in their moral weight, their value, their quality, their density, their depth. These inequalities endow totalization with its raison d'être and its leeway. Totalization is possible even if every being is total in every instant! Freedom is this very totalization. According to Bergson, the free act is the act into which the human being places himself entirely. It is the decision in which the whole person figures; the personal past weighs on it with all its weight and all its richness. Freedom thus cannot but go in the same direction as life, which tends to round itself off continually, to regenerate at every moment in a complete totality such that the parts themselves become total. It follows the example of Leibniz's monads: does not the monad, entirely like the person, suffice unto itself? Human beings can figure partially in what they decide; they can be petty, superficial, mean, mendacious, and act only on the cusp of the will, as it were, like those who think only on the cusp of thought. There are acts that are failures of the will instead of being true free acts.

Citing Plato, Bergson declares in the third chapter of *Time and Free Will* that the free act must be accomplished *xyn holē tē psychē*, "with the entire soul." These famous words appear twice in the *Republic*, in book IV and, above all, in book VII, where they apply to the conversion of the prisoners in the cave.[1] "With the entire soul" really means three things: first, that one must turn not only one's head toward the light, but the entire body; and, in the same way, that one must not turn a small portion of the soul toward the truth, or a little portion of that portion, but the entire soul. Second, which almost amounts to the same thing: one must not turn just a few degrees or at an acute angle; one must do an about-turn or about-face and turn around entirely. Conversion is a diametrical inversion, *epistrophē* or *peristrophē*. Third, it is not enough to convert and then to remain planted like a fence post while hailing those who leave: one must do it oneself. It is not enough to turn around, one still has to go ahead and walk. And because it is accomplished with the entire soul, the conversion itself is, above all, an essentially *serious* act. Does not Aristotle, in the *Nicomachean Ethics*, define the serious man as the one who desires "with all his soul" (*kata Pasan tēn psychēn*)?[2] The expression is not just Aristotelian and Platonic; the Old Testament and the New use it as well. For the first time in Deuteronomy, then in the book of Isaiah, the Eternal demands to be loved with the entire soul. Later, the apostles, varying the formula, say you must love God "with all your strength," "with all your understanding," "with all your mind."[3] In short, God is the one to whom human beings relate not with the cusp of the soul but with all their strength, all their knowledge, and all their willing, that is: fully. This is because the truth is not only an object of contemplation but an object of fruition and a true nourishment. Furthermore, Bergsonian intuition is not only knowledge, but an ecstatic identification with the object. The truth, for Bergson as for Scripture, wants to be known and loved with a heart that is not divided, that is to say, with a pure heart, simple, transparent, and undivided like a crystal.

De facto, Bergson's philosophy is not a philosophy like the others because it demands that we undertake, if not a veritable initiation, then at least particular modes of approach.

Bergson, as you know, spoke of the will twisting on itself.[4] This twisting implies a violent and radical reformation of our habits, an inversion of the conceptual method and, in sum, a true internal renewal. To approach the truth, then, one would need a new heart, and not a small piece of this heart, not just an auricle or a ventricle, but the entire heart. One would truly need a pure heart. The philosophical act itself demands this twisting or conversion: the human being gives himself to himself entirely, to the last drop of his blood and to the last globule of this drop.

But these formulas are still a little immanentist. *Time and Free Will* says that the free human being is the one who totalizes himself but it does not tell us what we must do, it does not tell us what our duty is. To totalize oneself is to be fully what one is, whoever one is: the one who is himself all the way down cannot be bad. In this respect, is *Time and Free Will* not a bit optimistic? It is by providing this totalization with a content that human beings will find a transcendent vocation once more.

When I spoke about the myth of the Cave, I said that one must not only turn one's head or a piece of one's soul, and not only turn and do an about-turn, but one must also go ahead and walk. One must not say it but do it. There is thus an intention to [act or] do, and in this intention, I aim at the other who is the object of my vocation and perhaps already the object of love. The difference between Saying and Doing [*le Dire et le Faire*] marks out the entire distance that separates a partitive and unilateral—because verbal—commitment and a total—because drastic— commitment. The veritable human being is the one who commits himself not only with the whole soul but for good, in a primary, immediate manner and without an exponent consciousness, because commitment is never a secondary act. If the virtue of totalization is seriousness, of which sincerity is the consequence, the virtue of courageous commitment will have to be called innocence. Bergson endows commitment with a lived sense once more. The verb "to commit oneself" is one much conjugated today, and generally in a secondary sense, notional and indirect. For the knights of verbal commitment, it is to commit oneself to committing oneself: it is a commitment in regard to commitment, a commitment to the power of two or three. Bergson's philosophy recovers the innocent effectiveness of Doing.

In *The Two Sources of Morality and Religion*, there is a phrase that returns often, a phrase to which we do not pay enough attention: "Don't listen to what they *say*, look at what they *do*."[5] This warning testifies, first of all, to the value Bergson assigns to experience in general, to everything that is perceived or perceptible. But there is something else: there is the idea that the language of acts—and this language of acts can be speech itself, when it is a question of courageously saying "no," for example—is a particularly eloquent and convincing manner of expressing oneself. Action, Aristotle says, is more eloquent and more convincing than words. Speaking of Eudoxus of Cnidus, he says in the *Nicomachean Ethics* that it is better to be an austere hedonist than a saucy rigorist.[6] What counts is the acts and not at all the words; what is important is "doing" or "not doing." To do as one says, or even doing without saying, would be the watchword of Bergsonian wisdom. In this respect, Bergson also reaches out to Tolstoy for whom the return to the immediate, the return to the things themselves, is the first imperative of a lived Christianity. Is this drastic wisdom not what Tolstoy himself tried to put into practice at Yasnaya Polyana? Also: for Tolstoy, ethics merges with hagiography, which narrates the *res gestae* of the saints. And according to *The Two Sources of Morality and Religion*, the saint acts by his very presence, not by sermons. What is important is not "saying" but "doing."

This is what Bergson's philosophy helps us to understand better: there are things—and they are the most important things, the most precious in life—that are not done to be talked about but are done to be done. One could say that this is the case for all of philosophy. What is incumbent on us is not at all to talk about philosophy, no, but to do philosophy. But the philosophers, avoiding the problems themselves in favor of a philosophy "with exponent," prefer talking about each other and never get beyond preliminaries. Bergson, for the first time, gives us a sense that philosophy is an act that each of us undertakes on his own account, as if he were alone in the world, as if he were the first to do it, as if no one had ever done it before him. Naturally, that is not true, but one must act *as if*. In this respect, the philosophical act resembles love. The one who does it redoes what millions of human beings have done before him. And yet he experiences what he does as something entirely new, unheard of, original, spring-like. For him, redoing is doing; for him, to start again is really to start; the one who loves for the first time is in his own way a brilliant inventor and improviser. Did not Descartes himself invite us to the re-creation that is creation? Bergson's intention was not that we do again *what* he did but that we do again *as* he did. It is Bergsonian to look in the direction he shows us but not at all to go on and on about Bergsonism, about the place it occupies, about the right drawer in which to stow it away.

It is in this sense that philosophy is poetry and that Bergson himself is a kind of poet. Poetry is not written [*fait*] to be talked about, it is written to be written, as Jean Wahl writes poems instead of composing a poetics. Stravinsky reminded us that poetics, after all, is an art of doing

[handwritten margin notes: Tolstoy & Bergson unify. Who else? What other thoughts began here? exemplarism. how far down does this go? Not to talk (i.e., philosophizes about action but just to act? / think he had rather better conceive of the talking of philosophy as the activity it is, not doctrine. Philosophy is philosophizing. but it isn't talking, put it that is the problem here.]

(*poiein*), doing understood as being without exponent, that is to say, in its immediate and primary sense. To be a poet is not to reflect on poetry and even less to reflect on this reflection, for poetry has nothing in common with gnoseology, which, for its part, is to the power of two or three... And that is true of music as well. But it is no less true of freedom, which must be thought directly and proves itself in action and by action, that is to say, freely. Those who abandon the perspective of the spectator, and even the point of view of the actor, abandon it for the destiny of the agent, convert themselves, they convert to doing without exponent. In this abandonment, they convert to movement and then mobilize others around them through a magical contagion and propagation.

First of all, the return to the immediacy of Doing conjures immobility. "Don't listen to what they say, look at what they do." That is to say: "Don't listen to what Zeno of Elea is saying, look at what Achilles is doing," or even, as Bergson often says, consult Achilles: he must well know how he does it because, in fact, he does catch up with the tortoise without otherwise troubling himself with aporias and sophisms... In sum, Bergson would willingly adopt the commonsense solution suggested by Diogenes of Sinope: to walk before witnesses. Movement resolved by movement: the evidence of this by no means vicious but healthy circle unties the paralytic. "Stand up and walk," says Jesus to the paralytic in Capernaum,[7] and the sick man gets up from his bedstead as if he had been tied to it by I don't know what Eleatic sophism, as if it had been the cruel Zeno who had held him back. He does not solve a problem—an inexistent problem because there is nothing to be resolved—but proves ipso facto that the problem does not exist, that this problem, a phantasm produced by spells and suggestion, was a pseudo-problem. The man who was tied down unties his bands and becomes free once more. One would like to say, paraphrasing Heinrich Heine: "And yet I am free; but don't ask me how."[8] Aristotle had an intuition of this act by means of which a man unties himself and breaks the enchanted circle into which immobilism locks him. Reflecting on the apprenticeship of virtue, he wonders in the *Nicomachean Ethics* how one can become a lyrist when one is not already, more or less, a lyrist...[9] Where does one find the support and grip necessary to learn to play the lyre when one is in no way a lyrist? And if one already is a lyrist, there is no need to become one—since, as Plato said, it is not possible to become what one already is. Yet the problem is very simply resolved by the fact: one becomes a lyrist by playing the lyre, just as it is by forging that one becomes a blacksmith. In the adventurous decision to throw himself into the water, the apprentice breaks the circle and, miraculously, irrationally, begins to swim. The solution germinates by itself and sketches itself in the initiative.

There is thus a kind of magical and immediate find that is already inherent in the drastic search. In *Creative Evolution*, Bergson expresses himself in approximately these terms: the intellect is capable of seeking no matter what, but by itself, it cannot find anything. Vice versa, instinct finds on the first try and infallibly but it finds only one thing: the one it is made for. Well, only intuition is capable of both, to find and to seek at the same time. Better than that: in the very act in which it seeks it has already found. "You would not seek me if you had not found me."[10] Thus the heuristic intention itself is the find; the thing sought had already been found, but one had to think of it...

And thus human beings begin with the discovery, that is to say with the end! To begin, one simply needs courage. Modifying Seneca's "*Velle non discitur* [One does not learn to will],"[11] we may well say "*Incipere non discitur* [One does not learn to begin]"—there are no recipes for creating, for beginning, and for giving, but only for imitating, for continuing, for conserving. On this point, Bergson agrees with Lequier for whom freedom is a beginning for itself.[12]

Two solutions might allow us to conjure the Eleatic Gorgon that stuns our consciousness, to find the simple truth with the whole soul and by an immediate decision. One solution is called love. Ariadne's thread, which guides Theseus lost in the labyrinth, is love. The amorous inspiration leads Theseus out of the maze. It is the beloved woman, the second person par excellence, who unravels the tortuous problem. The other solution is an even simpler find: it consists in flying over what one cannot resolve, by treating the problem as inexistent. This, we said, is what the pseudo-paralytic did. This is what Daedalus does. He is shut in on himself in the labyrinth he has built, bogged down in his artificial aporias, incapable of disentangling the imbroglio he had so carefully entangled. And suddenly, he has the idea of flying off into the air right under the nose of the flabbergasted monsters. He upsets the problem by making wings for himself, he resolves it by suppressing it in a levitation, and he acts as if the labyrinth did not exist.

And not only does this decision mobilize and repair a consciousness bewitched by the curses of the accursed philosophers (this is what Eugenio d'Ors calls Zeno of Elea[13]) but, moreover, the liberated man liberates the serfs who surround him. In a way, the saint and the hero of *The*

Two Sources of Morality and Religion are an exhortation to movement. They remind the human being that the right movement is, in fact, an entirely simple thing. Freedom acts a little like the magnetic rock Plato speaks of in the *Ion*.[14] Freedom is freedom not only to remain free in itself, in a bourgeois manner; freedom delivers others; freedom is liberating. Free human beings, resembling generous ones, deliver human beings not at all by what they say—even speakers—nor by what they write—like men of letters—but by what they *do*, like the heroes, and even more, like the saints, by what they *are*. Heroes do not give lectures on heroism, no more than nightingales give lectures on arpeggios; nightingales *make* arpeggios and prove the existence of arpeggios by singing them. Heroes posit the possibility of the impossible by doing the impossible. Impossibility becomes as simple as ABC. The lesson of heroism is the person itself and in its entirety; the presence of the hero is the message: this we read in *The Two Sources of Morality and Religion*. Only the example of a heroic life is rousing; it alone makes us want to resemble it; it alone is an infinite demand. Generosity is not obtained by preaching it; and Balzac talks somewhere about the preachers who make us change our opinions but in no way our behavior.[15] For it is about changing oneself in an effective way, and one can only do so in contact with a free being and in the radiance of its ipseity. As it is impossible to live close to a generous man without wanting to become generous in turn, so it is impossible to live next to a free mind and in the aura of freedom without liberating oneself. There is in someone's freedom a je ne sais quoi that does not stay in place, that in a way is outside of itself, and that is for us a rousing invitation to insurrection or, as the Psalms say, to the dilatation of the heart.[16]

Libera me de morte aeterna [Deliver me from death eternal]. The open ethics recalls not once but many times over the liturgical prose of the Requiem and of the sublime music Gabriel Fauré wrote for this prose. Addressing ourselves not at all to God but to those free human beings who will convert us to freedom, we want to say: us, too, liberate us. To the living dead that we are, to the deceased of the daily automatism, to those bewitched, fascinated by cruel Zeno, render the exercise of liberty. Make possible for them that which is impossible. Deliver us from the dark lake. Grant that we may not fall back into the deep shadows.

NOTES

The following abbreviations of Bergson's works have been used in the notes. Page references to DS, DSMR, EC, MM, and PM are, first, to the critical editions published by Presses Universitaires de France since 2007 (whose pagination is identical to their previous editions), then to the authorized translations published in Bergson's lifetime. The bibliography provides detailed bibliographic information on the translations and on other works by Bergson we refer to in the notes.

DS   *Durée et simultanéité*, 1922; *Duration and Simultaneity*
DSMR *Les deux sources de la morale et de la religion*, 1932; *The Two Sources of Morality and Religion*
Essai *Essai sur les données immédiates de la conscience*, 1889; *Time and Free Will: An Essay on the Immediate Data of Consciousness*
EC   *L'Évolution créatrice*, 1907; *Creative Evolution*
ES   *L'Énergie spirituelle*, 1919; *Mind-Energy*
MM   *Matière et mémoire*, 1896; *Matter and Memory*
PM   *La pensée et le mouvant*, 1934; *The Creative Mind*
Rire *Le rire*, 1900; *Laughter*

References to biblical texts are to the New Revised Standard Version.

Preface

1. Davidson, "Introductory Remarks," 545.

2. We have not included two long early essays Jankélévitch wrote on Bergson: "Deux philosophies de la vie: Bergson, Guyau" (1924) and "Bergsonisme et biologie" (1929), reproduced in *Premières et dernières pages*, 13–62 and 64–76. The themes and theses of these two texts are developed throughout *Henri Bergson*, especially in chapter 2, "Freedom," and chapter 4, "Life."

3. In a bibliographical note at the end of the introduction, page 3 of the French text.

1. "Two Philosophers of Life: Bergson, Guyau" was published in the *Revue philosophique* in 1924. Reproduced in Jankélévitch, *Premières et dernières pages*, 13–62.

2. The letter is included among the supplementary pieces in this volume.

3. In his testament, Bergson includes Jankélévitch among the close friends he calls upon to defend his memory. *Correspondances*, 1670.

4. Bergson's reply to the second of these articles is included in the appendix to this volume.

5. Jankélévitch, *Une vie en toutes lettres*, 158.

6. See, for example, Henri Gouhier's 1932 review in *Nouvelles littéraires, artistiques et scientifiques* and reproduced in Jankélévitch's *Une vie en toutes lettres*, 413–16.

7. This preface is also included among the supplementary pieces.

8. As a historian of Bergson and Bergsonism puts it, "The exegete [i.e., Jankélévitch] perceived what the author saw only confusedly... the elaboration of which will be a collaboration between interpreter and originator" (Azouvi, *La gloire de Bergson*, 276). Jankélévitch was, quite naturally, moved by this development. In the introduction to the second edition of *Henri Bergson* he admires the openness and generosity of his former teacher (see below, 1–2).

9. There are several good books on Bergson's impact on culture, arts, and politics. See Azouvi, *La gloire de Bergson*; Soulez, *Bergson politique*; Soulez and Worms, *Bergson*; Guerlac, *Literary Polemics* and *Thinking in Time*; Antliff, *Inventing Bergson*; Curle, *Humanité*; and Lefebvre and White, *Bergson, Politics, and Religion*.

10. See Soulez and Worms, *Bergson*, 73–118.

11. Indeed, the series in which Jankélévitch's *Henri Bergson* is published is itself a sign of the times: it includes volumes on Descartes and Pascal.

12. Cited in Azouvi, *La gloire de Bergson*, 318. Aron wrote these words in 1941.

13. On this point, see Jankélévitch's touching homage to Bergson on the hundred-year anniversary of his birth, "With the Whole Soul," included in the appendix to this volume. He begins with the claim that one way of being decidedly non-Bergsonian is to treat Bergson as a classic or "historical specimen."

14. Jankélévitch also makes small changes to the 1930 chapters but these are minor and usually make reference to a later work of Bergson's that had not yet appeared in 1930. Jankélévitch also removes Bergson's preface because, of course, Bergson did not live to see the second edition.

15. Bergson, "Philosophical Intuition," 88–89.

16. For a list in English of Jankélévitch's philosophical works, see the appendix of his *Forgiveness*, 167–68. For a list of his philosophical and musicological works, see his *Cours de philosophie morale*, 249–51.

17. Jankélévitch, *Une vie en toutes lettres*, 172–73.

18. Jankélévitch, *Une vie en toutes lettres*, 195–96. See also 345, 349.

19. For English-language introductions to the themes of time and irreversibility in Jankélévitch's writings on philosophy and music respectively, see Kelley's "Translator's Introduction" and Davidson's "The *Charme* of Jankélévitch."

20. Guerlac, *Thinking in Time*, 19.

21. Foley, *Life Lessons from Bergson*.

22. James, *A Pluralistic Universe*, 266, citing Gaston Rageot.

23. Worms, *Bergson ou les deux sens de la vie*, 8.

24. Hadot, *The Present Alone Is Our Happiness*, 125–26.

25. Lawlor and Moulard Leonard, "Henri Bergson."

26. Deleuze, *Bergsonism*, 13. Deleuze's concluding paragraph of *Bergsonism* repeats this language: "What progress [do these concepts] indicate in Bergson's philosophy?"

27. Guerlac, *Thinking in Time*, 180.

28. Deleuze, *Bergsonism*, 28.

29. Guerlac, *Thinking in Time*, 179–80.

30. See my *Human Rights as a Way of Life: on Bergson's Political Philosophy*.

31. I do not suggest that Bergson's *Two Sources* is unimportant for Deleuze, only that it receives little attention in *Bergsonism*. To the contrary, the influence of this text is evident from the beginning to the end of Deleuze's career. For example, in his book on Hume in 1953, Deleuze integrates a core insight from *Two Sources*, namely that what distinguishes human beings from other living creatures is the habit of contracting habits. See Deleuze, *Empiricism and Subjectivity*, 66. Similarly, I cannot help but feel that, in making the to and fro of territorialization and deterritoralization the centerpiece of *A Thousand Plateaus*, Deleuze and Félix Guattari adapt Bergson's insight that all human beings and human societies—and indeed, life in general—are caught in a continual process of opening and closing.

32. I note that while Deleuze did not cite Jankélévitch, neither did Jankélévitch cite Deleuze's early essays on Bergson: "Bergson, 1859–1941" and "Bergson's Conception of Difference" were both published in 1956 (reproduced in Deleuze, *Desert Islands and Other Texts*). It is plausible, however, that Jankélévitch didn't know of the work of the young Deleuze.

33. Nietzsche, *Posthumous Fragments*, Fall 1881. Cited in Hadot, *What Is Ancient Philosophy?*, 322.

34. These are themes, as we said earlier, that Bergson himself would go on to flesh out in his later essays.

35. This speech is included in the appendix to this volume.

36. Jankélévitch's 1930 preface is included in the appendix to this volume, 247.

Introduction

1. [Schelling, *Philosophie der Offenbarung, Werke*, VISupp:239.]

2. Pascal, *Pensées*, no. 298 [283], 94. [References to the *Pensées* are to the fragment numbers used by Krailsheimer and, in brackets, Brunschvicg, followed by the page number in the English translation.]

3. Letter to the author of 6 August 1930 [see below, 248–49]. In this *Bergson*, which was completed in January 1930, I developed a study on the Possible, the Nothing, and the illusion of retrospectivity that had appeared in the Revue de métaphysique et de morale under the title "Prolégomènes au bergsonisme" ["Prolegomena to Bergson's Philosophy"] in 1928. Bergson included the Swedish article of November 1930 in *The Creative Mind* in 1934 ["The Possible and the Real"], and it is in that book that he is for the first time systematically aware of a logic of retrospection (Introduction, part I).

4. [Schelling, Werke, VISupp:239.]

Chapter 1. Organic Totalities

[Epigraph. Pascal, *Pensées*, no. 919 (553), "The Mystery of Jesus Christ," 290.]

1. Brunschvicg, *Spinoza*, ch. 2, esp. 34–37.

2. *ES* 2/4; cf. *EC* 196/125.

3. Schlegel, *Philosophie des Lebens*, 1st lecture, *KSA* 10:7.

4. Letter to Harald Høffding, *Key Writings*, 366–68, esp. 367. In his article on Bergson, Richard Kroner correctly distinguishes in Bergson's philosophy between the point of view of intuitionist metaphysics and the spiritual perspective of duration. But, like Høffding, he wrongly begins with a metaphysical framework. Cf. Brunschvicg, *Progrès*, 2:659.

5. [*PM* 117–42/126–52.]

6. [Cf. Semon, *The Mneme.*]

7. [Jankélévitch here refers to the opening remarks, pp. 1–6, of the 1928 edition of Janet's *L'évolution de la mémoire et de la notion du temps*, which are not included in the 2006 reprint; compare, however, chapter 8 of that book, "Le problème de la mémoire," 145–62.]

8. [*EC* 2/1.]

9. [Cf. *MM* 250/297.]

10. Plato, *Philebus* 18–23, 548.

11. [Rostand, "Hymn to the Sun."]

12. [Cf. Alexander of Aphrodisias, *De Mixtione*, 16.]

13. *EC* 12/8. Cf. Simmel, *The View on Life*, 65–66, 74–75, and 123–24, "The Picture Frame," 11–14.

14. Plotinus, *Enneads*, IV.3.8, 56–60/57–61, cf. IV.2.1, 10/11: "but is a whole in each of the divided parts" and I.8.2, p. 280/281. [References are to the Loeb edition of the *Enneads*, with the first number indicating the page number of the Greek

text, the second that of the English.] On "parts that are wholes [*partes totales*]," see Leibniz, "On the Ultimate Origination of Things," 153; *EC* 119–20/77.

15. Schelling, *Philosophie der Offenbarung*, lecture 21, *Werke* VISupp:463. Cf. *DSMR* 229/216.

16. *EC* 96–97/57–63, 171–72/110, and 188–89/121.

17. Vialleton, *Origine*, 315.

18. Vialleton, "Le transformisme et la morphologie," 68, and *Origine*, 328–29. Hans Driesch shows (*The Science and Philosophy of the Organism*, esp. 1:59–65) that regeneration comes in to restore the complete individual as early as on the level of the blastula: the egg of the sea urchin, several of its blastomeres mutilated, will result in a reduced but complete individual.

19. *MM* 84/90 and 88/94–95; cf. 95–96/103–4.

20. *MM* 212/249–50; *EC* 92–96/59–62, 311/198–99, and 353–55/226; *ES* 209/253–54; Scheler, "The Idols of Self-Knowledge," 80–83; *PM* 192/202. We will see that, in just the same way, in amnesias there is no correspondence between this or that afflicted area of the cerebral cortex and this or that class of lost recollections.

21. [La Bruyère, *Characters* V.9, 87.] Cf. Schlegel, "Über die Philosophie," *KSA*, 8:54.

22. Leibniz, *Monadology* §64, p. 221; compare the letter to Arnauld of 9 October 1687, *Leibniz-Arnauld Correspondence*, 143–65.

23. Ravaisson, *Of Habit*, 26–31; Ravaisson's intuitions, however, are encumbered by abstract and Aristotelian formulas.—Boutroux, *The Contingency of the Laws of Nature*, 89–93.

24. [Descartes, *Discourse on the Method*, 120.]

25. "Note sur les origines psychologiques de notre croyance à la loi de causalité," *Mélanges*, 419–28, here 428.

26. [Goethe, *Faust*, ll. 1936–39.]

27. *MM* 148–50/171–73 and 184/215; *EC* 29n/19n9, 29/19–20, and 365–67/234–35; *PM* 151/160–61.

28. [*PM* 186/196.]

29. Taine, *On Intelligence*, 99–116; *EC* 92/59; *PM* 181–82/19, 190–92/199–202, 196/206, and 200/210–11.

30. *Essai* 106/141. Cf. "Philosophical Intuition," *PM* 117–42/126–52, and *ES* 186/225–26, where Bergson opposes unity and simplicity to one another, unity being the vital and concrete "simplicity" of *Essai*. Compare with Bergson's article on philosophical intuition the astonishing foreword Guyau wrote as early as 1876 for his *Morale d'Épicure* (1–8).

31. *EC* 90/58–59.

32. Cf. *PM* 291/300.

33. *MM* 130/148 [modified]. Some lines in *Essai* (122/162, cf. 178/237) seem to support our choice of example to illustrate the theory of the two simplicities. Cf. *PM* 133–34/142–43.

34. Delacroix, *Le langage et la pensée*, 492.

35. Hering, "On Memory as a Universal Function of Organized Matter," in Butler, *Works*, 6:85.

36. [The reference is to the third to last paragraph of the prologue in *Trois nouvelles exemplaires et un prologue*, which is not included in any recent translation of *Three Exemplary Novels*.]

37. *Essai* 106/14 1 [modified]. Cf. Ribot, *La logique des sentiments*, 31–32.

38. [Goblot, *Traité de Logique*, esp. ch. 2, pt. I, 85–90; cf. Émile Boutroux's preface in that volume, viii–xvi, esp. xi.]

39. [Compare Brunschvicg, *L'expérience humaine*, bk. XVII.]

40. *EC* 93–94/59–60.

41. *EC* 363/232–33; cf. 45/29: "even when it invents, [fabrication] proceeds, or imagines itself to proceed, by a new arrangement of elements already known." *PM* 16/25 and 181/191.

42. *EC* 47–49/30–31.

43. [Cf. Renouvier, *Histoire et solutions*, 385.]

44. "Prévision et nouveauté [Foresight and Newness]," 1920; see Raymond Lenoir's analysis of this lecture, "Le meeting d'Oxford," 101–3. It is in the Swedish article of 1930, included in 1934 in the collection *PM* under the title "The Possible and the Real," that Bergson for the first time takes up the expression I am using here (*PM* 110–11/118–20). *EC* mentions a "retroactive" finalism twice: chapter 1, 52/33 and chapter 4, 346/221; compare *EC* 238/152 and 293/188 as well as *MM* 213–15/250–53; *ES* 3/5–6 and 138/167–68; *DSMR* 71–72/71–72, 231/223, and 240/227.

45. *EC* 47–48/30. On the "delay," *EC* 282/181 and 292/187.

46. *Rire* 9/11–12.

47. *ES* 130/157 and 135/163–64.

48. This is how Bergson paraphrases Berkeley in *PM* 131/140.

49. Cf. Nietzsche, *Beyond Good and Evil*, §5, 8; also quoted in Ribot, *Logique des sentiments*, 114.

50. Plotinus, *Enneads*, III.7.8, 324/325.

51. *PM* 137146–47; *MM* 184/215.

52. *PM* 124/132–34 and 133–34/142–43.

53. *ES* 172/208; cf. *MM* 120/134–35, 127–28/143–44, 130/147, and 136–37/155–56.

54. [Leibniz, *New Essays*, IV.ii.7, 369.]

55. *MM* 183–88/214–20, 190–91/223, and 271/321; "Memory of the Present and False Recognition," *ES* 110–52/134–85.

56. Leibniz, *Theodicy*, pt. 1 §44, 147; "A Vindication of God's Justice" §36, 121; *Discourse on Metaphysics*, §§13 and 36, 44–46, and 67–68; "Elementa veræ pietatis," 16; "Résumé de métaphysique," 533; "Principles of Nature and Grace, Based on Reason" §7, 209–10. Compare Lequier, *La recherche d'une première vérité*.

57. *MM* 48–49/47, 62/63, and 264/312.

58. *EC* 7–78/49–50 and 95–97/61–62, cf. 169–71/109–10 and 175–77/112–13.

59. *DS* 155–56/106–7 and 164–65/113; *EC* 340/217; *DS* 165/113: "In the block which is *ready-made* and set free of the duration where it was *being made*, the

result, once obtained and cut off, no longer bears the stamp of the work with which we obtained it." Cf. MM 85/91: Motor recollection (as opposed to pure recollection) "bears upon it no mark which betrays its origin and classes it in the past."

60. DS 165/113.

61. MM 136/155–56, against those who "introduce into each term of the series elements which are only realized by those that follow." Cf. EC 192–201/123–25.

62. MM 120/134–35.

63. MM 48–49/47, 54–55/54–55, and 62/63 (cf. 219/258); Essai 69–70/92–94. In the same way, Herbart's intellectualism, seeing its task in a reduction of volition to representation, unwittingly rejoins the very dynamism it had reduced to relations. Compare the example of such a dilemma in Lachelier's reading of J. S. Mill ("The Basis of Induction," 317–18), as well as Boutroux 113–15 and EC 283/181.

64. Lequier quoted in Renouvier, Traité de psychologie, 2:110.

65. Le Roy, L'exigence idéaliste, x–xi.

66. [Pascal, Pensées, no. 919 [553], "The Mystery of Jesus Christ," 290.]

Chapter 2. Freedom

[Epigraph. de Maistre, Tenth Dialogue, 289.]

1. ES 1–28/3–36; cf. EC 16/10 and 105–6/68. This is the method of exposition in *Rire*.

2. EC 13/9 and 107/69.

3. [EC 105/68.]

4. DS, esp. 178–79/123.

5. [First articulated by Langevin in 1911, this problem is better known today as the Twin Paradox (see Langevin, "The Evolution of Space and Time," 295 and 297–98).]

6. MM 207–8/243–44; EC 309–10/198, and Essai 140–42/185–89; Brunschvicg, *Progrès*, 661.

7. Pascal, Pensées 427 [194], 128.

8. DS x–xi/xxvii–xxviii, 49–50/35–36, 65–66/45, 73–74/52, and 77–78/54–55. Cf. DSMR 255/241.

9. The German adjective *wirklich*, too, combines the ideas of the real and of the act.

10. [Cf. Poincaré, *Science and Method*, and Le Roy, "Science et philosophie."]

11. Essai 155/206. [Cf. William Thomson (Lord Kelvin), "On Vortex Atoms."]

12. EC 287–88/184.

13. EC 155/100; ES 35/43–44.

14. Essai 54–55/72–74; EC 222–23/142–43.

15. "vertigo": EC 307/196.

16. ES 191–210/231–55 (on the psycho-physiological paralogism).

17. EC 223/143.

18. *EC* 223/142–43, 235/150–51, and 274–75/175–76.

19. *EC* 278–80/178–79 and 294–95/188–89.

20. *MM* 174–75/202–4; cf. 141/162.

21. *Essai* 144–45/192–93, 162–64/215–18, *EC* 57–59/37–38, 67–69/43–44, and 70–71/45, as well as *DS* x/xxvii, 2/2, 50.38/27, 93–98/60–67, 135/93, and appendix 3.

22. *EC* 160/102–3.

23. *Essai* 40/54.

24. Proust 3:574.

25. *Essai* 137/181–83; *PM* 177–79/187–89; *Rire* 128/166–67 on the tragic poet's introspection. *EC* 4.4.2: "we only perceive what is coloured, or, in other words, psychic states."

26. Bergson articulates this methodological axiom on different occasions: *ES* 34–35/44, 59/73 (on the question of survival); *DS* 86/60, and 162/III (on the universality of real time) and 35–36/25–26 (on material extension).

27. Cf. Le Roy, *La pensée intuitive*, 57 and 63, and *L'exigence idéaliste*, xii.

28. Aristotle, *Physics*, IV.10, 217b32–34, 369.

29. Plato, *Philebus*, 14c, 565: "That one should be many or many one, are wonderful propositions; and he who affirms either is very open to attack."

30. [Lucretius, *De rerum natura*, III.1, 971]

31. See all of *Essai*; *EC* 14/9, 257–61/165–67 (and also 101/65); *PM* 197–98/207–8, cf. 137/146–47. Schelling's notion of becoming is quite similar.

32. Schopenhauer, *World*, 3:235.

33. Albert Gratieux (*A. S. Khomiakov et le mouvement slavophile*, 2:263) emphasizes certain traits shared by Bergson and Khomiakov.

34. [Cf., for example, *PM* 163/173.]

35. Damascius, *Problems and Solutions*, 80, and Plotinus, *Enneads*, IV.2.1, 10/11. Cf. Bréhier, *Études*, 280–81, n. 2.

36. See Bazaillas, *La vie personnelle*; cf. William James, *Some Problems of Philosophy*. See also Guyau, *Origin*, 103.

37. *ES* 166/201–2.

38. *ES* 189/228–29.

39. Kierkegaard, *The Concept of Anxiety*, and Wahl's preface to the French translation, 4–5.

40. Cf. *MM* 219/258.

41. *Essai* 40/54, 43/57–60, 47/64, 51/67–70, cf. 5/6–7, and 61–62/82–84.

42. [Descartes, *Rules for the Direction of the Mind*, *Philosophical Writings*, 1:40.]

43. [Plato, *Timaeus*, 37d, 723.]

44. de Maistre, 11th dialogue, 324.

45. Plato, *Timaeus*, 38a, 723. "When an ancient philosopher speaks of time, he thinks above all of the regular and periodical succession of days and nights, months, years. . . . Time is so intimately tied to diurnal movement that it is confused with the movement of the sphere and with the sphere itself" (Bréhier, "Note," 123).

46. Revelation 10:6.

47. The noun *durée* [duration], which implies a verb, is a much better expression of the transitive nature of becoming than the word Time, even if *Durée* also means permanence, persistence, resistance to becoming.

48. See PM 208–10/219–20; this is an abstract eternity, not at all the living eternity of which Guyau (*Origin*, 146) says that "eternity seems to be a notion that is incompatible with the notions of life and consciousness. . . . Life and consciousness presuppose change [*variété*], and change generates duration. For us, eternity is either nothingness or chaos." In "The Perception of Change," Bergson, too, speaks of "an eternity of life" and movement, which he opposes to an "eternity of immutability" (PM 176/186). Such would be the eternity the theosophist Franz von Baader speaks of.

49. [Aristotle uses the term frequently, but particularly often in the *Rhetoric*.]

50. Plotinus, *Enneads*, IV.8.1, 396/397. EC 201/128–29.

51. *Essai* 73–74/98–99, 81–82/109–10, 83/112, 94/126, 162–64/215–18, 168–72/229–32; DS 51/36, and 149–50/103; MM 69–70/71–73.

52. Bremond, *Prayer and Poetry*, 123 and 125.

53. *Essai* 125/166, 149/197–98; DS 42–43/30–31, 46–47/33, and 66–67/45–46 (Cf. ES 5/8 and 56/66–71; EC 22/14–15; PM 177–227/187–237).

54. *Essai* 171/227–28.

55. *Essai* 82/110.

56. *Essai* 94/126 and 102/136–37.

57. *Essai* 98–99/132–33, 102–3/137–38, 137/182–83, and 178/236–37.

58. The term is used, however, in the "Introduction to Metaphysics" (PM 181/191). Cf. PM 25–31/33–39, 216 n. 2/306, n. 26, and chapter 4, 117–42/126–52.

59. *Essai* 157/210 [amended].

60. *Essai* 171/227.

61. DS 61–63/42–44, 156/107, 160–62/110–11, and 166/114. Cf. EC 9–10/6–7 and 338–39/216–17.

62. [EC 9–10/6 and 338–39/216–17.]

63. DS 156/107 and 164–65/112–13; EC 338/216.

64. *Essai* 116–17/154–55, 145/194, and 148/197.

65. Following Vladimir Solovyov, contemporary Russian philosophy often uses the word *perezhivane*; cf. Hessen, "Mistika i metafizika," 132–33.

66. *Essai* 86–87/115–17, 145–47/193–95; EC 9–10/6–7 and 337–41/216–18; DS 56–57/40; PM 3/11. Cf. Janet, *L'évolution*, 460–61.

67. Montaigne, *Essays*, III.2, 907.

68. MM 76/80; cf. EC 277/177.

69. PM 177–227/187–237.

70. In DS (29/21), Bergson cites a rejoinder of Henry More's concerning Descartes's conception of physics. Also think of Dr. Arbuthnot's remark on Berkeley's illness. [Possibly a reference to Arbuthnot's letter of 19 October 1714 to Jonathan Swift, in which he writes that Berkeley "has now the idea of health, which

was very hard to produce in him, for he had an idea of a strange fever upon him so strong that it was very hard to destroy it by introducing a contrary one."] See Bénézé, "Qu'est-ce qu'un système de référence?," 356.

71. See vol. 2 of René Berthelot's book *Un Romantisme utilitaire*, entitled *Le pragmatisme chez Bergson* [*Bergson's Pragmatism*]. In December 1905, in the course of a discussion of "The Idea of Life in Guyau," Berthelot responded to Georges Dwelshauvers's lecture with a precise comparison of Guyau, Bergson, and Nietzsche ("L'idée de vie chez Guyau," 75–79).

72. The *Origin* was published by Fouillée in 1890, two years after Guyau's death and one year after Bergson's thesis [that is, *Time and Free Will*] was published. The *Origin*, however, reproduced an article that had appeared as early as 1885 in the *Revue philosophique* ["L'évolution de l'idée de temps dans la conscience"]. It is in any case possible (and this hypothesis Bergson himself suggested to me) that Fouillée, inspired by *Time and Free Will*, which had since been published, added something of his own to Guyau's posthumous book. To avoid neglecting any aspect of the question, however, we have to remember that in Fouillée, Bergson's philosophy has always had an opinionated opponent. The very Bergsonian tone of (Fouillée's) preface to the *Origin* is not at all the same tone as that of the *Psychologie des idées-forces* (2:109 and 2:112); cf. *La pensée et les nouvelles écoles anti-intellectualistes*.

73. *Essai* 74–76/99–102.

74. *Origin*, 126.

75. *Origin*, 125. This sentence was not in the 1885 article. Did Fouillée add it after reading the *Essai* (cf. *Origin* 99 and 134)?

76. *Origin*, 96, 103, 107.

77. *Origin*, 107 [modified].

78. Bergson, Review of Jean-Marie Guyau, *Mélanges*, 349–56, quote 355 [emphasis Jankélévitch]. A similar confession is made by Fouillée (*La psychologie des idées-forces*, 106), who takes the following words in his introduction to Guyau directly from Bergson (as he does the distinction between what is conceived and what is perceived): "the changing is grasped in the very moment in which it accomplishes itself, in transition, in dynamic form. This radical experience of change in the making ..." etc. (*Genèse*, xxxi–xxxxii).

79. *Origin*, 109–11; cf. Janet, *Évolution*, throughout.

80. *Origin* 111–12 (cf. 125: "So it is with time; we can envision the past only as a perspective *behind us*, and the future emerging from the present as a perspective *in front of us*."); compare to *DS* 48–53/35–38 and to *Origin*, 56 and 60.

81. Aristotle, *Physics*, IV.11, esp. 219a1, 371; 219b1, 372; 219b2, 372; 219b8, 372; and 220b33, 374.

82. *Origin*, 110, 113, and 116.

83. *Origin*, 146.

84. *Essai* 123/163, 136/181, and 137/183.

85. [See, for example, the chapter "The Elimination of Time" in Meyerson, *Identity and Reality*, 215–33, as well as Meyerson's *Explanation*, 135–37 and 165.]

86. I am here commenting on *Essai* 118–19/157.

87. On the meaning of this *future perfect*, see the already mentioned address to the Oxford meeting (Lenoir, 101); cf. *Essai* 138/183–84.

88. *être en règle avec*—Bergson himself uses this expression: *Essai* 119/158; on the idea of "recapitulation," see *Essai* 142/188.

89. Nietzsche, *Human, All Too Human*, II.I.82, 330.

90. Scheler, "Idols," 78–80.

91. Simmel, *The View on Life*, 78–82.

92. Pascal, *Pensées* no. 983 [276], 327–28. Cf. nos. 634 [97], 209–10, and 661 [81], 213. Compare the entries from Amiel's *Journal* cited by Brunschvicg, *Progrès*, 656.

93. Spinoza, *Ethics* III.9 sc., p. 500.

94. [La Rochefoucauld, *Maxims*, 31.]

95. Cf. Renouvier, *Traité de psychologie*, 1:314–16.

96. Nietzsche, *Human, All Too Human*, II.I.11, 306.

97. Bazaillas, *La vie personelle*, 63–64.

98. Kierkegaard, *Anxiety*, 49.

99. Lequier, *La Recherche d'une première vérité*, 45.

100. Plato, *Euthyphro*, 10a–11a, 318.

101. Renouvier, *Traité de psychologie*, 1:326.

102. *PM* 206/216–17 and 213/224.

103. *EC* 1–98/1–63 and esp. 40/25–26, 50–51/32–33, 54/35, 73/46–47, but also 104–5/67–68 and 322–32/206–7; cf. *EC* 73–75/46–48 for a classification of different types of causality. See also *Essai* 118–19/157, and *ES* 190/230.

104. Ravaisson uses an analogous expression to designate the "generative principle" of the person (*La philosophie en France au XIXe siècle*, 260).

105. [Cf. Meister Eckhart, *Wandering Joy*, 7, 41, 48, and 130.]

106. *Essai* 86/115–16, 114/151, and, especially, 146–48/194–97; *DS* 63/44.

107. *ES* 190/230.

108. [Aristotle, *Magna Moralia*, 1189a, 1880.]

109. *ES* 138/167–68 (and, generally, 137–40/165–70).

110. [*ES* 138/168.]

111. On this feeling of relativity, cf. Simmel, "Life as Transcendence," *The View on Life*, 1–17.

112. Renouvier, *Traité de psychologie*, 1:321, 1:326, 2:86, and 2:102.

113. *DS* 80/56.

114. *Essai* 84–86/112–15; *MM* 213–15/250–53; *EC* 308–13/197–200. *PM* 8/16, 156–57/166–67, and 160–61/170–71; *DSMR* 32/36–37, 51/54, 72/72, and 207–8/196–97.

115. *EC* 31/20 (cf. 240/154). These passages are concerned with an entirely different problem, but the two examples seem comparable. Philosophy, we

read in *MM*, "is a true work of integration" (206/242). Cf. Leibniz, "Tentamen ana-gogicum" ("Anagogical Essay on the Search for Causes"). See Le Roy, *La pensée intuitive*, 67.

116. Tolstoy, *War and Peace*, vol. III, pt. III, ch. 1, 821–22. Cf. *PM* 215/226.

117. Simmel, "Rodin," *GA* 14:330–48.

118. Aristotle, *Physics*, VIII.8, 263a12, 439; cf. VI.2, 233a3–31, 393, where Aris-totle writes, for example: "Hence Zeno's argument makes a false assumption in asserting that it is impossible for a thing to pass over or severally to come in contact with infinite things in a finite time. For there are two ways in which length and time and generally anything continuous are called infinite."

119. [*EC* 312/215 [modified]; *PM* 6/14.]

120. On the notion of *kinēma*, cf. Carteron, "Remarques sur la notion de temps d'après Aristote," esp. 74–79. Cf. Aristotle, *Physics*, VI.8, 216b, 367; *On the Soul*, III.6, 420b20–24, 685); *Physics*, IV.12, 220a18–20, 373: "Hence time is not number in the sense in which there is number of the same point because it is beginning and end, but rather as the extremities of a line form a number, and not as the parts of the line do so, both for the reason given (for we can use the middle point as two, so that on that analogy time might stand still), and further because obviously the 'now' is no *part* of time nor the section any part of the movement, any more than the points are parts of the line—for it is two *lines* that are *parts* of one line." The *kinēma* is an entirely dynamic position.

121. Aristotle, *Physics*, IV.12 220a21, 373: "In so far then as the 'now' is a bound-ary, it is not time, but an attribute of it; in so far as it numbers, it is number; for boundaries being only to that which they bound, but number (e.g. ten) is the number of these horses, and belongs also elsewhere." Carteron is right to point out the care with which Aristotle distinguishes between spatial trajectory and temporal continuity.

122. Leibniz, Letter to Fouchet, 238. The same kind of language is used by Descartes in a letter to Clerselier of June or July 1646.

123. Pascal, "Esprit géométrique," 165. See James, *Some Problems of Philosophy*, 180–83.

124. Renouvier, *Traité de logique*, 1:42–49 and 1:66. The infinity of time in no way resolves the infinity of space (?).

125. Pascal, "Esprit géometrique," 163–67. Cf. Leibniz, "New System" §§3 and 11, 139, and 142, and "On Nature Itself" §11, 161–2.

126. Proudhon, *Progrès*, 127 and note 1.

127. Aristotle, *Physics*, VI.2 233a3–31, 393.

128. Mill, *Hamilton's Philosophy*, 425–26.

129. On grace: *Essai* 9/11–12, *Rire* 22/28–29 and 38/49.

130. de Maistre, Tenth Dialogue, 289 [modified].

131. Cf. de Maistre, note vi on the 11th dialogue, 341–47.

132. [Cf. Aristotle, *On the Soul*, 404b, 644, and 410a27, 654.]

133. Simmel, "The Conflict of Modern Culture."

134. Plotinus, *Enneads*, I.6.9, 260/261; Plato, *Republic* VI, 508b, 370, and 509a, 371; *Phaedrus*, 250c, 157: "shining in pure light, pure ourselves."

135. Gide, *The Fruits of the Earth*, 42.

136. *EC* 193–94/124; *ES* 2/4–5 and *DS* 28–30/21–22.

137. Lequier, *Recherche*, 43 [modified].

138. Renouvier and Prat, *La nouvelle monadologie*, 254–55.

139. Renouvier, *Traité de logique*, 1:314–16.

140. Renouvier, *Traité de psychologie rationelle*, 2:82 [Jankélévitch modifies the quote, which ends, "without a necessary total connection with a certain eternal order of things"].

141. *Essai* 178n/237–8n.

142. [Jankélévitch's modification of Acts 17:28, "In Him we live and move and have our being."]

143. *MM* 207–8/243–44; Epictetus, *Diatribes*, in *Discourses*, 49: "it requires time. . . . Is then the fruit of a fig-tree not perfected suddenly and in one hour . . . ?"; Isaiah 66:8.

144. *Essai* 125–26/166–67, 129/172 ("emanate").

145. Renouvier, *Traité de psychologie rationelle*, 1:317.

146. Cf. Schopenhauer, *On the Basis of Morality*, §20, 195.

147. [Plato, *Republic* VII, 518c, 380] *Essai* 126/168; the entire beautiful passage 123–30/163–73 is worth rereading, as are 145–46 and 193–94.

148. *Rire* 60/79.

Chapter 3. Soul and Body

[Epigraph. Plotinus, *Enneads*, IV.8.1, 396/397.]

1. *MM* 6/xiii, 139/159, 193/226, and 201/236; *ES* 27/35, 30–31/39, 41–43/52–54, 47/58–59, 57–59/71–74, and 79/97–98, *EC* 181–82/116–17 and 263/168–69.

2. Janet, *L'évolution de la mémoire*, 145 and 230.

3. [Cf. Gracián y Morales, *Worldly Wisdom*, maxim 55, 31.]

4. *MM* 19/10, 25/18, 249/296, 253/299, and 280/332; *ES* 9/12, as well as *EC* 111–12/71–72, 125–27/81–82, and 252–53/161–62.

5. Compare what Monakow and Mourgue, in an important book of theirs, call the principle of the function's emigration toward the frontal pole (i.e., toward the central surfaces of projection and association): *Introduction biologique*, 14, 17, and 23.

6. Schopenhauer, *World*, 1:149–52.

7. Dr. Dumas shows how from simple irritability via "autochthonous movements" ("automatism of the centers") to volition, the disproportion between the peripheral excitation and the energy freed increases. When the capitalization of this energy in the brain has made the disproportion infinite, our reactions

are practically spontaneous and the centripetal impressions no longer count (see Tournay, "Physiologie spéciale"). Cf. *Essai* 25/33–34.

8. *Essai* 16–20/22–27 Cf. *MM* 218/254–56; Bergson, in *Time and Free Will*, goes so far as to admit the physiological theory of emotions, which is perhaps less suspect than the "ideological" theory of quantifying states of consciousness. Affects thus appear to be strangers to any measureable unit—which is proven by the theory of the "motor schema."

9. *MM* 26/19; cf. Larguier des Bancels, *Introduction à la psychologie*, 146; Alain, *Préliminaires*, 174–75.

10. *ES* 9/12 and 44/54. Ernst Kretschmer (*A Text-Book of Medical Psychology*, 16–17) uses the same term to name the thalamus, the *Schaltzentrale* or *Hauptzentrale* of general sensibility.

11. *MM* 7/xiv; *ES* 42–44/52–55, 47/58, and 74–75/92–93.

12. *MM* 6–7/xiii–xiv, 87/93, 172/201, 179/209, 180/211, 186/218, 251/298, 267/316, 273/323, and elsewhere, also *ES* 47/58 and 74/92, as well as *EC* 145/93, 146/94, 181/116, and 188/121. On the aesthetics of comical "play," see *Rire*; see Bergson's lecture "Le parallélisme psycho-physique et la métaphysique positive" and the discussion that followed at the meeting of the Société française de philosophie of 2 May 1901, *Mélanges*, 463–502.

13. Translation: *MM* 17/9 and 19/11; *Essai* 112/149.

14. [Spinoza, *Ethics*, I, prop. 10, sc., 416.] Cf. Brunschvicg, *Spinoza*, 64.

15. *EC* 184/118: Bergson would also refuse to treat intelligence "as a producer"; for him, it only "releases" certain effects by letting something pass that matter stops.

16. Descartes, "Treatise on Light and Other Principal Objects of the Senses," *The World*, 3.

17. [Roughly: generated as a whole.]

18. *MM* 18/9–10; *ES* 197–201/238–43, and *EC* 164/105.

19. See, for example, Claparède, *L'association des idées*, 312.

20. *MM* 4/xi; *ES* 36/45–46 and 210/253–54, and *EC* 354/226–27.

21. With the exception of Hughlings Jackson whose articles, while they were not republished until 1915 by Head, date from 1884. On this subject, compare Raoul Mourgue's interesting article, "Le point de vue neurobiologique dans l'œuvre de M. Bergson et les données actuelles de la science." Bergson cites the work of Pierre Marie and François Moutier (*Aphasie de Broca*, 141–56) in the preface to the seventh edition of *MM* [the "introduction" of the English translation] 8/xv; cf. *ES* 73–74/92.

22. *MM* 131/149, 196–97/231–32, and 266/315.

23. *MM* 131–34/149–53; Ribot, *Diseases of Memory*, 122; Ribot, *The Diseases of the Will*, 114–25; cf. also Hughlings Jackson, *Clinical and Physiological Researches on the Nervous System*.

24. *MM* 127–28/143–44 and 130–31/148; cf. *ES* 51–52/63–64.

25. *MM* 174–75/202–4.

26. *ES* 209/254.

27. *EC* 87–88/56.

28. *ES* 48/60 [modified], and compare 121–23/147–50. Cf. *EC* 181/116.

29. On this expression, see *MM* 7/14 and 193/226; *ES* 5/8, 47–48/59–60, 75–78/92–96, 107/130, 121–24/147–54, 145–47/178–81, and 151–52/184 as well as *Rire* 140/183 and 149/196.

30. Minkowski, *Lived Time*, 64–70 and 273.

31. Monakow and Mourgue, *Introduction biologique à l'étude de la neurologie et de la psychopathologie*, 20–25.

32. Arnold Pick attributes great importance to perseveration. Kretschmer (28) cites other lapses such as "confusion of letters and syllables" ("Silbenverwechslung") and "straying from the correct word-'sphere'" ("sphärische Entgleisung").

33. Ribot, *The Diseases of the Will*, ch. 1, pp. 26–53, esp. 41–42. Cf. Monakow and Mourgue, 284; *MM* 126–28/142–44.

34. For this word, see *MM* 142/163, 152/176, [155/181], and 197/231.

35. Pierre Janet, *Les obsessions*, 1:477 and 1:488–97; cf. *L'évolution* 271–74. Bergson cites Janet in *MM* 8/xv, 133/151, and 195–96/229–30; *ES* 113–15/137–40 and 122/148; and *DSMR* 242/228.

36. Delacroix, *Le langage et la pensée*, 477–573. In his *On Collective Memory*, Halbwachs insists above all on the social nature of the linguistic frameworks undone by aphasia because in memory, he sees above all the calendar aspect.

37. Delacroix 529 and 550 note; cf. Guyau, *Origin*, 123.

38. On this point, van Woerkom makes some remarks that are very close to Monakow and Mourgue's.

39. Ebbinghaus, *Psychology*, 80–81, where he also observes that a minuscule difference in excitation (for example two almost homonymous words) suffices to give rise to absolutely opposite representations. Cf. Hans Driesch, *Vitalismus*, 220–21.

40. [This map, charting the progress toward love, first appeared in Madeleine de Scudéry's novel *Clélie* (1654–61).]

41. *ES* 42–43/52–53, 193/233, and 200/241–42.

42. On the "principle of the common path," see Sherrington, *Integrative Action*, 115–17.

43. Cf. Monakow and Mourgue, 174, 175, and 261. Reciprocally, different lesions sometimes provoke the same symptom (Monakow and Mourgue, 22). In his book on aphasia, Head shows that one and the same motor center can, according to its prior activity and to the state of "vigilance" of the nervous system, govern movements in the opposite direction (*Aphasia*, 1:434 [on "vigilance," see Head, *Aphasia*, pt. I, ch. 4]).

44. The great philosopher Georg Simmel draws fascinating metaphysical consequences from this idea, an idea as Nietzschean as it is Bergsonian; see *The View on Life*, 1–17.

45. [Kierkegaard, *Philosophical Fragments*, 13.]

46. *MM* 150–51/173–75, 155/179–80, and 268/318; *ES* 132–33/161. Compare this criticism to the evidence Vialleton provides to support biological discontinuity.

[In *Origine*, 288–89, Vialleton quotes Buytendijk, *Psychologie des animaux*, 275: "the child is not a superior animal."]

47. MM 54–55/54–55 cf. 116/129–30.

48. Cicero, *Academica*, II.50, 530/531.

49. MM 47–48/45–46 and 62/63; cf. *Essai* 69–70/92–93.

50. MM 149–50/173: "We shall never reach the past unless we place ourselves within it from the outset" [modified]; cf. MM 269/319.

51. MM 58/59.

52. The gestalt theorists Köhler and Wertheimer try to explain the original *order* of sensible qualities (which associationism prohibits itself from understanding in any other way than as a projection of discrete elements) precisely by invoking a "secondary influx."

53. See Lossky, *Obocnovanie intuitivizma: Propedevticheskaya znaniya* [The Foundations of Intuitivism: Propaedeutics for an Epistemology] and "Umozrenie kak metod filosofi'i" [Contemplation as a Philosophical Method]. Simon L. Frank's ontologism is at a much further remove from Bergson's philosophy.

54. Rauh, "La conscience du devenir," and Heinrich Rickert, *Philosophie des Lebens*, who asserts the rights of "form" against Georg Simmel [see esp. chapter 4, "Lebensform und Lebensinhalt," 62–72].

55. *Zweck und Gesetz*, §4, "Der Biologismus," 44–58.

56. *Les obsessions*, 1:496–98.

57. MM 7/xiv, 115/128–29, 181/211–12, 269/318–19, and 280/331–32. See also Edouard Le Roy's article "Sur la logique de l'invention," 204, and Charles Blondel, *La conscience morbide*. In ES 95/116 and 160/194–95, Bergson speaks of a "pyramid" with the sensorimotor present at its summit. Cf. Guyau, *Origin*, 119. The concept of affective stratification also plays an important role in Max Scheler.

58. MM 69/71–72 and 95–96/103–4; cf. the preface to the 7th ed.

59. On this dialectic of antitheses, see Joseph Segond, *L'intuition bergsonienne*.

60. Lossky, *Obocnovanie intuitivizma*; "Esquisse," 63–65; and *L'Intuition, la matière et la vie*, 28–30.

61. It is worth noting that in the vocabulary of French psychology, the noun *sensation* today serves more to designate what Bergson calls "pure perception"; what it calls *perception*, on the contrary, is what we see as sensation interpreted, enriched with recollections. In *Matter and Memory*, sensation is opposed to representative perception as affection is to movement. See the entry "sensation" in Lalande, *Vocabulaire technique et critique de la philosophie*.

62. On this subject, compare Halbwachs, *On Collective Memory*, 45 and 46. In this important book Halbwachs refuses to understand how recollection can join something that it does not resemble in any way. The homogeneity of recollection and its spatial and intellectual framework are said to condition recall.

63. The expression can be found throughout *Matter and Memory*. Already familiar to Ribot, it seems to have been borrowed from the vocabulary of chem-

istry. Dr. Mourgue rightly insists on its importance ("Le point de vue neurobi-ologique," 37 and 42). The *dynamic schema*, which we shall discuss later, is the best example of a nascent state. The *élan vital* would be of the same order if it were a psychological reality, but it goes beyond the individual. On the idea of "nascent movement," see Dominique Parodi's ingenious remark on "Morality and Life" ("La moralité et la vie," 5).

64. Cf. Perry, "Le réalisme," 139.

65. Berkeley, *An Essay toward a New Theory of Vision*, esp. §§67–87, 30–40, but: MM 241–42/284–87.

66. [For William Molyneux's letter and Locke's response, see Locke, *An Essay concerning Human Understanding*, bk. 2, ch. 9, sect. 8, 993–94, and Berke-ley, *Theory of Vision*, 156–57.]

67. We take these words in the same sense as Høffding in his expression "*ge-bundene Erinnerung* [memory bound]." Høffding, as we know, defines perception as an "immediate recognition" (see his "Über Wiedererkennen"); cf. *Essai* 96/129.

68. ES, chapter 6, "Intellectual Effort," 153–90/186–239; cf. Le Roy, *La pensée intuitive*, 74–75; Scheler, "Idols," 80–83.

69. [Cf. von Baader, *Philosophische Schriften*, 1:53, 1:113–16, and 1:144.]

70. Plotinus, *Enneads*, III.8.6, 376/377: "round about"; VI.9.3, 314/315: "round it outside."

71. ES 169–70/205–7. In practice, this belief may well be regarded as a valid approximation. Generally, Delacroix remarks, the transition from meaning to sign is so instantaneous that the meaning justly seems to adhere immediately to language. This remark also aims at Bergson's idea of a motor schema, which plays so important a role in motor recognition. In many cases, language is said to directly fix thought (Delacroix, *Le langage et la pensée*, 405 and 442). The motor schema, incidentally, seems to play a less important role in *Mind-Energy* than it does in *Matter and Memory*.

72. MM 120/134–35; Delacroix (436–37) also shows that every effort at doing without spiritual totality—by which he understands, above all, a system of in-telligible values—condemns the interpreter to surreptitiously insert this very totality into the peripheral elements (image, action: Paulhan).

73. MM 114/126–27, 117/131, 128–29/145–46, and 135–37/153–56. MM is primarily concerned with the spontaneous and immediate form of interpretation that is *recognition*. Let us call, generically, *interpretation* (the phenomenologists would call this *Sinngebung* [endowment with meaning]) all these procedures for es-tablishing relations thanks to which the mind that recollects gives a meaning to the impressions that affect it, from instantaneous recognition to intense intellection. MM 113/125, 135–36/153–55, 141/162, and 147/170.

74. MM 142/163; cf. 113/136: "Our distinct perception is really comparable to a closed circle in which the perception-image, going toward the mind, and the memory-image, launched into space, career the one behind the other."

75. *MM* 145–46/168–69: "[W]e do not go from the perception to the idea, but from the idea to the perception; and the essential process of recognition is not centripetal, but centrifugal." At 119/134, Bergson speaks of an "excentric [*sic*] projection" of meaning; cf. *MM* 183–184/214–15.

76. *MM* 68/71 and 166–67/193–94. Cf. Høffding, *Outlines*, 141–44; *Rire* 52/68.

77. *ES* 165/200 and (on the issue of false recognition) 138/168 and 147–52/179–85. Compare *EC* 93–94/59–60; *MM* 132/150–51, 135/154, and 139/159. Cf. *DSMR* 58/60, 62/64, 79/78, 115–120/112–16, 208/197, 219/207, 229/216, 244/231, 250/236, 255/241, 265/250, 272/256, 282/265, 286/268–69, and 291/273–74; *PM* 65/72.

78. Bremond, *Prayer and Poetry*, 97 [amended]. Cf. Proust, 2:553.

79. [Claudel, "Jules," 156.]

80. [Cf. Charles Van Lerberghe, *Entrevisions*, and Gabriel Fauré's adaptations from this collection of poems in his opus 106, *Le jardin clos*, of 1911.]

81. Rather, it is the recollection that suggests the sensation (*ES* 113/137) the way a magnetizer suggests a hallucination. Cf. *MM* 112/124: the motor schema "suggests" pre-notions that we launch ahead of the perceived.

82. [Cf. Hesiod, *Works and Days*, line 111.]

83. *MM* 269/319. What is essential is not "evocation" but "recognition."

84. [On this criticism and the discussion in the remainder of this section, cf. James, *The Principles of Psychology*, 486–592.]

85. The essential passages in this respect are *ES* 166/201–2 and 189/228–30. [For the cone, see *MM* 169/197 and 181/211.]

86. *MM* 114–15/126–28, 184/215, and 191/224; cf. *Essai* 66/89: every feeling occupies the soul in its entirety.

87. [On this expression, cf. Jankélévitch's *Forgiveness*, esp. ch. 2, sect. III, 66–70: "The Total Excuse: To Understand Is to Forgive."]

88. *MM* 108/120–21 and 111–12/123–24; cf. *Essai* 13/17–18 and 33/44–45.

89. *ES* 99/120–21.

90. *MM* 103–4/113–14, 112/123, 116/129–30, and 125–26/141–42.

91. *MM* 266/315.

92. This is what is meant by Simmel's profound critique; cf. his "Henri Bergson." Yet compare *MM*, where Bergson describes motor memory as "follow[ing] the direction of nature"; dreams are not "natural" (94/102 and 88/94).

93. [Cf. Plato, *Theaetetus*, 155e, 251 (modified).]

94. *MM* 259/306.

95. *MM* 50–51/49–50. The same criticism could be addressed to Lossky who interprets the theory of specific nerve energy the way Bergson does and believes himself capable of thereby justifying his realist distinction between object and content. On this question generally, cf. Post 54–58. See also Meyerson's *Identity and Reality*, 286 and 354, as well as his *Explanation in the Sciences*, 150–51 and 526–27. [The reference is to the law of specific nerve energies, formulated in 1835 by Johannes Müller (1801–58), a German physiologist best known for his

synthetic work, *Elements of Physiology* (1833/1840, English translation 1837/1843), whose students included Hermann Helmholtz and Rudolf Virchow.]

96. Brunschvicg, *Progrès*, 670.

97. *MM* 156–65/181–93. Cf. *EC* 111–13/71–73 and 144–46/93–94 as well as 341/218: the past is the dead.

98. Rauh, "La conscience du devenir," 659.

99. *Essai* 82/110.

100. *MM* 68/71, among others; cf. *EC* 200/128 and 357–60/229–31 as well as 272–73/174–75.

101. *Rire*, ch. 3, 101–53/132–200; compare "Introduction to Metaphysics," *PM* 177–227/187–237.

102. [Biran, *Essai*, 44, quoted by Brunschvicg,] *L'expérience humaine et la causalité physique*, 20.

103. Cf. Le Roy, *L'exigence idéaliste*.

104. Plotinus, *Enneads*, I.6.9, 260/261.

105. *MM* 245/291 and 275/326. Cf. *DS* 35/25.

106. [*Rire* 118/154.]

107. [Cf. *Rules for the Direction of the Mind*.]

108. Pascal, *Pensées* no. 194 [72], 65; *EC* 359/230 on the necessary "distinctions."

109. Cf. Aristotle, *Nicomachean Ethics* I.3, 1094b26, 1730: "it is evidently equally foolish to accept probable reasoning from a mathematician and to demand from a rhetorician demonstrative proofs."

110. *Essai* 83/112, cf. *MM* 189/121 on the art of distinguishing levels of consciousness in literature; *EC* 227–28/146, 273–74/175, and ch. 4.

111. [Plato, *Theaetetus*, 173c, 272.]

112. [Plato, *Theaetetus*, 175d, 274.]

113. The clearest passages in this regard are *MM* 236–37/277–80 and 256/302–3. Georg Simmel attaches great importance to this tragic contradiction of spiritual life. But it is understood that motor habit is not the true memory of Bergson's; it does not, therefore, prove anything.

114. *EC* offers numerous examples of this spiritual parricide (in particular 104–5/67–68 and 128–29/83, 238–39/152–53, 269–70/173). At issue in *EC* 340–41/217–18 is the "given" memory. Cf. Proust, 2:140–44.

115. Do Bergson's two memories (motor habit and pure memory) not also have a common origin in one and the same property of life (which Høffding calls *law of exercise*, Semon *mnēmē*), an origin that the monism with which *Matter and Memory* ends will retroactively explain by the idea of a progressive relaxation of spiritual tension? Constituted memory is still much closer to constituting memory than habit is!

116. Cf. Ribot, *The Evolution of General Ideas*. An epistemologist like Mach ("On the Economical Nature of Physical Inquiry," 186–213) conceives of his "reading" above all in the past participle, in the skeletal symbols across which

the interpretative labor spreads. Bergson, on the contrary, conceives of it in the "present participle," in this labor itself (*MM* 113/126 as well as *ES* 97–98/118–20 and 170–71/206–7). On this question, cf. Delacroix, *Le langage et la pensée*, 330–37, and Nietzsche, *Beyond Good and Evil*, §192, 81–82. [On "suppositive" thought, cf. Leibniz, *Discourse on Metaphysics*, §§24–25, 55–58.]

117. [Nicolas Malebranche, *The Search after Truth*, xxxv.] La Bruyère, *The "Characters" of Jean de la Bruyère*, 36; cf. Descartes, "Letter to Voetius."

118. Janet, *L'évolution de la mémoire*. Pierre Janet shows how memory little by little emerges from "differed action" or, as Sherrington says, distant reflexes; the "erection" phase and the "consummation" phase grow increasingly distant, separated by a continuation of effort that allows us, little by little, to foresee and to wait. Cf. *EC* 111/71, 126–27/81–82, 179–80/115, and 182–83/117.

119. *MM* 170/198; *ES* 103/125, *Rire* 140–41/183–84 and 149/195; *EC* 162/104 and 214/137; *DSMR* 109/106, 241/228, and 259/245.

120. On breaking up, see Éduouard Le Roy's article "Science et philosophie" and his chapter "Le problème du morcelage." Damascius calls this "the divisions we have brought about in ourselves" (*Problems and Solutions*, 69).

121. Pascal, *Pensées*, no. 587 [34], 199.

122. Lévy-Bruhl has definitively shown that the progress of human reflection consists precisely in an increasing aptitude at maintaining separable series separate, at dissolving the "mystic preconnections that characterize the mentality of primitives" (378–79).

123. In *Essai*, "abstracting" abstraction is discussed on 67/90 and 91/122, "abstract" abstraction on 72–73/97.

Chapter 4. Life

1. *EC* 201–3/128–30 and the beginning of chapter 1.

2. *EC* x/xxxviii, 37–9/24–5, 46–8.29–30 and 51–2/33.

3. *Essai* 118/167–68 and *EC* 40/25–26.

4. Cf. *Essai* 137–48/183–97; on the notion *après coup*, *EC* 27–28/18, 52/33, and 224/144; and on the correlative expression *au fur et à mesure* ["as it goes on," "to the extent that," "in the order in which," "gradually"], *Essai* 9/6, 51/33, 104/67, 127/82, 146/94, 250/160, 340/217, and 353/226; cf. *MM* 168/195 and *Essai* 149/199.

5. *PM* 110/118–19. Cf. *EC* 51–52/33 and 238/152.

6. [Spinoza, *Ethics*, pt. I, appendix, 440 and 442.]

7. [Spinoza, *Ethics*, 442.]

8. [*ES* 190/190.]

9. [*EC* 87/56.]

10. [*EC* 125/81.]

11. [*EC* 51/33 and 104/67; cf. 54–55/35.]

12. [*EC* 93/60.]

13. [Cf. Le Roy, "Sur la logique," 201–2.]

14. Schopenhauer, *Will in Nature*, 367–70.

15. Schopenhauer, *Will in Nature*, 368. On the image of the magic lantern, cf. *World*, 2:332.

16. Brunschvicg, *Progrès*, 409 [who quotes Schopenhauer, *World*, 3:78–79].

17. Thibaudet, *Le Bergsonisme*, 2:33. The texts I am reading together here are EC 88–98/56–63 and Schopenhauer, *Will in Nature*, 368–70.

18. Schopenhauer, *World*, 3:77.

19. Leibniz, *Monadology*, §64, 221. Cf. EC 89/57: "The mechanism [*machine*] of the eye is, in short, composed of an infinity of mechanisms, all of extreme complexity."

20. As early as MM (276/327), Bergson denounces this mania. Cf. EC 217–18/139–40 and 251/160–61.

21. On vertigo, see DSMR 276/259.

22. [Kant, *Critique of the Power of Judgment*, 5:333, 209.]

23. Schopenhauer, *World*, 3:77–96; *Will in Nature*, 367–70.

24. Schopenhauer, *World*, 3:382–401.

25. [Aristotle, *On the Heavens*, I, XI, 281a, 465.]

26. ["Nature has had no more trouble in making an eye than I have in lifting my hand" (EC 92/59). "Nature's works, on the contrary, however artificial they may be, cost her absolutely no effort" (Schopenhauer, *World*, 3:79 [modified]).]

27. [In *The Fourfold Root*, 114, Schopenhauer speaks of having "dissected" practical reason; in the German original, the term used is *anatomisches Messer*.]

28. Cf. EC 129/83.

29. Guyau, *La morale d'Épicure*, 5.

30. DSMR 52/54 and 275/259.

31. [Spengler, *The Decline of the West*, 244.]

32. EC 90/58–59 and cf. 225–27/144–46; read together with ES 166/201–2.

33. [Giordano Bruno, *De Immenso et Innumerabili*, 8, 10, quoted in Schopenhauer, *Will in Nature*, 369 note.]

34. Plotinus, *Enneads*, VI.9.3, 314/315; III.8.6, 376/377: "and what they cannot get by going straight to it, so to speak, they seek to obtain by going round about."

35. Schelling speaks of the finality of nature in almost the same terms (*Philosophie der Mythologie*, 13th lecture, *Werke* V Supp, 24–151).

36. [Schopenhauer, *Will in Nature*, 369.]

37. EC 68–69/43–44, 78/50, and 86/55 as well as the entirety of chapter 2; on "grace," see *Rire* 21–22/28.

38. EC 211/135, 313/200, and 315–16/202.

39. [Schopenhauer, *Will in Nature*, 370.]

40. MM 114/126.

41. For example EC 54/35.

42. Cf. Monakow and Mourgue, 24. See also Louis Vialleton, *Origine*, esp. 343–44, which supports the discontinuity hypotheses with an exemplary

argument. But Vialleton, who is hostile to transformism, considers plurality to be original. See his chapter "Le transformisme et la morphologie" in the collection *Le transformisme*. On Vialleton, see Gaston Grua, "Un critique du transformisme," esp. 388.

43. *EC* 136/87–88.

44. *EC* 64–65/41–42.

45. *EC* 169–71/108–10 (and 175/112). Cf. Scheler, "Shame and Feelings of Modesty," 12–13.

46. Le Roy's *Exigence* includes a chapter sketching "a general framework" of "the evolution of life" (140–58). Cf. *DSMR* 313/294.

47. Vialleton, *Origine*, 345 and 373.

48. [Cf. *DSMR* 317–20/298–300.]

49. *EC* 258–59/165–66. Cf. *PM* 189/198–99.

50. *EC* 155/96.

51. Schopenhauer, *World*, 3:88.

52. *EC* 260/166. We may thus, in a certain sense at least, speak of a "division of labor," whatever Bergson may say on this point (*EC* 118/76). Are the separate tendencies not complementary? Cf. *EC* 255/163.

53. Schopenhauer, *World*, 3:88. Cf. *EC* 172–73/110–11 on the image of the circle. Evolution, it bears repeating, is not cyclical. Only matter, as we will see, "circularizes" it (*EC* 129–30/83–84 and 177–78/114).

54. Schelling, *Philosophie der Offenbarung*, *Werke* VISupp, 463 [modified].

55. Cf. *Rire* 49/65.

56. *EC* 129/83; *DSMR* 41–42n/44–45n2; *ES* 23–24/29–31.

57. Schopenhauer, *World*, 3:341.

58. To tell the truth, Guyau is more of a moralist, and he brings practical and pedagogical preoccupations to bear on these problems.

59. Scheler, *The Nature of Sympathy*, 18–36, esp. 28–30.

60. Russell, *The Analysis of Mind*, 55–56; Drever, *Instinct in Man*, 92–94: Ruyer, "Bergson et le sphex ammophile."

61. Cf. Ribot, *La psychologie des sentiments*, 193. It cannot be said often enough that instinct evolves and that it is exposed to singular aberrations. Henri Piéron cites some cases in his article "Les problèmes actuels de l'instinct."

62. Cf. Butler, *Life and Habit*, ch. 3 (36–48).

63. Piéron, "Les problèmes actuels," 358. Cf. Larguier des Bancels, *Introduction à la psychologie*, 178–86.

64. Plotinus, *Enneads*, III.7.8, 324/325.

65. *EC* 169/108.

66. Descartes, "Discourse 8 of the Meteors," *The World*, 89–91.

67. Cf. Armand Sabatier's excellent criticism of Romanes's and Edmond Perrier's intellectualist monism.

68. Schopenhauer, *World*, 3:90, 3:100, and 3:102. For Schopenhauer, sympathy and the sexual instinct triumph over time, which is merely a form of representation.

69. Cf. in particular Passavant, *Untersuchungen über den Lebensmagnetismus und das Hellsehen.*

70. *EC* 340/217.

71. Incompatible: *EC* 101/65 and 169/108. One must "choose."

72. Compare Bernoulli and Kern, eds., *Romantische Naturphilosophie*, 99–109.

73. Bernoulli and Kern, eds., *Romantische Naturphilosophie*, 288.

74. Like Bergson, the Romantics have insisted on the identity of instinct and the labor of organization; Bergson: "Where does the activity of instinct begin? And where does that of nature end? We cannot tell." (*EC* 140/90); Carus: "It is often difficult here to draw the line where growth [*Wachsen*], purely organic formation [*Bilden*], ends and artificial formation, the art drive begins"(*Psyche*, 134). Same remarks in Burdach and Treviranus (Bernoulli and Kern, eds., 177–220 and 282–300).

75. Maj. Richard William George Hingston, who has visited the Himalayas, cites some very amusing examples in his *Problems of Instinct and Intelligence.* For its demonstrative value, let us retain above all the very elegant experiment described by Henri Piéron [i.e. the example of the digger wasp *Sphex flavipennis* in "Les problèmes actuels de l'instinct," 363, taken from Fabre, *Souvenirs*, 93].

76. [Cf. Piéron 358.]

77. Russell, "Behaviorism," 153.

78. *EC* 152/98 [modified]; cf. Carus, *Psyche*, 156–58.

79. Pascal, "Préface sur le Traité du vide," 455.

80. See the first two chapters of *MM*, and especially 94–95/60–61; *EC* 120/77, 136–37/88, 178–79/114–15, and 183/117.

81. [Butler, *Erehwon, Works*, 2:172–205.]

82. [Cf. Maeterlinck, *Ariane et Barbe-Bleue*, 51–52.] Plato, *Republic* VII, 517a, 378.

83. *EC* 138–42/89–91 and 159–61/102–3.

84. Cuvier (31) and Schopenhauer (*World*, 3:98) compare instinct to a natural somnambulism; Carus (*Psyche*, 87) to a biological dream. That is von Kieser's idea.

85. *EC* 230–31/147–48 on the opposition of genera and laws and 329–35/211–14 on the "cinematographic mechanism" in modern science.

86. On the *quelconque*: *EC* 132/85, 141/91, 155–59/100–102; *Essai* already says of number that it "can be split up according to any law we please" (62/83 [modified]). Objectivity itself is but an apperception of possible subdivisions within the undivided. On space, *Essai* 84/113 and 155/206–7; cf. *DS* 164–65/112–13; *Essai* 136/181.

87. Carus, *Psyche*, 142–43. For a penetrating criticism of "transitions," cf. Vialleton, "Le transformisme et la morphologie," 76–80.

88. *EC* 160/103.

89. Carus, *Psyche*, 154.

90. For example *EC* 199–200/127–28 and, in the same vein, the introduction, vii/xxxvi.

91. *EC* 272–73/174–75 and 360/230.

92. *EC* 4/2, 33–35/21–23, 89–90/58, 164/105, 169/109, 231–32/148, 268–71/172–73, 305–7/195–96, 312/200, 363–65/232–34; *ES* 44/55; *DSMR* 7/14, 20/26, 59/60–61, 113/109, 257/242–43, 289/271, 295/277, and 331/310–11.

93. [Compare, for example, Leibniz, *Philosophical Essays*, 22 and 210.]

94. [Plotinus, *Enneads*, V.1.6, 28/29.]

95. [Aristotle, *On the Heavens*, I.11, 281a, 465.]

96. *EC* 94/60; *DSMR* 52/54, 118/114, and 335/314.

97. *EC* 88–98/56–63; cf. *ES* 22/29.

98. [Cf. Plato, *Gorgias* 493a2–3, 587: "the body is our tomb," and *Phaedrus* 250c.]

99. *EC* 94–95/60–61 and 103–4/66–67. Bergson uses the image of a canal and a road: the image of the tunnel seems even more clear-cut.

100. [Cf., for example, *Nicomachean Ethics* V.3, 1131b23, 1786.]

101. *EC* 103/107, 105/68, 128/83, 160/103, 162/104 (on 100/64, vice versa, the question is that of a magnetic action of life on matter); *Rire* 20/25 and 118/154; *Essai* (74/99, 75/101, 100/134, and 168/224) already discusses the "obsession" with space.

102. *MM* 87/93 and *ES* 97/118.

103. Plotinus, *Enneads*, V.1.2.

104. *Rire* 22/29 and 38–40/49–52.

105. Part of the collection *ES*: see 22/29. Cf. *EC* 259/166 ("matter divides actually what was but virtually manifold" in life [modified]) and 270/173 (the separation of individuals was so to speak inscribed between the lines in the *élan vital*, but it is matter which actualizes it); *Essai* 102–3/137–39: space forces our states of consciousness to express and to distinguish themselves from one another; *DSMR* 118/114.

106. [Seneca, Epistle 94.16.]

107. These paradoxical passages are *EC* 202–3/129–30 and 208–10/133–34.

108. *EC* 94–95/60–61 and 111/71.

109. Böhme, *Threefold Life of Man*, 5–6 and 9–10.

110. *EC* 99/64 [cf. 265/170 for the trampoline (or "springboard") image].

111. *Epibaseis* (footings or foothold): Plato, *Republic* VI, 511b: "footings" (cf. Plotinus, *Enneads*, VI.7.36, 198/199); *Epanabasmoi* (steps or rungs): *Symposium* 211c, 543; *Epibathrai* (stepping-stone): Plotinus, *Enneads*, I.6.1, 232/233. [For *hormai*, see *Republic* VI, 511b.]

112. *ES* 23/29.

113. *EC* 258–59/165–66; cf. 11/7.

114. *EC* 93/59–60.

115. *EC* 9–11/6–7, 39/25, 208–9/133–34, and 300/192 (every quality is change), cf. 202/129.

116. *EC* 179/115 and 186/119; cf. *ES* 18/23.

117. *EC* 342/219 and 368/236.

118. [That is, formative effort, drive or élan to reproduce; the term is an invention of Johann Friedrich Blumenbach's, *Bildungstrieb* in German.]

119. *Rire* 151–53/198–200.

120. *Rire* 21/28–29 and 37–39/48–51.

121. *EC* 129/83 and 270/173.

122. Aristotle, *Nicomachean Ethics* VII.14, 1154b26–27, 1825, and *Physics* IV.12, 221b12, 375.

123. Kierkegaard, *Purity*, 217–18.

124. The passages on which I am commenting here are *EC* 13/9 (conflict of individuation and reproduction), 259–60/166 (conflict of individuation and association), 255/163 (egotism of the species), 239/152 and 270/173 (conflict of the intellect and life), and, above all, 128–30/83–84. Cf. Simmel, "The Conflict of Modern Culture."

125. *DS* 80/56; *EC* 130/84.

126. There are several passages in *EC* that rehabilitate, at least propaedeutically, the approach taken by the intellect; see 160/103, 177–78/114–15, 183/117, 199–200/128, 249/159, and 273/174–75.

127. [*EC* 129/83.]

128. *EC* 127/82, 142/92, 150/97, and 254/161.

129. *ES* 14/9; *EC* 70–71/45.

130. *EC* 180–82/115–16, 184–85/117, and 264–65/169–70 [modified]; cf. 250/160: "Of these two currents the second runs counter to the first, but the first obtains, all the same, something from the second."

131. On the difference between "causing" and "triggering" (or "releasing"), see *EC* 73–74/47, 116/75, and 184/117.

132. Schelling, *Philosophie der Mythologie*, 5th lecture, *Werke* VI, 347.

133. Leibniz, *Theodicy*, pt. 1, §20, 136.

134. [*EC* 171/173.]

135. Especially in the 1913 lecture "'Phantasms of the Living' and 'Physical Research,'" *ES* 61–84/75–103.

136. *PM* 290/299, cf. 114/122.

137. "d'emblée" *EC* 298/191.

138. *EC* 200/128 and 357–60/229–31, cf. 273/175.

139. *EC* 200–201/128–29 and 298/191.

140. [In a letter to Zelter of 29 March 1827, Goethe writes, in French, *il faut croire à la simplicité*, "we must believe in simplicity" (456).]

Chapter 5. Heroism and Saintliness

1. [*ES* 138/168.]

2. "will have been [traced out]," *Essai* 137/182; *PM* 110/118–19; *DSMR* 72/72 and 313/294.

3. *PM* 110/118–19; cf. 13–16/21–25.

4. Proust 2:175–76.

5. [Alain, *Préliminaires*, 261.]

6. [Pascal, *Pensées* no. 194 (72), 65.]

7. Cohen, *Ethik des reinen Willens*, 588–89: the state is not an extension of the family but an original totality.

8. EC 191/122–23; cf. Kierkegaard, *Anxiety*, 30, 30n, 32, and 38.

9. For the use of the future perfect: DSMR 72/72 and 313/294; "after the fact," "retroactively" ["retrospectively," etc.]: 71–73/71–73, 78/78, 80/80, 189/180, 229/216, 231/218, 240/227, 313–14/294, and 328/308; "elements" and "parts": 109/106 and 313/294; cf. 70–72/70–72. Cf. PM 1–23/9–32 and 99–116/107–25 on the "retroactive," "retrospective," and "retrograde" movement of the present. These texts, the "Introduction (Part I)" and "The Possible and the Real" date from 1934 and 1930, respectively.

10. DSMR 79/78.

11. [In EC, 285/183, Bergson speaks of "a reality that drives into (*chasse dans*) the region of the ideal."]

12. [See, for example, *Nicomachean Ethics* IX.4, 1166a, 1843.]

13. DSMR 322–23/302–3.

14. In the same way that, in MM, the break is not between the cerebral and the spinal but between the cerebral and supra-biological recollection.

15. DSMR 44/47 ("at a bound"), 296/278 ("at a single stroke"), 51/53 ("at a stroke"), and 196/186 ("as an unbroken whole"), 196/186 ("as a whole"), 238/225 ("suddenly"), and 240/227 ("at a given moment"); cf. 73/73.

16. DSMR 28/33, 73/73, 119–20/115, 132/127, 146/140, 196/186–87, 208/197, 229/216, 291n/273n1, and 296/278.

17. DSMR 229/216, 132/127 and 140/134: transformations cannot but operate at one moment *rather than at* another. Cf. 301/279.

18. PM 168/177–8; cf. ES 5–6/8–9 and 30/38.

19. DSMR 24/29–30, 83/82–83, 106–7/103–4, 117/113, 132–33/126–28, 167–68/160–61, 289–91/271–75, and 321/301; cf. EC 77–85/49–55; on the repression of this simplified conscience: DSMR 293/275 and 331/310–11; DSMR 168/135: "the natural reappears, like the changeless star in the night."

20. Cf. DSMR 52/53–54 and 57/58 (on the interplay of resistances) as well as 134/128–29 (intellect opposing intellect); MM 246/291–93, 265/315–16, 279–80/331–32; EC 180–82/115–17, 184–85/117, and 264–65/169–70.

21. DSMR 144/138 and 216/204–5.

22. DSMR 255/241 and DS x/xxvii, 66/36, 88/45, 97–99/51–52, 104/54; on experience in general: DSMR 51/53, 247/233, 255–56/241, 263/247–48, 265–66/250–51, and 280/264.

23. DSMR 26/31, 149/143, 172/164, and 193/184.

24. DSMR 136–37/131–32; Georg Simmel, in "Death and Immortality," shows how we are absolutely certain of the "whether" and absolutely uncertain of the "when" (*The View on Life*, 66).

25. *EC* 129/83 and 269/173; *DSMR* 34/38, 44/47, 74/74, 196/186, 210/199, 221/209, 243/230, and 273/257.

26. [From *virtus in actione consistit*, a Latin commonplace.]

27. *DSMR* 57–58/60 [modified]; on intention, 99/97; on differential calculus, 58/60 and 188/179; *PM* 214–15/225–26; and *EC* ch. 4.

28. *DSMR* 7/14, 108/104–5, and 121/117.

29. [Cf. Kierkegaard, *Anxiety*, 100.]

30. *DSMR* 132/127.

31. *DSMR* 86/84–85; on the freedom of the saints, see 248/233–34.

32. Proust, 2:144–46.

33. *DSMR* 27/32 and 36/40.

34. *EC* 129/83; *DS* 78–80/55–56.

35. *DSMR* 48/50–51, 98/96–97, 119/115, 169/161–62, 249/235, and 273/257.

36. [*DSMR* 320/300.]

37. *DSMR* 18/23–24, cf. 182/173–74. See also *Essai* 73–74/98–99, 81–88/109–10, 83/112, 94/126, 162–64/215–18, 168–72/229–32; *DS* 52/37 and 149–50/103–4.

38. *DSMR* 130/125 and 187/178.

39. *DSMR* 5/12–13, 34/37–38, 47/49–50, 64/65, 141/135, 184/175, and 212–13/2012, 287/269.

40. *DSMR* 287/269, cf. 320/300.

41. *Revelation* 3:15–16. This is the passage that Stepan Trofimovich asks Sofya Matveevna to read to him at the end of *Demons* (pt. II, ch. 7, 653).

42. *PM* 164/174; cf. 166/176.

43. *DSMR* 53/55, 196/186–87, 210/199, 218/206–7, 225/212–13, 271–76/255–60, and 332/219, cf. 114/110–11. And compare *EC* 266/170–71; on the plurality of worlds: *EC* 256–57/164 and *DSMR* 271/255.

44. [Cf. Goethe, *Faust II*, act 5, ll. 11008–9.]

Chapter 6. The Nothingness of Concepts and the Plenitude of Spirit

[Epigraph. Plato, *Sophist*, 259d–e, 416.]

1. *EC* 220–38/141–52 and 273–98/175–90. Cf. *PM* 65–69/72–76 and 105–9/113–17; *DSMR* 266–67/251.

2. *EC* 296–98/189–90.

3. [Lafontaine, "The Sculptor and the Statue of Jupiter," Fable 6 of book IX (modified).]

4. [Hesiod, *Theogony*, ll. 124–25.]

5. Lachelier, *Du fondement de l'induction*, 46 [not included in the English translation].

6. Schopenhauer, *World*, 2:374.

7. For this vocabulary, see *EC* 238/152 and 283/180–82.

8. *MM* 109/120–21, to be read alongside *ES* 166/201–2.

9. *Essai* 40/54; EC 4/2: "We only perceive what is coloured, or, in other words, psychic states."

10. *Essai* 16/21.

11. MM 69/71–72, 141/162, 151/173–75, 155/181, and 266–67/315–17; cf. ES 130–35/158–64 and 208/252.

12. MM 85/91 and 88/94–95.

13. MM 52/51–52, 54–55/54–55, and 59/60.

14. EC 169–70/108–9.

15. MM 109/120–21 and 120/134–35; *Rire*, chapter 3, 101–53/132–200.

16. DSMR 132/127 and 240/227; MM 54–55/54–55, 69/71–72, and 141/162.

17. EC 96–97/61–62.

18. [Schopenhauer, *World*, 3:396.]

19. MM 114–15/126–28; cf. 184/215 and 191/224.

20. MM 131/149 and 195–96/230; ES 48/60 and 125–26/166–67.

21. ES 125–26/166–67 and 128/155.

22. Mourgue and Monakow, *Introduction biologique*, 113, 194, 283, and elsewhere.

23. ES 48/59–60, 76/93, and 100–101/122–23.

24. *Rire* 32/41, 36–37/47–48, 138–39/181, 143–44/187, and 149/195–96.

25. ES 128/155.

26. Such is the case, especially, for Hughlings Jackson's conceptions. For Schelling, see *Philosophical Investigations into the Essence of Human Freedom*, 38.

27. Cf. EC 172/110–11.

28. Pascal, "Esprit géométrique," 169.

29. Aristotle, *Physics*, VI.8, 216b, 367.

30. Cf. Delacroix, 553.

31. Bernard, *Experimental Medicine*, 45.

32. MM 130/147, 135–36/154, and 138–39/162–63; cf. ES 172/208.

33. Goblot, *Traité de logique*, 87. Cf. the quotation from Hannequin's *La méthode de Descartes*, 227, in Brunschvicg, *Progrès*, 682–83.

34. EC 286–88/183–84; Kant writes (CPR A708–709/B737–38) that the main purpose of negative judgments is to prevent error. They make up the content of *discipline* (as opposed to *culture*). Leibniz, *New Essays*, book III, ch. 1, §4, 276: "the act of denial is positive"; Montaigne, *Essays*, II.12 (Apology for Raymond Sebond), 488–683. [For Brochard, see his 1879 dissertation, *De l'erreur*.]

35. Montaigne, *Essays*, II.12: 590.

36. Plato, *Theaetetus*, 189a, 291; cf. *Sophist*, 237e, 387: "We cannot allow that one, who would fain express that which is not, ever speaks at all." Auguste Diès, in his editions of *Theaetetus* and *Sophist* (121 n2, 185 n2, and 186 n1), relates these passages to a large number of interesting texts, e.g. Malebranche, *Dialogue between a Christian Philosopher and a Chinese philosopher on the Existence and Nature of God*, 51 and 67 ("To think nothing and not to think . . . is the same thing") and *The Search after Truth* IV.2, §§ 4 and 5, 272–77, as well as Fénelon, *Demonstration*, pt. II, ch. 1, 160–63.

37. Plato, *Sophist*, 238c, 388.

38. EC 283/181.

39. Perry, "Le réalisme philosophique en Amérique," 139.

40. EC 280/179 and 283/181 as well as Carl Gustav Carus, "Das Organon der Erkenntnis [The Organon of Cognition]" in Bernoulli and Kern, eds., *Naturphilosophie*, 307–8. Here the relevant passage: "Since nonbeing or Nothingness is generally but a concept of the mind, namely insofar as every positive already presupposes its negation—and as every existence of a particular presupposes the nonbeing of another in its place—it is clear by itself that a Nothing, even if thought as a positive and as limiting other positives, must necessarily be a nonthing [*Unding*] and that it can no more exist than can a square circle." In this text, Carus defends the infinity of space.

41. Plato, *Sophist*, 257b, 413.

42. [Genesis 1:2.]

43. Jules Lequier in Renouvier, *Traité de psychologie*, 109–23; EC 101/65: "Each of us lives but one life" [modified].

44. Leibniz's Fifth Letter to Clarke, *Correspondence*, 39; cf. "Conversation sur la liberté et le destin," 482.

45. [Cf. Athaeneum fragment no. 226, *Lucinde*, 193.]

46. [*Pensées* no. 483 [726], 156, where Pascal transcribes Isaiah 50; cf. Matthew 12:30.]

47. Cf. Félicité Robert de Lamennais, *Indifference in Matters of Religion*.

48. [Leibniz's Fifth Letter to Clarke, *Correspondence*, 39.]

49. Plato, *Meno*, 77b and 78b.

50. [Letter to Louis Bourget of 3 January 1714, *Philosophische Schriften*, 3:562.]

51. EC 274/175.

52. Leibniz, *Discourse on Metaphysics*, §6, 39, on "geomancy."

53. [Schopenhauer, "On Ethics," 239.]

54. Descartes, *Meditations on First Philosophy*, 13. Cf. Pascal, *Pensées* no. 696 [22], 219.

55. Cf. PM 147/156–57.

56. DSMR 154–55/147–48.

57. "The Possible and the Real" (PM 99–116/107–25). See Leibniz, "On the Ultimate Origination of Things." As for Schelling, he speaks of a *Nothingness* that would be, following Plato's terms, another thing than being and not Not-Being. But to this Nothingness (*ēn on* [=nicht *Seiendes*]), he opposes *Nothing* (*ouk on* [=Nichts=Rien=*nicht* Seiendes]), which absolutely excludes being (*Darstellung des philosophischen Empirismus*, *Werke* V:271–332, here 281–82 and 328–31). On the positivity of the negative, compare a curious early piece by Kant, "Attempt to Introduce the Concept of Negative Magnitudes into Philosophy" (1763) as well as Solger, *Über Sein, Nichtsein und Erkennen*.

58. *Essai* 130–31/173–74.

59. EC 101/65 and *Essai* 7/9–10.

60. Kierkegaard, *Anxiety, Irony, Purity*, etc. [Schelling, *Werke* V, 281–82 and 328–31.]

61. [*EC* 101/65.]

62. *EC* 98/63 and 145/93–94.

63. *MM* 207/243; *Essai* 158–59/211–12.

64. *Essai* 158–59/211–12.

65. This difficulty already caused Aristotle embarrassment. In book VIII of the *Physics* (VIII.8, 263b9–26, 440), he says that change can only be conceived on the condition that the last moment of what comes before is being related to the future, i.e. the beginning of what comes after.

66. *EC* 209/134 and 211/135.

67. *MM* 247/293, 264/313, and 279/331.

68. *EC* 144–45/93; cf. 150/96–97.

69. *EC* 181–82/115–16, 184–85/117, and 264–65/169–70; cf. Kant, "Attempt to Introduce the Concept of Negative Magnitudes into Philosophy," and Schelling, *Philosophie der Mythologie, Werke* V supp, 51 (9th lecture) and VI:106 (5th lecture).

70. [Aristotle, *Physics*, IV.12, 221b12, 375.]

71. Thibaudet, *Le Bergsonisme*, I:121–31.

72. Spinoza, *Ethics*, part I, appendix, 442, and part III, preface, 492.

73. Spinoza, *Ethics*, part I, appendix, 441.

74. Brunschvicg, *Progrès*, 684.

75. [Spinoza, *Ethics*, part I, appendix, 443 [modified].]

76. *EC* 97/62, 116/75, 127/82, 137/89, 183/117, 246–47/157–58, 251/160–61, 264/169, and 266/170–71; *ES* 13/17–18. Cf. Guyau, *Non-Religion of the Future*, 496: "what we can affirm with certainty is that life, by the very fact of its development, tends to engender consciousness; and that progress in life ultimately comes to be one with progress in consciousness."

77. Stepun, "Tragediya tvorchestva (Fr. Schlegel)," 171.

78. On this radical contingency of evolution, see *EC* 103/66; Bergson discusses the "progress" of life on 104–5/67–68.

79. *EC* 277–88/177–84.

80. [A statue is the central device in Condillac's 1754 *Traité des sensations*.]

81. Spinoza, *Ethics*, part II, prop. 48 scol., 483–84 as well as prop. 32–35, 472, prop. 43 and 43 scol., 479–80, prop. 47 scol., 482–83, and prop. 49 scol, 485–91. Compare the scolium to prop. 45, 482: "nature of existence," and the appendix to part I. Compare to Bergson's critique of the possible in "The Possible and the Real" (*PM* 99–116/107–25).

82. *EC* 286/183; compare Descartes's first *Meditation* (*Philosophical Writings* II:12–15) cited above, 178–79.

83. *EC* 365/234.

84. Plotinus, *Enneads*, V.3.9. 102/103; see also I.4.12, 202/203; I.8.2, 280/281; VI.9.5, 318/319.

85. *EC* 281/180; *MM* 266/315.

86. *ES* 59–60/73–74.

87. [A Greek proverb; cf. Plato, *Greater Hippias*, 304e, 595.]

88. [Goethe, *Faust*, ll. 1938–39, 65.]

Chapter 7. Simplicity... and Joy

[Fénelon, *Christian Perfection*, no. 40, 194–204 (*Œuvres* 6:157).]

1. *Essai* 106/141. Cf. *PM* 223–25/233–35.

2. This is the abstract simplicity of which Bergson speaks in *MM* 69/71–72.

3. *PM* 189/198–99.

4. *ES* 186/22–26; cf. *PM* 226/236 on the concrete simplicity of intuition.

5. Plotinus, *Enneads*, II.9.1; V.3.13, 118/119; V.3.16, 128/129; V.4.1, 140/141; V.6.3, 208/209; V.6.4, 208/209. On "haplosis," see VI.9.11, 340–44/341–45.

6. Eugenio d'Ors, *Du baroque*, 19.

7. de Maistre, Tenth Dialogue, 289 [modified], and Nietzsche, "Schopenhauer as Educator," §1, 129.

8. *PM* 22/31, 160–61/170–71 (and 164/174). Cf. *ES* 2/4 ; *DSMR* 51/53–54.

9. Scheler, *The Nature of Sympathy*.

10. Fauré-Fremiet, *Pensée et re-création* and *La recréation du réel et l'équivoque*.

11. [Cf. Plato, *Symposium*, 202d–204a, 534–35.]

12. [A pedantic scholar in Molière's *Les Femmes savantes* (1672).]

13. Montaigne, *Essays*, I.25, 155.

14. Alain, *Préliminaires*, 164, and Bremond, *Prayer and Poetry*, ch. 12, 107–31.

15. Aristotle, *Nicomachean Ethics*, II.1, 1103b21–22, 1743.

16. [Aristotle, *Nicomachean Ethics*, I.7, 1098a, 1735.]

17. Pascal, *Pensées*, no. 919 [553], "The Mystery of Jesus," 290. Cf. Plotinus, *Enneads*, V.3.16, 128–30/129–31. Lequier, *Recherche*, pt. I and III. Plato, more dogmatic in this regard, says that Love only desires what it does not have and what it has, it does not desire (*Symposium*, e.g. 200b–e, 531–32).

18. *EC* 193/124.

19. Alain, *Préliminaires*, 191.

20. [Plato, *Phaedo*, 114d (modified).]

21. *DSMR* 78/78.

22. Lequier, *Recherche*, 138; cf. Renouvier, *Traité de psychologie*, 2:109–23.

23. Michelet, *The People*, pt. II, ch. 4, 92 (cf. 94).

24. *DSMR* 52/54.

25. [First articulated by Flaubert in 1841, the phrase now denotes a mathematical problem that cannot be solved with the information provided.]

26. *PM* 139/149; *DSMR* 51/53–54, 167/160, 241/228, 275/259, 320/300. Cf. Nietzsche, *Human, All Too Human*, II.I.196, 359.

27. *Essai* 54–55/72–74; EC 128/82–83; PM 8/16, 22/31, 32/40–41, 65–69/72–79, 99–116/107–25 (esp. 104/112), 157/167, 160/170, 173/183–84, 176/186, 205/215–16; DSMR 266–67/251.

28. This is how Bergson paraphrases Berkeley in PM 131/140.

29. Fénelon, Letter to countess Montberon of 22 April 1707, *Œuvres*, 8:676. This is the "not to resist the evil" of the Sermon of the Mount (Matthew 5:39). Cf. Tolstoy, *The Kingdom of God*.

30. DSMR 57/59.

31. PM 65/72.

32. Alain, *Préliminaires*, 204.

33. PM 157/167, 213/224, and 225/235.

34. Plato, *Republic* IV, 432d–432e, 285.

35. Tolstoy, *War and Peace*, vol. IV, pt. III, ch. 15, 1065 [modified]; "The Death of Ivan Ilyich," ch. 12, 160.

36. DSMR 51/53 and 246/232, cf. 244/230–31.

37. Matthew 9:5–7, Marc 2:9–11, Luke 5:23–25.

38. John 11:44: "hands and feet bound with strips of cloth." Cf. Marc 5:42, Luke 7:15 and 8:55. Compare Acts 2:4.

39. PM 66/73–74.

40. Plotinus, *Enneads*, II.9.1, 224–30/225–31. Cf. Spinoza, *Ethics*, part II, prop. 21 scol.: "For as soon as someone knows something, he thereby knows that he knows it, and at the same time knows that he knows that he knows, and so on, to infinity." Compare the *Treatise on the Emendation of the Intellect*.

41. PM 119/128; cf. 31/39, 133/142, 223–25/223–25.

42. PM 92/100.

43. "interposed" PM 4/12, 6/15, and 157/167; cf. MM 61/62 ; ES 2/4; EC 244/156 and 287/184.

44. [The quote is not from Fénelon, as Jankélévitch has it, but from Bossuet: Letter 144 to Sœur Cornuau, *Œuvres*, 17:726.]

45. Think also of Chopin's Andante spianato in G Major.

46. Plotinus, *Enneads*, II.9.14, 280–81 [modified]; Ruusbroec, 122.

47. DSMR 276–77/261.

48. La Ville de Mirmont, "L'horizon chimérique," 27.

49. PM 153–54/163–64.

50. PM 290/299.

51. [The word *problématique* used this way being an adaptation of the German *Problematik*, a set or complex of problems.]

52. [Fénelon, Letter to countess Montberon of 22 April 1707, *Œuvres*, 8:676.]

53. Bahnsen, *Das Tragische und der Humor* and *Der Widerspruch*.

54. Simmel, "Henri Bergson," 63–64.

55. [EC 271/173, emphasis Jankélévitch.]

56. Revelation 21:4.

57. [For Schopenhauer, see *World*, 1:254]

58. *ES* 23–24/29–31; *DSMR* 49/51, 57/58–59, 243–44/230, 277/261, and 338/317; *PM* 116/124, 142/152, and 290/298–99; Compare *Essai* 7–8/9–11; [Leibniz, *New Essays*, bk. 2, ch. 22, 166, and Spinoza, *Ethics*, pt. III, prop. 59, 529.] And cf. Marcel, 236–37 (entry of 29 February 1920); Jakob Böhme, *Mysterium magnum*, 268: "in the Conquest is joy [*in der Überwindung ist Freude*]." Koyré, 352: "La joie est dans la lutte et la victoire, et Dieu est éternellement victorieux [*Joy is in the struggle and in the victory, and God is eternally victorious*]."

59. *ES* 25/32; *PM* 291/299–300.

60. Cf. Aristotle, *Physics*, VIII.5 and VIII.12, and Plotinus, *Enneads*, V.3.17.

61. [Epicurus, Vatican Sayings no. 27, *Epicurus Reader*, 37.]

62. [From the "Drinking Song" of Ravel's *Don Quichotte à Dulcinée*, which sets to music poems by Paul Morand.]

Bergson and Judaism

["Bergson and Judaism" translated by Melissa McMahon.]

1. On the opposition between Spinoza's "monism" and Bergson's "dualism," see Gottlieb, "D'une erreur fondamentale dans les *Deux Sources* de M. Bergson."

2. [Plato, *Timaeus*, 37d, 1167.]

3. Genesis 1:6, 1:5, 1:7.

4. See Baudry, "Le problème de l'origine et de l'éternité du monde."

5. Pascal, Pensées, no. 17, 115 [modified]: "The God of Christians does not consist in a God who is merely the author of geometrical truths and of the order of the elements; that is the part given by the heathens and Epicureans."

6. Genesis 6:5, translated in Fleg, *Le livre du commencement* [Translator's note: Where there is a significant difference between the biblical passages cited in French and the most common English versions of these passages, I have translated directly from the French.]

7. Isaiah 66:8; see Epictetus, *Discourses*, book I, ch. 15, § 7; *Philebus*, 18 a–b.

8. *EC* 9–10/6 and 338–9/216–7.

9. Compare Genesis 3:19 and Ecclesiastes 3:20. See also Psalms 146:4.

10. Ecclesiastes 2:15. The Septuagint translates it: *Hinati* ("to what end"), the very word of abandonment on Calvary (Matthew 27:46; Mark 15:34: *eis ti* ["why"]).

11. Job 8:9 and 1 Chronicles 39:15.

12. Jeremiah 32:17.

13. Isaiah 42:16 and Jeremiah 31:13 and 31:16.

14. Leviticus 19:31 and Deuteronomy 13:2; see Exodus 22:18.

15. Isaiah 42:9 and 46:10, compare 48:3–5.

16. Isaiah 41:4, 44:6, and 48:12; see also Revelation 1:8, 1:17; 21:6, and 22:13: "I am the Alpha and the Omega, the First and the Last, the Beginning and the End."

17. *EC* 249/160 and 298/191; *DSMR* chapter 3, 221–82/209–65.

18. Silesius, *The Cherubinic Wanderer*, part I, 25 and III.

19. Rauh, "La conscience du devenir."

20. See Simmel, "Werde, was du bist," 307.

21. *Essai* 121/161.

22. *PM* 176/186 and 210/221 ("eternity of life") and 142/152 ("sub specie durationis").

23. *PM* 163–4/153–4.

24. [Cf. Plotinus, *Enneads*, I.6.8.]

25. See Cohen, *Ethik des reinen Willens*.

26. [Translator's note: A "garniture de cheminée" (the French phrase is also used in English) is a mantelpiece decoration consisting in a symmetrically arranged set of, most often, a clock with a candlestick on either side.]

27. Isaiah 25:8; compare Revelation 21:4, "There will be no more death," and 20:14: "It is the second death." Fleg, *Écoute Israël* 7.2, 583.

28. [Translator's note: See Epicurus, *Principal Doctrines*, n. 2.]

29. Huizinga, *Le déclin du Moyen Age*, 164–80.

30. Song of Songs 8.6.

31. See Cohen, *Le Talmud*, 45.

32. Exodus 3:6; cf. Matthew 22:33; Mark 12:27; Luke 20:38: "He is not the God of the dead, but of the living, for to him all are alive." But, see also Romans 14:8–9.

33. Isaiah 38:19.

34. Wisdom 1:12–14.

35. Proverbs 3:24–25.

36. Isaiah 43:1 and 43:5.

37. Proverbs 3:19.

38. Lewkowitz, *Das Judentum*.

39. Exodus 21:24–25.

40. Romans 13:10.

41. Matthew 22:40; see also 7:12.

42. Gottlieb, "D'une erreur fondamentale," 13–14.

43. Proverbs 20:22 and 34:29. It is not saying: "I'll pay them back for what they did" (see Romans 12:21 and Matthew 5:39, as well as Pascal, Pensées, 14/911).

44. Isaiah 2:4; see also 42:6.

45. Isaiah 66:18–20.

46. Deuteronomy 10:17. This is the "partiality" or "favouritism" Paul refers to in Romans 2:11 and Ephesians 6:9. See also 2 Chronicles 19:7.

47. Cohen, *Le Talmud*, 269.

48. Exodus 22:21, 23:9; Leviticus 19:33–34; Deuteronomy 10:18–19.

49. Exodus 33:4–5.

50. Fleg, *Nous de l'espérance*, 64.

51. Boulgakov, *L'orthodoxie*, 247–51.

52. [Translator's note: Jankélévitch plays here, as elsewhere in his work, on an invented opposition between "survenir," which means to arise or come to pass but which looks like it breaks down into "over" (sur)+"come" (venir), and "sub-venir," which looks like it shares a structure with "souvenir" (memory): "under" (sub/sou)+"come" (venir).]

53. Compare Wisdom 2:5 and Job 8:9.

54. Isaiah 65:17, cf. 43:18: "Remember ye not the former things, and consider not the ancient things."

55. Psalm 148; Tolstoy, *John of Damascus*. [Translator's note: Aleksey Konstantinovich Tolstoy (1817–75), second cousin to Leo, was a Russian poet whose narrative poem "John of Damascus" (1856) was put to verse by Pyotr Ilyich Tchaikovsky (1840–93). The song "I Bless You, Forests," is the fifth of Tchaikovsky's Seven Romances for voice and piano (op. 47, n. 5).]

56. Exodus 22:27; cf. Psalms 145:9.

57. Isaiah 66:2 and Job 5:15.

58. Leviticus 19:18 and Matthew 22:39, Mark 12:31, Romans 13:9, Galatians 5:14 and James 2:8.

59. Jeremiah 2:27.

60. Isaiah 29:13; see also Deuteronomy 10:17.

61. Book of Wisdom 1:1.

With the Whole Soul

1. On seriousness, cf. *Rire* 60/79. Plato, *Republic* VII, 518c, 380 [modified] (cf. *Republic* IV, 436b, 289). See also *Essai* 125–26/166–67 and PM 263/271 (on Ravaisson).

2. Deuteronomy 6:5, 10:12, 11:13, 13:3; Isaiah 26:9. Cf. Matthew 22:37 ("with all your heart, . . . soul, . . . mind"); Mark 12:30 and 12:33 ("with all the understanding, and with all the strength"); Luke 10:27.

3. Bossuet, *Méditations sur l'Evangile* I, 43rd and 44th day, *Œuvres* 4:132–35.

4. Fénelon, *Christian Perfection*, ch. 31: "Pure Love" (137–44); Aristotle, *Nicomachean Ethics*, IX.4, 1166a, 1843; Cicero, *De legibus* I.49, 351–52 (*toto pectore*); Saint Bernard, "On Loving God," II.6 and IX.29, 178, and 196–97.

5. Among others: PM 115/123.

6. DSMR 320–21/300–301.

7. Plato, *Republic* IX, 587a, 461, and Psalms 34:9.

8. See, for example, *Essai* 140–42/185–89.

9. [So the title of Gisèle Brelet's 1951 book.]

10. PM 92/100.

11. DSMR 26/31, 149/143, 172/164, and 193/184; Tolstoy, *The Kingdom of God*, ch. 5, 109–32.

12. Aristotle, *Nicomachean Ethics* X.2, 1172b, 1853: "His arguments were credited more because of the excellence of his character than for their own sake" (cf. *Nicomachean Ethics* X.1, 1172a–b, 1852). See also Xenophon, *Memorabilia*,

IV.4.10, p. 312/313: To Socrates's question, "Don't you think that deeds are better evidence than words?" Hippias answers, "for many say what is just and do what is unjust; but no one who does what is just can be unjust."Cf. Cicero, *De finibus bonorum et malorum*, II.25, 172/173, as well as Descartes, *Discourse on the Method*, part III, "The Visible Universe," *The Philosophical Writings*, 1:248–66.

13. [Honoré de Balzac, "Gobseck."]

14. [Luke 9:62.]

15. [*Ion* 533e, 107.]

16. DSMR 270/255, cf. 338/317.

17. PM 114/123, cf. 290/299.

18. Isaiah 42:7.

19. Luke 9:62.

20. PM 290/299.

21. [References to Rimsky-Korsakov's 1905 opera *The Legend of the Invisible City of Kitezh and the Maiden Fevroniya*.]

Preface to the First Edition of Henri Bergson *(1930)*

1. Vol. 35, no. 4: 437–90.

Letters to Vladimir Jankélévitch by Henri Bergson

1. This appendix assembles Bergson's published letters to Jankélévitch, with the exception of a short note of February 10, 1928 (*Correspondances* 1245). In that letter, Bergson thanks Jankélévitch for sending him his article, "Signification spirituelle du principe d'économie," which had just been published in the *Revue philosophique* (53:88–126).

2. "Deux philosophies de la vie: Bergson, Guyau," in *Premières et dernières pages*, 13–62.

3. "Bersonisme et biologie, à propos d'un ouvrage récent," *Revue de métaphysique et de morale* 36, no. 2 (April 1929): 2–256. Jankélévitch used most of this article in chapters 2 and 4 of the present volume.

4. Xavier Léon (1868–1935), most notably founder of the *Revue de métaphysique et de morale* and of the *Société française de philosophie*.

5. For the first edition of *Henri Bergson*, Fortuné Palhoriès (the editor of the series in which the volume appeared, *Les grands philosophes*), includes this letter as a preface, to which he adds:

These lines by the illustrious master are the best recommendation of Mr. V. Jankélévitch's work, which is why I personally insisted, despite some delicate scruples on the part of the one to whom they were addressed, on reproducing them here. In a conversation I had with him, Mr. Bergson already told me all the good he thought of this work. He stressed above all the way in which the author, instead of setting out to give a mere exposition, a reconstitution of ideas, applies himself to seeking out their genesis and to elaborate, if we may say so, their *substructions*. That is why this volume resembles none of the others that have appeared on Bergson's theory as a whole; it does not render them useless, it does not contradict them, at least in general; it completes them because it pushes them further, in extension and in depth. I won't dare add my compliments to those that so authoritative a judge addressed to Mr. V. Jankélévitch; I would like to express, however, my gratitude to Mr. Bergson for the honor he has done the *Collection*; which, incidentally, is not the only debt of acknowledgement I personally find I owe him.

6. *L'Alternative* (Paris: Alcan, 1938).
7. *Maurice Ravel* (Paris: Rieder, 1938).

Letter to Louis Beauduc on First Meeting Bergson (1923)

1. Jankélévitch's thesis supervisor, whose influence (and particularly his work on Plotinus and Schelling) is evident in this volume.

What Is the Value of Bergson's Thought?

[Jankélévitch was one of "three professors" to answer the question, What is the value of Bergson's thought today? in the weekly *Arts: Beaux-arts, littératures, spectacles* (no. 724, 27 May–2 June 1959: 3).]

1. [That is, around 1911; cf. PM 143–76/153–86.]

Solemn Homage to Henri Bergson

1. [*Essai* 125–26/166–67, and Plato, *Republic* VII, 518c, 380 and IV, 436b, 289 [modified].]
2. [Aristotle, *Nicomachean Ethics*, IX.4, 1166a, 1843.]
3. [Mark 12:30 and 12:33, Matthew 22:37.]
4. [Cf. EC 238/153 and 251/161.]
5. [DSMR 26/31, 149/143, 172/164, and 193/184.]
6. [Aristotle, *Nicomachean Ethics* X.2, 1172b, 1853.]
7. [Matthew 9:5–7, Marc 2:9–11, Luke 5:23–25.]
8. [Paraphrasing a poem from the collection *Buch der Lieder* [*Book of Songs*] set to music by Robert Schumann:

Anfangs wollt ich fast verzagen
Und ich glaubt, ich trüg es nie;
Und ich hab es doch getragen,—
Aber fragt mich nur nicht: wie?]

9. [Aristotle, *Nicomachean Ethics* I.7, 1098a, 1735.]

10. [Pascal, *Pensées*, no. 919 [553], "The Mystery of Jesus Christ," 290.]

11. [Seneca, letter LXXXI, §13, *Ad Lucilium Epistulae Morales*, 2:226.]

12. [Lequier, *Recherche*, pt. III.]

13. [Eugenio d'Ors, *Du baroque*, 19.]

14. [Plato, *Ion* 533e, 107.]

15. [Balzac, "Gobseck."]

16. [Psalms 119:32.]

BIBLIOGRAPHY

For a number of texts, the only translations available are heavily edited versions that do not include (all of) the passages Jankélévitch makes reference to. In these cases, the bibliographical information for the original text is given first, followed by the reference to the translation.

Alain, *Préliminaires à l'esthétique*. Paris: Gallimard, 1939.

Ansell-Pearson, Keith. *Philosophy and the Adventure of the Virtual: Bergson and the Time of Life*. London: Routledge, 2002.

Antliff, Mark. *Inventing Bergson: Cultural Politics and the Parisian Avant-Garde*. Princeton, NJ: Princeton University Press, 1992.

Aristotle, *The Complete Works of Aristotle*. Ed. Jonathan Barnes. Bollingen Series LXXI.2. Princeton, NJ: Princeton University Press, 1984.

———. *Magna Moralia*. Trans. St. George Stock. In *Complete Works*, 2:1868–1921.

———. *Nicomachean Ethics*. Trans. W. D. Ross, rev. J. O. Urmson. In *Complete Works*, 2:1729–1867.

———. *On the Heavens*. Trans. J. L. Stocks. In *Complete Works*, 1:447–551.

———. *On the Soul*. Trans. J. A. Smith. In *Complete Works*, 1:641–92.

———. *Physics*. Trans. R. P. Hardie and R. K. Gaye. In *Complete Works*, 1:315–446.

Azouvi, François. *La gloire de Bergson: Essai sur le magistère philosophique*. Paris: Gallimard, 2007.

Baader, Franz Xaver von. *Philosophische Schriften und Aufsätze*. Münster, Germany: Theissing, 1831.

Bahnsen, Julius. *Das Tragische als Weltgesetz und der Humor als ästhetische Gestalt des Metaphysischen*. Ed. Anselm Ruest. Leipzig, Germany: Barth, 1930.

———. *Der Widerspruch im Wissen und Wesen der Welt: Princip und Einzelbewährung der Realdialektik*. Vol. 1. Berlin: Grieben, 1880.

Balzac, Honoré de. "Gobseck." Trans. Ellen Marriage. Project Gutenberg. Accessed 20 November 2014. http://www.gutenberg.org/files/1389/1389-h/1389-h.htm.

Baudry, Jules. *Le problème de l'origine et de l'éternité du monde dans la philosophie grecque de Platon à l'ère chrétienne*. Paris: Belles lettres, 1931.

Bazaillas, Albert. *La vie personnelle, étude sur quelques illusions de la perception intérieure*. Paris: Alcan, 1904.

Bénézé, Georges. "Qu'est-ce qu'un système de référence?" *Revue de métaphysique et de morale* 32, no. 3 (July–September 1925): 321–58.

Bergson, Henri. *Correspondances*. Ed. André Robinet et al. Paris: PUF, 2002.

———. *Creative Evolution*. Trans. Arthur Mitchell. Ed. Keith Ansell Pearson, Michael Kolkman, and Michael Vaughan. Houndmills, UK: Palgrave Macmillan, 2007.

———. *The Creative Mind*. Trans. Mabelle M. Andison. New York: Philosophical Library, 1946.

———. *Duration and Simultaneity: Bergson and the Einsteinian Universe*. Ed. and trans. Robin Durie, 2nd ed. Manchester, UK: Clinamen Press, 1999.

———. *Key Writings*. Ed. Keith Ansell Pearson and John Mullarkey. New York: Continuum, 2002.

———. *Laughter: An Essay on the Meaning of the Comic*. Trans. Cloudesley Brereton and Fred Rothwell. New York: Macmillan, 1911.

———. *Matter and Memory*. Trans. Nancy Margaret Paul and W. Scott Palmer. New York: Macmillan, 1911.

———. *Mélanges*. Ed. André Robinet et al. Paris: PUF, 1972.

———. *Mind-Energy: Essays and Lectures*. Trans. H. Wildon Carr. New York: Holt, 1920.

———. *Time and Free Will: An Essay on the Immediate Data of Consciousness*. Trans. F. L. Pogson. New York: Macmillan, 1910.

———. *The Two Sources of Morality and Religion*. Trans. R. Ashley Audra and Cloudesley Brereton. Notre Dame, IN: University of Notre Dame Press, 1977.

Berkeley, George. *An Essay toward a New Theory of Vision*. In *Philosophical Writings*. Ed. Desmond M. Clarke, 1–66. Cambridge: Cambridge University Press, 2008.

Bernard of Clairvaux, "On Loving God [*De diligendo Deo*]." In *Selected Works*. Trans. G. R. Evans, 173–205. New York: Paulist Press, 1987.

Bernard, Claude. *An Introduction to the Study of Experimental Medicine*. Trans. Henry Copley Greene. New York: Schuman, 1949.

Bernoulli, Christoph, and Hans Kern, eds. *Romantische Naturphilosophie*. Jena, Germany: Diederichs, 1926.

Berthelot, René. *Le Pragmatisme chez Bergson*. In *Un romantisme utilitaire, étude sur le mouvement pragmatiste*, vol. 2. Paris: Alcan, 1911.

Berthelot, René, et al. "L'idée de vie chez Guyau: Séance du 28 décembre 1905." *Bulletin de la Société francaise de philosophie* 6 (1906): 42–79.

Blondel, Charles. *La conscience morbide: Essai de psycho-pathologie générale*. 2nd. augm. ed. Paris: Alcan, 1928.

Böhme, Jakob. *The High and Deep Searching of the Threefold Life of Man, through or according to the Three Principles*, vol. 2 of *The Works of Jacob Behmen, the*

Teutonic Theosopher [etc.]. Ed. G. Ward and T. Langcke. Trans. John Sparrow, John Ellistone, and H. Blunden. London: Richardson, 1764. Eighteenth Century Collections Online. Accessed 20 November 2014.

———. *Mysterium magnum, or An exposition of the first book of Moses called Genesis* [etc.]. Trans. John Sparrow and John Ellistone. London: Lloyd, 1656. Early English Books Online. Accessed 20 November 2014.

Bossuet, Jacques Bénigne. *Œuvres complètes*. Besançon: Outhenin-Chalandre, 1836.

Boulgakov, Sergeï. *L'orthodoxie*. Paris: Balzon, d'Allonnes et Cie, 1958.

Boutroux, Émile. *The Contingency of the Laws of Nature*. Trans. Fred Rothwell. Chicago: Open Court, 1916.

Bréhier, Émile. *Études de philosophie antique*. Paris: PUF, 1955.

———. "Note on treatise III.7." In *Ennéades*, by Plotinus. Vol. 3. Paris: Les Belles Lettres, 1924–38.

Brelet, Gisèle. *L'Interprétation créatrice: Essai sur l'exécution musicale*. Paris: PUF, 1951.

Bremond, Henri. *Prayer and Poetry: A Contribution to Poetical Theory*. Trans. Algar Labouchere Thorold. London: Burns, Oates and Washbourne, 1927.

Brochard, Victor. *De l'erreur*. 3rd ed. Paris: Alcan, 1926.

Brunschvicg, Léon. *L'expérience humaine et la causalité physique*. Paris: Alcan, 1949.

———. *Le progrès de la conscience dans la philosophie occidentale*. Paris: PUF, 1928.

———. *Spinoza*. Paris: Alcan, 1894.

Butler, Samuel. *Erehwon*. In *Works*, vol. 2.

———. *Life and Habit*. In *Works*, vol. 4.

———. *The Shrewsbury Edition of the Works of Samuel Butler*. Ed. Henry Festing Jones and A. T. Bartholomew. London: Cape, 1923–26.

Buytendijk, F. J. J. *Psychologie des animaux*. Trans. H. R. Bredo. Paris: Payot, 1928.

Carteron, Henri. "Remarques sur la notion de temps d'après Aristote." *Revue philosophique de la France et de l'étranger* 98 (July–December 1924): 67–81.

Carus, Carl Gustav. *Psyche: Zur Entwicklungsgeschichte der Seele*. 3rd ed. Pforzheim, Germany: Flammer, 1860. Reprint. Darmstadt: Wissenschaftliche Buchgesellschaft, 1975.

Cicero, M. Tullius. *Academica*. Trans. H. Rackham. In *Cicero in Twenty-Eight Volumes*, 19:406–659.

———. *Cicero in Twenty-Eight Volumes*. Cambridge, MA: Harvard University Press, 1965–79.

———. *De finibus bonorum et malorum* [*About the Ends of Goods and Evils*]. Trans. H. Rackham. In *Cicero in Twenty-Eight Volumes*, 17.

———. *De legibus* [*Laws*]. Trans. Clinton Walker Keyes. In *Cicero in Twenty-Eight Volumes*, 16:296–519.

Claparède, Édouard. *L'Association des idées*. Paris: Doin, 1903.

Claudel, Paul. "Jules ou l'Homme-aux-deux-cravates." In *Le poëte et le Shamisen, Le poëte et le vase d'encens, Jules ou l'Homme-aux-deux-cravates*. Ed. Michel Malicet, 153–72. Paris: Belles Lettres, 1970.

Cohen, Abraham. *Le Talmud*. Trans. Jacques Marty. Paris: Payot, 1950.

Cohen, Hermann. *Ethik des reinen Willens*. 5th ed. In *Werke*. Ed. Helmut Holzey. Vol. 7. Hildesheim, Germany: Olms, 1981.

Curle, Clinton. *Humanité: John Humphrey's Alternative Account of Human Rights*. Toronto: University of Toronto Press, 2007.

Cuvier, Georges. *Cuvier's Animal Kingdom, Arranged according to Its Organisation* [etc.]. London: Orr, 1840.

Damascius. *Damascius' Problems and Solutions concerning First Principles*. Trans. Sara Ahbel-Rappe. Oxford: Oxford University Press, 2010.

Davidson, Arnold I. "The *Charme* of Jankélévitch." In *Music and the Ineffable*, vii–xii. Princeton, NJ: Princeton University Press, 2003.

———. "Introductory Remarks." *Critical Inquiry* 22, no. 3 (spring 1996): 545–48.

Delacroix, Henri. *Le langage et la pensée*. Paris: PUF, 1924.

Deleuze, Gilles. *Bergsonism*. Trans. Hugh Tomlinson and Barbara Habberjam. New York: Zone Books, 1988.

———. *Desert Islands and Other Texts: 1953–1974*. Ed. David Lapoujade. Los Angeles, CA: Semiotext(e), 2004.

———. *Empiricism and Subjectivity: An Essay on Hume's Theory of Human Nature*. Trans. Constantin Boundas. New York: Columbia University Press, 1991.

Deleuze, Gilles, and Félix Guattari. *A Thousand Plateaus: Capitalism and Schizophrenia*. Trans. Brian Massumi. Minneapolis: University of Minnesota Press, 1987.

Descartes, René. *Discourse on the Method*. In *Philosophical Writings*, 1:111–51.

———. Letter 49 to Clerselier. In *Lettres de M. Descartes* [etc.], 603–7. Paris: Compagnie des librairies, 1724.

———. "Letter to Voetius, May 1643." In *Philosophical Writings*, 3:220–24.

———. *Meditations on First Philosophy*. In *Philosophical Writings*, 2:3–61.

———. *The Philosophical Writings of Descartes*. Trans. John Cottingham, Robert Stoothoff, Dugald Murdoch, and Anthony Kenny. 3 vols. Cambridge: Cambridge University Press, 1984–91.

———. *Rules for the Direction of the Mind*. In *Philosophical Writings*, 1:8–78.

———. *The World and Other Writings*. Trans. and ed. Stephen Gaukroger. Cambridge: Cambridge University Press, 1998.

Diès, Auguste, ed. and trans. *Parménide, Théétète, Le Sophiste*. By Plato. Paris: Gallimard, 1992.

Dostoevsky, Fyodor. *Demons*. Trans. Richard Pevear and Larissa Volokhonsky. London: Vintage, 1995.

Drever, James. *Instinct in Man: A Contribution to the Psychology of Education*. 2nd ed. Cambridge: Cambridge University Press, 1921.

Driesch, Hans. *The Science and Philosophy of the Organism: The Gifford Lectures Delivered Before the University of Aberdeen in the Year 1907*. London: Black, 1908.

———. *Der Vitalismus als Geschichte und als Lehre*. Leipzig, Germany: J. A. Barth, 1905 [*The History and Theory of Vitalism*. Trans. Charles Kay Ogden. London: Macmillan, 1914].

Dumas, Georges, et al. *Nouveau traité de psychologie*. 8 vols. Paris: Alcan, 1930–48.

Ebbinghaus, Hermann. *Psychology: An Elementary Text-Book*. Trans. and ed. Max Meyer. 1908. Reprint. New York: Arno Press, 1973.

Eckhart, Meister. *Wandering Joy: Meister Eckhart's Mystical Philosophy*. Trans. Reiner Schürmann. Great Barrington, MA: Lindisfarne, 2001.

Epictetus. *The Discourses of Epictetus, with the Encheridion and Fragments*. Trans. George Long. London: George Bell and Sons, 1890.

Epicurus. *The Epicurus Reader*. Ed. and trans. Brad Inwood and Lloyd P. Gerson. Indianapolis, IN: Hackett, 1994.

Fabre, Jean-Henri. *Souvenirs entomologiques: Première série*. Venette, France: Sciences NAT, 1985.

Fauré-Fremiet, Philippe. *Esquisse d'une philosophie concrète*. Pref. Vladimir Jankélévitch. Paris: PUF, 1954.

———. *Pensée et re-création*. Paris: Alcan, 1934.

———. *La recréation du réel et l'équivoque*. Paris: Alcan, 1940.

Fénelon, François de. *Christian Perfection*. Ed. Charles F. Whiston. Trans. Mildred Whitney Stillman. New York: Harper, 1947.

———. *A Demonstration of the Existence and Attributes of God* [etc.]. Harrisburgh, PA: Gillmor, 1811.

———. *Lettres spirituelles*. In *Oeuvres complètes de Fénelon*, vol. 8. Paris: Méquignon junior et J. Leroux / J. Leroux et Jouby, 1848–52.

Fleg, Edmond. *Écoute Israël*. Paris: Flammarion, 1954.

———. *Le livre du commencement: Genèse*. Paris: Minuit, 1959.

———. *Nous de l'espérance*. Angers, France: Masque d'Or, 1949.

Foley, Michael. *Life Lessons from Bergson*. London: Macmillan, 2013.

Fouillée, Alfred. *La Pensée et les nouvelles écoles anti-intellectualistes*. 2nd ed. Paris: Alcan, 1911.

———. "Préface." In *La genèse de l'idée de temps*. By Jean-Marie Guyau. Paris: Alcan, 1890.

———. *La psychologie des idées-forces*. Vol. 2. Paris: Alcan, 1893.

Gide, André. *The Fruits of the Earth*. Trans. Dorothy Bussy. New York: Knopf, 1949.

Goblot, Edmond. *Traité de logique*. Paris: Colin, 1918.

Goethe, Johann Wolfgang. *Faust: The First Part of the Tragedy*. Trans. David Constantinet. London: Penguin, 2005.

———. Letter to Zelter, 29 March 1827. In *Sämtliche Werke*, 37:456–59. Frankfurt, Germany: Deutscher Klassiker Verlag, 1993.

Gottlieb, Noé. "D'une erreur fondamentale dans les *Deux Sources* de M. Bergson." *Revue des Études Juives* 95, no. 189 (1933): 1–22.

Gracián y Morales, Baltasar. *The Art of Worldly Wisdom.* Trans. Martin Fisher. New York: Barnes and Noble, 2008.

Gratieux, Albert. *A. S. Khomiakov et le mouvement slavophile.* 2 vols. Paris: Cerf, 1939.

Grua, Gaston. "Un critique du transformisme: Louis Vialleton." *Revue de métaphysique et de morale* 37, no. 3 (1930): 383–421.

Guerlac, Suzanne. *Literary Polemics: Bataille, Sartre, Valery, Breton.* Stanford, CA: Stanford University Press, 1997.

———. *Thinking in Time: An Introduction to Henri Bergson.* Ithaca, NY: Cornell University Press, 2006.

Guyau, Jean-Marie. "L'évolution de l'idée de temps dans la conscience." *Revue philosophique de la France et de l'étranger* 19 (January–June 1885): 353–68.

———. *L'irréligion de l'avenir: étude sociologique.* Paris: Alcan, 1887 [*Non-Religion of the Future: A Sociological Study.* London: Heinemann, 1897.].

———. *La morale d'Épicure et ses rapports avec les doctrines contemporaines.* 7th ed. Paris: Alcan, 1927.

———. *The Origin of the Idea of Time.* Trans. John A. Michon, Viviane Pouthas, and Constance Greenbaum. In *Guyau and the Idea of Time.* Ed. John A. Michon, Viviane Pouthas, and Janet L. Jackson, 93–148. Amsterdam: North-Holland, 1988.

Hadot, Pierre. *The Present Alone Is Our Happiness: Conversations with Jeannie Carlier and Arnold I. Davidson.* Trans. Marc Djaballah. Stanford, CA: Stanford University Press, 2009.

———. *What Is Ancient Philosophy?* Trans. Michael Chase. Cambridge, MA: Harvard University Press, 2002.

Halbwachs, Maurice. *On Collective Memory.* Ed. and trans. Lewis A. Coser. Chicago: University of Chicago Press, 1992.

Hanna, Thomas, ed. *The Bergsonian Heritage.* New York: Columbia University Press, 1962.

Hannequin, Arthur. "La méthode de Descartes." In *Études d'histoire des sciences et d'histoire de la philosophie*, vol. 1. Paris: Alcan, 1908.

Head, Henry. *Aphasia and Kindred Disorders of Speech.* Cambridge: Cambridge University Press, 1926.

Hering, Ewald. "On Memory as a Universal Function of Organized Matter." Trans. Samuel Butler. In *Works*, by Samuel Butler, 6:69–94.

Hesiod. *Theogony. Works and Days. Shield.* Ed. and trans. Apostolos N. Athanassakis. Baltimore, MD: Johns Hopkins University Press, 1983.

Hessen, Sergeï Iosifovich. "Mistika i metafizika." *Logos* (in Russian) 1 (1910): 118–56.

Hingston, Richard William George. *Problems of Instinct and Intelligence*. London: Macmillan, 1928.

Høffding, Harald. *Outlines of Psychology*. Trans. Mary E. Lowndes. Bristol: Thoemmes Press, 1998.

———. *La philosophie de Bergson: Exposé et critique*. Trans. Jacques de Coussange. Paris: Alcan, 1916.

———. "Über Wiedererkennen, Association und psychische Aktivität." *Vierteljahresschrift für wissenschaftliche Philosophie* 13, no. 4 (1889): 420–58; 14, no. 1 (1890): 27–54; and no. 2:167–205.

Huizinga, Johan. *Le déclin du Moyen Age*. Paris: Payot, 1932.

Jackson, John Hughlings. *Clinical and Physiological Researches on the Nervous System*. London: Churchill, 1875.

James, William. *A Pluralistic Universe*. Lincoln: University of Nebraska Press, 1996.

———. *The Principles of Psychology*. New York: Holt, 1890.

———. *Some Problems of Philosophy: A Beginning of an Introduction to Philosophy*. New York: Longmans, Green, 1916.

Janet, Pierre. *L'évolution de la mémoire et de la notion du temps*. Paris: Chahine, 1928.

———. *Les obsessions et la psychasthénie*. Paris: Harmattan, 2005.

Jankélévitch, Vladimir. *L'alternative*. Paris: Alcan, 1938.

———. "Bersonisme et biologie, à propos d'un ouvrage récent." *Revue de métaphysique et de morale* 36, no. 2 (April 1929): 2–256.

———. *Cours de philosophie morale: 1962–1963*. Paris: Seuil, 2006.

———. "Do Not Listen to What They Say, Look at What They Do." *Critical Inquiry* 22, no. 3 (spring 1996): 549–51.

———. *Forgiveness*. Trans. Andrew Kelley. Chicago: University of Chicago Press, 2005.

———. *Maurice Ravel*. Paris: Rieder, 1938.

———. *Premières et dernières pages*. Ed. Françoise Schwab. Paris: Seuil, 1994.

———. "Should We Pardon Them?" *Critical Inquiry* 22, no. 3 (spring 1996): 552–72.

———. *Une vie en toutes lettres: Lettres à Louis Beauduc, 1923–1980*. Paris: Liana Levi, 1995.

Kant, Immanuel. "Attempt to Introduce the Concept of Negative Magnitudes into Philosophy." 1763. In *Theoretical Philosophy: 1755–1770*. Trans. and ed. David Walford and Ralf Meerbote, 203–41. Cambridge: Cambridge University Press, 2003.

———. *Critique of the Power of Judgment*. Ed. and trans. Paul Guyer and Eric Matthews. Cambridge: Cambridge University Press, 2001.

———. *Critique of Pure Reason*. Ed. and trans. Paul Guyer and Allen W. Wood. Cambridge: Cambridge University Press, 1998.

Kelley, Andrew. "Translator's Introduction." In *Forgiveness*, by Vladimir Janké-lévitch, vii–xxvii. Chicago: University of Chicago Press, 2005.

Kierkegaard, Søren. *The Concept of Anxiety: A Simple Psychologically Orienting Deliberation on the Dogmatic Issue of Hereditary Sin.* Ed. and trans. Reidar Thomte. In *Kierkegaard's Writings* 8.

———. *The Concept of Irony with Continual Reference to Socrates.* Ed. and trans. Howard V. Hong and Edna H. Hong. In *Kierkegaard's Writings* 2.

———. *Kierkegaard's Writings.* 25 Volumes. Ed. Howard V. Hong et al. Princeton, NJ: Princeton University Press, 1978–2000.

———. *Philosophical Fragments.* In *Kierkegaard's Writings*, 7:1–112.

———. *Purity of Heart Is to Will One Thing.* Ed. and trans. Douglas V. Steere. New York: Harper, 1956.

Koyré, Alexandre. *La philosophie de Jacob Boehme.* 3rd ed. Paris: Vrin, 1979.

Kretschmer, Ernst. *A Text-Book of Medical Psychology.* Trans. E. B. Strauss. London: Oxford University Press, 1934.

Kroner, Richard. "Henri Bergson," *Logos* (in German) 1 (1910): 125–50.

———. *Zweck und Gesetz in der Biologie: Eine logische Untersuchung.* Tübingen, Germany: J. C. B. Mohr, 1913.

La Bruyère, Jean de. *The "Characters" of Jean de la Bruyère.* Trans. Henri Van Laun. London: Nimmo, 1885.

La Rochefoucauld, François de. *Collected Maxims and Other Reflections.* Trans. E. H. Blackmore, A. M. Blackmore, and Francine Giguère. Oxford: Oxford University Press, 2007.

La Ville de Mirmont, Jean de. "L'horizon chimérique." *L'horizon chimérique, suivi de Les dimanches de Jean Dézert et Contes*, 23–26. Paris: Grasset, 2008.

Lachelier, Jules. *Du fondement de l'induction, suivi de: Psychologie et métaphysique.* 2nd ed. Paris: Alcan, 1896 [An excerpt published as "The Basis of Induction." Trans. Sarah A. Dorsey, *Journal of Speculative Philosophy* 10, no. 3 (July 1876): 307–19].

Lalande, André. s.v. Sensation. *Vocabulaire technique et critique de la philosophie.* 5th ed., 955–60. Paris: Alcan, 1947.

Lamennais, Félicité Robert de. *Essay on Indifference in Matters of Religion.* Trans. Henry Edward John Stanley. London: Macqueen, 1895.

Langevin, Paul. "The Evolution of Space and Time." Trans. J. B. Sykes. *Scientia* 108 (1973): 285–300.

Larguier des Bancels, Jean. *Introduction à la psychologie: L'Instinct et l'Emotion.* 2nd rev. and exp. ed. Paris: Payot, 1934.

Lawlor, Leonard. *The Challenge of Bergsonism: Phenomenology, Ontology, Ethics.* London: Continuum, 2003.

Lawlor, Leonard, and Valentine Moulard Leonard. "Henri Bergson." *The Stanford Encyclopedia of Philosophy* (winter 2013). Ed. Edward N. Zalta. http://plato.stanford.edu/archives/win2013/entries/bergson/.

Le Roy, Édouard. *L'exigence idéaliste et le fait de l'évolution.* Paris: Boivin, 1927.

———. *La pensée intuitive*. Paris: Boivin, 1929.

———. "Le problème du morcelage." In *Le continu et le discontinu*. Ed. Jacques Chevalier, 135–65. Paris: Bloud et Gay, 1929.

———. "Science et philosophie." *Revue de métaphysique et de morale* 7 (1899): 375–425, 503–62, and 706–31.

———. "Sur la logique de l'invention." *Revue de métaphysique et de morale* 13 (1905): 193–223.

Lefebvre, Alexandre. *Human Rights as a Way of Life: On Bergson's Political Philosophy*. Stanford, CA: Stanford University Press, 2013.

Lefebvre, Alexandre, and Melanie White, eds. *Bergson, Politics, and Religion*. Durham, NC: Duke University Press, 2011.

Leibniz, Gottfried Wilhelm. "Conversation sur la liberté et le destin." In *Textes inédits* no. V.32, 2:478–86.

———. *Discourse on Metaphysics*. In *Philosophical Essays*, 35–69.

———. *The Early Mathematical Manuscripts of Leibniz*. Trans. J. M. Child. Chicago: Open Court, 1920.

———. "Elementa veræ pietatis." In *Textes inédits*, no. I.4, 1:10–7.

———. "Introduction à l'*Horizon de la Doctrine humaine*." In *Opuscules et fragments inédits de Leibniz*. Ed. Louis Couturat, 530–33. Paris: Alcan, 1938.

———. *The Leibniz-Arnauld Correspondence*. Ed. and trans. H. T. Mason. Manchester, UK: Manchester University Press, 1967.

———. Letter to Simon Fouchet. In *Opera Omnia*. Ed. Louis Dutens, 2:238–39. Geneva: de Tournes, 1768.

———. *New Essays on Human Understanding*. Trans. and ed. Peter Remnant and Jonathan Bennett. Cambridge: Cambridge University Press, 1981.

———. "New System of Nature." In *Philosophical Essays*, 138–45.

———. "On Nature Itself." In *Philosophical Essays*, 155–67.

———. "On the Ultimate Origination of Things." In *Philosophical Essays*, 149–55.

———. *Philosophical Essays*. Ed. and trans. Roger Ariew and Daniel Garber. Indianapolis, IN: Hackett, 1989.

———. *Die philosophischen Schriften von Gottfried Wilhelm Leibniz*. Ed. C. J. Gerhardt. 7 vols. Leipzig: Lorentz, 1875–1931.

———. "Principles of Nature and Grace, Based on Reason." In *Philosophical Essays*, 206–13.

———. "The Principles of Philosophy, or, the Monadology." In *Philosophical Essays*, 213–25.

———. "Résumé de métaphysique." In *Opuscules et fragments inédits de Leibniz: Extraits des manuscrits de la Bibliothèque royale de Hanovre*. Ed. Louis Couturat, 533–36. Paris: Alcan, 1903.

———. "Tentamen anagogicum: Essai anagogique dans la recherche des causes." In *Philosophische Schriften*. 7:270–79.

————. *Textes inédits d'après les manuscrits de la Bibliothèque provinciale de Hanovre.* Ed. Gaston Grua. Paris: PUF, 1948.

————. *Theodicy: Essays on the Goodness of God, the Freedom of Man, and the Origin of Evil.* Ed. Austin Farrer. Trans. E. M. Huggard. London: Routledge and Kegan Paul, 1951.

————. "A Vindication of God's Justice Reconciled with His Other Perfections and All His Actions [*Causa Dei*]." In *Monadology and Other Philosophical Essays.* Trans. Paul Schrecker and Anne Martin Schrecker, 114–47. Indianapolis, IN: Bobbs-Merrill, 1965.

Leibniz, Gottfried Wilhelm, and Samuel Clarke. *Correspondence.* Ed. Roger Ariew. Indianapolis, IN: Hackett, 2000.

Lenoir, Raymond. "Le meeting d'Oxford." *Revue de métaphysique et de morale* 28, no. 1 (January–March 1921): 99–134.

Lequier, Jules. *La recherche d'une première vérité et autres textes.* Ed. André Clair. Paris: PUF, 1993.

Lévy-Bruhl, Lucien. *How Natives Think.* Trans. Lilian A. Clare. London: George Allen and Unwin, 1926. Reprint. New York: Arno Press, 1980.

Lewkowitz, Albert. *Das Judentum und die geistigen Strömungen des 19. Jahrhunderts.* Breslau, Germany: Marcus, 1935.

Locke, John. *An Essay concerning Human Understanding.* Amherst, MA: Prometheus, 1995.

Lossky, Nikolai Onufriyevich. "Esquisse d'une théorie intuitiviste de la connaissance," *Revue philosophique de la France et de l'étranger*, CV (January–June 1928): 50–87.

————. *L'Intuition, la matière et la vie.* Paris: Alcan, 1928.

————. *Intuitivism.* Prague: Russkiy Svobodnizh Universitet v Prage, 1935.

————. *Intuitivnaya filosofiya Bergsona.* Moscow: Put', 1914.

————. *Obocnovanie intuitivizma: Propedevticheskaya znaniya.* Berlin: Obelisk, 1924.

————. "Umozrenie kak metod filosofi'i." *Logos* (in Russian) 1 (1925).

Lucretius. *De rerum natura.* Trans. William Ellery Leonard. Madison: University of Wisconsin Press, 1942.

Mach, Ernst. "On the Economical Nature of Physical Inquiry." In *Popular Scientific Lectures.* Trans. Thomas J. McCormack, 3rd rev. ed., 186–213. Chicago: Open Court, 1898.

Maeterlinck, Maurice. *Ariane et Barbe-Bleue: Conte en trois actes tiré du théâtre de Maurice Maeterlinck; musique de Paul Dukas.* Brussels: Lacomblez, 1907.

Maine de Biran, Pierre. *Essai sur les fondements de la psychologie.* Ed. Francis Charles Timothy Moore. Paris: Vrin, 2001.

Maistre, Joseph de. *St. Petersburg Dialogues, or, Conversations on the Temporal Government of Providence.* Trans. Richard Lebrun. Montreal: McGill-Queen's University Press, 1993.

Malebranche, Nicolas de. *Dialogue between a Christian Philosopher and a Chinese Philosopher on the Existence and Nature of God.* Trans. Dominick A. Iorio. Washington, DC: University Press of America, 1980.

———. *The Search after Truth.* Ed. and trans. Thomas M. Lennon. Cambridge: Cambridge University Press, 1997.

Marcel, Gabriel. *Metaphyscial Journal.* Trans. Bernard Wall. London: Rockcliff, 1952

Meyerson, Émile. *Explanation in the Sciences.* Trans. Alice and David A. Sipfle. Dordrecht, the Netherlands [etc.]: Kluwer, 1991.

———. *Identité et réalité.* 3rd ed. Paris: Alcan, 1926 [*Identity and Reality.* Trans. Kate Loewenberg. New York: Dover, 1962].

Michelet, Jules. *The People.* Trans. C. Cocks. 3rd ed. London: Longman, Brown, Green and Longmans, 1846.

Mill, John Stuart. *An Examination of Sir William Hamilton's Philosophy and of The Principal Philosophical Questions Discussed in His Writings.* Ed. J. M. Robson. In *The Collected Works of John Stuart Mill*, vol. 9. Toronto: University of Toronto Press, 1979.

Minkowski, Eugène. *Lived Time: Phenomenological and Psychopathological Studies.* Trans. Nancy Metzel. Evanston, IL: Northwestern University Press, 1970.

Monakow, Constantin von, and Raoul Mourgue. *Introduction biologique à l'étude de la neurologie et de la psychopathologie, intégration et désintégration de la fonction.* Paris: Alcan, 1928.

Montaigne, Michel de. *The Complete Essays.* Trans. M. A. Screech. London: Penguin, 2003.

Mourgue, Raoul. "Le point de vue neurobiologique dans l'œuvre de M. Bergson et les données actuelles de la science." *Revue de métaphysique et de morale* 27, no. 1 (1920): 27–70.

Moutier, François. *L'Aphasie de Broca.* Paris: Steinheil, 1908.

Mullarkey, John. *Bergson and Philosophy.* Edinburgh: Edinburgh University Press, 1999.

Nietzsche, Friedrich Wilhelm. *Beyond Good and Evil.* Trans. Judith Norman. Cambridge: Cambridge University Press, 2002.

———. *Human, All Too Human.* Trans. R. J. Hollingdale. Cambridge: Cambridge University Press, 1986.

———. "Schopenhauer as Educator." In *Untimely Meditations.* Trans. R. J. Hollingdale, 125–94. Cambridge: Cambridge University Press, 1997.

Ors, Eugenio d'. *Du Baroque.* Trans. Agathe Rouart-Valéry. Paris: Gallimard, 2000.

Parodi, Domique. "La moralité et la vie: Séance du 26 janvier 1929." *Bulletin de la Société francaise de philosophie* 29 (1929): 1–71.

Pascal, Blaise. "De l'esprit géométrique." In *Œuvres complètes*, 2:154–82.

———. *Œuvres complètes.* Ed. Michel Le Guern. Paris: Gallimard, 2000.

———. *Pensées.* Trans. A. J. Krailsheimer. London: Penguin, 1995.

———. "Préface sur le Traité du vide." In *Œuvres complètes,* 1:452–58.

Passavant, Johann Carl. *Untersuchungen über den Lebensmagnetismus und das Hellsehen.* Frankfurt, Germany: Brönner, 1821.

Perry, Ralph Barton. "Le réalisme philosophique en Amérique." *Revue de métaphysique et de morale* 29, no. 2 (April–June 1922): 129–55.

Piéron, Henri. "Les problèmes actuels de l'instinct." *Revue philosophique de la France et de l'étranger* 65 (July–December 1908): 329–69.

Plato. *Collected Dialogues.* Trans. Benjamin Jowett. Oxford: Clarendon Press, 1953.

———. *Euthyphro.* In *Collected Dialogues,* 3:303–26.

———. *Gorgias.* In *Collected Dialogues,* 2:533–627.

———. *Greater Hippias.* In *Collected Dialogues,* 1:565–95.

———. *Ion.* In *Collected Dialogues,* 1:103–17.

———. *Meno.* In *Collected Dialogues,* 1:249–301.

———. *Phaedo.* In *Collected Dialogues,* 1:407–77.

———. *Phaedrus.* In *Collected Dialogues,* 3:107–93.

———. *Philebus.* In *Collected Dialogues,* 3:531–630.

———. *Republic.* In *Collected Dialogues,* 2:163–499.

———. *Sophist.* In *Collected Dialogues,* 3:321–428.

———. *Symposium.* In *Collected Dialogues,* 1:479–555.

———. *Theaetetus.* In *Collected Dialogues,* 3:191–319.

———. *Timaeus.* In *Collected Dialogues,* 3:631–780.

Plotinus. *Enneads.* In *Plotinus.* Trans. Arthur Hilary Armstrong. 7 vols. Cambridge, MA: Harvard University Press, 1966–88.

Poincaré, Henri. *Science and Method.* 1914. Reprint. London: Routledge/ Thoemmes Press, 1996.

Post, Karl. *Johannes Müller's philosophische Anschauungen.* Halle an der Saale, Germany: Niemeyer, 1905.

Proudhon, Pierre-Joseph. *Philosophie du progrès.* Ed. Théodore Ruyssen, Célestin Bouglé, Henri Moysset, and Jules-Louis Puech. In *Oeuvres complètes,* vol. 12. Paris: Rivière, 1946.

Proust, Marcel. *In Search of Lost Time.* Trans. Terence Kilmartin and C. K. Scott Moncrieff. Rev. D. J. Enright. 6 vols. New York: Modern Library, 1993.

Rauh, Frédéric. "La conscience du devenir." *Revue de métaphysique et de morale* 5 (1897): 659–81.

Ravaisson, Félix. *Of Habit.* Trans. and ed. Clare Carlisle and Mark Sinclair. London: Continuum, 2008.

———. *La Philosophie en France au XIXe siècle.* 5th ed. Paris: Hachette, 1904.

Renouvier, Charles. *Histoire et solutions des problème métaphysiques.* Paris: Alcan, 1901.

———. *Traité de logique générale et de logique formelle.* Paris: Colin, 1912.

———. *Traité de psychologie rationelle d'après les principes du criticisme.* Paris: Colin, 1912.

Renouvier, Charles, and Louis Prat. *La nouvelle monadologie.* Ed. Laurent Fedi and Guillaume Sibertin-Blanc. Paris: Fayard, 2004.

Ribot, Théodule. *Diseases of Memory: An Essay in Positive Psychology.* Trans. William Huntington Smith. New York: Appleton, 1882.

———. *Les maladies de la volonté,* 5th ed. Paris: F. Alcan, 1888 [*The Diseases of the Will.* Trans. Merwin-Marie Snell. Chicago: Open Court, 1894].

———. *The Evolution of General Ideas.* Trans. Frances A. Welby. Chicago: Open Court, 1899.

———. *La logique des sentiments.* Paris: F. Alcan, 1905.

———. *La psychologie des sentiments.* Paris: Alcan, 1896.

Rickert, Heinrich. *Die Philosophie des Lebens: Darstellung und Kritik der philosophischen Modeströmungen unserer Zeit.* Tübingen, Germany: J. C. B. Mohr, 1920.

Rodrigues, Gustave. *Bergsonisme et moralité.* Paris: Chiron, 1922.

Rostand, Edmond. "Hymn to the Sun." Trans. Margaret Franklin. *The Press* (Canterbury, New Zealand) 66, no. 13840 (17 September 1910): 7. http://paperspast.natlib.govt.nz/cgi-bin/paperspast?a=d&d=CHP19100917.2.28. Accessed 20 November 2014.

Russell, Bertrand. *The Analysis of Mind.* London: Routledge, 1992.

———. "Behaviorism: Its Effect on Ordinary Mortals Should It Become a Craze." *Century Magazine* (December 1926): 148–53.

Ruusbroec, John. *The Spiritual Espousals and Other Works.* Trans. James A. Wiseman. New York [etc.]: Paulist Press, 1985.

Ruyer, Raymond. "Bergson et le sphex ammophile." *Revue de métaphysique et de morale* 64, no. 2 (1959): 163–79.

Sabatier, Armand. "L'instinct." In *Philosophie de l'effort: Essais philosophiques d'un naturaliste,* 250–332. Paris: Alcan, 1908.

Scheler, Max Ferdinand. "Idols of Self-Knowledge." In *Selected Philosophical Essays.* Trans. David R. Lachterman, 3–97. Evanston, IL: Northwestern University Press, 1992.

———. *The Nature of Sympathy.* Trans. Peter Heath. Hamden, CT: Archon, 1970.

———. "Shame and Feelings of Modesty." In *Person and Self-Value: Three Essays.* Ed. and trans. M. S. Frings, 1–85. Dordrecht, the Netherlands: Nijhoff, 1987.

Schelling, Friedrich Wilhelm Joseph. *Philosophical Investigations into the Essence of Human Freedom.* Trans. Jeffrey Love and Johannes Schmidt. Buffalo: SUNY Press, 2010.

———. *Philosophie der Mythologie.* In *Werke,* vol. 5 Supplement.

———. *Philosophie der Offenbarung.* In *Werke,* vol. 6 Supplement.

————. *Schellings Werke*. Ed. Manfred Schröter, 1927–28, 4th ed. Munich: C. H. Beck und R. Oldenburg, 1984–.

Schlegel, Friedrich. *Friedrich Schlegel: Kritische Ausgabe seiner Werke*. Ed. Hans Behler with Jean-Jacques Anstett and Hans Eichner. 35 vols. Paderborn, Germany [etc.]: Schöningh, 1959– [*Kritische-Schlegel-Ausgabe=KSA*].

————. *Lucinde and the Fragments*. Trans. Peter Firchow. Minneapolis: University of Minnesota Press, 1971.

Schopenhauer, Arthur. *On the Basis of Morality*. Trans. E. F. J. Payne. Indianapolis, IN: Bobbs-Merrill, 1965.

————. *On the Fourfold Root of the Principle of Sufficient Reason and Other Writings* [*On Vision and Colours* and *On Will in Nature*]. Trans. and ed. David E. Cartwright, Edward E. Erdmann, and Christopher Janaway. Cambridge: Cambridge University Press, 2012.

————. "On Ethics." In *Parerga and Paralipomena: Short Philosophical Essays*. Trans. E. F. J. Payne. Oxford: Oxford University Press, 2000, 2:201–39.

————. *The World as Will and Idea*. Trans. R. B. Haldane and J. Kemp. 3rd ed. Boston: Ticknor, 1887.

Segond, Joseph. *L'intuition bergsonienne*. 3rd ed. Paris: Alcan, 1930.

Semon, Richard Wolfgang. *The Mneme*. Trans. Louis Simon. London: George Allen and Unwin, 1921.

Seneca. *Ad Lucilium Epistulae Morales*. Ed. and trans. Richard M. Gummere. 3 vols. Cambridge, MA: Harvard University Press, 1917–25.

Sherrington, Charles Scott. *The Integrative Action of the Nervous System*. New Haven, CT: Yale University Press, 1920.

Silesius, Angelus. *The Cherubinic Wanderer*. Mahwah, NJ: Paulist Press, 1986.

Simmel, Georg. "The Conflict of Modern Culture." Trans. Deena Weinstein. http://condor.depaul.edu/dweinste/theory/CoMC.html. Accessed 20 November 2014.

————. *Gesamtausgabe*. Ed. Otthein Rammstedt. 24 vols. Frankfurt, Germany: Suhrkamp, 1989– [=*GA*].

————. "Henri Bergson." In *GA* 13:53–69.

————. "The Picture Frame: An Aesthetic Study." Trans. Mark Ritter. *Theory, Culture and Society* 11, no. 1 (February 1994): 11–17.

————. "Rodin." In *GA* 14:330–48 ["Rodin's Work as an Expression of the Modern Spirit." Trans. John Anzalone. In *Rodin in Perspective*. Ed. Ruth Butler, 127–30. Englewood Cliffs, NJ: Prentice Hall, 1980].

————. *The View on Life: Four Metaphysical Essays with Journal Aphorisms*. Ed. and trans. John A. Y. Andrews and Donald N. Levine. Chicago: University of Chicago Press, 2010.

————. "Werde, was du bist." In *GA* 13:133–37.

Solger, Karl Wilhelm Ferdinand. "Philosophische Gespräche über Sein, Nichtsein und Erkennen." In *Nachgelassene Schriften und Briefwechsel*. Ed. Ludwig

Tieck and Friedrich von Raumer, 2:200–262. Leipzig, Germany: Brock-
haus, 1826.

Soulez, Philippe. *Bergson politique*. Paris: PUF, 1989.

Soulez, Philippe, and Frédéric Worms. *Bergson*. Paris: PUF, 2002.

Spengler, Oswald. *The Decline of the West*, vol. 1, *Form and Actuality*, trans. Charles
Francis Atkinson. New York: Knopf, 1927.

Spinoza, Benedictus de. *The Collected Works of Spinoza*. Ed. and trans. Edwin
Curley. Princeton, NJ: Princeton University Press, 1988.

———. *Ethics*. In *Collected Works*, 1: 408–617.

———. *Treatise on the Emendation of the Intellect*. In *Collected Works*, 1:6–45.

Stepun, Fyodor. "Tragediya misticheckogo soznaniya." *Logos* (in Russian) 2–3
(1911–12): 115–40.

———. "Tragediya tvorchestva (Fr. Schlegel)." *Logos* (in Russian) 1 (1910):
171–98.

———. *Zhizn i tvorchestvo*. Berlin: Obelisk, 1923.

Taine, Hippolyte-Adolphe. *On Intelligence*. Trans. T. D. Haye. Bristol, UK:
Maruzen, 1998.

Thibaudet, Albert. *Le Bergsonisme*. In *Trente ans de vie française*. 8th ed., vol. 3.
Paris: Nouvelle Revue française, 1924.

Thomson, William (Lord Kelvin). "On Vortex Atoms." *Proceedings of the Royal
Society of Edinburgh* 6 (1867): 94–105.

Tolstoy, Leo. "The Death of Ivan Ilyich." *The Death of Ivan Ilyich and Other
Stories*. Trans. Rosemary Edmonds, 99–161. London: Penguin, 1960.

———. *The Kingdom of God Is within You: Christianity Not as a Mystic Religion
but as a New Theory of Life*. Trans. Constance Garnett. Lincoln: University of
Nebraska Press, 1984.

———. *War and Peace*. Trans. Richard Pevear and Larissa Volokhonsky. London: Vintage, 2009.

Tournay, Auguste. "Physiologie spéciale du système nerveux." In Dumas, *Traité*,
223–92.

Unamuno, Miguel de. *Trois nouvelles exemplaires et un prologue*. Trans. Jean
Cassou and Mathilde Pomès. Paris: Éditions du Sagittaire, 1925.

Van Lerberghe, Charles. *Entrevisions*. Lyon, France: Les Editions Palimpseste,
2006.

Van Woerkom, Willem. "La signification de certains éléments de l'intelligence
dans la génèse des troubles aphasiques." *Journal de psychologie normale et
pathologique* 18, nos. 8–9 (October–November 1921): 731–51.

Vialleton, Louis. *L'origine des êtres vivants, l'illusion transformiste*. Paris: Plon
et Nourrit, 1929.

———. "Le transformisme et la morphologie." In *Le Transformisme*. Ed. Lucien Cuénot, Roland Dalbiez, Élie Gagnebin, W.-R. Thompson, and Louis
Vialleton, 61–122. Paris: Vrin, 1927.

Wahl, Jean. *Le malheur de la conscience dans la philosophie de Hegel.* Saint-Pierre-de-Salerne: Monfort, 1983.

———. "Préface." In *Le Concept d'angoisse.* By Søren Kierkegaard. Paris: Alcan, 1935.

Worms, Frédéric. *Bergson ou les deux sens de la vie.* Paris: PUF, 2004.

Xenophon. *Memorabilia.* Trans. E. C. Marchant. In *Xenophon in Seven Volumes,* 4:1–359. Cambridge, MA: Harvard University Press, 1923.

INDEX

absolute, 47, 212; duration and, 42

abstention, 67

abulia, 75

Achilles, 24–26, 44, 57–58, 81, 117, 152, 177, 193, 200–201, 244–45

action, 195; being and, 48; determinism and, 109; emergent action, 87, 95; forgetting and, 104; freedom and, 196; language and, 241–42; virtue in, 159, 242; wisdom and, 243

actor and spectator, 23–30, 241

amalgamate, 40, 45, 163

animal instinct, 129

anthropocentrism, 43

aphasia, 71–76, 96, 172

aporias, 24, 57, 80–81, 152, 159, 165, 177, 185, 188, 193, 196, 199, 201, 206, 221, 225, 240, 245, 258–59; freedom and, 49

arguments, 53

Aristotle, 30, 46, 58–59, 121, 152, 154; on habit and disposition, 194; list of movements of, 168

art, 118, 134

asceticism, 164–65

associationism, 19, 38, 79–80, 101, 120–21, 152

atomism, 53, 80–81, 122

autarky of organisms, 13, 173

Baroque period, 178

Bazaillas, Albert, 33, 54

becoming, 1–2, 10, 30–49, 98, 120–21, 155, 204–5; bare space and, 32; positivity of, 205; rectilinear, 125

Being, time and, 48–49

Bergson, Henri: Aristotle and, 121; chronological order of works of, 1–2, 23; critique of intensity of, 173; on death, 147, 149; on dreams, 141; ethics of, 151–52, 164–65; humanist theory of, 160–61; imitation theory and, 136; instinct and intellect and, 127–28, 130–35; interview of Jankélévitch with Françoise Reiss on Bergson, 251–53; letters to Jankélévitch by, 248–50; localization critique of, 71–78; on love, 126; on matter, 141–44; maximalism of, 159–66; realism of, 81–82; review of *The Origin of the Idea of Time* (Guyau) by, 45; Solemn Homage to Henri Bergson (1959), 253–60

Berkeley, George, 17, 19, 29, 188; *Essay toward a New Theory of Vision* of, 88; illusion of optics and, 40

Bernard, Claude, 174

Bible, 212–19

biology, 101, 113–14, 161–62

body and soul, 94–95, 137–40, 185

brain, 82, 96, 137, 147, 183, 186; freedom and, 69, 78, 104, 156; memory
and, 66, 72–74, 92, 137–38, 206;
movement and, 68, 83; as organ of
pantomime, 69
breaking up *(morcelage)*, 32–34, 105, 123
Bremond, Henri, 39, 92, 194
Broca, Paul, 71, 78
Bruno, Giordano, 118
Burdach, Karl Friedrich, 129–30, 132

causality, 52, 55–56, 168; finality and, 111
centralism, 92–93
centripetal psychologies, 66, 68, 71,
75, 93
cerebral symbolism, 70, 96
chance, 168, 179
charity, 153, 163–64
Christianity, 155, 158, 211, 240
chronological order of Bergson's
works, 1–2, 23
Cicero, 80
closed morality, 157–58; circle of, 158;
vital élan and, 163
closed obligation, 156
closed religion, 157
comical, 101–2, 140, 172, 198
common sense, 43, 68, 84, 104, 113, 152,
189; freedom and, 54, 60
complexity, 191
complication, 191
comportment, 47
conceptualism, 28, 174
confusion, 154
confusion of the state of mind with
its object, 153–54
confusionism, critique of Bergson's, 84
consciousness, 198; associationism and, 38; duration and, 40–41;
matter and, 156; organization of
in Bergson, 30; tragedy of, 162;
unprejudiced, 29–30
continuism, 32, 155

conversion: Bergson on, 238
Creation, 213
creative evolution, 165, 181–84, 186,
209, 211, 215–16, 220
Creative Evolution (Bergson), 39–42,
48, 55, 95, 101, 109–10, 114, 121–22,
140–41, 145–46, 148, 151–52, 161, 165,
183, 204, 206; corporeity and, 69;
freedom in, 244; global nature of
brain and, 74; intellect and instinct
and, 42, 135; negation in, 243; on
life, 23
Creative Mind (Bergson), 2, 251
Critique of the Power of Judgement
(Kant), 115

Daedalus, 202
Darwin, Charles, 20, 121, 155, 202
de Maistre, Joseph, 36, 193
death, 148, 158, 206–7, 225
Debussy, Claude, 160, 227
decision, 50–51, 53–55, 57
Decline of the West (Spengler), 118
Delacroix, Henri, 76
deliberation, 50, 55, 57, 177
demiurgic philosophy, 168–70, 181
Descartes, René, 35–36, 69–70, 100,
152, 158, 178, 188
despair, 205, 209
determinism, 110–11; action and, 109;
freedom and, 53–54, 56–57, 62, 65,
112
dialectics, 34, 57–62, 125, 195–96, 198;
of Bergson, 55, 79, 84, 109, 164; of
the organ-obstacle, 138–39, 141
Diogenes, 193
discontinuities, 32–36, 123, 155, 160,
252; of evolution, 121
disorder, 177, 179, 184, 187–88
Don Quixote, 102
dreams, 81, 95, 97–99, 101–2, 106–7,
109, 118, 122, 141, 172, 184; instinct
and, 135; reality and, 106

dualism, 81, 83, 98–99, 109, 121, 170; of
    Bergson, 39–41, 70, 79, 86, 95, 130,
    134, 141, 144, 162–64, 182
duration, 4–6, 30, 96–99, 159, 181; ab-
    solute and, 42; consciousness and,
    40–41; as experience of continua-
    tion, 37–38; creation and, 182; free-
    dom and, 245; Guyau on, 44–47; as
    heterogeneous, 32–33; intellection
    and instinct and, 129; intuition of,
    44, 47; memory and, 39, 104; move-
    ment and, 46; orientation and, 42;
    as privileged system, 43–44; space
    and, 44–45
Duration and Simultaneity (Bergson),
    25–26, 43, 145, 180
dynamic morality, 152, 155–56, 158–59
dynamic schema, 92, 129, 144, 167, 180

effective, *vs.* fictitious, 25–26
effort, 91–92, 94; matter as provoking,
    141–42; verticality of, 94
egoism, 154, 157
Einstein, Albert, 24–25, 152, 212
élan vital. *See* vital élan
Eleatics, 57–58, 60–61, 159, 171, 175, 177,
    193, 199, 201
emergent action, in Bergson, 87, 95
emerging states, 181
emotions, 6–7, 9, 31, 34–35, 38, 70, 78,
    104–5, 160–61, 174, 176, 239; spiri-
    tual weight of, 173
endomosis of space and mind, 101
error, 40, 86, 100
eschatology, 186
Essay toward a New Theory of Vision
    (Berkeley), 88
eternity, 37, 48
ethics, 151, 153; Bergson's, 164
Ethics (Spinoza), 110
Euthyphro (Plato), 54
evil, 144, 147–48, 162, 199; Bergson
    on, 211

evolution, 31, 48, 126, 130, 143–44,
    153, 159, 181, 186, 207; arborescent
    evolution, 122–23; of Bergson, 160;
    creative evolution, 165, 181–84,
    186, 209, 211, 215–16, 220; discon-
    tinuities of, 121; duration and,
    159; fabrication and, 119; finality
    and, 109–12, 114, 165; as pluri-
    dimensional, 120; rectilinear, 124,
    153; vital élan and, 140–42. *See also*
    becoming; *Creative Evolution*
    (Bergson)
exceptions, 178
expansion, 125
experience, 157
exteriority, 39, 72, 80, 82–86, 92,
    98–99
eye, 117–18, 138, 196, 198, 206

fabrication, 15–16, 20–21, 114–17, 119,
    182, 188, 190; logic and, 175; organi-
    zation and, 166–79
false recognition, 57
fascination, 140
Fauré, Gabriel, 35, 209–10
Fauré, Philippe, 5
Fechner, Gustav, 35, 39, 121, 152, 154
Fénelon, François de., 199, 203, 205,
    238
finality, 4, 109–19, 151–52, 165, 184–85;
    biological, 111; immanence of true,
    113; retrospective, 111, 113–14
finitism, 59–60
Fleg, Edmond, 216, 225–26, 231, 234
forgetting, 104, 190
forgiveness, 199
form and function, 118–19
freedom, 4, 27, 49–65, 131–32, 145, 149,
    181, 195, 231–32; action and, 196; as
    deliverance, 245–46; as inspired
    act, 56; brain and, 69, 78, 104, 156;
    determinism and, 53–54, 56–57, 62,
    65, 112; dynamic schema of, 56;

freedom (*continued*)
explanation and, 49; heroic, 244; intuition and, 61; Lequier on, 195; matter and, 142–43; vital élan and, 207
frenzy, law of, 122, 164–65
friendship, 154–55
future perfect, 2, 11, 16–17, 51, 110, 151, 153

generosity, 208
geometrical order, 185, 188
German philosophy, 252–53
gnoseological coordination, 84, 174
Goblot, Edmond, 14–15, 174
God, 148, 157, 169, 180, 213–14, 218–21, 225–26, 230–31, 233–35; Bergson on, 157, 219; love of, 187, 228, 237–38, 255
Goethe, Johann Wolfgang von, 150
grammar, 13–14, 72, 76, 174, 178–79. *See also* language; words
Greek philosophy, 168; Bergson's opposition to, 36
growth, 168–71, 182
Guyau, Jean-Marie, 44–47, 117, 126

hallucinations, 80–81, 172
haplosis (simplification), 200
Hegel, Georg Wilhelm Friedrich, 28, 180
heredity of acquired characteristics, 156
heroes and heroism, 4, 152–53, 158–60, 165–66, 179, 242–43; freedom and, 244; vital élan and, 162
Hesiod, 168, 175
hope, 187
Hufeland, Friedrich, 129
humanist theory, 160–61

idealism, 11–12, 27, 66, 68, 70–71, 80–82, 84, 97, 128, 170, 193, 239–40
Idols of Self-Knowledge (Scheler), 51

illusion of retrospectivity, 2, 10, 16–18, 50–51, 68, 89–90, 153
imagination, 185
imitation, theory of, 136, 163
immanence, 10, 98, 124
immediate given, 40, 239, 243
immediate thought, 100
immobilism, 59, 80, 145, 177, 244
impartiality, 107
impressionism, 29, 49, 170
improvisation, 129–30
indeterminism, 110, 175, 178
indifferentism, 62, 110, 175–76
infinite division, 58–59
infinite time, 59–60
innovation, 124
instinct, 7–8, 119–37, 121, 125–29, 142, 162; animal, 129; as ecstasy, 127, 137, 161; dreams and, 135; intellect and, 42, 148, 152, 161–63; wisdom and, 157
intellect, 119–37, 127–28, 134, 145–47, 153, 157; anthropometric, 182; instinct and, 42, 148, 152, 161–63; magic and, 158; memory and, 132; wisdom and, 157
intellection, 4, 61, 68, 86, 89–94, 106–7, 117, 125, 129, 161, 167, 195; as efferent and afferent, 194
intellectual effort, 34, 173
intensity, 68, 79–80, 165, 169, 173
intention, 46, 111, 196–97
internal reform, 238, 253
"Introduction to Metaphysics" (Bergson), 12
intuition, 2, 4, 25, 29–30, 40, 44, 99, 136, 149; asceticism and, 165; as ecstasy, 137; freedom and, 61; intellect and, 147; matter and, 40; optimism and, 207; as in the person, 239; the possible and, 181; simplicity and, 194, 206; as sympathy, 25
intuitivist gnoseology, 83

inverse movements, 39, 41, 144–46, 148

Isaiah, 214, 217, 219, 222, 225–26, 230, 233, 236, 238, 245, 255

James, William, 93, 155

Janet, Pierre, 46–47, 67, 75–76, 81, 85

Jankélévitch, Vladimir: Bergson's letters to, 248–50; interview with Françoise Reiss on Bergson, 251–53; letter to Louis Beauduc on meeting Bergson, 250–51

Jesus, 201, 226, 228, 237, 240, 258

joy, 104, 106, 142, 149, 159, 179, 204, 207–10, 240, 243, 245; simplicity and, 202–3. *See also* optimism

Judaism, 211, 220–37; dissimilarities with Bergson temporality and, 212–19

justifications, 52–53, 56

kairos, 16, 156

Kant, Immanuel, 115

Kierkegaard, Soren, 54, 155, 180, 209; immobility and, 145; modernity and, 209

kinship of species, 122–23

Kroner, Richard, 85

language, 28, 76, 96, 136, 138, 174, 194; action and, 241–42. *See also* grammar; words

laughter, 101–2

Laughter (Bergson), 17, 65, 100, 106, 144, 160, 182, 198

laziness, 199

Le Roy, Édouard, 14, 91

learned ignorance, 105

Leibniz, Gottfried Wilhelm, 9, 54, 61, 94, 114, 148, 177

Lequier, Jules, 62, 195, 222; on freedom, 195

Leviticus, 218, 230, 234

life, 31, 33, 186; irreversible order of, 134; matter and, 137–50; philosophy of, 23, 188; possibility and, 189

logic, 172; fabrication of, 175

Lossky, Nikolai, 83–84, 86

love, 126–27, 152, 158, 160, 163–64, 201–3, 206, 208–9, 228–29, 231, 233–34, 241–42, 244, 256–57, 259; death and, 225; friendship and, 154–55; of God, 187, 228, 237–38, 255; of humanity and family, 153–54; of self, 154

magic, 158, 163

Maistre, Joseph de, 60

Maritain, Jacques, 193

materialism, 152

mathematics, 30, 33, 39, 41, 121, 180, 185

matter, 118–19, 183–84, 186; art and, 118; consciousness and, 156; freedom and, 142–43; intuition and, 40; life and, 137–50; memory and, 94–108; as present, 99; as provoking effort, 141–42; as pure perception, 29

Matter and Memory (Bergson), 66, 76, 91–92, 94–96, 98, 103–4, 106, 109, 122–23, 140–41, 148, 151, 160–61, 164–65, 184; brain to thought in, 137; circular interpretation in, 91; duality of recollection and perception in, 79–80; intellect and instinct and, 135; intuition and, 40; pain in, 243; pure and impure knowledge and, 135; role of symbolism and, 70

maximalism, 165, 238

measurement, 37, 45–46, 121

mechanists and mechanism, 14–15, 19–21, 35–36, 110–11, 114, 119, 144, 147

Meditations (Descartes), 178

Megarian school, 81, 188, 199, 244

memory, 4–6, 97, 99, 106, 182–83, 189; brain and, 66, 72–74, 92, 137–38, 206; constituted, 145, 162; double aspect of, 102; duration and, 39, 104; as source of error, 86; as "giving" or as "given," 103; intellect and, 132; matter and, 94–108; prejudiced, 106–7; two levels of, 85. *See also* recollection

mental disorders, 76, 172, 185. *See also* aphasia

metaboles, 160

Mind-Energy (Bergson), 19, 91–92, 149, 198

miniature theory, 82–83, 128, 171

Minkowski, Eugène, 74

mixed perception, 88, 96

mobility, 61, 98, 204

modernity, Bergson and Schopenhauer's, 209

Monadology (Leibniz), 114

monads, 61, 94, 170, 254

Monakow, Constantin von, 85, 172

monism, 135, 143–44

moral obligation, 156, 160, 163–64

motives, 50–51, 53–55, 62, 190

motor schema, 95

Mourgue, Raoul, 85, 172

movement, 59–61, 195, 260; action and, 58; brain and, 68, 83; duration and, 46; simplicity of, 193–94, 196–98, 200–203

multiplicities, 45

muscular effort, 93

musical tonalities, 34–35, 85

mysticism, 128, 152, 163–64, 189, 227; heroism and, 160

mystics, 137, 159; learned ignorance and, 105; simplicity and, 201

nativism of Bergson, 86

nature, 116–18, 197; intellect and, 162

nervous system, 66–67, 77–78, 83, 142, 147–48

Nietzsche, Friedrich, 53

nominalism, 27–29, 88, 181, 188

nothingness, 2, 27–29, 34, 92, 167–70, 173, 175, 180–83, 188; optimism and, 206–7

numerical multiplicity, 45–46

open morality, 158

open religion, 158–59

optical illusions, 40, 88

optimism: intuition and, 207; of Bergson, 203, 208–10, 239. *See also* joy

order, 188; vital *vs.* mechanical, 27

organ-obstacle, 138–39, 141

organic possibility, 180–81

organicity, paradox of, 117

organisms, 9, 118; function in, 118–19; totalities and, 237

organization, 30

Origin of the Idea of Time (Guyau), 44–45

parallelist systems, 66, 69–70, 72–73, 87

Pascal, Blaise, 52, 55, 113, 152; infinite division and, 59; on joy, 209; on searching, 195

past, 79–80, 85, 87, 93–95, 97–98, 102–5

past participles of life, 16, 103, 110, 208

Pénélope (Fauré), 209–10

penetrance, 89, 94

perception, 26–27, 40, 44, 75–76, 95–98, 100, 128, 152–53, 171; idealism and, 170; mixed perception, 88; pure perception, 29, 85–88, 99, 135, 141, 149, 152, 182; recollection and, 79–89, 152–53; speculative, 101

"The Perception of Change" (Bergson), 48, 165

pessimism, 204, 207
Philosophical Intuition (lecture, Bergson), 4
physics, 28, 101, 114
Physics (Aristotle), 58
Plato, 30, 36, 54, 65, 142, 167; on justice, 201; One and the Many aporias of, 30
play (jeu), 25, 69–70, 72
plentitude, 173–75, 177–79, 184, 187–88, 191, 206, 223
Plotinus, 7, 61, 66, 84, 127, 137, 188, 202; cosmic tree image of, 122; on evil, 144; on simplicity, 192, 203
pluralism, 33–34, 36, 121
plurality of the real, 120
Poe, Edgar Allen, 200
poetry, 242
positivity, 188–89, 223, 243; of becoming, 205
possibility, 179–90; logical *vs.* organic, 180–81
"The Possible and the Real" (essay, Bergson), 2, 151
present participle, 110
privileged system, 43–44
prophecy, 217–18
Proudhon, Pierre-Joseph, 59
Proust, Marcel, 29, 151
pseudo-philosophers, 185
pure perception, 29, 85–88, 99, 135, 141, 149, 152, 182
pure recollection, 96–97, 99, 135, 149, 152

quoddity, 43, 133, 188, 242

Rauh, Frédéric, 97, 99, 221
realism, 83–84, 125; in Bergson, 43–44, 81–82, 125, 207, 239; dreams and, 106; mysticism and, 189; real *vs.* fictitious, 25–26; real *vs.* the virtual, 43–44

recollection, 8–9, 17, 38, 40, 44, 96, 122, 152–53, 171; aphasia and, 72; idealism and, 170; illusion of, 86–89; perception and, 79–89, 152–53; pure recollection, 96–97, 99, 135, 149, 152. *See also* memory
Reiss, Françoise, 251–53
relativist paradoxes, 24–25, 39, 42–44, 199, 212
relaxation, 94
Renouvier, Charles, 57, 59–60, 62–64, 75–76, 222
Ribot, Théodule, 17–18, 72, 75
Romantics of Philosophy of Nature, 128–30, 135

Saint Theresa, 189
saints and saintliness, 159, 165, 189, 242–43
Schelling, Friedrich Wilhelm Joseph, 7, 180
Schopenhauer, Arthur, 112–15, 118–19, 124, 126, 129, 159
sheaf, image of in Bergson, 31
signs, 90–92
Simmel, Georg, 212
simplicity, 12–13, 105, 117–19, 150, 152, 164–65, 191–203; complex and complicated, 191–92; *haplosis* (simplification) and, 200; of intuition, 194, 206; joy and, 202–3; of movement, 193–94, 196–98, 200–203; mystics and, 201; wisdom and, 198
sin, 213–14
sincerity, 65
Socrates, 54, 81, 199
Solemn Homage to Henri Bergson (1959), 253–60
sophism, 198–99, 201
space, 144; duration and, 44–45
Spencer, Herbert, 12–13, 45, 154, 181
Spengler, Oswald, 118
spinal cord, 67–68

Spinoza, Baruch, 19, 52, 110, 184–88; generositas and, 208; Judaism and, 212

spiritual bond, 190

spiritual centralism, 92–93

spiritual reality, 70–71

static morality, 152, 155–56, 157

static religion, 157–58

subjectivism, 82, 86–87

suddenness, 152–56, 182

symbolism, 26, 30, 69–70, 76–79, 98; cerebral symbolism, 70, 96

sympathy, 25, 126, 129

Taine, Hippolyte-Adolphe, 79, 154

teleological astonishment *(teleologisches Erstaunen)*, 114–17, 137–38, 185, 196

tellurism theory, 130

temporality, 48, 251; in the Bible, 212–19

The Two Sources of Morality and Religion (Bergson), 64, 145, 151, 155, 159–62, 164–65, 184, 189, 208; freedom in, 244; heroes in, 195

thought, 187–88; Bergson on, 174–75; brain and, 66–79

time, 31–32, 34, 36, 47–48, 204; Aristotle on, 30; Being and, 48–49; in Bergson, 37; mathematical, 39, 41, 47; the past, 79–80, 85, 87, 93–95, 97–98, 102–5; and space, 40, 44–46; true time, 42–43, 47

Time and Free Will (Bergson), 2, 14, 38–40, 64, 66, 95–97, 101, 103–5, 109, 117, 140, 151–52, 155, 159–61, 165, 208; brain and thought and, 74;

heterogeneity of states of consciousness in, 120; intensity in, 79, 169; memory in, 97; two simplicities of, 164, 191

Tolstoy, Leo, 58, 83, 157, 198–99, 225

totalities, 12, 14, 155, 168, 239

tragedy of consciousness, 162

Treviranus, Gottfried Reinhold, 130, 132

true *vs.* false, in Bergson, 39–40

understand, effort to, 35, 89–90

unity, 31–34, 37–38, 123–24

Vialleton, Louis, 7–8, 121, 135

virtual, *vs.* the real, 43–44

vision, 117–18

vital élan, 1, 18–19, 112, 118, 122, 126, 138, 154–55, 158–59, 180–81; closed morality and, 163; evolution and, 140–42; freedom and, 207; heroism and, 162; instinct and, 161; joy and optimism and, 208–9; simplicity and, 197; *vs.* Schopenhauer's *Will*, 159

von Baader, Franz Xaver, 89

von Kieser, Georg, 129–30

Wahl, Jean, 28, 32, 102

will, 111, 113, 126, 159, 200

wisdom, 152, 157–58; Bergson on, 240–41; simplicity and, 198

wonder, 104–5

words, 28, 72–74, 190; sounds and, 92–93. *See also* grammar; language

Zeno, 24, 60, 117, 177, 193, 196, 198–99